THE LITTLE

VEGAN

COOKBOOK

Brimming with creative inspiration, how-to projects, and useful information to enrich your everyday life, Quarto Knows is a favorite destination for those pursuing their interests and passions. Visit our site and dig deeper with our books into your area of interest: Quarto Creates, Quarto Cooks, Quarto Homes, Quarto Lives, Quarto Drives, Quarto Explores, Quarto Gifts, or Quarto Kids.

20 19 18 17   2 3 4 5

ISBN: 978-1-59233-732-3

Digital edition published in 2016
eISBN: 978-1-63159-175-4

Library of Congress Cataloging-in-Publication Data available

Cover Photo: Erin Alderson
Page Layout: Leanne Coppola
Photography:
  Bill Bettencourt
  Jack Deutsch
  Allyson Kramer
  Kate Lewis
  Glen Scott
  Ekaterina Smirnova
  Celine Steen

Printed in China

MIX
Paper from
responsible sources
FSC® C016973

THE LITTLE
VEGAN
COOKBOOK

500 of the Best Vegan Recipes Ever

Coconut Whipped Cream (See page 12)

Blackberry Breakfast Bars (See page 77)

Seared "Scallops" with White Truffle Sauce (See page 145)

Whole Wheat Bread (See page 13)

CONTENTS

PANTRY BASICS

See pages 10–11 for pantry basics photos.

VEGETABLE BROTH

This simple vegetable broth packs so much flavor you'll never miss the animal-product-laden versions. Freeze it in ice cube trays and use it to add flavor to stews, sautés, and sauces.

1 Vidalia onion, or about 1 cup (160 g), chopped
1 bunch celery, or about 3 to 4 cups (300 to 400 g), chopped
5 carrots, or about 2 cups (260 g), peeled and chopped
5 or 6 medium kale leaves
2 fresh tomatoes
2 cloves garlic, minced, optional
12 cups (2.9 L) water
Salt, to taste

Wash the vegetables and trim any tough or damaged parts. Chop the vegetables roughly and place in a stockpot. Add the water and cook over medium-low heat until the veggies are very soft, 25 to 30 minutes. Cool until easy to handle.

Strain the vegetables through cheesecloth into a large bowl or container. Squeeze the cheesecloth tightly to ensure no broth goes to waste and then discard the cooked veggies. Add salt to taste.

Store the broth in an airtight container in the fridge for up to 3 days or freeze for later use in a freezer-safe container or bag.

Yield: 12 servings, 1 cup (235 ml) each

CASHEW CREAM

This incredibly easy and useful recipe can be used in a variety of dishes, from a delicious condiment to incorporating into soups and stews for added creaminess.

2 cups (300 g) raw cashews, soaked in 4 cups (940 ml) water for at least 6 hours, then drained
1 cup (235 ml) cold water
3 tablespoons (45 ml) lemon juice
2 to 3 teaspoons (9 to 13 g) sugar, optional
Dash or two of salt

Place all of the ingredients in a food processor and blend until very smooth, about 5 minutes.

Store in a tightly sealed container in the fridge for up to 1 week.

Yield: 20 servings, 2 tablespoons (30 ml) each

PEACHY BUTTER

This very simple recipe makes a lightly sweet spread that's terrific on fresh-baked sweet bread, such as banana bread or even on oats for breakfast. For dessert, drizzle it over vegan ice cream.

3 cups (510 g) diced peaches
1 cup (235 ml) water
1 teaspoon ground cinnamon
1 teaspoon vegan butter

Add the peaches, water, and cinnamon to a pressure cooker. Cover and bring to pressure. Cook at high pressure for 3 minutes. Use a quick release method. Remove the cover. Using a potato masher, mash the peaches. Add the butter and simmer on low, uncovered, for 2 to 3 minutes to cook down any excess liquid to achieve a thick, jam-like consistency.

Yield: 2 cups (500 g)

CLASSIC STRAWBERRY JAM

This classic strawberry jam uses frozen berries so that you can make jam all year-round.

FOR THE JAM:
5 cups (1 kg) frozen strawberries
1 (1¾-ounce, or 49 g) box pectin
½ teaspoon nondairy butter, to reduce foaming
5 cups (1 kg) sugar
Zest of 1 lemon

FOR CANNING:
6 to 8 (8-ounce, or 235 ml) jars
6 to 8 rings and lids
OTHER "CANNING MATERIALS NEEDED" (SEE PAGE 8.)

Thaw and drain the frozen strawberries by placing them in a colander or strainer over a bowl in the fridge overnight.

In a saucepot, bring the thawed strawberries, pectin, and butter to a full boil over high heat, stirring constantly and mashing as necessary using a spoon as they cook. (There should be plenty of fruit bits.) Add the sugar and zest. Return to a full boil for 1 minute, stirring constantly.

Follow the "Canning Basics." (See page 8.) The processing time is 15 minutes. Any jars that did not seal need to be stored in the fridge and used within 1 week. Refrigerate after opening.

Yield: 6 to 8 (8-ounce, or 235 ml) jars

ORANGE BASIL MARMALADE

This marmalade tastes delicious spread on toast, crackers, or a bagel. It also makes a great glaze for seitan, tofu, or tempeh.

FOR THE MARMALADE:
8 medium navel oranges
4 cups (800 g) evaporated cane juice or granulated sugar
2 cups (470 ml) water
24 large fresh basil leaves, cut into a super-fine chiffonade
1 tablespoon (15 ml) vanilla extract

FOR CANNING:
8 (8-ounce, or 235 ml) jars
8 rings and lids
OTHER "CANNING MATERIALS NEEDED" (SEE PAGE 8.)

Cut the top and bottom off of each orange. Slice each orange into 8 segments and remove the seeds and center pith. Place in a food processor and pulse until the mixture has very tiny bits of peel.

In a saucepot, bring the orange purée, sugar, and water to a boil over high heat, reduce the heat to a simmer, and cook, uncovered, for 20 minutes, stirring often. Remove from the heat and stir in the basil and vanilla.

Follow the "Canning Basics." (See page 8.) The processing time is 15 minutes. Any jars that did not seal need to be stored in the fridge and used within 1 week. Refrigerate after opening.

Yield: 8 (8-ounce, or 235 ml) jars

LEMON LAVENDER CURD

Don't try to double this recipe. It can be difficult to handle if using more than what is listed here.

2 cups (400 g) sugar
1 cup (235 ml) lemon juice
Zest of 2 lemons
½ cup (112 g) nondairy butter, cubed
1 tablespoon (3 g) food-grade dried lavender flowers
½ cup (64 g) cornstarch mixed with ¾ cup (180 ml) water to make a slurry
For canning:
3 (8-ounce, or 235 ml) jars
3 rings and lids
OTHER "CANNING MATERIALS NEEDED" (SEE PAGE 8.)

In a pot, heat the sugar and lemon juice over medium-high heat until just beginning to boil, stirring constantly. As soon as it begins to bubble, reduce the heat to medium. Stir in the zest, and then add the butter and stir until melted. Stir in the lavender. Slowly stir in the cornstarch slurry and continue to stir and cook until thickened. (It will happen slowly at first and then all of a sudden, it will be very thick. When the lavender stays suspended in the mixture, it is the right consistency.)

Follow the "Canning Basics." (See page 8.) The processing time is 15 minutes. Any jars that did not seal need to be stored in the fridge and used within 1 week. Refrigerate after opening.

Yield: 3 (8-ounce, or 235 ml) jars

GINGER-CINNAMON WHITE BEAN GRAVY

This protein-packed gravy is perfect to serve over mashed potatoes or root vegetables. Puréed white beans replace the need for dairy.

1 cup (200 g) dried navy beans, soaked for 12 hours or overnight
1 teaspoon olive oil
3 cloves garlic, coarsely chopped
4 cups (940 ml) water
1 bay leaf
Juice of 1 lemon (about 2 tablespoons, or 30 ml)
4 tablespoons (56 g) vegan butter
½ cup (80 g) chopped yellow onion
⅛ teaspoon ground ginger
⅛ teaspoon ground cinnamon
⅛ teaspoon black pepper
1 cup (235 ml) vegetable broth
¼ cup (60 ml) soy sauce
2 tablespoons (14 g) nutritional yeast (flakes or powder)

Rinse and drain the beans.

In an uncovered pressure cooker, heat the oil on medium. Add the beans, garlic, water, and bay leaf. Cover and bring to pressure. Cook at high pressure for 6 to 8 minutes. Allow for a natural release. Remove the lid and stir in the lemon juice. Taste for doneness. If the beans are not fully cooked, simmer on low, uncovered.

In a large saucepan, heat the butter over medium-high heat. Once the butter is melted, sauté the onion for 2 to 3 minutes, or until translucent. Add the ginger, cinnamon, and pepper and stir well. Stir in the broth and soy sauce. Bring to a boil. Reduce the heat and add 1½ cups (1.3 kg) of the cooked beans, using a slotted spoon. Save the remaining beans for another use.

Using an immersion blender, blend the gravy in the saucepan. Stir in the yeast, cover the saucepan, and cook over medium heat for 5 minutes, stirring occasionally, or until slightly thickened.

Yield: 3 to 4 cups (780 to 1040 g)

▶ *Canning Materials Needed*
  - *Jars and lids with rings*
  - *Wide-mouth funnel*
  - *Canning pot, at least 12-quart (1.1 L) capacity*
  - *Canning tongs*
  - *Magnetic lid lifter, to lift lids and rings from hot water bath*

▶ *Canning Basics*
Place clean jars, lids, and rings in hot, not boiling, water until ready to fill. Prepare your recipe. Remove hot jars and drain. Ladle recipe into jars, using a wide-mouth funnel. Remove the lids and ring and apply so that it is finger tight. Do not overtighten the rings, because air needs to escape from the jars during the processing. Carefully lower the jars into the boiling water bath using the canning rack or canning tongs. Process according to the time given in the recipe. Carefully remove the jars from the water bath using canning tongs. Place the jars in a safe place, where they will remain undisturbed, to cool. Once completely cooled, remove rings and dry any excess moisture. Replace rings.

SUN-DRIED TOMATO, GARLIC, AND BASIL OLIVE OIL
Flavored oils like this one are great over pasta and for dipping fresh bread, sautéing veggies, and drizzling over salads. The longer the oil sits, the more flavor it gets.

6 tablespoons (1½ ounces, or 48 g) julienne-cut sun-dried tomatoes
1 head (about 8 cloves) garlic, peeled
1 tablespoon (2 g) dried basil
1¼ cups (295 ml) extra-virgin olive oil

Add all of the ingredients to a 12-ounce (355 ml) jar or bottle. Seal. Store in a cool, dark place.
    Use within 2 months.

Yield: 12 ounces (355 ml)

BUFFALO HOT SAUCE
Buffalo sauce is really easy to make. It's simply one part melted butter mixed with one part hot pepper sauce–Frank's on the East Coast, Tabasco on the West.

1 pound (454 g) fresh red jalapeños (or other spicy red pepper)
2 tablespoons (30 ml) olive oil
1 cup (235 ml) distilled white vinegar
2 teaspoons salt
2 cups (448 g) nondairy butter

1 tablespoon (15 g) minced garlic
1 teaspoon red pepper flakes, for extra heat, optional

To make the hot pepper sauce: Preheat the oven to 400°F (200°C, or gas mark 6). Line a rimmed baking sheet with foil.
    In a bowl, coat the jalapeños in the oil. Arrange the peppers in a single layer on the prepared baking sheet and roast for 1 hour, or until browned and charred. Remove the peppers from the oven and cool them completely. Remove and discard the stems.
    Transfer the peppers and juices to a food processor. Purée. Strain into a bowl through a fine-mesh sieve, pressing with the back of a wooden spoon, to get as much of the pulp as possible. Add the vinegar and salt and stir to combine.
    In a pot, combine 2 cups (470 ml) of the pepper sauce, butter, garlic, and red pepper flakes (if using) and heat over medium heat until the butter is completely melted.

Yield: 4 (8-ounce, or 235 ml) jars

SWEET WHISKEY BARBECUE SAUCE
This sweet and tangy barbecue sauce can do battle against any store-bought version.

¼ cup (60 ml) olive oil
1 medium yellow onion, roughly chopped
6 to 8 cloves garlic, minced
2 (15-ounce, or 425 g each) cans tomato sauce
¼ cup (60 ml) vegan Worcestershire sauce
½ cup (160 g) grape jelly
1 cup (220 g) firmly packed brown sugar
1 tablespoon (15 g) sriracha
½ cup (120 ml) whiskey
2 tablespoons (30 ml) liquid smoke
¼ cup (60 g) Dijon mustard
Salt, to taste
Black pepper, to taste

In a medium pot, heat the oil over medium-high heat. Sauté the onion and garlic for about 5 minutes, or until translucent. Add the tomato sauce, Worcestershire, jelly, sugar, sriracha, whiskey, liquid smoke, mustard, and salt and pepper to taste and stir to combine. Bring to a boil, reduce the heat to low, cover, and simmer for 30 minutes, or until thick and fragrant.
    If desired, use an immersion blender or carefully transfer to a tabletop blender and purée until smooth.

Yield: 6 (8-ounce, or 235 ml) jars

CALIFORNIA CHOW-CHOW

Chow-chow is pickled relish made from a combination of vegetables. This California chow-chow is a bit spicier and a tad sharper than the traditional Pennsylvania and Southern ones.

FOR BRINE:
For each 1 cup (235 ml) water, use 1 tablespoon (18 g) fine sea salt

FOR CHOW-CHOW:
1 tablespoon (6 g) black peppercorns
1 teaspoon whole mustard seed
1 teaspoon coriander seed
6 broccoli florets
6 cauliflower florets
24 carrot coins
2 cloves garlic, cut in half
1 tablespoon (7 g) chopped sun-dried tomatoes
1 bay leaf, broken into pieces
1 teaspoon fresh dill
½ teaspoon dried parsley
½ teaspoon dried chives
⅛ teaspoon red pepper flakes

To make the brine: In a saucepot, bring the water and salt to a boil over high heat. Boil until all the salt is dissolved. Reduce the heat to low and keep warm until ready to pour.

To make the chow-chow: In a very dry skillet, lightly toast the peppercorns, mustard seed, and coriander seed over medium-low heat.

Sterilize a 16-ounce (470 ml) canning jar with lid and ring. Pack the broccoli, cauliflower, and carrots into the jar. Add the garlic, sun-dried tomatoes, bay leaf, dill, parsley, chives, red pepper flakes, and toasted spices to the jar. Pour in the hot brine to fill the jar, allowing ½ inch (1.3 cm) of space at the top.

Place the lid and ring on the jar and give it a good shake to distribute all of the ingredients.

Place upright and allow to cool. (The lid should self-seal as the brine cools, creating a vacuum in the jar.) Place in a cool, dark place for 1 week, then refrigerate.

Yield: 1 (16-ounce, or 470 ml) jar

HOMEMADE TOFU MAYO

Store-bought vegan mayo might be delicious, but it can be pricey. This version is super easy and fast to make.

1 package (12 ounces, or 340 g) soft silken tofu, drained
⅓ cup (80 ml) extra-virgin olive oil
⅓ cup (80 ml) canola (or other mild-flavored vegetable) oil
1 tablespoon (15 ml) apple cider vinegar
1 tablespoon (15 ml) lemon juice

1 tablespoon (15 g) Dijon mustard
1 tablespoon (13 g) evaporated cane juice (or agave nectar)
1 tablespoon (8 g) nutritional yeast, optional
½ teaspoon salt

In a blender, purée all of the ingredients until silky smooth. Transfer the mixture to an airtight container and store in the fridge for up to 2 weeks.

Yield: Just over 2 cups (475 ml)

CASHEW "CHEESY" SAUCE

This sauce tastes great over pasta, potatoes, vegetables, or anywhere a tasty cheesy sauce would be used.

1 cup (112 g) raw cashews
2 cups (470 ml) vegetable broth
¼ cup (30 g) nutritional yeast
¼ cup (32 g) arrowroot powder or cornstarch
2 tablespoons (34 g) tomato ketchup
1 tablespoon (10 g) minced garlic
1 tablespoon (18 g) white or yellow miso paste
1 tablespoon (8 g) onion powder
1 tablespoon (15 ml) lemon juice
1 to 2 teaspoons Dijon mustard
½ teaspoon turmeric
½ teaspoon ground paprika

Soak cashews in water overnight. Rinse and drain.

In a blender, purée all of the ingredients until silky smooth. Transfer the mixture to a pot and heat over medium heat, whisking constantly, until thickened.

Use immediately or cool and store in an airtight container in the fridge for up to 1 week. (To reheat, warm on the stovetop or in the microwave, adding water or vegetable broth if needed to thin it out.)

Yield: 3 cups (705 ml)

CREAMY COCONUT CAESAR SALAD DRESSING

This dressing is delicious and similar in appearance and texture to Caesar dressing. It's also full of fiber and protein thanks to the white beans, which provide the creamy texture.

½ cup (91 g) cooked white beans
¼ cup (60 ml) canned coconut milk
1 tablespoon (14 g) raw, unrefined coconut oil, melted
1 tablespoon (15 ml) lemon juice
1 tablespoon (15 ml) apple cider vinegar

1 *Vegetable Broth*; 2 *Cashew Cream*; 3 *Peachy Butter*; 4 *Classic Strawberry Jam*; 5 *Orange Basil Marmalade*;
6 *Lemon Lavender Curd*; 7 *Ginger-Cinnamon White Bean Gravy*; 8 *Sun-Dried Tomato, Garlic, and Basil Olive Oil*

9 Buffalo Hot Sauce; 10 Sweet Whiskey Barbecue Sauce; 11 California Chow-Chow; 12 Homemade Tofu Mayo; 13 Cashew "Cheesy" Sauce; 14 Creamy Coconut Caesar Salad Dressing; 15 Basic Brown Bread; 16 Bizquix; 17 Pain Ordinaire

2 teaspoons chia seeds
¼ teaspoon salt
¼ teaspoon dried dill
⅛ teaspoon onion powder
⅛ teaspoon garlic powder

In a high-speed blender, blend all of the ingredients until creamy and smooth. Transfer to a glass jar. Serve chilled.

Yield: 1 cup (235 ml)

COCONUT WHIPPED CREAM (PHOTO PAGE 4)
Whipped cream is never considered a health food–unless you make coconut whipped cream. With this cream, you can enjoy a little sweet treat and a boost of health benefits.

1 can (13½ ounces, or 400 ml) coconut milk (full fat)
1 teaspoon pure vanilla extract

Refrigerate the can of coconut milk, upside down, for several hours or overnight to chill it thoroughly. While keeping the can of coconut milk upside down, carefully open the can. (Because the bottom of the can is now the "top," the water, or liquid coconut milk, will now be at the top of the can.) Spoon out the top layer of water and save it for other recipes. (It's perfect to use in smoothies.)

Spoon out the remaining thick white coconut milk into a medium bowl. Add the vanilla and beat with an electric mixer using the whisk attachment until soft peaks form. Serve chilled. (Store in an airtight container in the fridge for up to 3 days.)

Yield: About 2 cups (120 g)

BIZQUIX
This simple biscuit mix can be used where most traditional biscuit mixes are called for. Use in pancakes, biscuits, waffles, and other recipes instead of an all-purpose baking mix.

3 cups (474 g) superfine brown rice flour
1½ cups (195 g) sorghum flour
¾ cup (97 g) potato starch
¼ cup (32 g) tapioca starch
1 teaspoon xanthan gum
½ teaspoon salt
1¼ teaspoons (5 g) baking soda
3 tablespoons (21 g) baking powder
1 cup (240 ml) coconut oil, slightly softened but not liquefied

In a large bowl, combine the flours, starches, xanthan gum,

salt, baking soda, and baking powder. Stir in the oil and mix with a pastry blender or your hands until crumbly. Cover and chill in the fridge for a few hours until cold. In a food processor, pulse the crumbly mixture until it turns into a very uniform and fine mixture.

Store in an airtight container in the fridge for up to 3 weeks.

Yield: 10 servings, or 5½ cups (687 g)

PAIN ORDINAIRE
This crusty and toothsome white bread is great for serving fresh. It's also perfect for small bites such as mini cucumber tea sandwiches.

2½ cups (400 g) superfine brown rice flour
½ cup (65 g) cornstarch
1 tablespoon (18 g) psyllium husk powder
1½ teaspoons baking powder
1 teaspoon salt
2½ packets (20 g) dry active yeast
¼ cup (50 g) sugar
1 cup (235 ml) warm water
2 cups (475 ml) warm almond milk, divided
½ cup (120 ml) water
2 teaspoons vinegar
¼ cup (60 ml) + 2 tablespoons (28 ml) olive oil
1 tablespoon (12 g) ground chia seeds mixed with ¼ cup (60 ml) water
1 teaspoon olive oil + 1 tablespoon (15 ml) water

Lightly oil a standard-size loaf pan.

In a large bowl, sift together the flour, cornstarch, psyllium husk, baking powder, and salt.

In a small bowl, mix the yeast with the sugar, warm water, and 1½ cups (355 ml) of the milk until foamy and let rest for about 5 minutes. Add the water, vinegar, oil, and chia gel mixture.

Stir the wet ingredients into the flour mix. Add the remaining ½ cup (120 ml) almond milk. If using an electric mixer, mix on medium-high for about 2 minutes. If doing by hand, vigorously mix together the ingredients until a sticky dough forms and then continue to mix for 1 to 2 minutes until the dough becomes slightly fluffy.

Place the dough in the prepared pan. Let rise in a warm place for about 50 minutes.

Preheat the oven to 400°F (200°C, gas mark 6). Lightly brush the oil-water mixture onto the tops of the loaf. Bake on the middle rack for about 40 to 45 minutes or until golden brown on top. Cool for 20 minutes before removing from the pan. Cool completely before cutting with a serrated knife.

Yield: 1 loaf

BASIC BROWN BREAD

This bread is perfect for midday snacking, toasting, or using as bread crumbs. It's delicious toasted and topped with vegan mayonnaise, a garden tomato, and freshly ground black pepper.

1 tablespoon (7 g) active dry yeast
3 tablespoons (40 g) sugar
1½ cups (355 ml) warm water (110°F [43°C])
1¼ cups (150 g) buckwheat flour
¾ cup (97 g) sorghum flour
1 cup (130 g) potato starch
½ cup (60 g) tapioca starch
2 teaspoons (4 g) xanthan gum
1 teaspoon salt
3 tablespoons (45 ml) olive oil

In a large bowl, combine the yeast, sugar, and warm water and let proof until foamy, about 10 minutes. Lightly grease an 8 x 4-inch (20 x 10 cm) metal loaf pan.

In separate bowl, stir together the flours, starches, xanthan gum, and salt.

Add the oil to the yeast and mix well. Slowly incorporate the flour mixture until thoroughly combined. Mix on medium speed for about 1 minute or until the dough becomes sticky.

Spread the dough in the prepared pan. Smooth the top with wet fingertips.

Let the dough rest in a warm place for about 40 minutes or until the dough has risen a bit.

Preheat the oven to 450°F (230°C, or gas mark 8].
Bake on the center rack of the oven for 15 minutes.

Reduce the oven temperature to 385°F (195°C, or gas mark 5] and bake for 30 to 35 minutes longer or until golden brown on top and hollow sounding when tapped. Cool the bread in the pan for 10 minutes before transferring to a cooling rack, and then cool completely on the rack before cutting with a serrated knife. Store in an airtight container.

Yield: 10 servings

WHOLE WHEAT BREAD (PHOTO PAGE 4]

This bread is hearty and wholesome. It's perfect as sliced sandwich bread or as an accompaniment to a hot bowl of soup.

1 envelope active dry yeast
2 ¼ cups (530 ml) warm water
6 cups (750 g) whole wheat flour
1 teaspoon salt
2 tablespoons (30 ml) agave nectar
2 to 3 tablespoons (30 to 45 ml) olive oil, optional

Grease one 9-inch (23-cm) or two 8-inch (20-cm) loaf pans.

In a small bowl, add the yeast to the water and allow it to dissolve. (You can give it a little stir.) Let it sit for 10 minutes. The yeast should begin to form a creamy foam on the surface of the water. If not, the yeast is dead, and you need to start over with a new packet.

In a large bowl, mix together the flour and salt. Make a well in the center of the mixture. Pour the yeast and water mixture, agave, and oil, if using, into the well. Stir from the center outward, incorporating the liquid ingredients into the flour. Fold in the remaining flour from the sides of the bowl, and stir until the mixture forms a soft dough. If the dough is too dry, add a small amount of water. If the dough is too sticky, add a bit of flour.

Turn out the dough onto a breadboard (or continue using the stand mixer). For best results, knead the dough for about 10 minutes, without adding any more flour. If you're using a stand mixer, you won't need to do this for more than 5 minutes. (The dough should be elastic and smooth.)

Place the dough in a lightly oiled bowl, cover with a damp cloth, and let sit in a warm, draft-free spot to rise and double in size. (At 70°F (21°C], this should take about 2½ hours.) Then test the dough by poking a wet finger ½ inch (1.3 cm) into the dough. If the dough doesn't fill back in, it is ready. Gently press out the air, making the dough into a smooth ball. Return it to the bowl for a second rise, which will take about half as long as the first. After 1 hour, test the dough with your finger again. After the second rising, turn the dough onto a lightly floured countertop or breadboard. Deflate the dough by pressing it gently from one side to the other. Cut it in half and form each part into a round ball. Cover the balls and let them rest for about 10 minutes.

Shape each ball into a loaf, and place the loaves in the prepared pan(s). Let rise for about 30 minutes.

Preheat the oven to 425°F (220°C, or gas mark 7]. Bake for 10 minutes, and then lower the temperature to 325°F (170°C, or gas mark 3]. Bake for 45 to 60 minutes, or until the loaves turn a golden brown color. (The loaves should slip easily out of the pans. When you tap their bottoms, they should sound hollow.) Cool slightly before slicing.

Yield: 1 large or 2 standard-size loaves

APPETIZERS

See pages 20–21, 26–27, 34–35, 42–43, 50–51, and 56–57 for appetizer photos.

TOFU FETA

This isn't exactly like feta cheese, but it's pretty close. It makes a great addition to salads, pizzas, and hors d'oeuvres. Adjust the salt to your own taste.

1 block (1 pound, or 454 g) extra-firm tofu, drained and
    pressed to remove any extra water
3 tablespoons (45 ml) apple cider vinegar
3 tablespoons (45 ml) Kalamata or other olive juice
    (from a jar of olives packed in water, not oil)
6 tablespoons (90 ml) lemon juice
2 to 3 teaspoons (10 to 15 g) salt

The night before, freeze the pressed tofu overnight in a freezer-safe plastic bag.

The next day, let the frozen tofu thaw for about 4 hours, and then press it again to remove any moisture. Crumble into ½-inch (1.3 cm) chunks into a medium bowl.

In a separate small bowl, whisk together the vinegar, olive juice, lemon juice, and 2 teaspoons (10 g) of the salt. Drizzle the mixture over the tofu and stir to combine.

Let rest in the fridge for 1 hour, stir again, and let rest 1 hour longer. Add the remaining 1 teaspoon (5 g) salt, if using. Store in an airtight container for up to 1 week.

Yield: 10 servings, about 2 ounces (55 g) each

ALMOND-CRUSTED TOFU WITH BLACKBERRY SAUCE

This crispy, crunchy tofu pairs well with the sweetness and tartness of the sauce. Serve the crispy tofu with the sauce drizzled on it or on the side for dipping.

1 package (14 ounces, or 397 g) extra-firm tofu, drained
    and pressed at least 3 hours
¼ cup (30 g) gram flour
¼ cup (60 ml) water
½ teaspoon salt, plus a dash
1½ cups (168 g) almond meal
1 cup (145 g) fresh or frozen blackberries
2 tablespoons (28 ml) full-bodied red wine (such as
    Bordeaux)
2 tablespoons (26 g) sugar
1 tablespoon (8 g) cornstarch
2 tablespoons (28 g) very cold water

The day before making, place the tofu in a freezer-safe plastic bag and seal tightly. Freeze overnight, and then let thaw on the countertop for a few hours until thawed. Slice the tofu carefully into equal-size squares.

Preheat the oven to 400°F (200°C, gas mark 6). Line a baking sheet with parchment paper.

In a small bowl, whisk together the gram flour, water, and ½ teaspoon salt until no lumps remain.

In a separate bowl, place the almond meal. Dip each square of tofu first into the flour mixture to coat evenly. Next, dip each square into the almond meal to coat, and place on the prepared baking sheet. Bake for 20 minutes, flip, and then bake about 15 more minutes until the tofu is browned on all sides.

To make the sauce, in a small saucepan, combine the blackberries, wine, sugar, and dash of salt and heat over medium heat, stirring occasionally, for about 8 minutes, or until the berries begin to break apart.

In a small bowl, mix together the cornstarch with the cold water until very smooth and then stir into the blackberries. Turn off the burner and let the sauce thicken and cool, about 10 minutes.

Yield: 6 servings

BAKED BUFFALO TOFU BITES

Made with tofu, these cubes still cry out for the traditional sides of celery sticks and dip. Serve the cubes with the sauce. For super-spicy results, pour the sauce over the cubes just before serving.

FOR THE BITES:
2 tablespoons (30 ml) hot sauce (such as Frank's)
2 tablespoons (30 ml) tamari
2 teaspoons Dijon mustard
2 teaspoons onion powder, divided
1 teaspoon garlic powder, divided
¼ teaspoon black pepper, plus more to taste
15 ounces (425 g) extra-firm tofu, drained, pressed, and
    cut into 1-inch (2.5 cm) cubes
3 tablespoons (45 ml) unsweetened plain vegan milk
½ cup (64 g) arrowroot powder, more if needed
1 cup (80 g) panko crumbs
Salt, to taste

FOR THE SAUCE:
½ cup (120 ml) hot sauce (such as Frank's)
2 tablespoons (28 g) vegan butter, melted
2 teaspoons Dijon mustard
1 teaspoon pure maple syrup

To make the bites: In a medium bowl, combine the hot sauce, tamari, mustard, 1 teaspoon of the onion powder, ½ teaspoon of the garlic powder, and pepper. Add the tofu, stirring to coat. Cover and refrigerate for 1 hour, or up to 12 hours.

Preheat the oven to 400°F (200°C, or gas mark 6). Lightly coat a baking sheet with nonstick cooking spray.

Remove the cubes from the marinade. Add the milk to any remaining marinade.

Put the arrowroot powder on a plate.

On another plate, combine the panko, remaining 1 teaspoon onion powder, remaining ½ teaspoon garlic powder, salt, and pepper. Dip the cubes into the marinade mixture, shaking off any excess, then coat with the arrowroot. Dip them into the marinade mixture again, then generously coat with panko. Place the cubes on the prepared baking sheet and bake for 25 minutes. Turn the cubes and bake for 10 minutes longer, or until nicely golden.

To make the sauce: In a medium bowl, whisk together the hot sauce, butter, mustard, and syrup.

Yield: 4 servings

CINNAMON-ROASTED CAULIFLOWER
This cauliflower's light cinnamon flavor and crunchy corn-meal exterior make for an elegant, easy appetizer.

1 medium head cauliflower (about 2 pounds [910 g])
3 tablespoons (45 ml) olive oil, divided
3 tablespoons (27 g) cornmeal
1 teaspoon cinnamon
1 teaspoon salt

Preheat the oven to 400°F (200°C, or gas mark 6).

Cut the cauliflower into bite-size pieces (about 1 inch [2.5 cm] across). Discard the tough core. Place the cauliflower florets in a large bowl and coat evenly with 2 tablespoons (30 ml) of the oil.

In a small bowl, sift together the cornmeal, cinnamon, and salt. Sprinkle evenly onto the cauliflower and toss until each floret is well coated. Add a touch more cornmeal if needed to evenly cover. Transfer the cauliflower to an ungreased baking sheet (flat sides down), discarding any excess cornmeal. Drizzle lightly with the remaining 1 tablespoon (15 ml) oil. Bake for about 40 minutes without flipping, or until the cauliflower is crispy and browned on the edges and bottoms. Using a flat spatula, gently transfer the cauliflower to a plate.

Yield: 8 servings

BAKED CORN PUDDING
The easiest way to serve this classic dish, which is unlike sweet pudding and closer to a very wet cornbread, is by scooping it with a spoon, hence the name "corn pudding."

⅓ cup (80 ml) olive oil
½ cup (60 g) masa harina flour
¼ teaspoon salt
1 teaspoon baking powder
⅓ cup (47 g) finely ground cornmeal
¼ cup (60 ml) water
¼ cup (50 g) sugar
5 tablespoons (75 ml) canned coconut milk
2 cups (300 g) fresh or thawed frozen corn kernels

Preheat the oven to 325°F (170°C, or gas mark 3). Lightly grease an 8 x 8-inch (20 x 20 cm) glass baking dish.

In a large bowl, mix all of the ingredients together until well combined. Spread into the prepared pan and bake for 50 to 55 minutes, or until the edges are lightly golden brown.

Yield: 8 servings

GLAZED SUGAR SNAPS
These sugar snaps are delicious hot, warm, or at room temperature. The glaze is versatile: Try it with asparagus or green beans.

1½ tablespoons (23 ml) tamari
1½ tablespoons (23 ml) seasoned rice vinegar
1½ teaspoons pure maple syrup
1½ teaspoons light miso
¾ teaspoon Sriracha, or more to taste
1 teaspoon cornstarch
1 pound (454 g) fresh sugar snap peas, trimmed
3 cloves garlic, minced
¾ teaspoon minced fresh ginger
½ teaspoon toasted sesame oil
½ teaspoon toasted sesame seeds

In a small bowl, whisk together the tamari, vinegar, syrup, miso, Sriracha, and cornstarch.

In a wok or dry skillet over high heat, cook the peas for about 3 minutes, stirring frequently, or until black spots appear. (Do not overcook.) Add the garlic, ginger, oil, and seeds. Cook, stirring, for 1 minute. Add the tamari mixture. Cook and stir until thickened, about 2 minutes.

Yield: 4 servings

STUFFED CHERRY TOMATOES

This irresistible finger food should be eaten practically hot from the oven. Let 'em cool for just a few minutes before offering them up for munching.

1 cup (120 g) chopped walnuts
1 tablespoon (2.5 g) fresh sage
2 cloves garlic, minced
½ cup (75 g) chopped onion
1 tablespoon (15 g) apricot jam
1 teaspoon salt
26 cherry tomatoes
Olive oil

Preheat the oven to 350°F (180°C, or gas mark 4).

In a food processor, combine the walnuts, sage, garlic, onion, jam, and salt. Pulse several times until a paste is formed.

Slice the tops off of the tomatoes. Using a small spoon, scoop out the seeds of each tomato and discard the seedy filling. Fill each tomato with the walnut paste and replace the tomato cap. Arrange the tomatoes snugly in a small baking dish so the caps remain upright. Drizzle lightly with oil. Bake for about 30 minutes.

Yield: 13 servings, 2 tomatoes each

CHERRY TOMATOES STUFFED WITH GREEN OLIVE TAPENADE

These cherry tomatoes offer a world of flavor in each and every bite. They can be served immediately or chilled for 1 hour to let the flavors mingle.

20 cherry tomatoes
1 cup (100 g) pitted green olives
1 tablespoon (9 g) capers
1 clove garlic, minced
1 to 2 tablespoons (15 to 30 ml) lemon juice
2 tablespoons (30 ml) olive oil
Chopped parsley, for garnish
Lemon zest, for garnish

Cut the top off each cherry tomato. Using a small spoon, carefully scoop out the seeds and pulp. Place each tomato shell upside down on paper towels to drain.

In a blender or food processor, blend the olives, capers, garlic, juice, and oil until smooth. Divide the tapenade among each tomato shell, sprinkle with parsley and zest.

Yield: 20 servings

LEMON-ROASTED LEEKS

Lemon and leeks go hand in hand to make an incredibly easy and tangy appetizer.

4 large leeks
2 tablespoons (30 ml) olive oil
Zest and juice of 1 lemon
¼ cup (60 ml) water
¾ teaspoon salt
Black pepper to taste

Preheat the oven to 375°F (190°C, or gas mark 5).

Remove the outermost layer of skin on each leek and cut off and discard the root ends. Slice the leeks in half lengthwise and clean well under cold running water. Cut at the point where the leek begins to turn green, and reserve the remaining darker green tops for soup stock. Arrange the leeks in a baking dish so that they have room to lie flat.

In a small bowl, whisk together the oil, zest, juice, and water until well combined. Drizzle the dressing over the leeks. Season lightly and evenly with salt.

Roast for 35 to 45 minutes, or until the top layer is crispy and browned on the edges and the inner layers are tender and easy to cut with a knife. Remove the leeks from the oven, cut into bite-size pieces, and serve with pepper.

Yield: 4 servings

COMPASSIONATE CALAMARI

This dish is deliciously crispy and reminiscent of actual calamari. But happily, no squid were harmed in the making of this terrific appetizer. Serve it with your favorite dip.

Vegetable oil, for cooking

FOR THE COATING:
3 tablespoons (21 g) flaxseed meal mixed with 6 tablespoons (90 ml) warm water
¼ cup (60 ml) nondairy milk
¼ teaspoon sea salt

FOR THE DRY BATTER:
½ cup (30 g) brown rice flour
⅓ cup (47 g) ground yellow cornmeal
1 teaspoon dulse granules or flakes

FOR THE WET BATTER:
1 cup (140 g) finely ground yellow cornmeal
1½ cups (350 ml) nondairy milk
6 large king oyster mushrooms, tough bottoms removed, sliced into ¼- to ½-inch (6 mm to 1.3 cm)-wide strips
Salt, to taste

Pour the oil to a depth of 5 inches (13 cm) into a deep fryer or deep pot and heat to 360°F (182°C).

To make the coating: In a small bowl, mix all the coating ingredients together.

To make the dry batter: In a small bowl, sift together all the dry batter ingredients.

To make the wet batter: In a medium bowl, whisk the cornmeal and nondairy milk together until a thick batter forms.

When the oil is at temperature, dip one mushroom slice first into the coating, then into the dry batter, and finally into the wet batter, letting any excess drip off. (The mushroom should be evenly coated.) Drop the mushroom immediately into the hot oil and quickly repeat with a few more mushrooms until the fryer is filled. Fry for 6 minutes, or until dark golden brown. Remove with a skimmer and transfer to paper towels to absorb any excess grease. Season lightly with salt. Repeat until each mushroom slice has been cooked.

Yield: 8 servings

MEDITERRANEAN CROQUETTES

Reminiscent of baked falafel, these croquettes work as an appetizer, a main course, stuffed into bread and eaten as a sandwich, or topped with some grated veggies.

4 medium-size Yukon gold potatoes, unpeeled, cubed
    into small pieces
4 to 6 cloves garlic, minced
1½ cups (350 ml) water
1 heaping tablespoon (15 g) tahini
½ teaspoon salt
1¼ cups (162 g) chickpea flour
½ cup (75 g) diced roasted red bell pepper
½ cup (50 g) chopped Kalamata olives
⅔ cup (40 g) minced fresh parsley
1 teaspoon black pepper
Zest of 1 lemon
Olive oil, for baking

In a large frying pan, combine the potatoes, garlic, and water. Cover (with a slight vent) and cook over medium-high heat for about 15 minutes, stirring occasionally, or until the water has been cooked away and the potatoes are fork-tender. (You might need to add more water if the water cooks off before the potatoes are done.) Transfer the potatoes to a bowl and mix until mashed, or use a potato masher and mash by hand. Mash just until well blended, leaving some lumps. Stir the tahini and salt into the potatoes, mixing until just combined. Next, stir in the chickpea flour until well mixed. (Do not overstir.) Fold in the red pepper, olives, parsley, black pepper, and zest. Chill the dough in the freezer for about 15 minutes.

Preheat the oven to 400°F (200°C, or gas mark 6). Lightly oil a baking sheet.

Shape the dough into twenty 2-inch-wide x ¾-inch-thick (5 x 2 cm) patties and transfer to the prepared baking sheet. Brush both sides gently with oil. Bake for 20 minutes. Flip and bake for 20 minutes longer, or until golden brown on both sides.

Yield: 10 servings (20 croquettes)

SAVE THE FISHIES CAKES

Jackfruit and chickpeas create a texture for these cakes that is flaky, tender, undeniably delicious, and pretty similar in taste to a traditional fish cake.

1 tablespoon (15 ml) olive oil + more as needed
1 can (10 ounces, or 280 g) green jackfruit
1 tablespoon (3 g) dulse flakes
1 teaspoon minced fresh sage
1 teaspoon minced fresh thyme
1 teaspoon minced fresh tarragon
Salt, to taste
1½ cups (360 g) cooked chickpeas
1 large potato, unpeeled, baked, and chopped
½ cup (30 g) chopped fresh parsley
1 rib celery, minced
2 to 3 dashes liquid smoke
1 teaspoon salt
½ teaspoon Dijon mustard
4 shallots, minced
2 tablespoons (20 g) superfine brown rice flour

Preheat the oven to 400°F (200°C, gas mark 6). Line a baking sheet with parchment paper.

In a frying pan, heat 1 tablespoon (15 ml) of the oil over medium-high heat.

Combine the jackfruit with the dulse flakes in the pan and sauté for about 10 to 12 minutes, stirring often, or until the jackfruit becomes stringy and slightly golden brown. Add the sage, thyme, tarragon, and salt to taste. (You may need to break the jackfruit into smaller strands with a plastic spatula while cooking.) If the jackfruit sticks slightly to the pan, add more oil.

In a blender, combine the jackfruit with the chickpeas and pulse carefully just until it becomes slightly crumbly. Transfer to a medium bowl. Add the potato. Using a fork, mash the jackfruit and potato just until well combined. Stir in the parsley, celery, liquid smoke, salt, Dijon, and shallots and combine until uniform. Lightly dust the dough with the flour, distributing evenly.

Shape into 3-inch (7.5 cm) patties and place on the prepared baking sheet. Brush both sides of each patty with oil and bake for 25 minutes. Flip and bake an additional 15 to 20 minutes, or until the patties are golden brown on both sides.

Yield: 12 cakes

FRUIT SUSHI (A.K.A. FRUSHI) WITH STRAWBERRY REDUCTION SAUCE

This is a sweet, creamy variation on the traditional Japanese entrée. If you chill the rice after it cooks, it's easier to mold into oblong mounds.

FOR THE SUSHI:
1 cup (195 g) short-grain or other sushi rice, rinsed
1 cup (235 ml) water
1 cup unsweetened (235 ml) coconut milk
1 to 2 tablespoons (12 to 25 g) granulated sugar
Pinch of salt

FOR THE SAUCE:
2 cups (340 g) diced strawberries
½ teaspoon black pepper
2 teaspoons (10 ml) orange juice
½ cup (120 ml) water
2 tablespoons (30 ml) balsamic vinegar

4 ripe peaches or nectarines
¼ cup (80 g) fruit preserves
1 pint (290 g) fresh strawberries, thinly sliced
36 berries (fresh raspberries, blueberries, or blackberries)
48 large mint leaves or curly leaf lettuce, for garnish, optional
2 tablespoons (16 g) black sesame seeds, for garnish, optional

To make the sushi, in a pot, bring the rice, water, and coconut milk to a boil. Lower the heat, cover, and simmer until the liquid is absorbed and the rice is soft. (If the liquid evaporates before the rice is done, add a small amount of extra water or coconut milk.) Next, stir the sugar and salt in with the rice. Using a fork, fluff the rice to distribute evenly. Let the rice cool completely.

To prepare the sauce, in a pot, heat the strawberries, pepper, juice, water, and vinegar over medium heat until reduced to a syrupy consistency. Strain through a fine-mesh strainer until completely smooth.

In a pot of boiling water, blanch the peaches for 60 seconds. Cool the peaches in a bowl of ice water, and then peel the skin. Thinly slice half-moons from the fruit pits.

Press bits of rice between your hands to create oblong mounds. Carefully spread a thin layer of preserves on top of each mound, and top with a peach slice, a strawberry slice, and a berry.

On a serving plate, arrange the mint leaves, if using. Place the "frushi" rolls on the leaves and sprinkle with black sesame seeds, if using. Drizzle with the sauce.

Yield: 36 pieces

CUCUMBER PEANUT CHUTNEY

You can buy chaat masala at Indian markets and specialty spice stores. This is a great appetizer to eat with chips or chopped veggies. Serve it at room temperature or well chilled.

1 shallot, chopped
1 medium tomato, diced
1 medium cucumber, deseeded and chopped
½ cup (4 g) freshly chopped cilantro
1½ tablespoons (23 ml) lemon juice
2 tablespoons (30 ml) cooking oil
1 cup (150 g) raw peanuts
1 teaspoon black pepper
¼ teaspoon red chile powder
½ teaspoon chaat masala or garam masala

In a food processor, combine the shallot, tomato, cucumber, cilantro, and juice. Pulse briefly until well chopped but not puréed.

In a small pan, heat the oil over medium-high heat. Add the peanuts, pepper, chile powder, and chaat masala and cook for about 2 minutes, or until darkened, stirring occasionally. Combine the peanuts with the rest of the chutney.

Yield: 8 servings, about 3 tablespoons (45 g) each

BLUEBERRY AVOCADO SALSA

This fruity salsa is sure to delight as well as intrigue. It's best made with fresh blueberries, but frozen will also work just fine.

2 large tomatoes, quartered
2 cups (290 g) fresh blueberries
2 tablespoons (30 ml) lime juice, plus extra for drizzling
¼ cup (40 g) chopped green onion
½ cup (8 g) chopped fresh cilantro
1 teaspoon salt, or more to taste
1 jalapeño pepper, stemmed, seeded, and chopped (Leave the seeds in if you like more heat.)
1 ripe avocado, peeled, pitted, and cut into small chunks

In a food processor, combine the tomatoes, blueberries, 2 tablespoons (30 ml) juice, onion, cilantro, salt, and jalapeño and pulse a few times. Transfer to a bowl. Drizzle some more juice over the avocado chunks. Add to the salsa and stir to combine. Add a touch more salt if desired.

Yield: 3 servings, ¼ cup (62 g) each

SPINACH ARTICHOKE DIP

This richly flavored dip is great for movie night. Serve it hot with your favorite dipping chips or crackers.

1 recipe unsweetened Cashew Cream (See page 6.)
½ cup (110 g) vegan mayonnaise
½ cup (65 g) nutritional yeast
3 cloves garlic, minced
2 cups (60 g) packed chopped spinach leaves
1 can (14 ounces, or 392 g) large artichoke hearts, chopped
3 green onions, sliced into small rings
1 teaspoon lemon zest
½ teaspoon black pepper
Salt, to taste

Preheat the oven to 350°F (180°C, or gas mark 4).

In a small bowl, stir together the cream, mayonnaise, yeast, garlic, spinach, artichokes, onions, zest, and pepper until very well combined. Season with salt.

Place the mixture in an oven-safe dish. Bake for 25 minutes. Turn the oven to broil and cook for 2 to 3 minutes, or until the top becomes golden brown and crispy.

Yield: 8 servings

ALMOND, GARLIC, LEMON SPREAD AND DIP

This dip is wonderful on crackers, raw veggies, and pita. It also makes a great spread for sandwiches, on crostini, or mixed with chopped raw kale to make a kicky kale salad.

1 cup (120 g) raw almonds
4 to 6 cloves garlic, or to taste
½ cup (120 ml) olive oil
¼ cup (60 ml) mild-flavored vegetable oil (such as canola)
¼ cup (60 ml) lemon juice
½ teaspoon salt
½ teaspoon black pepper
½ teaspoon ground paprika
½ teaspoon dried dill or 1½ teaspoons fresh
½ teaspoon dried basil or 1½ teaspoons fresh

Soak the almonds overnight.

The next day, rinse the almonds and place in a blender or food processor with the remaining ingredients. Process until smooth, stopping occasionally to scrape down the sides of the container. (This can take up to 5 minutes.) Store the dip in an airtight container in the fridge until ready to use.

Yield: 1¾ cups (415 ml)

PINEAPPLE MANGO CHUTNEY

Use this incredibly flavorful and beautiful dish as a "salsa," a topping for rice, or the basis for a vegetable stir-fry. Sweet tropical fruit always pairs well with spicy flavors.

2 tablespoons (30 ml) oil or water, for sautéing
1 teaspoon crushed red pepper flakes
1 large yellow onion, minced
1 tablespoon (6 g) minced fresh ginger
1 large yellow bell pepper, seeded and diced
2 ripe mangoes, peeled and diced
1 small pineapple, peeled and diced
¼ cup (60 g) firmly packed brown sugar
1½ tablespoons (9.5 g) curry powder
½ cup (120 ml) apple cider vinegar

In a large sauté pan, heat the oil over medium heat. Stir in the red pepper flakes. Cook until they begin to sizzle, about 1 minute, and then add the onion. Reduce the heat to low and cook for about 7 minutes, stirring occasionally, or until the onion has softened.

Increase the heat to medium and stir in the ginger, bell pepper, mangoes, pineapple, sugar, curry powder, and vinegar. Bring to a simmer and cook for 25 to 30 minutes, stirring occasionally. Cool the chutney completely. Store in airtight containers in the fridge.

Yield: 32 servings, about 2 tablespoons (30 g) each

SOCAL SALSA FRESCA

This fresh salsa screams with California sunshine.

2 cups (330 g) diced fresh mango
1 cup (13 g) finely diced cilantro
1 cup (160 g) finely diced red onion
1 tablespoon (15 g) minced garlic
1 teaspoon salt
½ teaspoon black pepper
2 jalapeño or serrano chiles, seeded, deveined, and finely diced
¼ cup (60 ml) lime juice
2 tablespoons (30 ml) white vinegar

FOR CANNING:
4 (8-ounce, or 235 ml) jars
4 rings and lids
Other "Canning Materials Needed" (See page 8.)

Place all the ingredients in a bowl and stir to combine.

Follow "Canning Basics" on page 8. Processing time is 15 minutes. Any jars that did not seal need to be stored in the fridge and used within 1 week. Refrigerate after opening.

Yield: 4 (8-ounce, or 235 ml) jars

S
N 1 *Tofu Feta;* 2 *Almond-Crusted Tofu with Blackberry Sauce;* 3 *Baked Buffalo Tofu Bites;* 4 *Cinnamon-Roasted Cauliflower;*
L 5 *Baked Corn Pudding;* 6 *Glazed Sugar Snaps;* 7 *Stuffed Cherry Tomatoes;* 8 *Cherry Tomatoes Stuffed with Green Olive Tapenade*

20 • THE LITTLE VEGAN COOKBOOK

9 Lemon-Roasted Leeks; 10 Compassionate Calamari; 11 Mediterranean Croquettes; 12 Save the Fishies Cakes; 13 Fruit Sushi (A.K.A. Frushi) with Strawberry Reduction Sauce; 14 Cucumber Peanut Chutney; 15 Blueberry Avocado Salsa; 16 Spinach Artichoke Dip

SEASIDE AVOCADO DIP

This recipe is modeled after a dip from Madagascar that's similar to guacamole but has anchovies as a main ingredient. Serve it with your favorite crackers.

FOR THE MARINATED MUSHROOMS:
1½ cups (105 g) sliced button mushrooms
3 tablespoons (9 g) dulse flakes
5 to 10 dashes liquid smoke
1 tablespoon (15 ml) olive oil
1½ teaspoons salt
½ tablespoon vegan Worcestershire sauce
⅔ cup (160 ml) water

FOR THE REST OF THE DIP:
4 ripe avocados, peeled and pitted
1½ tablespoons (23 ml) lime juice
1 teaspoon lime zest
1 tablespoon (15 ml) white wine
Salt, to taste
¼ cup (40 g) minced red onion or shallots

To make the marinated mushrooms: At least 2 hours before making the dip, place the sliced mushrooms in a small bowl and toss with all the other ingredients until well coated. Cover and let rest between 1 and 4 hours. Squeeze all the liquid from the mushrooms until they are fairly dry. Chop into ½-inch (1 cm) pieces.

To make the dip: In medium bowl, smash the avocados until they are smooth. Stir in the juice, zest, wine, and salt to taste. Fold in the onions and mushrooms.

Yield: 3 cups (780 g) dip

CHICKPEA HUMMUS

In this recipe, add key ingredients such as onion and garlic into the cooking process itself–rather than after.

1 cup (200 g) dried chickpeas, soaked for 12 hours or
   overnight
1 tablespoon (15 ml) sesame oil
½ cup (80 g) diced yellow onion
4 or 5 cloves garlic, minced
½ to 1 teaspoon salt
¼ cup (60 g) tahini
¼ cup (60 ml) lemon juice

Rinse and drain the chickpeas.

In an uncovered pressure cooker, heat the oil on medium-high. Add the onion and garlic and sauté for 3 minutes, or until the onion is translucent. Add the chickpeas and enough water to cover, plus another 1 inch (2.5 cm). Cover the cooker and bring it to pressure. Cook at high pressure for 13 to 15 minutes. Allow for a natural release. Remove the lid and stir in the salt. Drain the chickpeas,

reserving the cooking broth.

In a food processor, pulse the chickpeas, tahini, and juice to a creamy texture. If the mixture is too dry, add the cooking broth as needed.

Yield: 4 to 6 servings

CREAMY DREAMY KALAMATA HUMMUS

To make the creamiest hummus ever, use dried chickpeas (not canned), soaked overnight, slightly overcooked, and peeled. Cool the chickpeas completely before blending.

3 cups (600 g) dried chickpeas
½ cup (120 ml) Kalamata olive juice
2 tablespoons (30 g) tahini
¼ cup (60 ml) water
Zest and juice of 1 lime
Dash of salt
1 cup (380 g) minced Kalamata olives

Soak the chickpeas in water at least 6 hours and up to overnight. Place the chickpeas in a large stockpot, cover with water at least 5 inches (13 cm) above the chickpeas, and bring to a boil. Reduce the heat to a constant simmer and cook for about 2 hours, or until the chickpeas are very tender. Rinse under cold water and rub between your hands to remove the thin skins. Let the chickpeas cool completely.

In a food processor, combine the chickpeas, olive juice, tahini, water, zest, lime juice, and salt until very smooth, for at least 7 minutes. Fold in the olives and blend until they become chopped evenly. Chill for 2 hours before serving.

Yield: 3 cups (738 g)

DAL DIP

Traditional Indian dal is a soup with red lentils. Keeping true to the spices but using less liquid, this healthy dip is perfect on Indian breads, such as naan or roti.

1 tablespoon (15 ml) sesame oil
2 cloves garlic, minced
1 cup (130 g) diced carrot
1-inch (2.5 cm) piece ginger root, minced or grated
   (about 2 teaspoons)
½ teaspoon cumin
½ teaspoon fennel seeds
1 cup (180 g) diced fresh tomato
1 cup (200 g) dried red lentils
2¼ cups (530 ml) water
2 tablespoons (30 ml) lemon juice

In an uncovered pressure cooker, heat the oil on

medium-high. Add the garlic, carrot, and ginger and sauté for 2 minutes. Add the cumin, fennel seeds, tomato, lentils, and water. Stir to combine.

Cover and bring to pressure. Cook at high pressure for 5 minutes. Allow for a natural release.

Remove the lid. Stir in the juice. Transfer to a food processor and pulse quickly. (This should not take more than 10 seconds.) Refrigerate for at least 2 hours but overnight is best. Serve cold.

Yield: 8 to 6 servings

ROASTED RED PEPPER AND WALNUT SPREAD
This may very well become your favorite spread.

2 to 3 whole roasted red bell peppers (fresh or from a jar)
⅔ cup (75 g) bread crumbs
1 cup (120 g) walnuts, raw or toasted
4 large whole cloves garlic, peeled
½ teaspoon salt
1 tablespoon (15 ml) lemon juice
2 teaspoons (13 g) agave nectar
1 teaspoon (2 g) ground cumin
¼ teaspoon red pepper flakes

In a blender or food processor, purée the peppers, bread crumbs, walnuts, garlic, salt, juice, agave, cumin, and red pepper flakes to a smooth consistency. Scrape down the sides of the machine to make sure all ingredients are thoroughly combined. Season to taste.

Yield: 1 cup (225 g), or 8 (2-tablespoon [30 g]) servings

BLACK OLIVE AND SUN-DRIED TOMATO TAPENADE
This tapenade features some of the finest flavors in European cuisine. It's a delicious starter to any meal.

15 sun-dried tomatoes
½ cup (120 ml) water (substitute 3 tablespoons [45 ml] of water with white wine for extra zing)
1 tablespoon (15 ml) olive oil
1 small red onion, diced
1 clove garlic, sliced
1 teaspoon salt, divided
1½ cups (255 g) black olives

In a small bowl, soak the tomatoes in the water for about 1 hour, or until softened.

Meanwhile, in a medium frying pan, heat the oil. Add the onion, garlic, and ½ teaspoon of salt. Sauté over medium-high heat until the onions are evenly browned and

translucent, about 10 minutes. Once the tomatoes have soaked, drain well and combine with the onions and olives in a food processor. Add the remaining salt and pulse until all ingredients are combined and the olives and tomatoes are very finely chopped.

Yield: 1½ cups (203 g) tapenade

GREEN SNACKERS
Flaky and crisp, these crackers are a welcome addition to any get-together. They're even popular with kids! The thinner the dough is rolled, the crisper the crackers will be.

¾ cup (90 g) whole wheat pastry flour
¼ cup (31 g) all-purpose flour
½ teaspoon salt
Pinch of black pepper
2 tablespoons (28 g) vegan butter
1 cup (40 g) packed fresh spinach
¼ cup (60 ml) cold water

Preheat the oven to 375°F (190°C, or gas mark 5).

In a medium bowl, whisk together the flours, salt, and pepper. Cut in the butter to the consistency of small peas.

In a mini blender, combine the spinach and water. Process until smooth. Pour into the flour mixture. Using a fork, stir to combine. If the mixture is too wet or dry, add additional flour or water 1 teaspoon at a time. The mixture should form a ball.

Lightly flour a work surface, and roll the dough out to between ⅛- (3 mm) and ¼-inch (6 mm) thick. Using a 2-inch (5 cm) round cutter, cut the dough into crackers. Transfer to a baking sheet. Using a fork, poke each cracker twice. Bake for 20 to 24 minutes (for biscuit-like crackers) or 24 to 28 minutes (for crisp crackers), or until firm and the bottoms are starting to brown. Transfer to a wire rack to cool. Store in an airtight container for up to 4 days.

Yield: 24 to 28 crackers

UMAMI ANASAZI BEANS
The secret vegan ingredient in this dish is umami, the Japanese word for "pleasant savory taste," which is considered the fifth taste in the culinary world (along with sweet, sour, bitter, and salty).

1 tablespoon (15 ml) olive oil
2 cups (320 g) half-moon slices onion
½ teaspoon sugar
1 cup (200 g) dried Anasazi beans, soaked for 12 hours or overnight, rinsed and drained
½ cup (35 g) finely diced mushrooms

¼ teaspoon liquid smoke
1 teaspoon smoked paprika
2 cups (470 ml) vegan beef-style broth
¼ cup (60 ml) water
2 teaspoons red miso
1 teaspoon tamari, optional

In an uncovered pressure cooker, heat the oil on high. Add the onion and sugar and cook on high for 10 minutes, stirring frequently and adding water as necessary to avoid sticking. Add the beans, mushrooms, liquid smoke, paprika, broth, and water. Stir to combine. Cover and bring to pressure. Cook at high pressure for 5 to 7 minutes. Allow for a natural release. Remove the lid and stir in the miso. For a saltier flavor, add the tamari.

Yield: 4 servings

THREE BEAN DELIGHT
You could also serve this dish as an entrée, surrounded by steamed vegetables and a simple grain side dish.

1 teaspoon olive oil
½ cup (80 g) diced sweet onion
2 cloves garlic, minced
2 cups (400 g) mixed dried pinto, red kidney, and adzuki beans
1-inch (2.5 cm) strip kombu
4 to 5 cups (940 to 1175 ml) water
½ to 1 teaspoon dulse flakes

In an uncovered pressure cooker, heat the oil on medium heat. Add the onion and garlic and sauté for 3 minutes, or until the onion is translucent. Stir in the beans, kombu, and water. Cover and bring to pressure. Cook at high pressure for 22 to 25 minutes. Allow for a natural release. Remove the lid and taste for doneness. If the beans need to be cooked a bit longer, simmer until done. Stir in the dulse flakes.

Yield: 4 to 6 servings

PIZZA CRACKERS
With their addictive pizza flavor, these crackers satisfy the late-night munchies!

2 cups (260 g) chickpea flour
½ cup (65 g) sorghum flour, plus more for rolling
½ cup (65 g) potato starch
½ cup (65 g) nutritional yeast
1 teaspoon xanthan gum
1 teaspoon salt
2 to 3 teaspoons ground pizza seasoning, plus more for sprinkling
⅓ cup (80 ml) olive oil
¼ cup (60 g) tomato paste
¾ cup (180 ml) cold water

Preheat the oven to 350°F (180°C, or gas mark 4).

In a large bowl, combine the flours, starch, yeast, xanthan, salt, and seasoning until well mixed. Using a large spoon, stir in the oil, paste, and water. Mix until very well combined. Turn the dough out onto a lightly floured surface and knead just until the dough is a uniform texture and color.

Add a little more flour to your rolling surface and pat out the dough to about 1 inch (2.5 cm) thick. Sprinkle the top with more sorghum flour and flip over.

Using a lightly floured rolling pin, roll out the dough until it is about ⅛-inch (3 mm) thick. Use a circular cookie cutter or a pizza wheel to cut out 1½-inch (3.8 cm) shapes of dough. Sprinkle with additional pizza seasoning.

Using a flat metal spatula, scoop up the shapes and place on an ungreased baking sheet, pacing them about 1 inch (2.5 cm) apart. Bake for about 30 minutes, flipping once halfway through the cooking time. (The crackers will have a reddish hue [from the tomato paste] but should be slightly puffy and golden brown on both sides when they are done.

Let cool completely.

Yield: About 70 crackers, 3 crackers per serving

CURRIED CHICKPEAS
This wonderful dish is bursting with flavor.

2 cups (470 ml) plus 2 tablespoons (30 ml) water, divided
2 large onions, finely chopped
1 teaspoon (2 g) minced fresh ginger
1 tablespoon (6 g) ground coriander
1 tablespoon (6 g) garam masala
1 tablespoon (7 g) ground cumin
1 teaspoon (2 g) ground cinnamon
1 teaspoon (2 g) ground cloves
1½ teaspoons (3 g) chili powder
2 tablespoons (25 g) sugar
1 can (6 ounces, or 170 g) tomato paste
4 cans (15 ounce, or 420 g, each) chickpeas, drained and rinsed
1 teaspoon (6 g) salt

In a large saucepan, heat 2 tablespoons (30 ml) water. Add the onions and ginger and sauté for about 5 minutes, or until the onions become translucent. Add the coriander, garam masala, cumin, cinnamon, cloves, chili powder, and sugar. Stir for 30 seconds. Add the paste. Cook for 5 minutes. Stir to combine. Add the chickpeas and remaining 2 cups (470 ml) water, and cook for 10 to 20 minutes, stirring occasionally. (To vary the thickness of the curry, either add water or let the water cook down.) Add the salt.

Yield: 8 to 10 servings

RED LENTILS

This appetizer is amazingly simple and delicious. Red lentils cook faster than most other types, making this both a tasty and quick dish.

1 tablespoon (15 ml) coconut or canola oil
3 cloves garlic, minced
1 large yellow onion, finely chopped
1 teaspoon (2 g) cumin seeds
5½ cups (1.3 L) water
2 cups (385 g) red lentils, picked over, rinsed and drained
1 tablespoon (6 g) ground coriander
¼ teaspoon cayenne pepper
1 teaspoon (6 g) salt

In a large saucepan, heat the oil over medium heat. Add the garlic, onion, and cumin seeds, and cook, stirring frequently, for about 3 minutes, or until the garlic begins to turn golden brown and the onion becomes translucent. Add the water, lentils, coriander, pepper, and salt, and cook over medium-low heat until the beans are mushy, about 25 minutes.

Yield: 8 to 10 servings

QUINOA-MILLET-PEA BOWL

This recipe is lightly seasoned to allow the contrasting textures of the peas, grains, and vegetables to come through. Rosemary offers a hint of seasoning to this light appetizer.

½ cup (100 g) dried whole peas, soaked for 12 hours or overnight, rinsed and drained
½ cup (60 g) sliced zucchini
½ cup (60 g) chopped celery
¼ cup (40 g) finely diced onion
1 cup (175 g) quinoa, drained and rinsed
½ cup (90 g) millet, drained and rinsed
2 cups (470 ml) vegetable broth
½ to 1 cup (120 to 235 ml) water
1 teaspoon whole rosemary, crumbled
½ to 1 teaspoon salt

Place all of the ingredients, except the salt, in the pressure cooker. Stir to combine. Cover and bring to pressure. Cook at high pressure for 8 to 10 minutes. Allow for a natural release. Remove the lid and stir in the salt to taste. Using a fork, fluff the millet. Leave uncovered for about 5 minutes, then fluff again before serving.

Yield: 4 to 6 servings

MUSHROOM RICE

Serve this before an Asian stir-fry.

1 teaspoon sesame oil
1 cup (70 g) chopped mushrooms
1 cup (190 g) long-grain brown rice
1½ cups (355 ml) vegetable broth
1 to 2 tablespoons (15 to 30 ml) tamari

In an uncovered pressure cooker, heat the oil on medium heat. Add the mushrooms and sauté for 3 minutes. Add the rice and broth. Stir to combine. Cover and bring to pressure. Cook at high pressure for 22 minutes. Allow for a natural release. Remove the lid and stir in the tamari to taste.

Yield: 4 servings

SPICY GARLIC DILL PICKLES

This recipe is so simple, you'll have your pickles jarred in about the time it takes to boil the water and slice the cucumbers. You can adjust this recipe to make one jar or 10.

FOR THE BRINE:
For each 1 cup (235 ml) water, use 1 tablespoon (18 g) salt

FOR THE PICKLES:
1 tablespoon (6 g) black peppercorns
1 teaspoon whole mustard seed
1 to 2 cucumbers, cut into desired shapes to fit jar
4 cloves garlic, halved
1 bay leaf, broken into pieces
1 tablespoon (3 g) fresh dill
1 teaspoon red pepper flakes, or to taste

FOR CANNING:
1 (16-ounce, or 470 ml) jar, plus ring and lid

To make the brine: In a saucepot, bring the water and salt to a boil over high heat. Boil until all the salt is dissolved. Reduce the heat to low and keep warm until ready to pour.

To make the pickles: In a very dry skillet, lightly toast the peppercorns and mustard seed over medium-low heat.

Pack the cucumbers into the sterilized jar. Add the garlic, bay leaf, dill, red pepper flakes, toasted peppercorns, and mustard seed to the jar. Pour in the hot brine to fill the jars, allowing ½ inch (1.3 cm) of space at the top. Place the lid and ring on the jar and give it a good shake to distribute all of the ingredients. Place upright and allow to cool. The lid should self-seal as the brine cools, creating a vacuum in the jar. Place in a cool, dark place for 1 week, and then refrigerate.

Yield: 1 (16-ounce, or 470 ml) jar

17 Almond, Garlic, Lemon Spread and Dip; 18 Pineapple Mango Chutney; 19 SoCal Salsa Fresca; 20 Seaside Avocado Dip; 21 Chickpea Hummus; 22 Creamy Dreamy Kalamata Hummus; 23 Dal Dip; 24 Roasted Red Pepper and Walnut Spread

25 Black Olive and Sun-Dried Tomato Tapenade; 26 Green Snackers; 27 Umami Anasazi Beans; 28 Three Bean Delight; 29 Pizza Crackers; 30 Curried Chickpeas; 31 Red Lentils; 32 Quinoa-Millet-Pea Bowl

NEW WORLD SZÉKELY GOULASH

This recipe is a blend of the traditional Székely goulash ingredients—specifically the sauerkraut and sour cream—with the Midwest addition of tomatoes.

1 teaspoon olive oil
2 cloves garlic, minced
½ cup (80 g) half-moon slices yellow onion
1½ cups (195 g) chopped carrots
2 tablespoons (14 g) paprika, plus more for garnish
1 teaspoon black pepper, plus more for serving
1 cup (200 g) dried chickpeas, soaked for 12 hours or
      overnight, rinsed and drained
2 cups (470 ml) vegetable broth
1 cup (245 g) tomato sauce
1 bay leaf
1 to 1½ cups (235 to 355 ml) water, or as needed
1 teaspoon salt
32 ounces (896 g) sauerkraut, drained
½ cup (120 g) vegan sour cream

In an uncovered pressure cooker, heat the oil on medium-high heat. Add the garlic, onion, and carrots and sauté for 3 minutes, or until the onion softens. Stir in the paprika and pepper. Add the chickpeas, broth, sauce, bay leaf, and enough water to cover everything, plus an additional ½ inch (1.3 cm). Cover and bring to pressure. Cook at high pressure for 13 to 15 minutes. Allow for a natural release. Remove the cover and stir in the salt. If the chickpeas are not quite done, simmer on low until thoroughly cooked. Remove and discard the bay leaf. Stir in the sauerkraut and sour cream and simmer on low until everything is completely heated through. Garnish with a dash of paprika and serve with more pepper.

Yield: 6 servings

NO-QUESO QUESADILLAS

If the combination of Middle Eastern hummus and Mexican tortillas seems strange, don't worry. The result is absolutely delightful. It comes out as an incredibly fast appetizer.

3 cups (675 g) vegan hummus, divided
8 (10-inch, or 25-cm) flour tortillas
½ cup (50 g) chopped green onions
½ to 1 cup (130 to 260 g) salsa

Spread 3 heaping tablespoons (45 g) hummus on a tortilla and place (hummus side up) in a large nonstick skillet over medium heat. Sprinkle with the onions and spread on a thin layer of salsa. Top with a second tortilla, and cook until the bottom tortilla is warm and turning golden brown, 3 to 5 minutes. Turn the quesadilla over and cook the second side for another few minutes, or until golden brown. (This process becomes a lot quicker once the pan is hot, so stay close to the stove! The first one always takes the longest because the pan isn't totally hot.) Cut the quesadillas in half or into pizza-shaped triangles. Repeat with the remaining ingredients.

Yield: 4 to 8 servings

PLUM-TILLAS WITH VANILLA DIPPING SAUCE

The slight tartness of the plum is paired with the sweet, almost buttery flavor and super creaminess of the vanilla dipping sauce here.

1 cup (235 ml) unsweetened plain or vanilla soymilk
¼ cup (50 g) granulated sugar
2 teaspoons vanilla extract
⅛ to ¼ teaspoon xanthan gum
¼ cup (60 ml) coconut cream or full-fat coconut milk
6 firm medium plums (1 pound, or 454 g), pitted and cut
      into bite-size pieces
1 teaspoon nondairy butter, melted
1 tablespoon (14 g) packed light brown sugar
1 teaspoon balsamic vinegar
1 teaspoon water
Four 9-inch (23-cm) flour tortillas

In a blender, combine the soymilk, sugar, vanilla, xanthan (start with only ⅛ teaspoon xanthan, adding more if needed to obtain a yogurt-like texture), and milk. Blend until perfectly smooth and somewhat thick, like yogurt. Refrigerate in an airtight container for at least 3 hours before using.

In a skillet, sauté the plums with the butter, sugar, vinegar, and water over medium heat until all of the liquid evaporates and the plums are just tender but not mushy, about 4 minutes. Remove from the heat.

Preheat a panini press fitted with smooth or grill plates on high heat. Place the equivalent of 1½ plums evenly on half of each tortilla and fold over the other half. Lightly coat both sides of the tortilla with nonstick cooking spray, close the panini press, and cook until golden brown and crispy, about 6 minutes in all. Cut each tortilla into 4 triangles and serve with the Vanilla Sauce.

Yield: 4 tortillas, 1½ cups (355 ml) Vanilla Sauce

SESAME CUCUMBER SANDWICHES

The filling can be made ahead, covered, and refrigerated for up to 24 hours. The cucumbers can be sliced ahead of time. Fill the sandwiches near serving time..

4 ounces (113 g) tempeh, crumbled
1 cup (235 ml) water

1 tablespoon (15 ml) tamari
2 teaspoons toasted sesame oil
1 teaspoon sesame chile oil
¼ to ½ teaspoon Chinese five-spice powder
½ teaspoon grated fresh ginger
1 clove garlic, minced
¼ cup (40 g) finely chopped snow peas
1 tablespoon (7 g) grated carrot
1 tablespoon (10 g) minced green onion
2 tablespoons (30 g) vegan mayonnaise
½ teaspoon Sriracha, plus more to taste
Salt, to taste
Black pepper, to taste
48 very thin, round slices cucumber, about 2 English
cucumbers
3 tablespoons (24 g) black sesame seeds

In a small skillet, bring the tempeh, water, and tamari to a
boil over high heat. Reduce the heat to medium and
continue to boil until all the liquid is absorbed, about 15
minutes. Transfer the tempeh to a plate. Using a paper
towel, wipe the skillet dry.

Add the oils to the skillet and return the heat to medium.
Add the tempeh, and cook for about 5 minutes, stirring
occasionally, or until lightly browned. Stir in the ¼ teaspoon
five-spice powder, ginger, and garlic and cook for 1 minute
longer. Taste a piece of the tempeh, and add the remaining
¼ teaspoon five-spice powder if using. Remove from the
heat and let cool.

In a medium bowl, combine the cooled tempeh mixture,
snow peas, carrot, onion, mayonnaise, and Sriracha. Taste
and add salt and pepper to taste. Scoop 1 teaspoon of the
filling onto half of the cucumber slices. Top with the
remaining cucumber slices and press down so the filling
reaches the edges of the cucumber. Roll the filling part in
the sesame seeds so the seeds will adhere to the middle of
the sandwich. Gently press the filling back to line up with
the cucumbers. Refrigerate until ready to serve, up to
1 hour.

Yield: 24 sandwiches

HOLLANDAZE'D ASPARAGUS ROUNDS
Hollandaise sauce is one of the five "mother" sauces in
French cooking. That means it's the base that's used in
other sauces. This unique version is very adaptable.

½ cup (69 g) cashews, soaked in water for 1 hour, rinsed,
and drained
⅓ cup plus 1 tablespoon (95 ml) nondairy milk
¼ cup (60 g) sauerkraut, drained but not squeezed dry
2 tablespoons (30 ml) lemon juice
1 tablespoon plus 1 teaspoon (20 ml) apple cider vinegar
2 tablespoons (30 ml) olive oil, divided
1 teaspoon Dijon mustard
1 teaspoon nutritional yeast

¼ teaspoon salt, plus more to taste
¼ teaspoon Sriracha
Pinch of white pepper, plus more to taste
12 ounces (340 g) asparagus, cut into 4-inch (10-cm)
pieces
1 large tomato, cut into four ½-inch (1.3-cm) slices
2 English muffins, split and toasted
Minced fresh chives, for serving

In a blender, combine the cashews, milk, sauerkraut, juice,
vinegar, 1 tablespoon (15 ml) of the oil, mustard, yeast, ¼
teaspoon salt, Siracha, and pinch of pepper. Blend until
smooth. Taste and adjust the seasonings.

Just before serving, heat over medium heat in a small
saucepan, stirring often. Add an extra tablespoon (15 ml)
milk if needed for a pourable consistency.

Preheat the oven to 400°F (200°C, or gas mark 6). In a 9
x 13-inch (23 x 33-cm) pan, toss the asparagus with the
remaining 1 tablespoon (15 ml) oil and salt and pepper to
taste. Roast in the oven for 10 minutes, or until tender.

Place the tomato slices on the muffin halves. Divide the
asparagus evenly on top. Pour a generous ¼ cup (60 ml)
sauce over each half and sprinkle with the chives.

Yield: 4 sandwiches

ORANGE FENNEL SUMMER ROLLS
Always fancy and refreshing, these summer rolls are an
appetizer. They're also perfect to take on-the-go for lunch
because they're not susceptible to sogginess.

2 tablespoons (30 ml) sesame oil
2 tablespoons (30 ml) seasoned rice vinegar
1 tablespoon (15 ml) orange juice
1 teaspoon ground ginger
1 clove garlic, pressed
¼ teaspoon salt
¼ teaspoon red pepper flakes
16 rice paper wraps
2 cups (175 g) thinly sliced fennel (about 10 ounces, or
280 g untrimmed)
1 can (11 ounces, or 312 g) mandarin orange slices,
drained
2 teaspoons black sesame seeds

In a medium bowl, whisk together the oil, vinegar, juice,
ginger, garlic, salt, and pepper flakes.

Immerse the rice paper 1 sheet at a time in warm water
to soften. Soak for a few seconds, or until pliable. Handle
carefully because rice paper breaks easily. Drain on a clean
kitchen towel before rolling. Add 2 tablespoons (11 g) fennel,
2 slices mandarin orange, and a pinch of sesame seeds.
Roll tightly, folding the ends in and rolling closed. Serve
with the dipping sauce.

Yield: 16 summer rolls

APPLE TEMPEH TRIANGLE DIPPERS

These turnover-like triangle dippers can be served any time.

1 cup (150 g) peeled, cored, and diced crisp apple
¾ cup (94 g) cooked, diced tempeh bacon
¼ cup (45 g) pomegranate seeds
2 tablespoons (30 ml) lemon juice, divided
Pinch of ground cinnamon
All-purpose flour, for dusting
2 sheets vegan puff pastry, thawed
¾ cup (180 ml) pomegranate juice, divided
2 tablespoons (30 ml) pure maple syrup
1 tablespoon (8 g) cornstarch

Preheat the oven to 400°F (200°C, or gas mark 6). Lightly spray two baking sheets with nonstick cooking spray.

In a medium bowl, combine the apple, tempeh, pomegranate seeds, 1 tablespoon (15 ml) of the lemon juice, and cinnamon.

On a lightly floured surface, roll 1 pastry sheet into a 12 x 12-inch (30 x 30-cm) square. Cut into 4 equal squares, and then cut the squares on the diagonal to form 8 triangles. Repeat with the remaining sheet puff pastry. Place 1 tablespoon (11 g) filling in each triangle. (Be sure to get apple, seeds, and tempeh in each for a balance of flavor and texture.) Fold the triangles closed, pressing the seams with your fingers. Repeat with the remaining triangles and filling. Place on the baking sheets and bake for 15 minutes, or until golden.

Meanwhile, in a small saucepan, heat ½ cup (120 ml) of the pomegranate juice, the maple syrup, and the remaining 1 tablespoon (15 ml) lemon juice over medium-high heat.

In a small bowl, whisk together the remaining ¼ cup (60 ml) pomegranate juice and the cornstarch. When the mixture is boiling, add the cornstarch slurry and whisk constantly until the sauce thickens, 3 to 4 minutes. (It should be a syrupy consistency.) Serve the triangles with the sauce.

Yield: 4 servings

FIGS STUFFED WITH ROSEMARY AND WALNUT-CASHEW CREAM

This appetizer features a delicious cashew cream.

½ yellow onion, finely chopped
1 tablespoon (15 ml) olive oil, plus more for brushing
1 cup (145 g) raw cashews, soaked overnight, rinsed, and drained
1 teaspoon yellow/light miso
1 tablespoon (15 ml) lemon juice
1 tablespoon (15 ml) water
¼ cup (25 g) raw walnuts
1 tablespoon (12 g) nutritional yeast
1 tablespoon (2 g) minced rosemary
Salt, to taste

Black pepper, to taste
12 figs, stemmed
Agave nectar, for drizzling
Rosemary sprigs, for garnish

In a medium pan, sauté the onion in the oil until translucent and tender, 5 to 7 minutes.

Place the cashews, onion, miso, juice, and water in a blender and process until smooth. Transfer to a bowl.

In a food processor, pulse the walnuts until coarsely chopped. Stir the walnuts, yeast, and minced rosemary into the cashew mixture. Season with salt and pepper. (At this point, you may store the cream in the fridge for up to 3 days or continue on to stuff and roast the figs.)

Preheat the oven to 425°F (220°C, or gas mark 7). Lightly oil a glass roasting pan.

Set each fig upright on the cutting board. Working from the top down, carefully cut crosswise into the top of each fig, as if you were quartering it, but without cutting all the way through. (You don't want to cut them all the way to separate them; you want them to remain intact but open enough to pipe in the creamy filling.)

Use a spoon to place 1 tablespoon (15 g) of the cashew cream into the cavity of each fig.

Transfer the filled figs to the prepared roasting pan, brush or lightly spray the figs with a little oil, and roast for about 12 minutes, or until the figs are soft. Just before serving, drizzle some agave over the figs and garnish the serving platter with rosemary sprigs.

Yield: 12 servings

BLACK OLIVE BRUSCHETTA

This is a beautiful and delicious appetizer. The contrast between the white cashew cream and black olives is striking

FOR THE CASHEW CREAM:
½ yellow onion, finely chopped
1 tablespoon (15 ml) olive oil, plus more for brushing
1 cup (150 g) raw cashews, soaked in water overnight, rinsed and drained
1 teaspoon yellow/light miso
1 tablespoon (15 ml) lemon juice
1 tablespoon (15 ml) water

FOR THE BRUSCHETTA:
2 tablespoons (30 ml) olive oil, plus more for brushing
3 cloves garlic, finely minced
2 shallots, finely minced
Pinch of salt
Pinch of black pepper
¼ cup (35 g) pine nuts, coarsely chopped
½ cup (50 g) pitted black olives, finely minced
1 teaspoon balsamic vinegar
1 whole grain baguette, sliced

1 tablespoon (4 g) finely minced fresh parsley
1 tablespoon (4 g) finely minced fresh basil

To make the Cashew Cream: In a medium pan, sauté the onion in the oil until translucent and tender, 5 to 7 minutes.

In a blender, process the cashews, onion, miso, juice, and water until smooth.

To make the Bruschetta: Preheat the oven to 400°F (200°C, or gas mark 6). Line a baking sheet with parchment paper.

In a large pan, heat the oil over medium heat. Sauté the garlic, shallots, salt, and pepper until the shallots begin to glisten, about 5 minutes. Stir in the pine nuts and olives and sauté for 3 minutes longer. Stir in the vinegar and turn off the heat.

Lightly brush both sides of the bread slices with oil. Arrange on the prepared baking sheet and bake until the ends of the bread begin to turn golden brown and crispy, 5 to 7 minutes.

Remove from the oven and let cool for 10 minutes.

Spread a generous amount of Cashew Cream on each bread slice and carefully spoon the olive mixture on top. Sprinkle with the parsley and basil.

Yield: 20 to 25 slices

TOMATO, BASIL, AND ARUGULA BRUSCHETTA
Traditional bruschetta consists of grilled bread rubbed with garlic and topped with olive oil, salt, and pepper. This variation is oh-so-satisfying and pretty!

1 loaf fresh Italian bread or baguette
2 tablespoons (30 ml) olive oil, plus more for brushing
3 large cloves garlic (1 peeled and left whole, 2 peeled and minced or pressed)
1 pint (300 g) cherry tomatoes, sliced
4 cups (80 g) chopped arugula
1 cup (40 g) finely chopped fresh basil, divided
2 teaspoons (10 ml) balsamic vinegar
Salt, to taste
Black pepper, to taste

Preheat the oven to broil.

Cut the bread into ½-inch-thick (1 cm) slices. Brush each side of each slice with oil. Broil for 2 to 3 minutes on one side (being careful not to burn), turn, and broil the other side for 2 minutes longer.

Remove the bread from the oven. Rub the whole peeled garlic clove on each slice. Place the bread on a serving platter.

In a small bowl, combine the remaining minced or pressed garlic, tomatoes, arugula, ½ cup (20 g) basil, 2 tablespoons (30 ml) oil, and vinegar. Toss to coat the greens with the dressing.

Divide the mixture among the bread, season with salt

and pepper, and sprinkle with the remaining ½ cup (20 g) basil.

Yield: 20 to 25 slices

PORTOBELLO HORSERADISH BRUSCHETTA
Bruschetta gets a makeover in this recipe. The seasoned bread is topped with horseradish- and arugula-spiked mayonnaise and grilled-to-perfection portabellas.

FOR THE BREAD:
3 tablespoons (45 ml) olive oil
1 teaspoon garlic salt
¼ teaspoon lemon pepper
¼ teaspoon black pepper
1 baguette, cut into ½-inch (1.3 cm) slices (about 20 pieces)

FOR THE DRESSING:
½ cup (112 g) vegan mayonnaise
½ teaspoon to 1 teaspoon prepared horseradish, to taste
¼ cup (5 g) fresh baby arugula, minced
Salt, to taste
Black pepper, to taste

FOR THE PORTOBELLOS:
¼ cup (60 ml) dry red wine
1 tablespoon (15 ml) tamari
1 tablespoon (15 ml) lemon juice
1 teaspoon Dijon mustard
¼ teaspoon liquid smoke
¼ teaspoon herbes de Provence
4 large portobello mushroom caps, stemmed, gills removed
1 tablespoon (15 ml) olive oil

Large handful pea shoots

To make the bread: Preheat the oven to 400°F (200°C, or gas mark 6).

In a small bowl, stir together the oil, garlic salt, lemon pepper, and black pepper. Brush the mixture on one side of each slice of bread, and place on a baking sheet, oil-side up.

Bake for 12 to 15 minutes, or until golden brown. Remove and let cool on a wire rack. (Once cool, the slices can be stored in an airtight container for up to 2 days before using.)

To make the dressing: In a bowl, stir together the mayonnaise, horseradish, and arugula. Season with salt and pepper to taste. (The sauce can be stored in the fridge in an airtight container for up to 24 hours.)

To make the portobellos: In a 9 x 13-inch (23 x 33 cm) glass dish, combine the wine, tamari, juice, mustard, liquid smoke, and herbes. Add the mushrooms and turn to coat. Let marinate for 30 minutes.

Heat a grill pan over high heat. Right before cooking, brush the mushrooms with oil. Cook the mushrooms for 3 to 5 minutes, or until grill marks are visible, brushing with the remaining marinade as they cook. Turn over to cook the second side in the same way, about 3 minutes. Transfer to a cutting board and slice into ½-inch (1.3 cm) strips.

To assemble, spread the dressing evenly on the bread slices. Divide the pea shoots on top of the slices, and top with the mushroom slices.

Yield: 20 slices

CUCUMBER AND CREAM CHEESE SANDWICHES

Simplify this recipe by placing paper-thin slices of cucumber between two thin slices of lightly buttered (nondairy, of course) white bread, with the crusts cut off.

1 container (8 ounces, or 225 g) nondairy cream cheese, softened
3 tablespoons (9 g) finely chopped fresh chives
2 tablespoons (8 g) finely chopped fresh dill
2 tablespoons (12 g) finely chopped fresh mint
1 seedless cucumber, peeled and very thinly sliced into rounds (about 32 slices)
16 slices bread (whole wheat, white, rice, rye, or pumpernickel), crusts removed
½ pound (225 g) arugula
Salt, to taste
Black pepper, to taste

In a small bowl, combine the cream cheese, chives, dill, and mint.

Place the cucumber slices between layers of paper towels to remove excess moisture.

Spread a thin layer of the cream cheese mixture on each slice of bread. Top every other slice with cucumber and arugula, season with salt and pepper, and assemble the sandwiches. Cut the sandwiches in half diagonally and then in half again.

Yield: 32 servings

PURPLE POTATOES WITH CASHEW CREAM

If you serve these little gems, people will talk about them for years. They are delicious warm or at room temperature.

30 small purple potatoes
1 tablespoon (15 ml) olive oil, plus more for roasting and frying
Salt, to taste
Black pepper, to taste
1 yellow onion, chopped

3 cloves garlic, minced
1 tablespoon (14 g) nondairy butter
1 teaspoon (5 g) sugar
4 large sage leaves
½ cup (60 g) walnuts, toasted
1 cup (125 g) unsalted raw cashews, toasted
1 tablespoon (12 g) nutritional yeast flakes
1 cup (235 ml) vegetable broth, non-tomato-based (to preserve cream color), if available

Preheat the oven to 425°F (220°C, or gas mark 7).

Wash the potatoes under running water, and then dry them with a towel. Roast or bake them.

To roast: Toss whole potatoes with enough oil to coat lightly. Season with salt and pepper. Arrange in an even layer on a lightly oiled baking pan. Roast for 20 to 30 minutes, or until tender, moving them around occasionally. Let cool on a towel-lined plate to soak up excess oil.

To bake: Using a small fork, pierce whole potatoes in several places so steam can escape. (Because you will later cut the potatoes in half, consider making the piercing marks where you'll be cutting.) Place the potatoes on an oven rack or baking sheet. Bake for 40 minutes, or until tender when pierced with a fork.

Meanwhile, in a large pan, sauté the onion and garlic in the butter over medium-high heat until they begin to brown slightly, about 5 minutes. Stir in the sugar and a pinch of salt, and continue cooking for 20 to 25 minutes, or until the onion turns brown.

Meanwhile, in a small pan, sauté the sage in 1 tablespoon (15 ml) oil for 30 to 60 seconds, or until crispy. Transfer the sage to a towel-lined plate to soak up extra oil, and then place it with the walnuts in a blender. Pulse to a coarse crumble. Add salt to taste. Transfer the mixture to a bowl.

When the onion is ready, blend it with the cashews, yeast, and broth on high until the mixture is creamy. (This could take several minutes.) Add more cashews or broth as necessary, to get a creamy, thick consistency. Season with salt.

Once the potatoes have cooled, cut them in half without tearing the skin. Using a melon baller, scoop out the centers, leaving ¼-inch (6 mm) walls. Cut a small slice off the bottom of each potato to help it sit level. Spoon the cashew mixture into the halved potatoes, and sprinkle with the walnut/sage mixture.

Yield: 60 potato halves

TEMPEH AND EGGPLANT POT PIES

Use any combination of vegetables for the filling here. The dough is perfect for making drop biscuits, and the topping is perfect for fruit-based cobblers.

FOR THE FILLING:
2 cups (165 g) diced eggplant (1 small globe eggplant or 2 Asian eggplants)
1 package (8 ounces, or 225 g) tempeh, cut into ½-inch (1 cm) cubes
1 small yellow onion, chopped
1 rib celery, chopped
2 tablespoons (30 ml) water
1 teaspoon (2 g) fennel seeds
1 to 2 tablespoons (8 to 16 g) capers, rinsed
2 tablespoons (30 ml) balsamic vinegar
1 jar (15 ounces, or 420 g) tomato sauce
½ teaspoon red pepper flakes
Salt, to taste
Black pepper, to taste

FOR THE DOUGH:
1⅔ cups (210 g) all-purpose flour
1 tablespoon (15 g) baking powder
½ teaspoon salt
⅔ cup (160 ml) nondairy milk
⅓ cup (80 ml) canola oil

Preheat the oven to 425°F (220°C, or gas mark 7). Coat 4 or 6 individual ramekins, a 9-inch (23 cm) square pan, or a rectangular pan with oil.

To make the filling, steam the eggplant and tempeh for 10 to 15 minutes, or until the eggplant is soft and translucent.

Meanwhile, in a large pan, sauté the onion and celery in the water until soft. Add the fennel seeds, capers, and vinegar and sauté for 1 minute. Add the sauce, red peppers, and tempeh and eggplant. Simmer for 10 minutes, stirring occasionally.

Meanwhile, to make the dough: In a bowl, stir together the flour, baking powder, and salt. Pour in the milk and oil, and mix just until the dry ingredients are evenly moistened. (The dough should be lumpy and sticky, not smooth like cake batter.)

Remove the pan from the heat, and season the filling with salt and pepper. Divide the filling evenly among the prepared pans. Drop the dough by small spoonful on top of each ramekin. Use the back of the spoon to spread the dough so it evenly covers the filling. Bake the pot pies for about 15 minutes, or until the crust is golden.

Yield: 4 to 6 servings

POTATO LATKES

Frying foods during Hanukkah is an ancient tradition, connected with the oil used to light the menorah during the "festival of lights."

2 tablespoons (14 g) ground flaxseed
¼ cup (60 ml) water
4 cups (440 g) peeled and shredded potatoes (about 5 medium potatoes)
6 green onions, finely chopped
1 tablespoon (8 g) all-purpose flour
1 teaspoon (6 g) salt, plus more to taste
Canola oil, for frying
Nondairy sour cream and/or applesauce, for accompaniments
Chopped chives, for garnish

In a food processor or blender, whip the flaxseed and water together for 1 to 2 minutes, or until thick and creamy, almost gelatinous.

Spread the potatoes on a clean towel, and roll up jelly-roll style. Twist the towel tightly to wring out as much liquid as possible. (You may need to do this again with a second towel to extract all of the water.) Transfer the potatoes to a bowl. Add the flaxseed, onions, flour, and salt. Use your hands to combine the ingredients and get a feel for the mixture. (You want it moist but not too wet.)

In a large nonstick pan, heat some oil over medium heat until hot but not smoking. Using a tablespoon, scoop a large spoonful of the potato mixture into the hot oil, pressing down to form a ¼- to ½-inch- (6 mm to 1 cm) thick patty. (You aren't trying to create dense patties, but the batter should stick together enough to be flipped without falling apart.) Slide a spatula underneath latkes while they're cooking to make sure they don't stick to the pan.

Brown on one side, turn over, and brown on the other. (You may need more oil as you add more latkes to the pan.) Transfer the latkes to a paper towel–lined plate to soak up excess oil. Season with salt. Serve the latkes hot with the sour cream and sprinkled with chives.

Yield: 15 to 20 latkes

33 Mushroom Rice; 34 Spicy Garlic Dill Pickles; 35 New World Székely Goulash; 36 No-Queso Quesadillas; 37 Plum-Tillas with Vanilla Dipping Sauce; 38 Sesame Cucumber Sandwiches; 39 Hollandaze'd Asparagus Rounds; 40 Orange Fennel Summer Rolls

41 Apple Tempeh Triangle Dippers; 42 Figs Stuffed with Rosemary and Walnut-Cashew Cream; 43 Black Olive Bruschetta; 44 Tomato, Basil, and Arugula Bruschetta; 45 Portobello Horseradish Bruschetta; 46 Cucumber and Cream Cheese Sandwiches 47 Purple Potatoes with Cashew Cream; 48 Tempeh and Eggplant Pot Pies

YEAR-ROUND RATATOUILLE

In winter, this ratatouille works well with canned tomatoes and dried herbs. However, in summer, use peeled, seeded, diced fresh tomatoes and adjust for the fresh herbs.

1 tablespoon (15 ml) olive oil
¾ cup (120 g) minced onion
½ cup (41 g) finely chopped eggplant
½ cup (62 g) finely chopped zucchini
½ cup (75 g) finely chopped bell pepper (any color)
3 cloves garlic, minced
¾ teaspoon dried basil (or 2 teaspoons fresh, minced)
¾ teaspoon dried thyme (or 2 teaspoons fresh, minced)
½ teaspoon dried parsley (or 1 teaspoon fresh, minced)
½ teaspoon salt
¼ teaspoon dried rosemary (or ½ teaspoon fresh, minced)
¼ teaspoon celery seed
¼ teaspoon black pepper
Pinch red pepper flakes
2 tablespoons (30 ml) vegan dry red wine, optional
1 can (14½ ounces, or 411 g) petite diced tomatoes, drained, or 1 cup (180 g) peeled, seeded, diced tomatoes
2 teaspoons minced fresh parsley

In a large skillet, heat the oil, onion, eggplant, zucchini, bell pepper, garlic, basil, thyme, dried parsley, salt, rosemary, celery seed, black pepper, and red pepper flakes over medium heat. Cook, stirring often, for 3 to 4 minutes, or until the onion is translucent. Add the wine and cook for about 3 minutes, or until it's absorbed. Add the tomatoes and reduce the heat to a simmer. Cook for 10 minutes, stirring occasionally. Stir in the fresh parsley. This is best at room temperature but benefits from sitting for 1 hour, or covered and refrigerated overnight to allow the flavors to blend. Bring the ratatouille to room temperature for serving.

Yield: 2 cups (400 g)

PARTY OLIVES

Baking these olives infuses them with incredible flavor, the almonds bring crunch, and the onions are a favorite with people who aren't even onion fans! For an even easier preparation, have the dish ready to go hours before serving. Just pop it in the oven when your guests arrive.

½ cup (80 g) pitted green olives, pimento- or garlic-stuffed
½ cup (80 g) pitted Kalamata olives
4 cipollini onions, peeled, or shallots, peeled, cut in half vertically
2 tablespoons (15 g) whole raw almonds
2 tablespoons (30 ml) vegan dry red wine or vegetable broth

4 cloves garlic
¼ to ½ teaspoon berbere, to taste
1 dundicut dried pepper or other dried pepper of choice

Preheat the oven to 400°F (200°C, or gas mark 6).

In a small cast-iron or ovenproof skillet, combine all of the ingredients. Bake for 25 to 30 minutes. (Most of the liquid will evaporate, but don't overcook or the almonds and garlic will burn.) Remove the dried pepper before serving hot or at room temperature.

Yield: 1½ cups (215 g)

HARISSA CARROT ZUCCHINI CUPS

With Moroccan influences thanks to the harissa, a North-African chili sauce, this is a new take on zesty carrot salad. It can be made ahead and refrigerated for up to 24 hours.

2 zucchini (7 inches [18 cm] long, 1 to 1½ inches [2.5 to 3.7 cm] wide)
1 tablespoon (15 ml) tamari
½ teaspoon liquid smoke
½ teaspoon olive oil
½ teaspoon ground coriander
2 teaspoons harissa paste, or more to taste
2 teaspoons red wine vinegar
1 cup (110 g) grated carrot
2 teaspoons fresh minced parsley
Salt, to taste
Black pepper, to taste
36 raisins

Cut the ends from the zucchini, and then cut each into six 1-inch (2.5 cm) rounds. Using a sharp paring knife, a metal measuring spoon, or a melon baller, cut the center of each slice into a cup, leaving the edges and bottom intact.

In a small bowl, stir together the tamari, liquid smoke, oil, and coriander.

Heat a grill pan over medium-high heat. Lightly coat the pan with cooking spray. Brush the cut sides of the zucchini with the tamari mixture. Put the rounds on the grill with the cup side down. Grill until marked, about 4 minutes. Turn one-quarter turn and grill again for 3 to 4 minutes, or until marked. Baste and turn over to grill the smooth sides of the rounds for 3 to 4 minutes, or until marked. Turn one-quarter turn and grill again until marked. Remove the rounds from the grill. (The zucchini should retain their texture rather than be overly soft.)

Stir the harissa and vinegar into the remaining basting liquid. Pour over the carrot, and add the parsley. Stir to combine, and season to taste with salt and pepper. Add more harissa, if desired. Spoon the mixture evenly into the zucchini cups, mounding the mixture. Top each with three raisins.

Yield: 12 zucchini cups

KALE CUCUMBER CUPS

Hurray, kale! The most super of the superfoods! This kale salad can be made ahead of time and stored in a covered container in the fridge for up to 8 hours, but it will continue to reduce in amount, so make extra.

2 cups (120 g) packed very finely chopped kale leaves (stems discarded)
2 teaspoons tamari
2 teaspoons lemon juice
1 teaspoon toasted sesame oil
½ teaspoon Sriracha, or more to taste
½ teaspoon white sesame seeds, or more to taste
Salt, to taste
Black pepper, to taste
14 ½-inch (1.3 cm) thick round slices cucumber

In a medium bowl, stir together the kale, tamari, and juice. Using your hands, rub it together for a few minutes, or until the kale wilts and softens. Stir in the oil, Sriracha, and seeds. Let it sit for 15 minutes for the flavors to meld. The kale will reduce in amount.

Using a ½-teaspoon measuring spoon or a melon baller, carefully scoop out the center of the cucumbers to create a bowl. (Do not scoop all the way through the cucumber.) Taste the salad and adjust the seasonings. Fill each cucumber with 1 teaspoon kale salad.

Yield: 14 cups

BAKED JALAPEÑOS

Creamy filling is hidden by a crunchy coating, all inside a spicy jalapeño, making an easy snack with layers of flavor and texture. Safety first: Wear plastic gloves when handling the peppers.

FOR THE FILLING:
½ cup (70 g) raw cashews, soaked in ½ cup (120 ml) water for 3 hours, drained
½ cup (131 g) cooked navy beans
2 tablespoons (30 ml) vegan dry white wine
2 tablespoons (30 ml) lemon juice
1 tablespoon (8 g) nutritional yeast flakes
2 teaspoons ume plum vinegar
1 teaspoon light miso
½ teaspoon onion powder
Salt, to taste
Black pepper, to taste

FOR THE PEPPERS:
8 to 12 medium whole jalapeño peppers
2 cups (56 g) cornflakes, crushed
½ cup (40 g) whole wheat panko crumbs
Salsa, for serving

To make the filling: In a blender, combine all the filling ingredients and blend until completely smooth. Cover and refrigerate for at least 1 hour for the flavors to meld. Taste and adjust the seasonings. This can be made up to 4 days in advance. Store covered in the fridge.

To make the peppers: Preheat the oven to 400°F (200°C, or gas mark 6). Lightly coat a baking sheet with nonstick cooking spray.

Cut the peppers in half and remove the seeds. Fill each half with up to 1 tablespoon (17 g) filling (depending on the size of the halves).

On a plate, stir together the cornflakes and the panko. Dip the filling-stuffed side of each pepper into the cornflake mixture, patting the crumbs to adhere to the filling. Bake the peppers for 20 minutes, or until the crumbs are golden brown and the peppers are slightly deflated. Serve with salsa.

Yield: 16 to 24 pepper halves, ⅔ cup (200 g) filling

POTATO PUFFS WITH TAPENADE

You'll have extra tapenade for another use, such as a sandwich spread. The tapenade can be made ahead and stored in the fridge, covered, for up to 4 days.

FOR THE TAPENADE:
¼ cup (40 g) pitted Kalamata olives
4 large pitted green olives
1 tablespoon (4 g) soft sun-dried tomato halves, not oil-packed
3 leaves fresh basil
Pinch of ground black pepper

FOR THE PUFFS:
About 2 cups (244 g) potato insides from Nacho Potato Skins (see page 38) or cooked potato pieces
½ cup (40 g) vegan instant potatoes
½ cup (120 ml) unsweetened plain vegan milk
2 tablespoons (30 ml) olive oil
½ teaspoon salt
Generous pinch of black pepper

To make the tapenade: Finely chop all the tapenade ingredients, and stir together, or combine them in a mini blender used on pulse.

To make the puffs: Preheat the oven to 400°F (200°C, or gas mark 6). Lightly coat a mini muffin pan with nonstick cooking spray.

In a medium saucepan, heat the potato pieces, instant potatoes, milk, and oil over medium heat. Cook for 2 to 3 minutes, mashing the potatoes as they cook. (The mixture should easily form a ball.) Season with salt and pepper. When the mixture is cool enough to handle comfortably, scoop 1 tablespoon [47 g] into your hand and form into a small ball. Make a small indentation with your finger. Spoon ½ teaspoon tapenade into the indentation. Seal the ball closed with another 1 to 1 ½ teaspoons of the potato mixture. Roll the ball closed and put in the mini muffin pan. Continue until all of the potato mixture is used. Lightly coat the balls with nonstick cooking spray. Bake for 35 minutes, or until lightly browned and slightly crusty.

Yield: 14 to 18 puffs, ⅓ cup [85 g] tapenade

NACHO POTATO SKINS

Potato skins, the epitome of bar finger food, get a vegan remake that doesn't miss a beat in flavor. Save the insides of the potatoes to make Potato Puffs. [See page 37.]

6 medium russet potatoes [each about 5 ounces, or 140 g]
1 can [15 ounces, or 425 g] black beans, drained and rinsed
½ cup [90 g] chopped tomato
¼ cup [40 g] minced red onion
2 tablespoons [18 g] minced poblano pepper
2 tablespoons [30 ml] lime juice
2 teaspoons minced fresh cilantro
½ teaspoon ground cumin
Salt, to taste
Black pepper, to taste
2 tablespoons [30 ml] olive oil
1 tablespoon [15 ml] canned chipotle pepper in adobo, with sauce
Your favorite Nacho Sauce
1 medium avocado, pitted, peeled, and diced, optional

Preheat the oven to 400°F [200°C, or gas mark 6].

Pierce the potatoes a couple of times so they can release steam. Bake the potatoes for 45 minutes, or 1 hour if larger, or until tender. Let cool, slice in half, and scoop the insides from the potatoes, leaving about ¼ inch [6 mm] from the skin intact.

Meanwhile, in a medium bowl, combine the beans, tomato, onion, pepper, juice, cilantro, and cumin. Season to taste with salt and pepper.

Preheat the oven to 475°F [240°C, or gas mark 9].

In a mortar and pestle, combine the oil and chipotle and pound until combined. Add a pinch of salt and pepper. Using a fork, pierce the inside of the potato skins a few times. Brush the oil on the insides of the potatoes, and place on a baking sheet. Bake for 15 minutes, or until starting to crisp. For extra crispness, broil the potato skins for a few minutes after baking. Fill each potato with a heaping tablespoon [28 g] of filling, dividing the filling evenly among the potatoes. Top each potato with Nacho Saucy Dip and a few pieces of avocado, if using.

Yield: 12 potato skins

CORN FRITTERS WITH TOMATO-THYME GRAVY

These are delicious with Tomato-Thyme Gravy, but if you're short on time, just spike some vegan mayonnaise with hot sauce, and dip away! If you happen to have extra gravy, save it to pour over a tofu scramble, or use it as a dip with the Baked Frittata Minis. [See page 41.]

FOR THE FRITTERS:
½ cup [60 g] garbanzo flour
¼ cup [31 g] all-purpose flour
2 tablespoons [15 g] fine cornmeal [not corn flour]
½ teaspoon baking powder
½ teaspoon ground cumin
¼ teaspoon dried thyme
¼ teaspoon paprika
¼ teaspoon salt
Generous pinch of black pepper
1 cup [135 g] frozen corn kernels, thawed
2 tablespoons [14 g] finely grated carrot
1 tablespoon plus 1 teaspoon [4 g] minced chives, plus more for garnish, if desired
¼ cup [60 ml] unsweetened plain vegan milk, more if needed
High-heat neutral-flavored oil, for cooking

FOR THE TOMATO-THYME GRAVY:
½ cup [80 g] finely minced onion
2 tablespoons [16 g] all-purpose flour
2 tablespoons [30 ml] olive oil
1 teaspoon dried thyme or 1 tablespoon [2 g] minced fresh thyme
½ teaspoon salt
¼ teaspoon black pepper
1 can [15 ounces, or 425 g] diced tomatoes with juice [preferably no-salt-added]
¾ cup [180 ml] tomato juice
1 tablespoon [15 ml] Frank's Hot Sauce, or more to taste
2 teaspoons liquid smoke

To make the fritters: In a medium bowl, combine the flours, cornmeal, baking powder, spices, salt, and pepper. Whisk to combine. Stir in the corn, carrot, and chives, followed by the milk. [The mixture will be sticky, but it should be shapeable. If not, add an extra 1 tablespoon [15 ml] milk.]

In a large skillet, pour a thin layer of oil. Heat over medium-high heat. Using a heaping tablespoon [20 g] of the mixture, shape into a small patty about 1½ inches [4 cm] across and ½- to ¾-inch [1.3 to 2 cm] thick. Put the fritters into the oil and cook until golden, 4 to 6 minutes. Turn the fritters over to cook the second side, 4 to 6 minutes.

Drain the fritters on a paper towel and serve with the gravy.

To make the tomato-thyme gravy: In a medium saucepan, heat the onion, flour, oil, thyme, salt, and pepper over medium heat. Cook for 3 to 4 minutes, stirring, or until the flour is cooked. Add the remaining ingredients, and simmer over low heat for 15 to 20 minutes. (The gravy may be made ahead, covered, and refrigerated for up to 48 hours. Reheat over low heat.)

Yield: 16 to 18 fritters, 2 cups (470 ml) gravy

FRESH CORN FRITTERS

For incredible fritters, use corn that has just been cut from the cob. Serve the fritters hot with a zesty dip.

1 quart (946 ml) vegetable oil (such as canola)
2½ cups (385 g) corn fresh cut from the cob, or (410 g) frozen and thawed
1 cup (225 g) masa harina
1½ teaspoons salt
1 teaspoon baking powder
2 teaspoons minced thyme
1 teaspoon ground chia seeds mixed with ¼ cup (60 ml) water
Squeeze of lime juice
1 cup (235 ml) water

In a deep fryer or deep pan using a thermometer, preheat the oil to 360°F (182°C). Line a plate with paper towels.

In a large bowl, stir together all of the ingredients for about 1 minute, or until a thick batter forms. Drop by the tablespoonful (15 g) into the preheated oil and cook about 3 minutes, OR until deep golden brown. Transfer to the prepared plate to catch any excess oil.

Yield: about 20 fritters

INDIAN POTATO FRITTERS

These fritters are made of ingredients similar to a samosa, minus the pastry. Serve them with your favorite chutney.

Vegetable oil for deep fryer
3 large shallots
1 teaspoon mustard seed
1 teaspoon cumin seed
1 teaspoon asafetida
2½ teaspoons salt, divided
1 teaspoon olive oil
3 medium yellow potatoes, boiled whole until fork-tender
1 cup (130 g) frozen peas, thawed
1 cup (110 g) gram flour
1 cup (235 ml) water
Pinch of additional salt

Preheat the oil for a deep fryer to 360°F (182°C). Line a plate with paper towels.

In a medium frying pan, sauté the shallots, mustard seed, cumin seed, asafetida, 1 teaspoon of the salt, and olive oil over medium-high heat for about 10 minutes, or until the shallots are golden brown on the edges. Remove from the heat.

In a medium bowl, mash the potatoes, leaving a few big lumps remaining throughout. Stir in the shallot mixture, peas, and 1 teaspoon of the salt.

In a separate bowl, whisk together the flour, water, and remaining ½ teaspoon salt until smooth. Roll the mashed potatoes into 18 golf-ball-size balls and then dip into the flour batter, letting any excess drip back into the bowl. Fry about 3 at a time for 10 minutes. Transfer to a prepared plate to absorb any excess oil.

Yield: about 18 fritters

KIMCHI-STUFFED SAUSAGES

If you aren't able to find the Korean hot pepper powder, substitute cayenne pepper. It will still taste great.

4 ounces (113 g) extra-firm tofu, drained and crumbled
1¾ cups (396 g) drained kimchi, not squeezed, divided
½ cup (120 ml) water, plus more if needed
3 tablespoons (50 g) ketchup
1 tablespoon (15 ml) tamari
2 teaspoons ground coriander
1 teaspoon ground ginger
1 teaspoon ground cumin
1 teaspoon garlic powder
1 teaspoon onion powder
1 teaspoon Korean hot pepper powder
1 teaspoon ground white pepper
1½ cups (216 g) vital wheat gluten
¼ cup (30 g) nutritional yeast
1 tablespoon (15 ml) neutral-flavored oil
Korean sauce from Baked Buffalo Tofu Bites (See page 14.)
Minced green onions, for garnish
Sesame seeds, for garnish

In a blender, combine the tofu, 1 cup (226 g) of the kimchi, water, ketchup, tamari, coriander, ginger, cumin, garlic powder, onion powder, and peppers and process until smooth.

In a medium bowl, whisk together the vital wheat gluten and nutritional yeast. Add the tofu mixture. Using a fork, stir to combine. Mix together well. (The mixture should be cohesive and able to be formed.) Add 1 tablespoon (15 ml) water or (9 g) vital wheat gluten if needed to make a dough.

Prepare a steamer and six 10-inch (25 cm) pieces of foil. Divide the mixture evenly among the foil pieces: each piece will be 4 ounces (113 g). Shape each into a 6-inch (15 cm) log.

Make a deep indentation down the center, leaving the ends intact. Fill with a generous 2 tablespoons (28 g) of the remaining kimchi, and pinch the well closed. Try to center the filling so the sausages will not tear when cooking. Shape into a sausage and close the foil, twisting the ends. If the log isn't sealed well, the kimchi may fall out when slicing or cooking. Repeat with the remaining sausages, and steam for 1 hour 10 minutes.

Use a serrated knife to carefully cut the sausages into ½-inch (1.3 cm) rounds. Heat the oil in a large skillet over medium heat. Cooking in batches, cook the sausages until browned, about 4 minutes per side. Turn over to cook the second side, about 3 minutes. Keep warm. When all of the sausages are browned, return them to the skillet along with the sauce. Stir to coat, and cook for 1 minute.

Transfer to a plate and sprinkle with the onions and sesame seeds.

Yield: 72 rounds

MEDITERRANEAN MEATLESS BALLS
With such a large amount of fresh basil, this appetizer is a show-stealer. Add the olives and sun-dried tomatoes, and a star is born! Try it with Tomato-Thyme Gravy. (See page 38.)

¼ cup (40 g) pitted Kalamata olives
¼ cup (16 g) soft sun-dried tomato halves, not oil-packed
½ cup (12 g) packed fresh basil
8 ounces (227 g) extra-firm tofu, drained, pressed, and crumbled
¼ cup (40 g) finely minced onion
3 tablespoons (28 g) minced green bell pepper
2 tablespoons (30 ml) lemon juice
2 tablespoons (15 g) nutritional yeast
2 cloves garlic, minced
½ teaspoon dried thyme
½ teaspoon dried oregano
½ teaspoon salt
¼ teaspoon black pepper
Pinch of red pepper flakes
¼ cup (66 g) tomato paste, plus more if needed
½ cup (63 g) all-purpose flour, divided
Neutral-flavored oil, for cooking

In a small blender, combine the olives and tomatoes. Process until finely chopped. Add the basil, and process until combined.

In a medium bowl, place the tofu and add the basil mixture, mashing the tofu with a fork and mixing together. Stir in the onion, bell pepper, juice, yeast, garlic, thyme, oregano, salt, black pepper, and red pepper until well combined. Combine with your hands, if necessary, to make a uniform mixture. Stir in the paste and ¼ cup (31 g) of the

flour. If the mixture isn't shapeable, add 1 tablespoon (17 g) extra tomato paste.

Preheat the oven to 325°F (170°C, or gas mark 3). Lightly coat a baking sheet with nonstick cooking spray.

Scoop 1 tablespoon (25 g) of the mixture and form a ball. Place the ball on the sheet. Repeat until all the mixture is used. Lightly coat the balls with nonstick cooking spray. Bake for 20 minutes, or until lightly browned. Turn over carefully, and spray again. Bake for 20 minutes longer, or until golden. Broil the balls for 5 minutes.

Alternately, for pan frying: Place the remaining ¼ cup (31 g) flour on a plate. Scoop 1 tablespoon (25 g) of the mixture, and form a ball. Roll the ball in the flour, and place the ball on the sheet. Repeat until all the mixture is used. Heat a thin layer of oil in a large skillet over medium heat. Line a plate with a paper towel for draining. Fry the balls for 8 to 10 minutes, turning occasionally, or until golden. Drain briefly on the paper towel–lined plate. Serve the balls hot, warm, or at room temperature with the sauce and toothpicks.

Yield: 14 to 16 balls

JAMAICAN JERK TEMPEH SKEWERS
This is a very mild jerk sauce. Sweet pineapple and brilliant red bell peppers make for a gorgeous presentation. For more heat, use the full jalapeño or a Scotch bonnet.

FOR THE SAUCE:
½ cup (120 ml) vegetable broth
2 green onions, trimmed
1 tablespoon (17 g) tomato paste
1 tablespoon (15 ml) apple cider vinegar
2 teaspoons pure maple syrup
2 teaspoons olive oil
½ jalapeño pepper, stemmed and seeded, more to taste
3 cloves garlic, minced
½-inch (1.3 cm) round fresh ginger, peeled
½ teaspoon salt
½ teaspoon dried thyme
½ teaspoon sweet paprika
½ teaspoon ground cumin
¼ teaspoon ground allspice
¼ teaspoon black pepper
8 ounces (227 g) tempeh, steamed, cut into 1-inch (2.5 cm) cubes

FOR THE SKEWERS:
32 toothpicks, soaked in water for at least 30 minutes
Two ½-inch (1.3 cm) round slices red onion, each cut into 16 pieces
Four ½-inch (1.3 cm) round slices fresh pineapple, each cut into 8 pieces
2 medium red bell peppers, each seeded and cut into sixteen 1-inch (2.5 cm) pieces

To make the sauce: In a blender, combine all of the sauce ingredients except the tempeh and process until smooth. Place the tempeh cubes in a 9-inch [23 cm] square baking dish. Pour the sauce over the tempeh cubes and toss to coat. Cover and refrigerate for at least 24 hours or up to 3 days, turning occasionally.

To make the skewers: On each of 32 toothpicks, skewer a piece of onion, a tempeh cube [letting the extra sauce drip back into the dish], a piece of pineapple, and a piece of bell pepper.

Heat a grill pan over high heat. Lightly coat the grill pan with nonstick cooking spray.

Transfer the toothpicks to the grill pan, and cook until marked, about 5 minutes, while basting with the remaining jerk sauce. Turn to cook the second side until marked, about 5 minutes, still basting.

Yield: 32 toothpicks

BAKED FRITTATA MINIS

Broccoli and pasta in a frittata? Yes, please! Feel free to serve the red sauce with other recipes in this book.

FOR THE RED SAUCE:
¾ cup [135 g] chopped tomato
⅓ cup [49 g] chopped red bell pepper
3 tablespoons [30 g] chopped shallot
2 cloves garlic, minced
1 teaspoon minced fresh ginger
1 teaspoon olive oil
¼ teaspoon ground cinnamon
¼ teaspoon cayenne pepper, plus more to taste
1 tablespoon [15 ml] red wine vinegar
1 tablespoon [15 ml] water, plus more if needed
Salt, to taste
Black pepper, to taste

FOR THE FRITTATA MINIS:
1 ounce [28 g] dry capellini or angel hair noodles, broken into 1-inch [2.5 cm] pieces
2 teaspoons olive oil
1 cup [91 g] minced broccoli
¼ cup [40 g] minced onion
2 tablespoons [8 g] soft sun-dried tomato halves, not oil-packed, minced
¼ teaspoon dried dill
2 cloves garlic, minced
Salt, to taste
Black pepper, to taste
10 ounces [283 g] extra-firm tofu, drained and crumbled
¼ cup [60 ml] unsweetened plain vegan milk
1 tablespoon plus 1 teaspoon [11 g] nutritional yeast
1 tablespoon plus 1 teaspoon [20 ml] lemon juice
1 tablespoon [15 ml] ume plum vinegar

To make the red sauce: In a small skillet, combine all of the red sauce ingredients over high heat. Bring to a boil, and then reduce the heat to a simmer. Cook for 10 minutes, stirring occasionally. Remove from the heat and process in a blender until smooth. Let the flavors meld for at least 30 minutes.

To make the frittata minis: Preheat the oven to 400°F [200°C, or gas mark 6]. Lightly coat 22 cups of a mini muffin pan with nonstick cooking spray.

Cook the noodles according to the package directions, and drain.

In a large skillet, heat the oil, broccoli, onion, tomatoes, and dill over medium heat. Cook for about 3 minutes, stirring occasionally, or until the broccoli is bright green. Remove from the heat and stir in the garlic. Season with salt and pepper.

In a blender, combine the tofu, milk, yeast, juice, and vinegar. Process until smooth. Pour into the broccoli mixture and add the noodles. Stir to combine. Scoop by 1 tablespoon [20 g], and drop in the muffin cups. Pat the tops smooth. Continue until all the tofu mixture has been used.

Bake for 25 to 30 minutes, or until the tops are slightly golden and firm to the touch. Remove from the tin and serve hot, warm, or at room temperature.

Yield: 22 mini frittatas, ¾ cup [142 g] sauce

FALAFEL FRITTERS WITH SPICY TAHINI SAUCE

These fritters are full of the falafel flavors you know and love. The cashew-based tahini sauce is spiked with harissa [a North-African chili sauce]. Extra sauce is great over salads.

FOR THE SPICY TAHINI SAUCE:
¼ cup [35 g] raw cashews
3 tablespoons [45 ml] vegetable broth
2 tablespoons [32 g] tahini
2 tablespoons [30 ml] seasoned rice vinegar
1 tablespoon [15 ml] lemon juice
2 cloves garlic, minced
1 teaspoon harissa, plus more to taste
½ teaspoon salt

FOR THE FALAFEL:
1 can [15 ounces, or 425 g] chickpeas, drained and rinsed
1/4 cup [40 g] finely minced red onion
3 tablespoons [28 g] finely minced green bell pepper
2 tablespoons [30 ml] lemon juice
1 tablespoon [4 g] finely minced fresh parsley
2 cloves garlic, minced
1 teaspoon ground cumin
1 teaspoon ground coriander
½ teaspoon salt
½ teaspoon ground white pepper

49 Potato Latkes; 50 Year-Round Ratatouille; 51 Party Olives; 52 Harissa Carrot Zucchini Cups; 53 Kale Cucumber Cups;
54 Baked Jalepeños; 55 Potato Puffs with Tapenade; 56 Nacho Potato Skins

57 Corn Fritters with Tomato-Thyme Gravy; 58 Fresh Corn Fritters; 59 Indian Potato Fritters; 60 Kimchi-Stuffed Sausages; 61 Mediterranean Meatless Balls; 62 Jamaican Jerk Tempeh Skewers; 63 Baked Frittata Minis; 64 Falafel Fritters with Spicy Tahini Sauce

¼ cup (31 g) all-purpose flour, plus more if needed
High-heat neutral-flavored oil, for cooking

To make the spicy tahini sauce: In a small high-powered blender, combine all of the sauce ingredients. Process until completely smooth. (Taste and adjust the seasonings. Serve immediately, or cover and refrigerate for up to 4 days.

To make the falafel: In a food processor, process the chickpeas until crumbly, but not a paste. Transfer to a medium bowl and add the onion, bell pepper, juice, parsley, garlic, cumin, coriander, salt, and white pepper. Stir to combine, and then use your hands to mash a little. Add the flour, and mix together. The mixture should hold its shape. If not, add a bit more flour.

Using a slightly heaping tablespoon (20 g), shape into 18 small flat rounds, about 1 inch (2.5 cm) in diameter.

In a large skillet, heat a thin layer of oil over medium-high heat. Cook the falafel until lightly browned, about 4 minutes. Turn over to cook the second side until golden, about 4 minutes.

Drain on a paper towel–lined plate.

Yield: 18 falafels, ¾ cup (140 g) sauce

MEAN BEAN TACO CUPS
You'll fall in love with this method of making tortilla cups. They are versatile, so let your ideas run wild. Shake up the seasoning on them, and then concoct your own filling.

3 8-inch (20 cm) flour tortillas
½ teaspoon smoked salt
½ cup (86 g) cooked black beans
½ cup (52 g) minced cucumber
1 tablespoon (9 g) minced red bell pepper
1 tablespoon (10 g) finely minced red onion
1 teaspoon minced fresh cilantro
½ teaspoon chipotle in adobo sauce
1 tablespoon (15 ml) red wine vinegar
½ avocado, pitted, peeled, and diced
Juice of ½ lemon
Salt, to taste
Black pepper, to taste

Preheat the oven to 400°F (200°C, or gas mark 6).

Using a 3-inch (8 cm) round cutter, cut 4 rounds from each tortilla. Lightly coat one side of each round with nonstick cooking spray and sprinkle evenly with smoked salt. Using two 12-cup inverted regular muffin pans, tuck a round–salted side up–in between 4 of the cups, curving the sides up to form a small bowl. Repeat until all the rounds are used. Bake for 6 minutes, or until the edges are lightly browned. Cool on a wire rack. (The bowls can be stored in an airtight container for up to 3 days before using.)

In a small bowl, combine the beans, cucumber, bell pepper, onion, and cilantro.

Using a mortar and pestle, pound the chipotle into the vinegar until smooth. Pour over the bean mixture, stirring to coat. Spoon about 1 tablespoon (12 g) into each cup.

In a small bowl, toss the avocado with the juice and season with salt and pepper. Sprinkle a few pieces on each cup. Serve immediately.

Yield: 12 cups

TINY TOMATO PIES
These little pies fly off the table at any gathering.

FOR THE CRUSTS:
2 cups (240 g) whole wheat pastry flour
½ teaspoon salt
¼ cup plus 2 tablespoons (90 ml) olive oil
¼ cup plus 2 tablespoons (90 ml) cold water

FOR THE FILLING:
½ cup (20 g) packed spinach leaves
¼ cup (10 g) packed basil leaves
2 tablespoons (18 g) raw cashews
2 tablespoons (20 g) chopped onion
1 tablespoon plus 1 teaspoon (11 g) nutritional yeast
Juice of 1 lemon
8 ounces (227 g) extra-firm tofu, drained, pressed, and crumbled
½ cup (120 ml) unsweetened plain vegan milk
½ teaspoon salt
Pinch of black pepper
12 cherry tomatoes, halved

Preheat the oven to 400°F (200°C, or gas mark 6). Lightly coat a 24-cup mini muffin pan with nonstick cooking spray.

To make the crusts: In a medium bowl, stir together the flour and salt. Drizzle in the oil. Using a fork, stir to create crumbs. Add the water 1 tablespoon (15 ml) at a time, stirring with the fork, until it forms a dough. Scoop a generous 2 teaspoons of dough and form into a ball. Put in one of the muffin cups, and press to line the whole cup. Repeat until all of the dough has been used.

To make the filling: In a food processor, process the spinach, basil, and cashews until finely chopped. Add the onion, yeast, and juice and pulse again. Add the tofu, milk, salt, and pepper. Process until smooth. Fill each cup with about 2 teaspoons filling, using all the filling. Top each with a cherry tomato half, cut-side down. Bake for 25 to 30 minutes, or until the tops are golden brown and the crusts are done.

Yield: 24 mini pies

ANTIPASTA TOFU-STUFFED SHELLS

The tofu is seasoned with a vegan favorite, nutritional yeast, as well as other goodies.

1 tablespoon (8 g) nutritional yeast
1 tablespoon (15 ml) tamari
1 tablespoon (15 ml) olive oil
1 tablespoon (15 ml) liquid smoke
1 tablespoon (15 ml) vegan dry red wine
½ teaspoon pure maple syrup
½ teaspoon garlic powder
Salt, to taste
Black pepper, to taste
1 pound (454 g) extra-firm tofu, drained, pressed, and cut into ¼-inch (6 mm) cubes
6 stalks roasted asparagus, cut into ¼-inch (6 mm) pieces
3 tablespoons (30 g) minced green onions
4 artichoke hearts, minced
2 tablespoons (8 g) soft sun-dried tomato halves, not oil-packed
1 tablespoon (9 g) capers, drained and minced
1 cup (40 g) packed baby arugula, minced
¼ cup (11 g) chopped fresh basil
2 tablespoons (30 ml) red wine vinegar
Pinch of red pepper flakes
2 tablespoons (28 g) vegan mayonnaise, or more to taste
14 to 18 dry, jumbo, vegan pasta shells, cooked al dente, drained

Preheat the oven to 400°F (200°C, or gas mark 6). Lightly coat a large rimmed baking sheet with nonstick cooking spray.

In a medium bowl, combine the yeast, tamari, oil, liquid smoke, wine, syrup, garlic powder, and salt and black pepper to taste. Stir in the tofu to coat. Spread the tofu on the prepared sheet and bake for 30 to 35 minutes, or until golden and firm in texture. Let cool.

In a bowl, combine the tofu, asparagus, onions, artichokes, tomatoes, capers, arugula, basil, vinegar, red pepper, and mayonnaise.

Fill each shell with about 2 tablespoons (34 g) of the filling.

Yield: 14 to 18 shells

TWISTED BREAD STICKS

Beer brings plenty of extra flavor to bread dough. Serve these with the red sauce for dipping.

1 cup (235 ml) flat vegan beer, at room temperature
1 teaspoon light agave nectar
2¼ teaspoons active dry yeast
5 tablespoons (75 ml) olive oil, divided
2 cups (240 g) white or regular whole wheat flour

1 cup minus 1½ teaspoons (120 g) all-purpose flour
½ teaspoon salt
2 teaspoons garlic salt, or more to taste

In the bowl of a stand mixer fitted with a dough hook, combine the beer, agave, and yeast. Stir and let sit for 5 minutes for the yeast to get bubbly. Add 2 tablespoons (30 ml) of the oil, the flours, and the salt. Knead for 6 to 8 minutes, until a smooth, cohesive dough is formed. (Alternatively, knead by hand on a lightly floured surface for 10 minutes.) Add an extra 1 tablespoon (15 ml) beer or water or (8 g) flour if needed. Shape the dough into a ball.

Lightly coat a medium bowl with nonstick cooking spray. Put the dough in the bowl, and turn over so the oiled side is up. Cover with plastic wrap and let rise in a warm place until doubled, about 1½ hours.

In a small bowl, combine the garlic salt and the remaining 3 tablespoons (45 ml) oil.

Lightly coat two baking sheets with nonstick cooking spray. Lightly flour a work surface.

Roll the dough out to an 8 x 15-inch (20 x 38 cm) rectangle. Cut into ten 1½-inch (4 cm) strips.

Brush with about 1 tablespoon (15 ml) of the oil mixture. Twist both ends of the dough in opposite directions to form a rope about ½ inch (1.3 cm) thick. Cut in half to make two sticks, and place on the baking sheet. Continue until all the sticks are formed, placing them about 2 inches (5 cm) apart. Brush with another 1 tablespoon (15 ml) of the remaining oil mixture, and let rise for about 30 minutes, or until puffy.

Preheat the oven to 400°F (200°C, or gas mark 6).

Bake for 13 to 16 minutes, or until golden brown. Brush with the remaining 1 tablespoon (15 ml) oil.

Yield: 20 bread sticks

SPINACH SWIRLS

These easy little spinach bites are an impressive part of an appetizer spread. Try to resist eating the filling with a spoon, but we won't blame you if you do.

FOR THE DOUGH:
½ cup (120 ml) warm water
1 teaspoon Sucanat
1 teaspoon active dry yeast
1 cup (120 g) white or regular whole wheat flour
½ cup (63 g) all-purpose flour
2 tablespoons (30 ml) olive oil
½ teaspoon Italian herb blend
½ teaspoon salt

FOR THE FILLING:
3 cups (90 g) finely chopped spinach
2 tablespoons (15 g) nutritional yeast
1 tablespoon (15 ml) olive oil
¼ teaspoon black pepper

To make the dough: In the bowl of a stand mixer fitted with a dough hook, stir together the water, Sucanat, and yeast. Let sit for 5 minutes, or until the yeast bubbles. Add the flours, oil, herb blend, and salt. Mix on low for about 6 minutes, or until the dough forms a smooth ball. (Alternatively, knead by hand on a lightly floured surface for 10 minutes.) Add an extra 1 tablespoon (8 g) flour or (15 ml) water if needed to make a cohesive dough.

Coat a large bowl with nonstick cooking spray.

Round the dough into a ball and place it in the bowl, turning so the oiled side is up. Cover with plastic wrap and let rise until doubled, about 1½ hours.

Lightly dust a work surface with flour. Divide the dough in half and roll each half into an 8 x 10-inch (20 x 25 cm) rectangle.

Preheat the oven to 375°F (190°C, or gas mark 5).

To make the filling: In a medium bowl, combine the spinach, yeast, oil, and pepper. Spread half of the filling evenly on each rectangle. Roll from the 10-inch (25 cm) side, pinching the dough together as you go, including the ends and the last edge of the dough, so the swirls don't unwind in the oven. Cut each roll into 1-inch (2.5 cm) slices, and place on a baking sheet with the filling side on top. Bake the rolls for 18 to 22 minutes, or until lightly browned and the centers are cooked.

Yield: 20 swirls

PORTOBELLO BLTS

Spread toasted bread slices with creamy, spicy (if you choose) guacamole, and top it with smoky, crisp vegan bacon to create this open-faced appetizer.

FOR THE GUACAMOLE:
2 small ripe avocados, halved, pitted, and peeled
2 tablespoons (8 g) soft sun-dried tomato halves, not oil-packed, minced, optional
1½ tablespoons (15 g) minced red onion
½ teaspoon (up to 1 teaspoon) minced jalapeño pepper, to taste, optional
1½ tablespoons (2 g) chopped fresh cilantro or fresh parsley, optional
1 to 1½ tablespoons (15 to 23 ml) lime or lemon juice
Salt, to taste

FOR THE BLTS:
16 slices (½-inch, or 1.3 cm, thick) baguette, toasted
16 portobello mushroom slices, grilled
4 romaine leaves, torn into pieces
1 large tomato, sliced into ¼-inch (6 mm) rounds and cut in half to make 16 slices
7 ounces (198 g total) vegan bacon
6 portobello mushroom slices, grilled

To make the guacamole: In a small bowl, mash the avocado with the tomatoes, onion, jalapeño and cilantro, if using, juice, and salt to taste. (You can leave the guacamole slightly chunky if you prefer.) Use promptly after preparation.

To make the BLTs: Place a slice of portobello on each baguette slice. Spread the guacamole evenly on the toasted baguette slices. Divide the lettuce leaves evenly on the toast, and top each with a tomato and a few slices of bacon. Serve promptly to prevent the guacamole from discoloring.

Yield: 16 BLTs, about 1 heaping cup (320 g) guacamole

FIG AND NUT CANAPÉS

You'll love the mousse-like texture, creaminess, and white-ness the coconut cream imparts to this spread. These canapés are also excellent without the fig spread.

FOR THE CASHEW ALMOND SPREAD:
1½ cups (210 g) raw cashews
½ cup (56 g) slivered almonds
¼ cup plus 2 tablespoons (90 ml) water, plus extra 2 tablespoons (30 ml) if needed
1 tablespoon plus 1 teaspoon (20 ml) lemon juice
¼ cup (50 g) coconut cream (scooped from the top of a chilled can of full-fat coconut milk)
½ teaspoon salt

FOR THE FIG SPREAD:
1 pound (454 g) dried figs, stemmed and chopped
Zest of 1 orange
2 cups (470 ml) fresh orange juice
4 tablespoons (48 g) Sucanat
Pinch of salt
1 teaspoon vanilla extract

FOR THE CANAPÉS:
1½ cups (389 g) Fig Spread
1 sourdough (16-inch, or 41 cm, long), baguette, cut into ½-inch (1.3 cm) slices, lightly toasted
2 cups (544 g) Cashew Almond Spread
2 ripe, firm pears, each sliced into 32 thin wedges
Brown rice syrup, for drizzling
¾ cup (90 g) chopped toasted walnuts

To make the cashew almond spread: In a 4-cup (940 ml) glass measuring cup, place the cashews and almonds and generously cover with water. Cover with plastic wrap, and let stand at room temperature for 8 hours to soften the nuts. Drain the nuts (discard the soaking water); give them a quick rinse. Place them in a food processor or high-speed blender, along with the ¼ cup plus 2 tablespoons (90 ml) water, juice, coconut cream, and salt. Process until perfectly smooth, stopping to scrape the sides occasionally with a rubber spatula. (If you see that the nuts need extra moisture to blend easily, add up to 2 extra tablespoons (30 ml) water, 1 tablespoon (15 ml) at a time.) This might take up to 10 minutes, depending on the machine.

Transfer the spread into a medium bowl fitted with a lid, and let stand at room temperature for 24 hours. After 24 hours, the top of the spread will look slightly crackled, and the spread will be mousse-like; store in an airtight container in the fridge for up to 2 weeks.

To make the fig spread: In a medium saucepan, bring the figs, zest, juice, Sucanat, and salt to a boil, lower the heat, and simmer for 15 minutes, stirring occasionally.

Remove from the heat, add the vanilla, and stir. Cover with a lid and let cool. In a blender, blend until mostly smooth. Refrigerate until ready to use.

To make the canapés: Spread 2 teaspoons of Fig Spread on each slice of bread, or enough to thinly cover the surface of the bread. Add 1 tablespoon (17 g) Cashew Almond Spread on top, or enough to generously cover the surface of the bread. Add two pear wedges per slice. Using a fork, lightly drizzle with the syrup. Drop a few chopped walnuts on top.

Yield: 32 canapés, about 2 cups (544 g) Cashew Almond Spread, about 3 cups (876 g) Fig Spread

EGGPLANT STACKERS

Think eggplant Parmesan, boosted with pesto, topped with tomato, and made vegan. Voila: You get this mouthwatering stacker. Leftover pesto can be stored covered in the fridge for up to 4 days.

FOR THE BREAD:
2 tablespoons (30 ml) olive oil
1 teaspoon nutritional yeast
Pinch of Italian herb blend
Pinch of salt
Pinch of black pepper
16 slices (½-inch, or 1.3 cm, thick) French bread

FOR THE EGGPLANT:
¾ cup (60 g) panko crumbs
½ teaspoon Italian herb blend
Salt, to taste
Black pepper, to taste
3 tablespoons (45 ml) unsweetened plain vegan milk
1 tablespoon (8 g) cornstarch
½ teaspoon garlic powder
16 slices (½-inch, or 1.3 cm, thick) eggplant

FOR THE PESTO:
¾ cup (18 g) fresh basil leaves, plus 16 leaves for garnish

1 or 2 cloves garlic, pressed, to taste
2 tablespoons (18 g) toasted pine nuts or (15 g) toasted walnut pieces
Salt, to taste
Black pepper, to taste
1 tablespoon (15 ml) lemon juice
2 tablespoons to ¼ cup (30 to 60 ml) olive oil, as needed
16 tomato slices (¼-inch, or 6 mm, thick)

To make the bread: Preheat the oven to 400°F (200°C, or gas mark 6).

In a small bowl, stir together the oil, yeast, and seasonings. Brush on one side of each bread slice. Place on a baking sheet, and bake for 10 minutes. (These can be made in advance, cooled, and stored in an airtight container for up to 2 days.)

To make the eggplant: If you have prepared the bread ahead of time, preheat the oven to 400°F (200°C, or gas mark 6) again.

On a plate, combine the panko, herb blend, and a generous pinch of salt and pepper on a plate.

In a shallow dish, whisk together the milk, cornstarch, garlic powder, and a generous pinch of salt and pepper. Lightly coat a baking sheet with nonstick cooking spray.

Dip the eggplant slices into the milk mixture, and then dredge in the crumb mixture, patting to coat. Put the slices on the baking sheet, and bake for 25 minutes. Flip and bake for 10 minutes longer, or until golden.

To make the pesto: In a food processor, pulse the ¾ cup (18 g) basil, garlic, and nuts a few times to chop the basil and nuts. Add salt and pepper to taste, and then add the juice.

While the machine is running, slowly add the oil through the hole in the lid, until a paste forms. To assemble, spread a layer of pesto on each slice of bread, dividing it evenly among the slices. Top with a tomato slice and an eggplant slice. Top with a basil leaf.

Yield: 16 stackers

SWEET-AND-SOUR SLOPPY JOES

Open-faced Sloppy Joes as finger food? Absolutely!

1 tablespoon (15 ml) neutral-flavored oil
8 ounces (227 g) tempeh, steamed and crumbled
¼ cup plus 2 tablespoons (56 g) minced green bell pepper
¼ cup (40 g) minced red onion
2 tablespoons (31 g) minced pineapple, plus extra for garnish
1 teaspoon ground cumin
2 cloves garlic, minced
1½ teaspoons minced fresh thyme, plus extra for garnish
½ cup (132 g) ketchup

2 tablespoons (28 g) packed light brown sugar
1 to 2 tablespoons (15 to 30 ml) red wine vinegar, to taste
2 tablespoons (30 ml) tamari
1 teaspoon vegan Worcestershire sauce
1 teaspoon Dijon mustard
½ teaspoon liquid smoke, optional
Salt, to taste
Black pepper, to taste
4 vegan English muffins, split and toasted

In a large skillet, heat the oil over medium-high heat. Add the tempeh and cook until lightly browned, stirring occasionally, about 5 minutes. Add the bell pepper, onion, pineapple, cumin, garlic, and thyme. Cook and stir for 1 minute longer. Add the ketchup, sugar, vinegar, tamari, Worcestershire sauce, mustard, and liquid smoke, if using. Reduce the heat to low. Simmer for 10 minutes, stirring occasionally. (The sauce will thicken.) Season with salt and pepper.

Spoon ¼ cup (65 g) onto each English muffin half and garnish with a few pieces of pineapple and a sprinkle of thyme.

Yield: 8 open-faced sandwiches

GRANOLA TRAIL MIX

The granola part of the mix is excellent without the extras and paired with vegan milk for breakfast, turning a rad snack into a spoon-tastic morning cereal.

¼ cup (60 ml) pure maple syrup
¼ cup (60 ml) brown rice syrup
¼ cup (48 g) Sucanat
1 cup (256 g) unsalted crunchy almond butter or peanut butter
1½ teaspoons vanilla extract
¼ cup (60 ml) neutral-flavored oil
Scant ½ teaspoon salt
2 teaspoons ground cinnamon
½ teaspoon ground ginger
¼ teaspoon allspice
¼ teaspoon ground nutmeg
3 cups (240 g) rolled oats (or other rolled flakes like spelt or rye)
¾ cup (90 g) wheat germ
1 cup (176 g) vegan semisweet chocolate chips
1 cup (147 g) dry-roasted peanuts (or coarsely chopped dry-roasted almonds)
1 cup (160 g) dried cherries or raisins (or a combination)

Preheat the oven to 300°F (150°C or gas mark 2).

In a large bowl, combine the syrups, Sucanat, nut butter, vanilla, oil, salt, and spices. Stir to emulsify. Add the oats and wheat germ. Stir to thoroughly coat.

Evenly spread the granola on a large rimmed baking sheet: Break it into large clusters so it bakes evenly. Bake in 12-minute increments, flipping the granola with a spatula after each increment, being careful not to break the large clusters, for a total of approximately 24 minutes. Continue to bake in shorter (4-minute) increments until the granola is lightly browned and mostly dry. (A slight moistness is okay at the end.) Let cool on the sheet. The granola will crisp as it cools.

Let cool completely before combining with the chocolate chips, peanuts, and cherries.

Store leftovers in an airtight container at room temperature or in the fridge for up to 2 weeks.

Yield: 3 pounds (1.4 kg)

HEART-HEALTHY TRAIL MIX

Trail mix is a great snack for anyone wanting to eat healthy, and it is specifically great for people eating to improve their heart health. Nuts contain a variety of vitamins and minerals.

1 cup (145 g) shelled raw pistachios
1 cup (145 g) raw almonds
½ cup (80 g) unsweetened dried cranberries
½ cup (43 g) unsweetened shredded coconut

In a medium bowl, mix all of the ingredients together with your hands or a spoon. Store in an airtight container.

NOTE: Reach for this when you need a healthy snack. Almonds provide the body with antioxidant vitamin E. Pistachios are the lowest-fat nut, and cranberries and coconut give the body a boost of energy without a sugar rush.

Yield: 4 servings

KALE CHIPS

Kale chips are easy to make and help satisfy the craving to munch! They're low in calories and full of flavor. Baking these chips with coconut oil provides an added nutritional benefit.

1 large bunch kale
2 tablespoons (28 g) coconut oil, melted
½ teaspoon salt

Preheat the oven to 375°F (190°C, or gas mark 5).

Remove the thick kale stems by grabbing hold of the leaves and then "zipping" them off the stem. Cut or tear the leaves into bite-size pieces. Dry the kale completely in a salad spinner or on a clean kitchen towel. Arrange the kale on a baking sheet and drizzle with the oil. Sprinkle with the salt and toss to evenly coat the kale. Spread out into an even layer. Bake for 8 to 10 minutes, or until the chips have shrunk slightly and are crisp and darker in color. (Watch carefully because kale can burn quickly.)

Yield: 2 servings

PATATAS BRAVAS

Tapas are a variety of small snacks, or appetizers, served in Spain and oftentimes ordered in groups.

FOR THE PATATAS BRAVAS SAUCE:
1 tablespoon (15 ml) olive oil
1 teaspoon chile pepper powder (or 1 whole small spicy red chile)
2 cloves garlic, minced
1 small onion, diced
1 teaspoon salt
1 can (15 ounces, or 425 g) stewed tomatoes
2 teaspoons agave
1 teaspoon smoked paprika
1 tablespoon (16 g) tomato paste

FOR THE PATATAS:
3 large yellow-skinned potatoes
Salted water, for boiling
Vegetable oil, for frying

To make the Patatas Bravas sauce: In a medium frying pan, heat the oil and sauté the chile pepper, garlic, onion, and salt over medium-high heat for about 10 minutes, or until the onion is golden brown, stirring often. Reduce the heat to medium-low and add the tomatoes, agave, smoked paprika, and paste. Simmer for about 10 minutes, or until the flavors have melded and the sauce is fragrant.

To make the Patatas: Bring a large stockpot of water filled 2/3 of the way full to a rolling boil. Cut each potato into 1-inch (2.5 cm) cubes, drop in the pot, and cook for 3 to 4 minutes. Remove from the water and pat dry with a clean towel.

Preheat a deep fryer to 360°F (182°C).
Once the oil is hot, deep-fry the potatoes for 7 to 8 minutes, or until crispy and deep golden brown. Place on a paper towel to drain any excess oil, salt lightly, place on a plate, and smother with the Patas Bravas Sauce.

Yield: 6 servings

COCONUT BACON

You'll love how similar this tastes to bacon. It's perfect to add on top of a salad.

1 tablespoon (14 ml) liquid smoke
1½ teaspoons Bragg's Liquid Aminos
1½ teaspoons maple syrup
1½ teaspoons water
1¾ cups (150 g) unsweetened dried coconut flakes
1½ teaspoons coconut oil

Preheat the oven to 325°F (170°C, or gas mark 3).
In a medium bowl, combine the liquid smoke, liquid aminos, syrup, and water, blending the ingredients together evenly. Add the coconut and gently fold to combine.
Grease a baking sheet with the oil and evenly disperse the coconut onto the baking sheet. Bake for 20 to 25 minutes. Use a spoon or spatula to flip the coconut bacon every 5 to 8 minutes to allow all sides to cook evenly. (This can burn easily, so watch it carefully.) Let cool, then store in an airtight container in the fridge for up to 3 days.

Yield: 14 (2-tablespoon, or 28 g) servings

65 Mean Bean Taco Cups; 66 Tiny Tomato Pies; 67 Antipasta Tofu-Stuffed Shells; 68 Twisted Bread Sticks; 69 Spinach Swirls; 70 Portobello BLTS; 71 Fig and Nut Canapés; 72 Eggplant Stackers

73 Sweet-and-Sour Sloppy Joes; 74 Granola Trail Mix; 75 Heart-Healthy Trail Mix; 76 Kale Chips; 77 Coconut Bacon; 78 Patatas Bravas; 79 Stuffed Olives; 80 Garlic Mushrooms

STUFFED OLIVES

These olives are best served at room temperature.

1 cup (110 g) crumbled soyrizo
2 tablespoons (12 g) nutritional yeast
16 colossal black olives, pitted
Olive oil, for drizzling

In a bowl, mix the Soyrizo with the yeast. Spoon to fill the cavity of each olive. Place the olives upright on a plate and drizzle with the oil.

Yield: 16 olives

GARLIC MUSHROOMS

The small "bite-size" nature of tapas like this is thought to encourage conversation among diners—much like finger foods served at parties.

2 tablespoons (28 ml) olive oil
20 ounces (560 g) fresh white button mushrooms, halved if large
5 cloves garlic, minced
½ cup (30 g) finely chopped packed fresh parsley, divided
1 small onion, minced
1 teaspoon salt

In a large frying pan, heat the oil over medium-high heat. Sauté the mushrooms, garlic, ¼ cup (15 g) of the parsley, onion, and salt, stirring often, for about 10 to 15 minutes. When the mushrooms are tender and the onion is translucent, remove from the heat. Stir in the remainder of the parsley and sauté just to wilt the parsley.

Yield: 4 servings

BAKED PIEROGI WITH DILLED SOUR CREAM

This recipe is a combination of traditional pierogi mixed with pastry and portability. The result is a flaky, cheesy pocket pie.

FOR THE PASTRY:
2 cups (320 g) superfine brown rice flour
1 cup (112 g) almond meal/flour
¼ cup (51 g) sweet white rice flour
¼ cup (30 g) tapioca flour
2 teaspoons xanthan gum
½ cup (85 g) potato starch
1 teaspoon baking powder
7 tablespoons (98 g) cold vegan margarine
¾ cup (175 ml) plus 2 tablespoons (28 ml) ice-cold water
½ tablespoon ground chia seeds mixed with 2 tablespoons (28 ml) water

FOR THE DILLED SOUR CREAM:
1 tablespoon (4 g) minced dill leaves
½ cup (115 g) vegan sour cream
Salt, to taste
Lime juice, to taste

FOR THE FILLING:
1 tablespoon (15 ml) olive oil, plus more for drizzling
1 Vidalia onion, chopped
Dash of salt + 1 teaspoon
3 large baked yellow potatoes
1 tablespoon (14 g) vegan margarine
¾ cup (90 g) shredded Cheddar-style vegan cheese
Black pepper

To make the pastry: In a large bowl, whisk together the flours, gum, starch, and baking powder.

Use a pastry blender to cut in the margarine until it forms even crumbles. Make a well in the center of the mixture. Using a fork, stir in the water. Stir in the chia seed mixture. Combine into a dough, knead a few times, and separate into 2 disks. Wrap in waxed paper and chill while you make the Dilled Sour Cream and filling.

To make the dilled sour cream: In a small bowl, combine the dill and sour cream. Add salt and juice to taste.

To make the filling: In a skillet, heat the oil over medium-high heat. Add the onion and a dash of salt and sauté until browned, about 10 minutes. Reduce the heat slightly and cook until soft and deep golden brown, about 10 minutes. Transfer to a bowl and combine with the potatoes, 1 teaspoon salt, and margarine. Using a potato masher, mash until smooth. Stir in the vegan cheese and pepper. Let cool.

To assemble: Preheat the oven to 375°F (190°C, gas mark 5).

Between 2 sheets of plastic wrap, roll out the dough to about ¼-inch (6 mm) thickness. Using an inverted cereal bowl, cut out circular shapes. Place 2 tablespoons (28 g) filling on half of each circle. Flip over half of the dough to form half-moon shapes. Using a fork, crimp and seal the edges. Cut 1-inch (2.5 cm) slits into the tops and drizzle lightly with oil. Bake for 30 minutes. Increase the oven temperature to 400° F (200°C, gas mark 6) and bake for an additional 10 minutes, or until golden brown and crispy. Serve with the Dilled Sour Cream.

Yield: 20 pierogies

COLOMBIAN EMPANADAS
Empanadas are made in various ways all over South America–from savory to sweet and everything in between. This recipe uses a corn-based dough. Its filling is traditional to Colombia.

FOR THE DOUGH:
2½ cups (560 g) masa harina flour
3 cups (700 ml) hot water
1½ teaspoons salt

FOR THE FILLING:
1 tablespoon (15 ml) olive oil
1 cup (70 g) chopped mushrooms
1 small potato, diced
1 onion, diced
1 clove garlic, minced
Salt, to taste
¼ cup (4 g) packed cilantro
1 cup (130 g) frozen peas, thawed
1 teaspoon ground cumin
¾ cup (84 g) vegan cheese shreds (Daiya brand works best.)

Vegetable oil, for frying

To make the dough: In a medium bowl, combine the flour, water, and salt into a dough using a fork. Cover and let rest about 20 minutes.

To prepare the filling: In a large pan, heat the oil over medium-high heat. Sauté the mushrooms, potato, onion, and garlic until the potato is softened and the onion is translucent, about 10 to 15 minutes. Salt lightly while cooking. Stir in the cilantro, peas, cumin, and vegan cheese. Transfer the mixture to a bowl and chill in the fridge.

To assemble the empanadas: Grab a piece of dough a bit larger than a golf ball and roll out between 2 pieces of plastic wrap, forming a 5-inch (13 cm) diameter circle.
    Place about 1 heaping tablespoon (15 g) of the filling on half of the dough and using the plastic wrap, gently coax the other half of the circle to cover the filling. Use your fingers to seal the dough and form a half moon–shaped

pocket. Make sure there aren't any breaks or tears in the empanada. Seal any small holes using your wet fingers. Place the empanadas on a parchment-covered surface and repeat until all dough and filling has been used.

To cook the empanadas: Preheat a deep fryer to 360°F (182°C). Prepare a surface with either paper bags or paper towels to place the empanadas on once they have cooked.
    Drop about 3 empanadas at a time into the preheated oil and cook for 6 minutes, or until golden yellow in color. Place on the prepared surface and let cool briefly before serving.

Yield: 12 empanadas

JAMAICAN JACKFRUIT PATTIES
Similar to empanadas, these patties are baked, not fried. They feature the color and flavor of turmeric in the dough.

FOR THE PASTRY:
1 cup (160 g) superfine brown rice flour
1 cup (136 g) sorghum flour
½ cup (96 g) potato starch
¼ cup (51 g) sweet white rice flour
¾ teaspoon salt
1 teaspoon xanthan gum
2 teaspoons turmeric
7 tablespoons (98 g) cold vegan margarine, chopped
1 cup (235 ml) very cold water

FOR THE FILLING:
2 tablespoons (28 ml) olive oil
1 can (10 ounces, or 280 g) green jackfruit
1 small red onion, minced
2 cloves garlic, minced
1 teaspoon salt
½ tablespoon ground chia seeds mixed with ¼ cup (60 ml) water
1 tablespoon (15 ml) vegan Worcestershire sauce
1 tablespoon (16 g) tomato paste
1 tablespoon (15 g) brown sugar
Few drops of liquid smoke
Dash of red pepper
1 teaspoon paprika
¼ cup (30 g) bread crumbs
¼ cup (60 ml) water

To make the pastry: In a large bowl, whisk together all the ingredients except the margarine and water. Using a pastry blender, cut in the margarine until the mixture resembles coarse crumbs. Make a well in the center of the mixture and stir in the water using a fork until all is combined. Pat into a patty and chill the dough for about 30 minutes.

To make the filling: In a large frying pan, heat the oil over medium-high heat. Add the jackfruit, onion, garlic, and salt. Sauté until the onion is translucent and the jackfruit starts to shred, about 12 minutes. (You may need to use a wooden fork to get it to shred into thin pieces.) Add the chia mixture, Worcestershire, paste, sugar, liquid smoke, pepper, and paprika. Simmer for a few minutes, or until fragrant. Stir in the bread crumbs and water. Cook gently over medium heat for about 5 to 7 minutes, or until thickened. Cook for an additional 2 minutes. Take off of the heat.

To assemble: Preheat the oven to 375°F (190°C, gas mark 5).

Between 2 sheets of plastic wrap, roll out the dough until about ⅓-inch (5 mm) thick. Using a small bowl (about 3 inches [7.5 cm] in diameter), cut 12 circle shapes out of the dough.

Place about 1 tablespoon (15 g) of the filling on half of the dough, and then gently pull the other side of the dough over to cover. Using a fork, press and seal the edges of the dough.

Place on an ungreased baking sheet and bake for 30 minutes, or until golden brown and crispy on the edges.

Yield: 12 patties

PANAMANIAN TAMALES

You can buy banana leaves at Asian groceries. Thaw them before using. Be sure they are de-ribbed before using. When assembling, avoid folding against the ridges and use as much of the natural shape as possible to prevent tearing.

FOR THE DOUGH:
1 cup (224 g) vegan margarine
3 cups (680 g) masa harina
2¾ cups (650 ml) vegetable broth, warmed

FOR THE FILLING:
1 tablespoon (15 ml) olive oil
5 cremini mushrooms, minced
1 cup (120 g) zucchini, diced
1 teaspoon cumin
1 tablespoon (1 g) minced cilantro leaves
1 small onion, diced
1 clove garlic, minced
1 teaspoon salt
½ cup (56 g) vegan cheese shreds (Daiya brand recommended.)
5 large banana leaves, cut into 15 even-size squares, about 10 x 12 inches (25 x 30 cm)

For the dough: Using a pastry blender, cut the margarine into the masa harina until uniform. Use a fork to stir in the broth and mix well. Let rest while you prepare the filling.

For the filling: In a large frying pan, heat the oil over medium-high heat. Sauté all of the ingredients except for the vegan cheese until all the vegetables are tender and the onion is translucent and slightly browned on the edges, about 10 minutes. Stir in the vegan cheese, letting the pan remain over the heat, until the cheese has melted. Let cool slightly.

If the banana leaves are too tough to fold easily, blanch in boiling water for 1 minute.

To assemble the tamales: Lay 1 banana leaf smooth side up onto a clean, flat surface. Press about 2 tablespoons (28 g) of the masa harina mixture into the middle of the leaf, forming as close to a rectangle as possible. In the very center of the masa dough, place about 1 tablespoon (15 g) filling so that it stretches the length of the dough but remains in the very center. Roll up, trying to get each end of the tamale to touch and wrapping the banana leaf snugly so that it is watertight. (Wrap it as you would a package: one end rolled up, sides turned in, holding it down to keep sealed.) Tie tightly on 2 ends with kitchen twine to seal. Repeat with all the leaves until the dough has been used up.

Bring a very large pot of water to a rolling boil. Carefully drop the tamales into the water. To prevent them from floating, place a metal strainer on top of the pot to press the tamales down gently and then cover with an oversize lid. Let cook 1 hour over medium heat (remaining at a constant bubble) and then transfer to a wire rack for about 20 minutes.

Yield: 15 tamales

MINI POTATO SKINS

Use a vegan cheese that doesn't get too runny when melted, such as Daiya, to retain the desired balance of crispy skins to chewy cheese.

10 fingerling potatoes

FOR THE RUB:
2 tablespoons (28 ml) olive oil
1 tablespoon (6 g) nutritional yeast
1 clove garlic, grated
1 teaspoon salt
1 teaspoon smoked paprika
Black pepper

FOR THE TOPPINGS:
1 cup (112 g) Cheddar-style shredded vegan cheese
¼ cup (17 g) shredded kale
½ cup (115 g) vegan sour cream
1 green onion, sliced very thin
¼ cup (20 g) vegan bacon bits

Preheat the oven to 400°F (200°C, gas mark 6).

Using a fork, poke a few holes in the potatoes. Bake for 30 minutes, or until softened and skin is crackly. Remove from the oven to cool.

Increase the oven temperature to 450°F (230°C, gas mark 8).

When the potatoes are cool enough to handle, halve them lengthwise. Scrape out a good portion of the filling, leaving about ¼ inch (6 mm) of potato clinging to the skins.

To make the rub: In a small bowl, combine all the rub ingredients.

To make the potatoes: Sprinkle the rub mixture onto both sides of the potato skins. Place on a baking sheet. Bake for 5 minutes, flip over, and bake for an additional 5 minutes.

Remove from the oven, fill with the cheese, sprinkle with kale, bake for 5 minutes, and broil for 2 minutes. Remove from the oven, plate, and top with the sour cream, onion, and bacon.

Yield: 20 mini potato skins

STUFFED ZUCCHINI FLOWERS

Zucchini flowers are usually battered and fried, but they're more delectable raw. You can really taste the floral notes and the zucchini this way. Serve these flowers with your favorite dip.

11 zucchini blossoms
1 cup (230 g) vegan cream cheese
2 teaspoons cumin
⅓ cup (16 g) chopped chives
½ tablespoon nutritional yeast

Wash the flowers by soaking them in salty water for about 10 minutes. Remove and gently pat dry.

In a small bowl, combine the cream cheese, cumin, chives, and yeast. Place in a piping bag. From the bottom of the flower, where the sturdy green base is, slice off enough of the green just to create an opening. Pipe in the filling until well filled, gently clasping the ends closed so the filling does not come out the other side. Chill before serving.

Yield: 11 blossoms

"CHEDDAR AND BACON" DILLED DEVILED TOFU BITES

These bites offer a variety of presentation options. Cut them into "rustic egg shapes," or use small, basic-shaped cookie cutters (such as stars and hearts) to add a little pizzazz.

1 block (14 ounces, or 397 g) extra-firm tofu, pressed for 8 hours
Black salt, to taste
¾ cup (180 g) cooked and drained chickpeas
1 tablespoon (6 g) nutritional yeast
2 tablespoons (22 g) yellow mustard
2 teaspoons turmeric
¼ cup (20 g) crumbled Smokey Tempeh "Bacon" (See page 67.)
¼ cup (16 g) fresh dill leaves
Smoked paprika

Cut the pressed tofu into about 8 even blocks. Using a small melon baller, scoop out a cavity about ½-inch (1 cm) deep and 1-inch (2.5 cm) wide in each. Sprinkle with the salt.

In a food processor, combine the scooped-out tofu and the rest of the filling ingredients. Pulse several times, until very smooth, scraping down the sides as necessary.

Transfer the filling into a piping bag fit with a large tip. Pipe into the tofu blocks. Top with the bacon, dill, and paprika. Chill for 2 hours before serving.

Yield: 8 appetizers

"PEPPERONI" ROLLS

These delicious rolls are straight from the wild, wonderful hills of West Virginia. You'll love this animal-friendly version. They're made in hoagie rolls.

FOR THE "PEPPERONI":
1 block (14 ounces, or 397 g) extra-firm tofu, well pressed for about 3 hours
2 cloves garlic, grated
1 large shallot, grated
3 tablespoons (48 g) tomato paste
1 teaspoon cumin seeds
1 teaspoon coriander
1 teaspoon white pepper
2 teaspoons black pepper
3 teaspoons (4 g) red chile pepper flakes
2 teaspoons fennel seeds
1 teaspoon black mustard seeds
1½ teaspoons smoked paprika
1 teaspoon salt
¼ cup (60 ml) + 2 tablespoons (28 ml) olive oil
¼ cup (60 ml) + 2 tablespoons (28 ml) water
1 tablespoon (20 g) red jam (e.g., lingonberry, cherry, or red raspberry)

81 Baked Pierogi with Dilled Sour Cream; 82 Colombian Empanadas; 83 Jamaican Jackfruit Patties; 84 Panamanian Tamales;
85 Mini Potato Skins; 86 Stuffed Zucchini Flowers; 87 "Cheddar and Bacon" Dilled Deviled Tofu Bites; 88 "Pepperoni" Rolls

FOR THE HOAGIES:
1½ cups (240 g) superfine brown rice flour
1 cup (136 g) sorghum flour
½ cup (96 g) potato starch
3 teaspoons (9 g) xanthan gum
1½ teaspoons baking powder
1 teaspoon salt
2 packets (18 g) dry active yeast
¼ cup (48 g) sugar
2 cups (475 ml) warm water
2 teaspoons vinegar
1 tablespoon (12 g) ground flaxseed meal mixed with ¼
    cup (60 ml) water
¼ cup (60 ml) olive oil

To make the "pepperoni": Slice the block of tofu into about 20 small sticks. Place in a shallow dish.

In a bowl, combine the rest of the pepperoni ingredients. Pour the mixture over the tofu. Let marinate overnight.

Preheat the oven to 300°F (150°C, gas mark 2). Line a baking sheet with parchment paper.

Remove the tofu from the dish, reserving the marinade, and transfer to the prepared baking sheet. Top with the marinade. Bake for 3 hours, flipping halfway through.

Prepare the dough for the hoagies (below) and then lightly grease 4 miniature loaf pans. Spread about ½ cup (115 g) dough onto the bottom of each of the pans and snugly place 4 to 5 strips of pepperoni on top of the dough. Top with about ½ cup (115 g) more dough to completely cover the pepperoni. Let rest 30 minutes in a warm spot.

Preheat the oven to 375°F (190°C, gas mark 5).

Bake for 30 to 35 minutes. Let cool completely before serving.

To make the hoagies: In a large bowl, sift together the flours, starch, xanthan, baking powder, and salt.

In a small bowl, dissolve the yeast in sugar and water and let sit until foamy, about 5 minutes. Add the vinegar, flaxseed mixture, and oil.

Stir the wet ingredients into the flour mix. (If using an electric mixer, mix on medium high for about 2 minutes.) (When making Pepperoni Rolls, stop here and continue with the baking instructions above.)

Using lightly oiled hands, divide the dough in half and shape into two 9-inch (23 cm) long hoagie loaves. Place on a lightly oiled baking sheet or mat. Let rise in a warm place for 50 minutes.

Preheat the oven to 375° F (190°C, gas mark 5). Bake the loaves for about 25 to 30 minutes or until golden brown on top. Let cool and then slice in half with serrated knife.

Yield: 4 rolls or 8 servings

88 "Pepperoni" Rolls

BREAKFASTS

See pages 68–69 and 74–75 for pantry basics photos.

BISCUITS AND HERBED COUNTRY GRAVY

This dish is perfect for a lazy Sunday afternoon brunch, and it also makes a wonderful main course when having breakfast for dinner.

FOR BISCUITS:
4 cups (500 g) Bizquix (See page 12.)
1¼ cups plus 2 tablespoons (325 ml) nondairy milk

FOR HERBED COUNTRY GRAVY:
¼ cup (32 g) sorghum flour
¼ cup (32 g) millet flour
5 tablespoons (70 g) nondairy margarine
1 tablespoon (2.5 g) minced fresh herbs (such as rosemary, thyme, or sage)
3 cups (705 ml) nondairy milk (Lightly sweetened and non-flavored is best.)
1¼ teaspoons salt
½ teaspoon black pepper

To make the Biscuits:
Preheat the oven to 400°F (200°C, or gas mark 6). In a bowl, mix together the Bizquix and milk until well combined. Use your hands to shape into 9 biscuits, each about 1½ inches (3.8 cm) in diameter. Place on an ungreased baking sheet.

Bake for 13 to 15 minutes, or until lightly golden brown on the edges. Let cool briefly, and then use a flat metal spatula to gently remove from the baking sheet.

To make the herbed country gravy: In a medium pan, warm the flours, margarine, and herbs and warm over medium heat. Stir to combine as the margarine melts to create a thick roux, about 1 minute. Using a whisk, add the milk and continue to stir to prevent lumps from forming. Stir in the salt and pepper. Cook over medium to medium-high heat for about 7 minutes, or until the gravy becomes thick, stirring constantly. Serve the gravy over the biscuits.

Yield: 9 biscuits

STRAWBERRY SHORTCAKE MUFFINS

Like quaint little shortcakes with strawberries hiding inside, these muffins aren't overly sweet. They make a great breakfast on the go.

1 cup (200 g) sugar
½ cup (120 ml) olive oil
1½ cups (350 ml) nondairy milk
1/3 cup (80 g) strawberry soy yogurt
1 teaspoon salt
3½ teaspoons (16 g) baking powder
2 cups (316 g) superfine brown rice flour
¾ cup (97 g) sorghum flour
¾ cup (97 g) potato starch
1 teaspoon xanthan gum
2 cups (340 g) chopped strawberries

Preheat the oven to 375°F (190°C, or gas mark 5). Lightly grease or line 16 muffin cups with paper liners.

In a medium bowl, combine the sugar, oil, milk, and yogurt.

In a large bowl, combine the salt, baking powder, flours, starch, and xanthan. Fold in the strawberries and stir to coat with the flour mixture. Gradually stir in the wet ingredients until well combined. Fill the muffin cups with about 1/3 cup (80 g) batter. Bake for 22 to 25 minutes, or until lightly golden brown on top. Allow to cool for 15 minutes before serving.

Yield: 16 muffins

APPLE PECAN MUFFINS

These muffins are prized for their flavor and also for their rustic appearance. So easy to prepare, they are very healthful and contain lots of dietary fiber.

1½ cups (188 g) unbleached all-purpose flour
½ cup (63 g) whole wheat flour
1 tablespoon (4.6 g) baking powder
1 teaspoon cinnamon
½ teaspoon salt
2 tablespoons (30 g) ground flaxseed
6 tablespoons (90 ml) water
½ cup (125 g) unsweetened applesauce
1/3 cup (80 ml) canola oil
½ cup (100 g) sugar
1 teaspoon vanilla extract
1½ cups (225 g) peeled and chopped raw apples
½ to 1 cup (60 to 125 g) chopped pecans

Preheat the oven to 350°F (180°C, or gas mark 4). Lightly grease 12 muffin cups.

In a medium bowl, combine the flours, baking powder, cinnamon, and salt.

In a food processor or blender, whip the flaxseed and water together until it reaches a thick and creamy consistency.

In a separate bowl, combine the applesauce, oil, sugar, vanilla, and flax mixture. Using an electric hand mixer or wire whisk, beat until creamy smooth. Add to the flour mixture, stirring until well blended. (Do not overmix.) Fold in the apples and nuts. (The batter will be thick rather than smooth and wet. If it's too stiff, add 1 or 2 tablespoons (15 or 30 ml) of water.)

Fill the prepared muffin cups about three-quarters full. Bake until a wooden skewer inserted into the center comes out clean, about 20 minutes. Cool in the tins for 5 minutes, and then transfer to a wire rack.

Yield: 12 muffins

DOUBLE-CHOCOLATE MUFFINS

These muffins are great for breakfast, but equally as good if eaten as a dessert. Teff flour adds a nutritional boost to these moist and almost brownie-like muffins.

1 cup (130 g) brown rice flour
½ cup (65 g) teff flour
¼ cup (32 g) tapioca starch
½ cup (65 g) cornstarch
½ cup (40 g) cocoa powder
1 teaspoon xanthan gum
½ teaspoon baking soda
2 teaspoons (4 g) baking powder
½ teaspoon salt
1⅓ cups (265 g) sugar
2 tablespoons (30 ml) olive oil
1½ cups (350 ml) nondairy milk
2 tablespoons (30 ml) apple cider vinegar
1 teaspoon almond or vanilla extract
1 cup (183 g) nondairy chocolate chips
½ cup (74 g) crushed walnuts

Preheat the oven to 350°F (180°C, or gas mark 4). Line 15 muffin cups with liners or grease and lightly dust with brown rice flour.

In a medium bowl, sift together the flours, starch, cornstarch, cocoa, xanthan, baking soda, baking powder, salt, and sugar until well blended. Make a well in the center of the mixture, and then stir in the oil, milk, vinegar, and almond extract. Mix vigorously until very smooth. Stir in the chocolate. Fill the muffin cups about two-thirds full. Top with the walnuts. Bake for about 25 minutes, or until slightly risen and firm to the touch.

Yield: 15 muffins

JAM-FILLED OAT BRAN MUFFINS

These special little muffins have a surprise inside! Filling these healthful, hearty muffins with strawberry jam ensures they don't taste like "health food."

2 tablespoons (30 g) ground flaxseed
6 tablespoons (90 ml) water
2 cups (200 g) oat bran
1 cup (125 g) all-purpose pastry flour
½ cup (115 g) firmly packed brown sugar
4 teaspoons (6.1 g) baking powder
1 teaspoon ground cinnamon
½ teaspoon salt
1¼ cups (294 ml) nondairy milk
⅓ cup (80 ml) canola oil
1 cup (150 g) chopped walnuts, optional
½ cup (160 g) strawberry jam

Preheat the oven to 425°F (220°C, or gas mark 7). Lightly grease 16 muffin cups.

In a food processor, whip the flaxseed and water together for 1 to 2 minutes, or until it's thick and creamy.

In a large bowl, combine the oat bran, flour, sugar, baking powder, cinnamon, and salt.

In a small bowl, whisk together the flaxseed mixture, milk, and oil. Stir in the walnuts, if using. Add to the dry ingredients. Mix just until blended. Fill the prepared muffin cups less than half full with the batter. Place a dab of jam in the center of each cup. Add more batter to fill the cups two-thirds full, concealing the jam. Bake for 15 to 20 minutes. Cool in the tins for 3 minutes, and then remove to cool on a wire rack.

Yield: 16 muffins

G'MORNIN' MUFFINS

These fluffy muffins have all the makings of a delicious breakfast or an anytime snack. How about adding home-made Classic Strawberry Jam? (See page 6.)

2 cups (250 g) all-purpose flour
3 tablespoons (24 g) arrowroot powder
½ teaspoon baking powder
½ teaspoon baking soda
½ teaspoon salt
1 cup (200 g) evaporated cane juice or sugar
6 ounces (170 g) nondairy yogurt (lemon, vanilla, or plain)
½ cup (120 ml) canola oil
½ cup (120 ml) nondairy milk
1 teaspoon vanilla extract
1 teaspoon lemon extract
Zest and juice of 1 lemon
2 cups (290 g) fresh or frozen blueberries (If frozen, you may need to increase the baking time.)

Preheat the oven to 350°F (180°C, or gas mark 4). Line 14 muffin cups with paper liners.

In a large bowl, sift together the flour, arrowroot, baking powder, baking soda, and salt.

In a medium bowl, mix together the cane juice, yogurt, oil, milk, vanilla, lemon, lemon zest, and lemon juice. Add to the flour mixture and mix until well combined. (Do not overmix.) Fold in the blueberries. Fill the prepared cups three-quarters full. Bake for 30 to 40 minutes, or until the tops are golden brown and a wooden pick inserted into the center comes out clean. Remove from the oven, let cool enough to touch, and then transfer to a cooling rack to cool completely.

Yield: 14 muffins

BLUEBERRY CAKE DONUTS

These donuts are vegan and delicious donutty goodness. The addition of fresh blueberries makes these an extra-special breakfast-time treat.

FOR THE DONUTS:
2¼ cups (292 g) sorghum flour
1½ cups (237 g) brown rice flour
¾ cup (97 g) potato starch
¼ cup (32 g) tapioca starch
1 teaspoon xanthan gum
4 teaspoons (8 g) baking powder
¾ teaspoon salt
1 cup (225 g) packed brown sugar
3 tablespoons (42 g) nondairy margarine
2 tablespoons (14 g) flaxseed meal mixed with ¼ cup (60 ml) warm water
1 teaspoon vanilla extract
½ cup (115 g) coconut cream (scooped from the top of a chilled can of full-fat coconut milk)
1 cup (245 g) applesauce
1 cup (145 g) fresh blueberries
Vegetable oil, for frying

FOR THE GLAZE:
1 cup (120 g) confectioners' sugar
1 tablespoon (15 ml) nondairy milk
½ teaspoon lemon extract

To make the donuts: In a medium bowl, sift together the flours, starch, tapioca, xanthan, baking powder, and salt.

In a large bowl, cream together the sugar and margarine until smooth. Add the flaxseed mixture, vanilla, cream, and applesauce. Fold in the blueberries and mix well. (Don't break the blueberries up too much.) Gradually add in the flour mixture and stir well. (The dough will be somewhat sticky.) Chill for at least 1 hour.

Pour the oil to a depth of 5 inches (13 cm) into a deep fryer and preheat to 365°F (185°C).

Turn the dough out onto a lightly floured surface, adding just enough sorghum to make the dough workable, but still soft. Flatten gently using lightly floured hands to make a patty 1 to 1½ inches (2.5 to 3.8 cm)-thick. Using two circular cookie cutters (one 3 inches [7.5 cm] and one ¾ inch [2 cm] across, cut out 12 of the bigger circles and then use the smaller cutter to cut out the middles. Reserve the middles for frying into donut holes.

Carefully drop a few donuts into the oil and fry for 3 minutes. Using a slotted metal spoon, remove the donuts from the oil and place on a paper towels to absorb any excess oil. Return the oil to temperature and repeat until all of the donuts have been fried. Cook all donut holes at once for 3 minutes. Let cool.

To make the glaze: In a small bowl, whisk all the ingredients together until very smooth.

Once the donuts have cooled, place them on a wire rack (with a baking sheet underneath to catch any drips) and drizzle with the glaze. Let rest for about 1 hour, or until the glaze has hardened.

Yield: 12 donuts and donut holes

CRANBERRY SPICE BAGELS

This easy breakfast treat is great to make ahead and freeze for later. Like gluten-filled bagels, these are best eaten toasted and slathered with your favorite bagel topper.

FOR WET INGREDIENTS:
1 tablespoon (7 g) active dry yeast
¼ cup (50 g) sugar
1 cup (235 ml) warm water
½ cup (125 g) applesauce
2 tablespoons (30 ml) olive oil
1 tablespoon (15 ml) apple cider vinegar
3 tablespoons (21 g) flaxseed meal mixed with 6 tablespoons (90 ml) warm water
¾ cup (90 g) dried cranberries

FOR THE DRY INGREDIENTS:
1½ cups (180 g) buckwheat flour
½ cup (65 g) teff flour
1 cup (130 g) sorghum flour
1 cup (130 g) cornstarch
½ cup (65 g) tapioca starch
2 teaspoons (6 g) xanthan gum
½ teaspoon ground nutmeg
¼ teaspoon ground cloves
2 teaspoons (6 g) orange zest
1 teaspoon salt
½ cup (65 g) additional sorghum or buckwheat flour
Cornmeal, for dusting baking sheet
Sugar, for dusting

To prepare the wet ingredients: In a large bowl, combine the yeast, sugar, and warm water and proof until foamy, about 10 minutes. Add the applesauce, oil, vinegar, flaxseed mixture, and cranberries. Mix well.

To prepare the dry ingredients: In a large bowl, sift together the flours, cornstarch, tapioca, xanthan, nutmeg, cloves, zest, and salt. Gradually add the dry ingredients to the wet, about ½ cup (65 g) at a time until well incorporated. Mix vigorously until the dough is sticky. Scrape the sides of the bowl and gather the dough into a tacky ball. Sprinkle in about ¼ cup (30 g) of the additional sorghum flour to make the dough workable, knead the dough briefly, and then add as much as needed of the remaining ¼ cup (30 g) sorghum flour until the dough is easy to handle.

Divide the dough into 8 equal size balls. Flatten with floured hands to about 1¾ inches (4.5 cm) thick. Using your finger, poke a hole in the center to form a bagel shape. Repeat until all the dough has been shaped. Smooth the tops and sides with wet fingers to make a uniform shape. Let the bagels rest for about 25 minutes.

Preheat the oven to 375°F (190°C, or gas mark 5). Sprinkle a baking sheet with the cornmeal.

Bring a large pot of water to a boil and drop 1 or 2 bagels at a time into the boiling water. Boil for 2 minutes. Using a slotted spoon, remove and place on a wire rack until nearly dry.

Transfer the bagels to the prepared baking sheet and sprinkle the tops of the barely wet bagels with the sugar. Bake for 30 minutes, or until golden brown on the edges.

Yield: 8 bagels

BANANA BREAD SCONES

These scones are like little personal banana breads and are sure to impress any guest. They smell heavenly when baking in the oven. They taste best served warm, fresh from the oven.

1 tablespoon (14 g) flaxseed meal mixed with 2 tablespoons (30 ml) warm water
¾ cup (173 g) sugar, plus more for sprinkling
3 very ripe medium bananas, about 2 cups (300 g) mashed
1 teaspoon vanilla extract
1 teaspoon salt
¼ teaspoon ground cloves
1 teaspoon cinnamon
¼ teaspoon cardamom
1 teaspoon baking powder
1 teaspoon baking soda
1 teaspoon xanthan gum
1 ⅓ cups (173 g) sorghum flour
1 ⅓ cups (173 g) buckwheat flour
1 cup (130 g) potato starch
1 cup (120 g) walnuts pieces, optional

Preheat the oven to 400°F (200°C, or gas mark 6). Line a baking sheet with parchment paper.

In a large bowl, combine the flaxseed mixture, ¾ cup (173 g) sugar, bananas, and vanilla. Stir until smooth.

In a medium bowl, sift together the salt, cloves, cinnamon, cardamom, baking powder, baking soda, xanthan, flours, and starch. Slowly add the dry ingredients to the wet and stir until well incorporated. Fold in the walnuts, if using.

Drop the batter by heaping ¼-cup (60 g) portions onto the prepared baking sheet, placing each about 2 inches (5 cm) apart. Sprinkle lightly with sugar. Bake for 15 minutes, or until the bottoms are dark golden brown.

Yield: 10 scones

CLASSIC CURRANT SCONES

In Great Britain, it's traditional for scones to include raisins, currants, or dates. Enjoy these for breakfast or a mid-afternoon snack with some black tea.

1½ teaspoons Ener-G Egg Replacer (equivalent of 1 egg)
2 tablespoons (30 ml) water
2½ cups (313 g) all-purpose flour
⅓ cup (67 g) sugar
4 teaspoons (6.1 g) baking powder
½ teaspoon salt
¾ cup (169 g) nondairy butter, cold
1 cup currants
½ cup (120 ml) nondairy milk, plus 2 to 3 tablespoons (30 to 45 ml) for brushing tops
Extra milk or water as needed
Cinnamon, for sprinkling
Sugar, for sprinkling

Preheat the oven to 425°F (220°C, or gas mark 7). Lightly oil a baking sheet.

In a food processor, whip the egg replacer and water together until thick and creamy.

In a large bowl, combine the flour, sugar, baking powder, and salt. Add the butter to the dry ingredients and cut it into small pieces with two knives or with a pastry blender until a coarse crumbly batter forms. (To make flaky scones, leave some of the butter pieces as large as peas.) Stir in the currants. Add the milk and egg replacer mixture. (Minimize the mixing to avoid developing the gluten in the flour, which produces tough scones.) Using a wooden spoon, mix just until the dry ingredients are moistened or nearly moistened. (The dough will not be completely smooth like bread dough.)

Gather the dough into a ball. (You may need to add just 1 more teaspoon of nondairy milk or water, but you will be able to form it into a ball.) Place the ball on a lightly floured surface. (You may want to lightly flour your hands, as well.) Pat or roll the dough out to a ½-inch-thick (1.3-cm) round, and cut into 8 or 10 pieces. (Triangles are a traditional shape.) Place them ½ inch (1.3 cm) apart on the baking sheet, brush the tops with nondairy milk, and sprinkle with cinnamon and sugar. Bake until the tops are golden brown, 12 to 15 minutes. Let cool on a rack or serve warm.

Yield: 8 to 10 scones

BUTTER PECAN STICKY ROLLS
These are similar to cinnamon rolls in texture, but with the addition of buttery pecans. These are best eaten warm from the oven while the icing is still gooey.

FOR THE ROLLS:
2 tablespoons (14 g) active dry yeast
1 cup (235 ml) almond milk, warmed to about 110°F (43°C)
¾ cup (150 g) granulated sugar, divided
¼ cup (60 ml) olive oil
1 teaspoon vanilla extract
¼ cup (32 g) brown rice flour
½ cup (65 g) sorghum flour
¾ cup (97 g) tapioca starch
½ cup (65 g) cornstarch
½ teaspoon baking soda
2 teaspoons (6 g) baking powder
2 teaspoons xanthan gum
½ teaspoon salt
¼ cup (60 g) nondairy margarine, melted
¾ cup (170 g) packed brown sugar
1 cup (110 g) chopped pecans, toasted for about 5 minutes at 400°F (200°C, or gas mark 6)

FOR THE ICING:
2 cups (240 g) confectioners' sugar
2 tablespoons (30 g) nondairy margarine, slightly softened
1 teaspoon vanilla extract
2 tablespoon (30 ml) almond milk

To make the rolls: In a large bowl, combine the yeast, milk, and ¼ cup (50 g) of the granulated sugar and proof until foamy, about 10 minutes. Stir in the oil, the remaining ½ cup (120 g) granulated sugar, and vanilla.

In a separate bowl, sift together the flours, starch, cornstarch, baking soda, baking powder, xanthan, and salt. Gradually stir the dry mixture into the wet until a very sticky dough is formed.

Tape a 25-inch (63.5 cm)-long sheet of plastic wrap to your countertop. Place the dough in the center and top carefully with a second piece of plastic wrap. Roll out into a 20 x 12-inch (51 x 30.5 cm) rectangle. Remove the top layer of plastic wrap. Lightly brush the margarine onto the dough, covering evenly with a thin layer. Sprinkle on the brown sugar and pecans.

Using the plastic wrap as a guide, roll up the dough tightly, starting with shortest side of the rectangle. Hold the plastic wrap taut as you lift up so that gravity helps roll up the dough. Discard the plastic wrap and cut the rolled dough into eight 2-inch (5 cm) sections. Using a flat spatula, transfer the rolls into an 8-inch (20 cm) cake pan so they fit snugly in the pan. Cover with a lightly greased sheet of plastic wrap and let rise in a warm place for 45 minutes.

Preheat the oven to 350°F (180°C, or gas mark 4).

Transfer the rolls to the center rack and bake for about 30 minutes, or until the tops are golden brown.

To make the icing: In a medium bowl, stir the icing ingredients together until smooth. Spread or pipe over the warm rolls while they are still in the pan.

Yield: 8 rolls

CINNAMON ROLLS
Prepare these the night before and let them rise overnight while you slumber. The next morning, finish off the recipe and bake them while your loved ones sleep in.

TO MAKE THE DOUGH:
4½ teaspoons Ener-G Egg Replacer (equivalent of 3 eggs)
6 tablespoons (90 ml) water
4½ to 5 cups (565 to 625 g) all-purpose flour, divided
1 packet active dry yeast
1 cup (235 ml) nondairy milk, plus more for brushing
⅓ cup (37 g) nondairy butter
⅓ cup (66 g) granulated sugar
½ teaspoon salt

FOR THE FILLING:
¾ cup (170 g) firmly packed brown sugar
1 tablespoon (8 g) cinnamon
½ cup (112 g) nondairy butter, softened
½ cup (75 g) raisins, optional
¾ cup (112 g) chopped walnuts

FOR THE ICING:
1 cup (100 g) confectioners' sugar
2 tablespoons (28 g) nondairy butter, melted
½ teaspoon vanilla extract
2 tablespoons (30 ml) nondairy milk

To make the dough: In a food processor, whip together the egg replacer powder with the water until thick and creamy.

Using the paddle attachment in the bowl of an electric stand mixer, combine 2¼ cups (280 g) of the flour and the yeast.

In a small saucepan, heat 1 cup (235 ml) of the milk, butter, sugar, and salt, stirring constantly, until warm and the butter is almost melted. Pour the milk mixture into the flour mixture, with the mixer on low speed. Add the egg replacer mixture. Scrape down the sides of the bowl. Turn the speed to high and beat the mixture for 3 minutes. Replace the paddle attachment with the dough hook. Knead in as much of the remaining 2¼ to 2¾ cups (280 to 345 g) flour as needed until the dough is moderately soft, smooth, and elastic, 3 to 5 minutes. (The dough will no longer be sticky to the touch.) Shape into a ball. Place in a greased bowl. Cover and let rise in a warm place for 1 to 2 hours. When the dough has doubled in size, punch it down. Place on a lightly floured surface, cover with a clean towel, and let rest for 10 minutes.

To make the filling: Combine the sugar, cinnamon, butter, raisins (if using), and nuts.

After the dough has rested for about 10 minutes, roll the dough into a 12-inch (30-cm) square. Brush the filling evenly over the rolled-out dough. Carefully roll the dough into a log and pinch the edges to seal. Slice the log into 8 equal-sized pieces. Arrange these pieces on a greased cookie or baking sheet. Cover the dough loosely with clear plastic wrap, leaving room for the rolls to rise. Let the dough rise in a warm place until the rolls are nearly double in size, 45 minutes to 1 hour.

Preheat the oven to 375°F (190°C, or gas mark 5).

Brush the dough with the nondairy milk. Bake for 25 to 30 minutes, or until golden brown.

To prepare the icing: In a bowl, combine the sugar, butter, vanilla, and milk.

When the rolls are ready, remove them from the oven, and let them cool for 5 minutes. Drizzle with the icing.

Yield: 8 rolls

ESPRESSO CHOCOLATE CHIP LOAVES
They are good, dependable gifts. Who doesn't love choco-late cake? These are perfect to make for bake sales. Wrap them in plastic wrap or place them in cellophane bags.

6 ounces (170 g) plain soy yogurt
1 cup (235 ml) canola oil
1 tablespoon (15 ml) vanilla extract
1 tablespoon (15 ml) chocolate extract
2 cups (400 g) sugar
2 tablespoons (44 g) molasses
½ cup (120 ml) coffee-flavored liqueur
1 cup (235 ml) nondairy milk
½ cup (22 g) instant coffee crystals
3½ cups (438 g) all-purpose flour
1 cup (120 g) whole wheat pastry flour
½ cup (40 g) unsweetened cocoa powder
2 teaspoons baking powder
2 teaspoons baking soda
2 tablespoons (16 g) cornstarch

1 teaspoon salt
1½ cups (264 g) nondairy semisweet chocolate chips

To make the loaves: Preheat the oven to 350°F (180°C, or gas mark 4). Coat 5 mini loaf tins (5 x 3½ x 2 inches [12.5 x 8.3 x 5 cm]) or 2 standard loaf tins (9 x 5 x 3 inches [23 x 12.5 x 7.5 cm]) with nonstick cooking spray

In a large bowl, mix together the yogurt, oil, vanilla, chocolate, sugar, molasses, liqueur, milk, and coffee crystals.

In a separate bowl, sift together the flours, cocoa, baking powder, baking soda, cornstarch, and salt. Add to the sugar mixture and mix well. Fold in the chocolate chips.

Fill the loaf tins two-thirds full. Bake mini loaves for 35 to 45 minutes or standard loaves for 45 to 60 minutes, or until a wooden pick inserted into the center comes out clean. Let cool completely before turning out the loaves.

Yield: 5 mini or 2 standard loaves

PUMPKIN CHOCOLATE CHIP LOAF
These loaves freeze well!

3 cups (375 g) all-purpose flour
1 teaspoon baking soda
1 teaspoon baking powder
½ teaspoon salt
½ teaspoon ground cinnamon
½ teaspoon ground cloves
½ teaspoon ground nutmeg
3½ cups (15 ounces, or 425 g) pumpkin purée
1 cup (200 g) sugar
½ cup (120 ml) nondairy milk
½ cup (120 ml) canola oil
1 teaspoon vanilla extract
1 cup (176 g) vegan chocolate chips

To make the loaves: Preheat the oven to 350°F (180°C, or gas mark 4). Coat 5 mini loaf tins (5 x 3½ x 2 inches [12.5 x 8.3 x 5 cm]) or 2 standard loaf tins (9 x 5 x 3 inches [23 x 12.5 x 7.5 cm]) with nonstick cooking spray.

In a large bowl, combine the flour, baking soda, baking powder, salt, cinnamon, cloves, and nutmeg.

In a medium bowl, mix together the pumpkin, sugar, milk, oil, and vanilla. Add to the flour mixture and stir to combine. Fold in the chocolate.

Fill each loaf tin three-fourths full. Smooth the tops with the back of a spoon. Bake for 40 to 60 minutes for mini loaves or 45 to 60 minutes for standard loaves, or until the tops have cracked and a wooden pick inserted into the center comes out clean. Let cool completely before turning out the loaves.

Yield: 5 mini or 2 standard loaves

MEDITERRANEAN OLIVE BREAD

For an artisan bread look, use a round pan instead of a loaf pan. A lovely breakfast or snack bread, this is also perfect for serving with Mediterranean dishes, particularly soups.

3 tablespoons (45 g) ground flaxseed
½ cup (120 ml) water
1½ cups (188 g) all-purpose flour
¾ cup (94 g) whole wheat flour
2½ teaspoons baking powder
1 teaspoon chopped fresh rosemary (or ¾ teaspoon dried)
1 teaspoon chopped fresh basil (or ¾ teaspoon dried)
½ teaspoon salt
1 cup (235 ml) nondairy milk
¼ cup (60 ml) olive oil
⅓ cup (50 g) finely chopped walnuts
⅓ cup (33 g) chopped pitted black olives
⅓ cup (33 g) chopped sundried tomatoes

Preheat the oven to 350°F (180°C, or gas mark 4). Lightly grease an 8-inch (20-cm) or 9-inch (23-cm) loaf pan.

In a food processor, whip the flaxseed and water together until thick and creamy.

In a large bowl, thoroughly combine the flours, baking powder, rosemary, basil, and salt.

In a separate bowl, combine the flaxseed mixture, milk, and oil. Add the wet mixture to the dry and fold until about three-quarters of the dry ingredients are moistened. Add the walnuts, olives, and tomatoes, and fold just until the pieces are distributed and the dry ingredients are moistened. (The batter will be stiff and a little sticky.) Scrape the batter into the prepared pan and spread evenly. Bake until a wooden pick inserted into the center comes out clean, about 40 minutes. Let cool in the pan on a rack for 5 to 10 minutes before unmolding to cool completely on the rack.

Yield: 1 standard loaf

PUMPKIN SPICE BREAD

This delicious, fat-free fragrant bread is perfect as dessert or a side dish for a winter holiday meal. Full or mini loaves make great gifts. This recipe was adapted from La Dolce Vegan.

3 tablespoons (45 g) ground flaxseed
½ cup (120 ml) water
2 cups (400 g) sugar
1½ cups (370 g) unsweetened applesauce
1 (14-ounce or 392-g) can pumpkin puree
3 cups (375 g) all-purpose flour
1 teaspoon ground cloves
1 teaspoon ground cinnamon
1 teaspoon nutmeg
1 teaspoon baking soda

½ teaspoon baking powder
½ teaspoon salt

Preheat the oven to 350°F (180°C, or gas mark 4). Lightly oil two 8-inch (20-cm) loaf pans or four 6 × 3 × 2-inch (15 × 7.5 × 5-cm) mini-loaf pans.

In a food processor, whip the flaxseed and water together until thick and creamy.

In a large bowl, stir together the sugar, applesauce, puree, and flaxseed mixture.

In a medium bowl, stir together the flour, cloves, cinnamon, nutmeg, baking soda, baking powder, and salt. Thoroughly combine the dry ingredients, then add them to the wet. Stir until just combined. Spoon the batter into the prepared pans. Bake for 55 to 60 minutes, or until a wooden pick inserted into the center comes out clean. If using mini-loaf pans, check for doneness after 30 minutes. Let the breads cool for at least 20 minutes before removing from the pans. (The bread is still baking and needs time to coalesce in the hot pan.)

Yield: 4 mini or 2 standard loaves

COCONUT ZUCCHINI BREAD

Zucchini bread is a classic baked-good favorite. This version replaces the butter and sugar with coconut butter and coconut sugar. Now you can have your bread and eat it too.

1 to 2 teaspoons coconut oil
1 tablespoon (7 g) ground flaxseeds
3 tablespoons (45 ml) warm water
1½ cups (125 g) whole wheat pastry flour
¾ teaspoon baking soda
½ teaspoon baking powder
½ teaspoon salt
½ teaspoon ground cinnamon
¼ teaspoon ground nutmeg
¾ cup (150 g) coconut sugar
1½ cups (180 g) grated zucchini
⅓ to ½ cup (80 to 120 ml) unsweetened plain almond milk
1 teaspoon vanilla extract
⅓ cup (75 g) coconut butter, melted
¾ cup (62 g) unsweetened shredded coconut

Preheat the oven to 350°F (180°C, or gas mark 4). Grease a 5 × 9-inch (13 × 23 cm) loaf pan with the oil.

In a small bowl, combine the flaxseeds with the water

In a large bowl, combine the flour, baking soda, baking powder, salt, cinnamon, and nutmeg.

In a medium bowl, combine the sugar, flaxseed mixture, zucchini, milk, and vanilla. Mix well. Add the butter. Add the wet ingredients to the dry ingredients and blend to combine. Fold in the coconut. Pour the batter into the prepared pan. Bake for 50 to 60 minutes. (If the top of the bread darkens too quickly, cover with foil.) Cool the bread for 10 minutes before removing from the pan. Transfer to a wire rack to cool completely before serving. Store leftovers in the fridge, wrapped in plastic wrap.

Yield: 8 to 10 servings

FENNEL AND KALE CORN BREAD

This corn bread is deliciously savory and marbled with kale for color and texture. To achieve a better texture and even cooking, use finely ground cornmeal rather than coarsely ground.

1½ cups (210 g) yellow cornmeal
¾ cup (300 g) masa harina flour
½ cup (48 g) nutritional yeast
2 teaspoons fennel seeds
2 teaspoons baking powder
1 teaspoon salt
2 tablespoons (24 g) ground chia seeds mixed with 6 tablespoons (90 ml) water
1 cup (164 g) cooked corn kernels
2 cups (470 ml) nondairy milk
⅓ cup (80 ml) olive oil
1 cup (67 g) packed finely chopped kale

Preheat the oven to 350°F (180°C, gas mark 4). Lightly grease 4 mini loaf pans.

In a large bowl, combine the cornmeal, flour, yeast, fennel, baking powder, and salt. Make a well in the center of the mixture and add the chia mixture, corn, milk, and oil. Stir well to incorporate. Fold in the kale. Spread the batter evenly into the prepared dish. Bake for 40 to 60 minutes.

Yield: 4 mini loaves

CORNBREAD

This recipe takes no time at all to prepare and is out of the oven in 30 minutes–hot, moist, and delicious. You can eliminate the whole corn kernels if you want. It's best served hot.

1½ cups (355 ml) nondairy milk
1½ tablespoons (23 ml) white vinegar
1 cup (140 g) cornmeal
1 cup (125 g) all-purpose flour
3 tablespoons (39 g) sugar
½ teaspoon salt
1 teaspoon baking powder
1 teaspoon baking soda
2 tablespoons (30 ml) canola oil
½ to 1 cup (80 to 155 g) whole corn kernels, optional

Preheat the oven to 425°F (220°C, or gas mark 7). Lightly oil a 9 × 9-inch (23 × 23-cm) baking dish.

In a small bowl, combine the milk and vinegar.

In a large bowl, mix the cornmeal, flour, sugar, salt, baking powder, and baking soda. Add the milk mixture and oil. Add the corn, if using. Stir until just blended. Spread the batter evenly in the prepared baking dish. Bake for 25 to 30 minutes, or until the top is golden brown.

Yield: 9 servings

LEMON POPPY SEED CAKES

Moist and delicious, these cakes have just enough sweetness and the right amount of tang.

FOR THE CAKES:
2 (6-ounce, or 170 g each) containers lemon soy yogurt
1 cup (235 ml) plain or vanilla soy milk
1 cup (235 ml) canola oil
2 cups (400 g) sugar
1 tablespoon (15 ml) vanilla extract
1 teaspoon lemon extract
Zest and juice of 1 lemon
½ cup (120 g) vegan sour cream
2 tablespoons (18 g) poppy seeds
5 cups (625 g) all-purpose flour
3 tablespoons (24 g) cornstarch
1 tablespoon (12 g) baking powder
1 tablespoon (12 g) baking soda
1 teaspoon salt

FOR THE GLAZE, OPTIONAL:
1 cup (120 g) confectioners' sugar
2 tablespoons (30 ml) lemon juice

To make the cakes: Preheat the oven to 350°F (180°C, or gas mark 4). Coat 5 mini loaf tins (5 x 3½ x 2 inches [12.5 x 8.3 x 5 cm]), or 2 standard loaf tins (9 x 5 x 3 inches [23 x 12.5 x 7.5 cm]) with nonstick cooking spray.

In a large bowl, mix together the yogurt, milk, oil, sugar, vanilla, lemon extract, zest, juice, sour cream, and poppy seeds.

In a separate bowl, sift together the flour, cornstarch, baking powder, baking soda, and salt. Add to the yogurt mixture and stir to combine. (The mixture will be thick, not runny.) Fill the loaf tins two-thirds full. Bake for about 45 minutes for mini tins or 45 to 60 minutes for standard tins, or until a wooden pick inserted into the center comes out clean. Let cool completely before turning out the loaves.

To make the glaze: In a bowl, whisk together the sugar and lemon juice until smooth. Drizzle over the cakes.

Yield: 5 mini or 2 standard loaves

CHERRY VANILLA BEAN PANCAKES

Fragrant and flavorful, these pancakes are a delicious start to the morning. Fluffy and laced with vanilla beans and cherries, they don't need any syrup at all.

1¼ cups (162 g) sorghum flour
¼ cup (32 g) tapioca starch
¼ cup (50 g) sugar
½ teaspoon xanthan gum
2 teaspoons (9 g) baking powder
½ teaspoon salt
1½ cups (350 ml) nondairy milk
1 tablespoon (15 ml) apple cider vinegar
3 tablespoons (45 ml) olive oil
2 teaspoons (10 g) vanilla bean paste or 2 scraped
    vanilla beans
¾ cup (117 g) pitted and chopped fresh cherries
Nondairy margarine, for cooking

In a large bowl, sift together the flour, starch, sugar, xanthan, baking powder, and salt. Stir in the milk, vinegar, oil, and vanilla. Fold in the cherries.

Preheat a well-seasoned cast-iron or nonstick skillet over medium-low heat. Melt about ½ teaspoon margarine in the hot skillet. Drop ¼ cup (60 ml) of the batter onto the preheated pan and cook for about 3 minutes, without touching, or until little holes form on top of the pancake. Using a flat spatula, flip over carefully and cook on the other side for 1 to 2 minutes, or until no batter remains visibly wet from the sides. Transfer to a plate. Repeat with the remaining batter.

Yield: About 7 pancakes

NUTTY FRUITCAKE PANCAKES

You can use spiced, light, dark, or even coconut rum in these pancakes. Use 100 percent pure grade A or B maple syrup. It's so much better for you than the maple-flavored sugar stuff.

FOR THE TOPPING:
½ cup (55 g) chopped pecans
¼ cup (30 g) chopped walnuts
¼ cup (26 g) sliced or slivered almonds
¼ cup (30 g) dried cranberries
¼ cup (22 g) crushed banana chips
¼ cup (30 g) sweetened shredded coconut
⅓ cup (80 ml) rum
1 cup (235 ml) maple syrup

FOR THE PANCAKES:
2 tablespoons (22 g) ground flaxseed
¼ cup (60 ml) warm water
1¼ cups (295 ml) coconut milk
¼ cup (60 ml) rum

2 tablespoons (30 ml) lime juice
1 cup (125 g) all-purpose flour
1 cup (120 g) whole wheat pastry flour
1 teaspoon baking powder
1 teaspoon baking soda
½ teaspoon salt
¼ teaspoon ground allspice
¼ cup (60 ml) mild-flavored vegetable oil
2 tablespoons (30 ml) maple syrup
¼ cup (26 g) sliced almonds
¼ cup (27 g) chopped pecans
¼ cup (30 g) chopped walnuts
¼ cup (10 g) freeze-dried blueberries
¼ cup (30 g) dried cranberries
¼ cup (30 g) sweetened shredded coconut

To make the topping: In a bowl, combine all of the ingredients.

To make the pancakes: In a small bowl, mix together the flaxseed and water.

In a bowl, mix together the milk, rum, and juice. (The mixture will curdle and become like buttermilk.)

In a large bowl, mix together the flours, baking powder, baking soda, salt, and allspice.

Stir the flaxseed mixture, oil, and syrup into the milk mixture. Add the wet mixture into the flour mixture. Stir to combine. Fold in the almonds, pecans, walnuts, blueberries, cranberries, and coconut.

Preheat a nonstick griddle or skillet over medium heat.

Using a ⅓-cup measure, pour ⅓ cup (3.25 ounces, or 92 g) of the batter onto the griddle. Cook until bubbles begin to pop and edges begin to lift, and then flip. Repeat with the remaining batter.

Spoon the topping over the top of the pancakes.

Yield: 8 pancakes

BANANA NEPALESE PANCAKES WITH "BACON"

Traditional Nepalese pancakes are deep-fried. To save a few calories, this batter works with light pan frying instead. Serve the pancakes with sliced bananas on top.

FOR THE BANANA NEPALESE PANCAKES:
2 bananas, mashed
1 tablespoon (12 g) ground chia seeds mixed with ¼ cup
    (60 ml) water
½ cup (100 g) sugar
1½ teaspoons baking powder
1 teaspoon cardamom
¾ teaspoon salt
1 teaspoon xanthan gum
½ cup (80 g) superfine brown rice flour
½ cup (60 g) gram flour

2 tablespoons (28 ml) olive oil
½ cup (120 ml) nondairy milk

FOR THE SMOKEY TEMPEH "BACON":
1 package (8 ounces, or 227 g) tempeh
⅓ cup (80 ml) red wine
½ tablespoon liquid smoke
¼ cup (80 g) maple syrup
⅛ cup (28 ml) soy sauce
⅓ cup (80 ml) olive oil
1 teaspoon vegetable broth seasoning
Dash of allspice
½ teaspoon smoked paprika
Black pepper
½ teaspoon salt

To make the Banana Nepalese Pancakes: In a medium bowl, combine all the ingredients and whisk until smooth.

Heat a nonstick skillet just above medium heat. Drop about ½ teaspoon margarine or coconut oil onto the hot skillet. Pour approximately ⅛ cup (28 g) of the batter onto the pan and let cook for 1½ to 2 minutes before attempting to flip. (There should be bubbles on the surface, and it should be easy to flip the cakes over.) Flip gently and cook about 1 more minute on the other side.

To make the Smokey Tempeh "Bacon": Slice the tempeh into 12 long, thin strips. Place in a shallow dish, about 9 x 9 inches (23 x 23 cm).

In a small bowl, whisk together all of the remaining ingredients. Pour over the tempeh to cover.

Let marinate for at least 8 hours, up to overnight, flipping once halfway through.

Preheat the oven to 300°F (150°C, gas mark 2). Line a baking sheet with parchment. Transfer the tempeh to the prepared baking sheet. Bake for 1 hour to 1 hour 20 minutes, flipping once halfway through, or until the "bacon" is dark brown and crispy.

Yield: 12 mini pancakes, 12 strips "bacon"

STRAWBERRY CRÊPES WITH SPICED COCONUT CREAM

This is a sweet and spicy take on classic fruit-filled crêpes. The classic method of macerating the fruit creates soft, sweet, supple strawberries, which make a perfect filling for these tender crêpes.

FOR THE CRÊPES:
2 tablespoons (28 ml) olive oil
¼ cup (50 g) sugar
½ cup (64 g) cornstarch
½ cup (80 g) superfine brown rice flour
⅓ cup (80 g) silken tofu
1 cup (235 ml) almond milk

Dash of salt
Dash of cinnamon
½ teaspoon vegan margarine

FOR THE STRAWBERRY FILLING:
4 cups (580 g) whole strawberries
2 tablespoons (26 g) sugar

FOR THE SPICED COCONUT CREAM:
1 can (15 ounces, or 440 ml) full-fat coconut milk
½ teaspoon cinnamon
¼ teaspoon white pepper

To make the crêpes: In a bowl, whisk together all of the ingredients and chill for at least 2 hours, up to overnight.

To make the strawberry filling: Slice the strawberries about ¼-inch (6 mm) thick, discarding the tops and toss with the sugar. Chill in the fridge for about 2 hours, up to overnight.

For the coconut cream: Chill the can of coconut milk in the freezer for about 20 minutes. Once a solid layer of cream has formed on top of the can, carefully scoop out and mix with cinnamon and white pepper. Reserve the rest of the coconut milk for another use.

Warm a large, nonstick crêpe pan or skillet over medium heat. Drop about ½ teaspoon nondairy margarine into the pan to coat. Add ⅓ cup (80 ml) of the batter into the hot pan and quickly swirl around to coat the pan with an even circle of batter. Place back onto the heat and let cook about 2 minutes without trying to flip over the crêpe. When it bubbles up slightly and the edges remove easily from the pan, use a flat, flexible spatula to gently lift up and flip it. Heat the other side for about 1 to 2 more minutes, or until golden brown on both sides. Repeat with the remaining batter.

Fill each crepe with about ¼ cup (65 g) of the strawberries. Drizzle the tops with the coconut cream.

Yield: 7 crêpes

CRISPY TOASTER WAFFLES

You can cook the whole batch and freeze the leftovers. Pop them into the toaster for a quick breakfast during the week.

¼ cup (26 g) ground flaxseeds
¾ cup (180 ml) warm water
1½ cups (180 g) whole wheat flour
½ cup (79 g) rice flour
½ cup (100 g) date paste or maple syrup
2 teaspoons vanilla extract
1 teaspoon ground cinnamon
1 cup (235 ml) water or unsweetened almond milk

1 Biscuits and Herbed Country Gravy; 2 Strawberry Shortcake Muffins; 3 Apple Pecan Muffins; 4 Double-Chocolate Muffins; 5 Jam-Filled Oat Bran Muffins; 6 G'Mornin' Muffins; 7 Blueberry Cake Donuts; 8 Cranberry Spice Bagels

9 Banana Bread Scones; 10 Classic Currant Scones; 11 Butter Pecan Sticky Rolls; 12 Cinnamon Rolls; 13 Espresso Chocolate Chip Loaves; 14 Pumpkin Chocolate Chip Loaf; 15 Mediterranean Olive Bread; 16 Pumpkin Spice Bread

In a bowl, mix the flaxseeds and water. Set aside to thicken. (For a quicker preparation, place flaxseeds and water into a hot pan and cook for approximately 4 minutes over medium heat, stirring constantly, or until mixture becomes gelatinous, similar to an egg white.)

In another bowl, mix the flours. Once the flaxseed mixture has thickened, add it to the flours. Add the date paste or maple syrup, vanilla, and cinnamon. Stir in the water or milk until the mixture has a batter consistency. (It should be thick, but still pourable.)

Cook the waffles according to the waffle iron instructions.

Yield: 6 to 8 waffles

CREAM OF JASMINE RICE

This hot cereal is made with rice, but it has the same nostalgic feel as the kind made with wheat. Serve it hot.

1 cup (195 g) white jasmine rice
5½ cups (1.3 L) water, divided
Dash or two of salt
Brown sugar, for topping
Fresh fruit, for topping

Preheat the oven to 375°F (190°C, or gas mark 5).

Onto an ungreased baking sheet, spread the rice evenly. Bake for 10 to 15 minutes, stirring occasionally, or until the rice turns golden brown. Remove from the oven and let cool.

In a clean coffee grinder or spice grinder, grind the rice, in batches if necessary, until the rice is ground up into small granules.

In a bowl, mix the rice with 1 cup (235 ml) of the water.

In a saucepan, bring the remaining 4½ cups (1 L) water to a boil. Slowly add the rice mixture to the boiling water and reduce the heat to medium-low. Cover and cook until the water has been absorbed and the rice is tender, about 8 minutes. Serve with sugar to taste and top with fruit.

Yield: 6 servings

APPLE PIE STEEL-CUT OATS

This is an especially sweet, hot breakfast. Peaches and berries are a great substitute for the apple, as are raisins or dried cranberries for the dates.

1 cup (80 g) steel-cut oats
1 cup (235 ml) almond milk
2 cups (470 ml) water

1 cup (150 g) diced apple
1 large medjool date, chopped
½ teaspoon ground cinnamon
Pinch of salt

Add all the ingredients to a pressure cooker. Cover and bring to pressure. Cook at pressure for 3 minutes. Allow for a natural release.

Yield: 4 servings

LOADED OATMEAL

If you're looking for a quick-and-easy way to make a big impact on your family's breakfast, you've found it. This energy-packed breakfast can be on the table in 10 minutes flat.

2 cups (156 g) quick cooking oats
2 tablespoons (13 g) ground flaxseeds
2 tablespoons (12 g) ground hemp seeds or hearts, optional
½ teaspoon ground cinnamon
1 apple, peeled, cored, and diced
1 banana, peeled and sliced
2 cups (470 ml) almond milk
2 cups (470 ml) water
1 cup (220 g) packed brown sugar, divided
1 teaspoon vanilla extract
1 cup (145 g) fresh or frozen blueberries
½ cup (120 ml) maple syrup
½ cup (55 g) sliced almonds

In a large pot with tight-fitting lid, combine the oats, flaxseeds, hemp, if using, cinnamon, apple, banana, milk, water, and ½ cup (110 g) of the brown sugar. Cover and heat over medium heat until the oatmeal begins to bubble. Stir in the vanilla and cook for about 5 minutes, or until soft and hot. Remove from the heat. Stir in the blueberries. Spoon into serving bowls and top with the remaining sugar, syrup, and almonds.

Yield: 4 servings

OATMEAL WITH FLAXSEEDS, CINNAMON, AND COCONUT MILK

This meal is comforting, satisfying, and definitely good for the heart.

½ cup (40 g) steel-cut or quick-cooking rolled oats
1 tablespoon (7 g) ground flaxseeds
1 tablespoon (7 g) sliced raw almonds

1 teaspoon ground cinnamon
1 teaspoon unsweetened shredded coconut
1 cup (235 ml) cold unsweetened coconut milk from a
   carton

Prepare the oats according to the package directions. At the end of cooking, stir in the flaxseeds, almonds, cinnamon, and coconut. Pour the milk over the hot cereal.

Yield: 1 serving

OAT, AMARANTH, AND CARROT PORRIDGE

Consider replacing the carrots with 1 cup (150 g) of vegetables that cook up in about 4 minutes, such as cubed butternut squash or cauliflower florets.

2 tablespoons (28 g) vegan butter
¼ cup (40 g) diced yellow onion
2 carrots, diced
1 cup (80 g) rolled oats
1 cup (130 g) amaranth
2½ cups (588 ml) water
1 teaspoon salt
½ teaspoon ground cinnamon

In an uncovered pressure cooker, heat the butter over medium heat. Add the onion and carrots and sauté until the onions are translucent, 3 to 4 minutes. Add the oats, amaranth, water, salt, and cinnamon. Stir to combine. Cover and bring to pressure. Cook at high pressure for 4 minutes. Allow for a natural release.

Yield: 4 servings

BROWN RICE AND FARRO PORRIDGE

Farro has twice the fiber and protein of traditional wheat, making this a healthy breakfast alternative.

½ cup (95 g) short-grain brown rice, drained and rinsed
½ cup (90 g) farro, drained and rinsed
½ cup (65 g) frozen corn
2¼ cups (530 ml) water
Pinch of salt
Fresh basil, for garnish, optional

Add the rice, farro, corn, water, and salt to a pressure cooker. Stir to combine.
   Cover and bring to pressure. Cook at high pressure for 20 minutes. Allow for a natural release; if after 10 minutes the pressure has still not come down fully, manually release. Garnish with basil, if using.

Yield: 4 to 6 servings

GROOVY GRANOLA

If eating granola promotes peace on Earth, free love, and happiness, well, then, pour another bowl, man!

2 cups (164 g) old-fashioned rolled oats
½ cup (45 g) sliced almonds
½ teaspoon ground cinnamon
¼ teaspoon salt
½ cup (120 ml) agave nectar
1 teaspoon vanilla extract
¼ cup (56 g) nondairy butter, melted
1 cup (14 g) freeze-dried blueberries

Preheat the oven to 300°F (150°C, or gas mark 2). Line a rimmed baking sheet with parchment.
   In a large bowl, combine the oats, almonds, cinnamon, and salt.
   In a small bowl, combine the agave, vanilla, and butter. Add to the oat mixture and toss to coat. Transfer the mixture to the prepared baking sheet and spread in a single layer. Bake for 30 minutes, turning with a spatula every 10 minutes. Remove from the oven and allow to cool.
   Return the mixture to the bowl and mix in the blueberries, breaking up any large clumps.

Yield: 1 pound (454 g)

DOWN-HOME COUNTRY TOFU SCRAMBLE

This recipe uses potatoes, tofu, and tempeh to re-create a healthier vegan version of a diner favorite.

1 block (10 to 12 ounces, or 280 to 340 g) extra- or
   super-firm tofu, pressed and drained
¼ cup (30 g) nutritional yeast
½ teaspoon turmeric
1 tablespoon (11 g) Dijon mustard
2 tablespoons (28 ml) oil, optional
2 cups (220 g) shredded potatoes, rinsed in cool water
   to remove excess starch
1 medium yellow onion, julienned
1 tablespoon (10 g) minced garlic
½ recipe, "Sweet and Smoky Tempeh Strips" (See page
   72.), cut into bite-size chunks
1 cup (30 g) baby spinach
Pinch of black salt, optional, plus more to taste
Salt, to taste
Ground black pepper, to taste

In a small bowl, crumble the tofu and toss with the yeast, turmeric, and mustard to coat.
   In a large skillet, heat the oil, if using, over medium-high heat. Sauté the potatoes and onion for about 5 minutes, tossing constantly. Add the garlic. Cook an additional 2 to 3 minutes, or until the garlic is fragrant and the onion is translucent. Add the tofu and tempeh. Toss to mix. Cook for

an additional 5 minutes, or until the tofu is heated through.
Remove from the heat and toss in the spinach to wilt.
Add the black salt, if using, and toss.

Season with salt and pepper.

Yield: 4 to 6 servings

▶ *Recipe Variation*
Tofu Scramble can also be made into an awesome break-
fast or brunch casserole by tossing together all the ingredi-
ents and spreading them in a 9 x 9 inch (23 x 23 cm) baking
dish. Sprinkle the top with your favorite shredded nondairy
cheese and bake at 350oF (180oC, or gas mark 4), covered
with foil, for 30 minutes. Remove the foil and bake for an
additional 20 minutes, or until the top is slightly browned
and most of the liquid is evaporated.

VEGGIE-GOOD BREAKFAST TACOS

Potatoes and vegetables fill you up with lots of nutrients
and keep you going for hours. When you add avocado,
corn tortillas, and salsa, it makes for a breakfast delight.

5 cloves garlic, chopped
1 cup (160 g) diced onion
Low-sodium, oil-free vegetable broth
1 red bell pepper, seeded and chopped
2½ pounds (1107 g) Yukon gold potatoes, cut into ¼-inch
    (6 mm) cubes and boiled until fork tender
½ teaspoon black pepper
1 tablespoon (3 g) ancho or chipotle chili powder
1 can (15 ounces, or 378 g) no-sodium-added black or
    kidney beans, drained and rinsed
1 cup (225 g) baby spinach
12 (6-inch, or 15 cm) corn tortillas
2 ripe avocados, chopped
1 cup (235 ml) salsa

Heat a large saucepan over medium heat. Sauté the garlic
and onion for about 5 minutes, or until onion becomes
translucent. If the onion sticks, add broth. Add the bell
pepper, potatoes, black pepper, and chili powder. Cook for
about 5 minutes, or until the bell pepper softens. Add the
beans. Cook for 2 to 3 minutes, or until heated through. Add
the spinach. Cook for 3 to 4 minutes, or until wilted.

With a tortilla warmer, heat the tortillas. (Alternately,
place the tortillas on a plate. Wrap them with a damp paper
towel and cover with another plate. Microwave on high for 3
minutes.)

To assemble, add the potatoes mixture to the tortilla.
Top with the avocados and salsa.

Yield: 12 tacos

SWEET AND SMOKY TEMPEH STRIPS

This bacon is perfect for making in big batches and keep-
ing on hand in the fridge. Eat the strips cold; reheat in a
toaster oven or microwave; or pan fry in a bit of oil to get
'em nice and crispy.

1 block (8 ounces, or 227 g) plain soy tempeh
¼ cup (60 ml) maple syrup
2 tablespoons (30 ml) liquid smoke
2 tablespoons (30 ml) mild-flavored vegetable oil,
    optional
2 tablespoons (30 ml) soy sauce
1 tablespoon (14 g) packed brown sugar
2 teaspoons apple cider vinegar
½ teaspoon salt, or to taste
½ teaspoon black pepper
½ teaspoon garlic powder
½ teaspoon onion powder
¼ teaspoon smoked paprika

Steam or simmer the tempeh for 20 minutes to reduce
bitterness, if desired.

In a bowl, combine the remaining ingredients, including
the oil, if using, to make the marinade.

Slice the tempeh into thin strips. In a shallow dish,
combine the tempeh and marinade. Allow to marinate for at
least 1 hour in the fridge.

Preheat the oven to 350°F (180°C, or gas mark 4). Line a
rimmed baking sheet with parchment. Arrange the tempeh
in a single layer on the prepared baking sheet. Pour any
excess marinade over the tempeh. Bake for 15 minutes, flip,
and bake for an additional 15 minutes, or until the tempeh is
a rich chocolate-brown color, dry but still flexible.

Use immediately, or store in an airtight container in the
fridge until ready to use.

Yield: 18 to 20 pieces

BERRY-STUFFED FRENCH TOAST POCKETS

Buttery and rich, with a fruity surprise hidden inside, this
unconventional French toast will make a popular (and
short-lived) appearance on the breakfast table.

4 slices (1½ inches, or 4 cm thick) slightly stale brioche
    or vegan challah bread
½ cup (70 g) raspberries
1 cup (235 ml) full-fat coconut milk or coconut cream,
    divided
1 tablespoon (8 g) arrowroot powder
1 tablespoon (15 g) maca powder, optional
2 tablespoons (25 g) sugar
½ teaspoon vanilla extract
Pinch of salt
Syrup, for serving

Using a paring knife, cut a deep slit across the top in the middle of each slice of bread to create a pocket. Stuff with about 2 tablespoons (31 g) fruit. Close the opening by gently pressing the bread together.

In a medium, shallow dish, combine 2 tablespoons (30 ml) of the milk with the arrowroot. Stir to dissolve the powder. Add the remaining 14 tablespoons (205 ml) milk, maca, sugar, vanilla, and salt. Whisk until smooth.

Dip the pockets into the mixture, one at a time, and soak for a few seconds on each side. Let the extra batter drip back down into the dish.

Heat a panini press fitted with smooth plates or a large skillet over high heat. Lightly coat both sides of the pockets with nonstick cooking spray. Cook the pockets on medium-low heat until golden brown, about 4 minutes in all if using a closed panini press, or 4 minutes on each side in a skillet. Drizzle the syrup on top.

Yield: 4 stuffed pockets

▶ *Recipe Variation*
Not a fan of raspberries? That's not a problem because any sort of berry will fit here, be it blueberries, strawberries, or even blackberries. Just be sure to chop larger berries such as strawberries so that they fit nicely in the pocket.

MAPLE-NUT PIE WAFFLEWICH
A little autumnal, spicy decadence bright and early is a good thing. You might want to double the recipe for the walnut filling here. It's delicious on top of ice cream or stirred into oatmeal.

FOR THE FILLING:
2 tablespoons (30 ml) water
2 tablespoons (28 g) nondairy butter
⅓ cup (73 g) packed brown sugar
2 teaspoons ground cinnamon
Pinch of salt
1 cup (100 g) pecan pieces
½ teaspoon vanilla extract

FOR THE WAFFLES:
1 cup (235 ml) soy milk
1 tablespoon (15 ml) apple cider vinegar
3 tablespoons (45 ml) canola oil
¼ cup (55 g) packed brown sugar
2 teaspoons maple extract
½ teaspoon salt
1½ cups (180 g) whole wheat pastry flour
1 teaspoon baking powder
½ teaspoon baking soda

To make the filling:
In a small saucepan, combine the water, butter, sugar, cinnamon, and salt. Cook over medium-high heat for about 1 minute, stirring constantly, or until the butter is melted. Remove from the heat, add the pecans, and stir for about 1 minute. Add the vanilla. Stir to combine. (The mixture will thicken a little as it cools.)

To make the waffles: In a large bowl, combine the milk and vinegar. (The mixture will curdle and become like buttermilk.) Stir in the oil, sugar, maple, and salt. Add the flour, baking powder, and baking soda. Stir until smooth, being careful not to overmix.

Cook the waffles according to the waffle iron instructions. (For extra crispness, toast the waffles in a toaster oven before assembling.)

To serve, break the waffles into quarters. Add 2 tablespoons to ¼ cup (34 to 68 g) of filling on top of one quarter, and then top with another quarter.

Yield: 4 to 8 wafflewiches

APRICOT BREAKFAST PANINI
The jam thickens as it cools, so make it ahead of time and refrigerate in an airtight container until you're ready to use it.

FOR THE QUICK APRICOT JAM:
12 ounces (340 g) fresh apricots, halved, pitted, and chopped
2 tablespoons (15 g) dried sweetened tart cherries
¼ cup plus 2 tablespoons (90 ml) orange juice, divided
1 to 2 tablespoons (21 to 42 g) agave nectar
Pinch of grated nutmeg
2 tablespoons (16 g) cornstarch

FOR THE SANDWICHES:
2 tablespoons (28 g) nondairy butter
8 slices bread
¼ cup (60 g) nondairy cream cheese

To make the quick apricot jam: In a small saucepan, heat the apricots, cherries, ¼ cup (60 ml) of the juice, 1 tablespoon (21 g) of the agave, and nutmeg over medium heat. Bring the mixture to a boil, reduce the heat to a simmer, and allow the apricots to break down some, for 4 to 5 minutes. (It should be chunky, but not have large pieces of fruit.)

In a small bowl, combine the remaining 2 tablespoons (30 ml) juice and cornstarch. Add to the saucepan. Stir until thickened, 3 to 4 minutes. Taste and add the remaining 1 tablespoon (21 g) agave if needed.

17 Coconut Zucchini Bread; 18 Fennel and Kale Corn Bread; 19 Cornbread; 20 Lemon Poppy Seed Cakes; 21 Cherry Vanilla Bean Pancakes; 22 Nutty Fruitcake Pancakes; 23 Banana Nepalese Pancakes with "Bacon"; 24 Strawberry Crêpes with Spiced Coconut Cream

25 Crispy Toaster Waffles; 26 Cream of Jasmine Rice; 27 Apple Pie Steel-Cut Oats; 28 Loaded Oatmeal; 29 Oatmeal with Flaxseeds, Cinnamon, and Coconut Milk; 30 Oat, Amaranth, and Carrot Porridge; 31 Brown Rice and Farro Porridge; 32 Groovy Granola

To assemble the sandwiches: Preheat a panini press.

Butter one side of each slice of bread. On the unbuttered sides, spread 1 tablespoon (15 g) of the cream cheese and 2 tablespoons (40 g) of the jam, keeping the jam away from the edges of the bread so it will not seep out. Put the top slice of bread on so that both the buttered sides are facing out. Close the panini press and cook for 5 to 7 minutes, or until golden brown.

Yield: 4 sandwiches, 1½ cups (300 g) jam

Blueberry and Corn Pancakes Sandwiches with Lemony Filling

BLUEBERRY AND CORN PANCAKE SANDWICHES WITH LEMONY FILLING

There's no need to cook the corn on the cob, but if yours is precooked, that's fine, too. Bursting with blueberries and cream, these sandwiches feel like you're having dessert for breakfast.

FOR THE FILLING:
¼ cup plus 2 tablespoons (51 g) cashews, soaked in water for 1 hour, then drained
¼ cup plus 2 tablespoons (89 ml) lemon juice
1 tablespoon (6 g) lemon zest
1 tablespoon plus 2 teaspoons (25 g) nondairy cream cheese
1 tablespoon plus 1 teaspoon (28 g) agave nectar
Pinch of salt

FOR THE PANCAKES:
1 cup plus 2 tablespoons (265 ml) soy milk
2 tablespoons (30 ml) lemon juice
2 tablespoons (25 g) granulated sugar
1 tablespoon (15 ml) canola oil
½ teaspoon salt
½ teaspoon dried thyme
½ teaspoon lemon zest
1 cup (125 g) all-purpose flour
¼ cup (32 g) finely ground cornmeal
1 tablespoon (12 g) baking powder
1¼cups (183 g) blueberries, divided
½ cup (77 g) fresh or frozen corn, rinsed
Canola oil, for cooking
Confectioners' sugar, for serving

To make the filling: In a blender, blend all the ingredients until completely smooth. Refrigerate in an airtight container until ready to use.

To make the pancakes: In a medium bowl, combine the milk and juice. (The mixture will curdle and become like buttermilk.) Stir in the granulated sugar, oil, salt, thyme, and zest. Add the flour, cornmeal, and baking powder. Stir to combine. (A few lumps are okay.) Stir in ¾ cup (110 g) of the blueberries and the corn.

Preheat the oven to 300°F (150°C, or gas mark 2).

Lightly coat a large skillet with oil and place over medium heat. Working in batches, scoop ¼ cup (57 g) of the batter into the skillet. Cook for 3 to 4 minutes, or until the edges look set and bubbles are appearing on the tops of the pancakes. Flip and cook the other side for 2 to 3 minutes. Keep warm in the oven until all the pancakes are cooked.

To assemble the sandwiches: Place 6 pancakes on plates. Top each with a generous tablespoon (14 g) of the filling and a generous tablespoon (9 g) of the remaining blueberries. Top with the remaining 6 pancakes. Dust with confectioners' sugar.

Yield: 6 sandwiches

BEANS NOT ON TOAST

You'll like how these waffles won't get floppy on you.

FOR THE WAFFLES:
2 tablespoons (30 ml) sesame oil
1 tablespoon (21 g) agave nectar
1 cup (235 ml) plain nondairy milk, lukewarm
2 tablespoons (30 ml) lemon juice
1 teaspoon salt
Scant 3 cups (360 g) all-purpose flour
2 teaspoons instant yeast

FOR THE BEANS:
1 tablespoon (15 ml) olive oil
4 large tomatoes, diced small
⅓ cup (50 g) minced shallot
6 cloves garlic, minced
¼ cup (60 ml) apple cider vinegar
¼ cup (66 g) tomato paste
2 teaspoons vegan Worcestershire sauce
2 cans (15 ounces, or 425 g each) pinto beans, drained
  and rinsed
½ teaspoon smoked sea salt, to taste
¼ teaspoon black pepper, to taste

FOR THE SANDWICHES:
Nondairy butter, for serving
Chopped fresh parsley, for serving

To make the waffles: In a large bowl, combine the oil, agave, milk, juice, and salt. Add the flour and yeast. Stir for a few minutes, stabbing the dough with a spatula to knead it. Cover and let rise for 2 hours, or until doubled in size. Punch down the dough. Divide it into 4 or 8 equal portions. (The dough will be sticky, so moisten your hands if needed.) Use a heaping ½ cup (155 g) dough for 4 portions or ¼ cup (78 g) for 8 portions. Place the portions on parchment and let rest for 15 minutes.

Place one (if using a standard waffle iron) or two (if using a large and wide Belgian waffle iron) portions of dough on the iron and press closed for a few seconds to spread the dough. Bake for 8 minutes, or until golden brown and the edges of the waffles aren't doughy.

Cool waffles on a wire rack. Repeat with the remaining dough.

To make the beans: In a large skillet, heat the oil over medium-high heat. Cook the tomatoes, shallot, and garlic for 2 minutes, or until the tomatoes get saucy.

In a small bowl, combine the vinegar, paste, and Worcestershire. Add to the skillet. Cook for 1 minute. Add the beans, salt, and pepper. Cook for 2 minutes longer, stirring occasionally.

To assemble the sandwiches: Spread butter on each waffle. Divide the bean mixture among the waffles. Sprinkle with parsley.

Yield: 4 or 8 sandwiches

BLACKBERRY BREAKFAST BARS (PHOTO PAGE 4)

A delicious breakfast–or snack or dessert–you can serve these bars on their own or with some nondairy yogurt. They're a cross between a breakfast bar and a mini cobbler.

2 cups (290 g) blackberries, rinsed
2 tablespoons (9 g) granulated sugar
2 tablespoons (30 ml) water
1 tablespoon (15 ml) fresh lemon juice
¾ teaspoon ground cinnamon, divided
1 cup (120 g) all-purpose pastry flour
1 cup (80 g) quick-cooking oats
⅔ cup (150 g) packed brown sugar
¼ cup (28 g) ground flaxseed
⅛ teaspoon baking soda
½ cup (112 g) nondairy butter, melted

Preheat the oven to 350°F (180°C, or gas mark 4).

In a medium saucepan, combine the blackberries, sugar, water, juice, and ½ teaspoon of the cinnamon. Cover and bring to a boil. Reduce the heat and uncover. Simmer, uncovered, for about 8 minutes, stirring frequently. (The mixture may begin to thicken up a bit by this point.) Remove from the heat.

In a medium bowl, combine the flour, oats, brown sugar, flaxseed, the remaining ¼ teaspoon cinnamon, and the baking soda. Stir in the butter until thoroughly combined.

Press half of the flour-oat mixture into an ungreased 8 x 8-inch (20 x 20 cm) pan. (Reserve the other half to use as a topping.) Bake for 20 to 25 minutes, or until the blackberries begin to bubble a bit. Remove from the oven.

Spread the berry mixture on top of the crust. Sprinkle with the reserved oat mixture. Lightly press it into the berry filling. Bake for 20 minutes longer, or until the topping turns a golden brown. Cool in the pan on a wire rack. Cut into bars.

Yield: 12 to 16 bars

33 Down-Home Country Tofu Scramble; 34 Veggie-Good Breakfast Tacos; 35 Sweet and Smoky Tempeh Strips; 36 Berry-Stuffed French Toast Pockets; 37 Maple-Nut Pie Wafflewich; 38 Apricot Breakfast Panini

39 Beans Not on Toast

VEGAN "LOOSE MEAT" SANDWICHES

Not a sloppy Joe and not quite a Maid-rite, this vegan version of a loose meat sandwich is oh so simple and tasty! This filling is terrific served on a toasted bun with yellow mustard and onions.

2 tablespoons (28 g) vegan butter
½ cup (80 g) diced onion
1 cup (70 g) diced mushrooms
½ teaspoon cumin
½ teaspoon garlic powder
¼ teaspoon salt, or more to taste
¼ teaspoon liquid smoke
½ cup (120 ml) almond milk
1 cup (100 g) textured vegetable protein (TVP)
½ cup (120 ml) vegetable broth
½ teaspoon black pepper
4 hamburger buns, toasted

In an uncovered pressure cooker, heat the butter on medium-high. Sauté the onion and mushrooms for 3 minutes, or until the onion softens. Add the seasonings and milk. Bring to a light boil. Add the TVP and broth. Stir well. Cover and bring to pressure. Cook at high pressure for 3 minutes. Use a quick release. Remove the lid, stir in the pepper and salt to taste. Spoon onto the buns.

Yield: 4 sandwiches

SUMMER SQUASH VEGGIE SLOPPY JOES

Who doesn't like sloppy joes? Make your sloppy joes soy free by using beans in place of tofu. You can use tortillas instead of the hamburger buns.

1 cup (160 g) diced yellow or white onion
¼ cup (60 ml) low-sodium vegetable broth
½ cup (54 g) chopped carrot
1 cup (101 g) chopped celery
12 ounces (340 g) extra-firm tofu, drained and mashed
    up, or 1 can (15 ounces, or 425 g) black or pinto beans
1½ cups (170 g) peeled and chopped summer squash
6 ounces (170 g) tomato paste
3 cups (705 ml) tomato sauce
3 cloves garlic, minced
1 teaspoon chili powder
1 teaspoon ground paprika
1 teaspoon dried oregano
1 teaspoon black pepper
1½ cups (355 ml) water

6 hamburger buns, toasted
1 cup (120 g) nutritional yeast

In a large pan, sauté the onion. Once the onion starts to brown, add the broth. Add the carrot and celery. Cook, stirring occasionally, for 2 minutes. Add the tofu or beans and squash, mixing well. Cook for 2 minutes. Add the paste and sauce, stirring to dissolve completely. Add the garlic, chili powder, paprika, oregano, and pepper. Mix until thoroughly combined. Reduce the heat to medium-low. Add the water. Cook for 8 to 10 minutes, or until the mixture is thickened, stirring occasionally.

Once the mixture has thickened, divide it on the buns. Top with the yeast.

Yield: 6 sandwiches

PAV BHAJI

Pav bhaji is a popular street food dish in India, consisting of a thick potato-based curry (bhaji) and soft rolls (pav)– sort of like sloppy joes, only way kinder and way spicier.

1 large white potato (10 ounces, or 280 g), diced
2 heaping cups (290 g) frozen cauliflower florets
2 tablespoons (30 ml) olive oil
⅓ cup (50 g) chopped red onion
1 small hot green pepper, seeded and minced
1 red bell pepper, seeded and diced
2 cloves garlic, pressed
1 to 1½ teaspoons grated fresh ginger, to taste
¼ teaspoon turmeric
1 tablespoon (5 g) pav bhaji masala or garam masala
1 cup (260 g) crushed tomatoes
½ cup (80 g) cooked petite green peas
Salt, to taste
Nondairy butter, for rolls
8 large soft rolls, halved and lightly toasted
½ cup (8 g) chopped fresh cilantro

In a large pot, place the potato and cauliflower and cover with water. Boil over high heat until tender, 10 to 15 minutes, and then drain. Mash.

In a large skillet, heat the oil over medium-high heat. Sauté the onion, green pepper, and bell pepper until tender, about 5 minutes. Add the garlic, ginger, turmeric, and masala and cook for 1 minute longer. Add the tomatoes, peas, and salt to taste. Add the potato mixture, stir well, cover with a lid, and simmer on low heat for 15 minutes, stirring occasionally. (The mixture should be very thick but not dry. If it gets dry before the cooking is done, add a little water or vegetable broth to moisten it just a bit.)

To assemble the sandwiches, lightly butter both halves of the rolls. Scoop ½ cup (120 g) pav bhaji on the bottom half. Sprinkle with 1 tablespoon (1 g) chopped cilantro. Replace the tops of the rolls or leave open-faced.

Yield: 8 sandwiches

TEMPEH SLOPPY JOES

Here's a great way to use tempeh instead of tofu, although the latter is perfectly acceptable. This is a hearty dish that can be a sandwich or a main event.

1 package (8 ounces, or 225 g) tempeh, cubed
1 tablespoon (15 ml) olive oil
1 onion, finely chopped
1 bell pepper, seeded and finely chopped
1 can (15 ounces, or 420 g) tomato sauce
1 tablespoon (8 g) chili powder, or to taste
½ teaspoon salt
¼ teaspoon black pepper
2 tablespoons (30 ml) vegan Worcestershire sauce
1 teaspoon (5 ml) hot sauce, optional
4 buns, toasted

In a steamer basket placed in a pot filled with 2 to 3 inches (5 to 7.5 cm) of water, steam the tempeh for 10 minutes. Transfer the tempeh to a bowl, and crumble with your hands.

In a large saucepan, heat the oil over medium heat. Sauté the onion until translucent. Add the bell pepper and tempeh. Sauté for a few minutes more, stirring constantly. Add the sauce, chili powder, salt, pepper, Worcestershire, and hot sauce, if using. Cover, reduce heat, and simmer for 10 minutes. Serve on the buns.

Yield: 4 sandwiches

CARNITAS SANDWICHES

Jackfruit is a wonderful substitute for shredded meat because it has the perfect texture. It also absorbs the flavors of whatever sauce you marinate it in.

FOR THE CARNITAS:
2 cans (20 ounces, or 565 g each) jackfruit in brine or water (not syrup)
½ cup (120 ml) orange juice
2 tablespoons (14 g) onion powder
6 cloves garlic, minced, divided
3 tablespoons (45 ml) lime juice, divided
¼ cup plus 2 tablespoons (90 ml) tamari, divided
1 tablespoon (15 ml) hot sauce

1 tablespoon (2 g) dried cilantro
1 teaspoon ground cumin
1 tablespoon (22 g) brown rice syrup
2 tablespoons (30 ml) olive oil
¼ cup (40 g) minced shallot

FOR THE CHILI CRÈME:
6 ounces (170 g) drained firm silken tofu
2 tablespoons (30 ml) olive oil
1 tablespoon (15 ml) lime juice
½ teaspoon salt, or to taste
1 teaspoon chili powder, or to taste
½ teaspoon onion powder
1 tablespoon (1 g) chopped fresh cilantro

FOR THE SANDWICHES:
¾ cup (192 g) guacamole
4 sub sandwich rolls, 6 inches (15 cm) long, lightly toasted

To make the carnitas: Rinse, drain, and roughly shred the jackfruit.

In a large pot, combine the jackfruit, juice, onion powder, 4 cloves of the garlic, 1 tablespoon (15 ml) of the juice, ¼ cup (60 ml) of the tamari, hot sauce, cilantro, cumin, and syrup. Add enough water to reach about ¾ inch (2 cm) above the jackfruit. Cover and bring to a boil over high heat. Lower the heat and simmer for 1 hour, stirring occasionally. Stop simmering if so much liquid evaporates that the jackfruit isn't fully immersed. Do not drain. Let cool, cover, and chill the jackfruit in the liquid overnight, up to 24 hours.

When ready to cook, drain the jackfruit.

In a large skillet, heat the oil over medium-high heat. Add the jackfruit, the remaining 2 cloves garlic, and the shallot. Cook for 10 minutes, or until the jackfruit starts to brown. Stir occasionally. Add the remaining 2 tablespoons (30 ml) juice and the remaining 2 tablespoons (30 ml) tamari. Cook for 5 minutes longer.

To make the crème: In a food processor, process all of the ingredients until smooth, scraping the sides with a rubber spatula as needed. Store in an airtight container in the fridge for up to 1 week.

To assemble the sandwiches: Spread 3 tablespoons (48 g) guacamole on one half of each roll. Spread 2 generous tablespoons (36 g) chili crème on the other side of each roll. Pile ½ cup (100 g) jackfruit on top, or enough to fit on the roll without spilling over.

Yield: 4 sandwiches, 1 scant cup (215 g) Chili Crème

BEET-N-BARLEY BURGERS

These delectable burgers hit the mark even with non–beet lovers. The slightly earthy undertone is the perfect spring-board for the black-eyed peas and barley. Keep in mind that beets stain.

4 cups (940 ml) water
½ cup (100 g) dry pearl barley
Pinch of salt
1 tablespoon (15 ml) olive oil
1 cup (160 g) minced onion
1 cup (225 g) peeled, finely diced raw beets
½ cup (75 g) minced green bell pepper
3 tablespoons (24 g) minced carrot
3 cloves garlic, pressed
1 teaspoon smoked paprika
1 teaspoon ground cumin
1 teaspoon dried thyme
½ cup (86 g) cooked black-eyed peas, drained and rinsed
¼ cup (65 g) barbecue sauce
2 teaspoons Dijon mustard
1 teaspoon liquid smoke
1 teaspoon ume plum vinegar
½ teaspoon salt
¼ teaspoon black pepper
⅔ to 1 cup (60 to 90 g) old-fashioned or quick oats, ground
Canola oil, for cooking
8 burger buns
Vegan mayonnaise, onions, lettuce, tomato, pickles, or other burger toppings

In a medium saucepan, bring the water, barley, and salt to a boil over high heat. Reduce the heat to a simmer. Cook, uncovered, for 30 to 35 minutes, or until the barley is quite tender. Drain.

In a large skillet, heat the oil over medium heat. Add the onion, beets, pepper, carrot, garlic, and spices. Cook for about 10 minutes, stirring, or until the vegetables are tender.

In a large bowl, mash the peas with a fork until pasty. Add the sauce, mustard, liquid smoke, vinegar, salt, and pepper. Stir to combine. Add the barley and vegetables. Stir well to combine. Add ⅔ cup (60 g) of the oats and mix well. Add more oats, 1 tablespoon (8 g) at a time, until the mixture can be shaped into burgers. Refrigerate the mixture for 1 hour or longer.

Line a baking sheet with parchment paper.

Using ½ cup (112 g) of the mixture, form into 8 patties about 3 inches (8 cm) wide and ½ inch (1.3 cm) thick.

In a large skillet, heat enough oil to cover the bottom over medium-high heat. Add the burgers and cook for 5 to 6 minutes, or until the bottom is blackened and slightly crisp. Turn and cook the other side for 4 to 5 minutes. Serve on the buns with the toppings.

Yield: 8 burgers

SUPER STACKED VEGGIE "BURGER"

This isn't your usual burger. It's even better! Grill up extra veggies to save and use for other meals during the week.

FOR THE MARINADE:
⅓ cup (80 ml) coconut aminos, low-sodium soy sauce, or Bragg's Liquid Aminos
2 tablespoons (30 ml) balsamic vinegar
1 tablespoon (7 g) smoked paprika
2 teaspoons black pepper
1 teaspoon garlic powder
1 teaspoon onion powder
1 teaspoon chipotle powder or cayenne pepper
½ teaspoon dried oregano
½ teaspoon dried thyme
About ½ cup water (120 ml)

FOR THE "BURGER":
1 medium sweet onion, cut into round slices
4 medium portobello mushrooms, brushed clean
3 medium zucchinis, sliced lengthwise in ¼-inch- (6 mm) thick slices
1 large red bell pepper, seeded and sliced lengthwise
1 medium eggplant, sliced in ¼-inch (6 mm) round slices

FOR THE TOPPINGS:
1 large tomato, sliced
2 large avocados, sliced in quarters
1 head Romaine lettuce, washed, dried, and pulled into separate pieces
4 hamburger buns
1 tablespoon (11 g) mustard or ketchup

To make the marinade: In a bowl, combine all of the marinade ingredients. Taste and adjust the seasonings. This marinade is very concentrated, so add approximately ½ cup (120 ml) water to thin out.

To make the "burgers": To the marinade, add the onion, mushrooms, zucchinis, pepper, and eggplant. Toss until vegetables are covered, but don't leave in marinade beyond 2 minutes.

Preheat the grill.

Grill the vegetables until soft.

Assemble the sandwich in this order: bottom of bun, mushroom, eggplant, lettuce, tomato, 2 or 3 slices zucchini, 2 slices pepper, onion, and avocado. Spread the condiment on the bun top and place atop vegetables.

Yield: 4 "burgers"

BEET BURGERS

This burger pairs perfectly with a side of Carrot Fries. (See page 186.) Serve each burger on a whole wheat bun, topped with tomatoes, onions, avocado, and eggless mayonnaise.

2 cups (240 g) grated beets (about 2 large beets)
1½ cups (300 g) cooked bulgur wheat
1 cup (130 g) toasted sunflower seeds
½ cup (120 g) toasted sesame seeds
½ cup (80 g) minced onion (about 1 small onion)
½ cup (60 g) bread crumbs
¼ cup (60 ml) oil
3 tablespoons (24 g) all-purpose flour
3 tablespoons (8 g) finely chopped fresh parsley
4 cloves garlic, finely chopped
2 to 3 tablespoons (30 to 45 ml) tamari soy sauce
¼ teaspoon cayenne pepper
Salt, to taste

Preheat the oven to 350°F (180°C, or gas mark 4). Line a baking sheet with parchment.

In a large bowl, combine the beets, bulgur, sunflower, sesame, onion, bread crumbs, oil, flour, parsley, garlic, tamari, cayenne, and salt to taste.

Try to create a patty that will stay together. If it falls apart, add a little more bulgur or flour until you have a firm patty that won't fall apart while baking.

Form the mixture into 10 to 12 patties. Bake for 25 minutes, or until firm. Carefully flip halfway during the cooking time.

Yield: 10 to 12 patties

"BACON 'N EGG," PINEAPPLE BEETROOT BURGER

In Australia, this assortment of toppings is standard for enjoying a burger. For best results, prepare everything separately and assemble right before eating.

FOR THE BURGERS:
1½ cups (257 g) cooked pinto beans
1 cup (96 g) textured vegetable protein (TVP) rehydrated in 1 cup (235 ml) vegetable broth for 10 minutes
2 cloves garlic, grated
1 carrot, grated
1 small beet, peeled and grated
½ teaspoon salt
½ cup (60 g) bread crumbs

FOR THE "EGGS":
1 block tofu (14 ounces, or 397 g), extra firm, drained and pressed slightly
2 teaspoons black salt
½ cup (60 g) gram flour mixed with 1/2 cup (120 ml) water

FOR THE ASSEMBLED BURGER:
12 hamburger buns
½ cup (115 g) vegan mayonnaise
1½ cups (30 g) arugula leaves
12 slices canned pineapple, drained
12 burgers
1 large avocado, sliced into 24 thin pieces
24 pieces vegan bacon
12 "eggs"
2 medium tomatoes, sliced into about 12 slices
12 slices pickled beetroot, drained

To make the burger: Preheat the oven to 375°F (190°C, gas mark 5).

In a large bowl, smash together the pinto beans and prepared TVP using a potato masher until very well combined. Blend in the rest of the ingredients using a large fork to make a homogenous mixture.

Brush a large baking pan with oil. Shape the mixture into about 12 patties and place on the pan. Brush the tops of the patties with a little more oil. Bake for 45 to 60 minutes, flipping once halfway through.

To make the "eggs": In a small bowl, combine all of the ingredients with a fork.

Coat a medium frying pan with a little oil, heat over medium high, and drop ¼ cup (55 g) "egg" onto pan. Cook for about 3 minutes, flip, and cook for 3 minutes more.

To assemble: Lightly toast the buns. Spread the mayonnaise on the insides of each half of the bun. Assemble in this order: bottom bun, arugula, pineapple, burger, avocado, "bacon," "egg," tomato, beetroot, top bun.

Yield: 12 burgers

TU-NOT SALAD

Jackfruit stands in for tuna in this salad, and the seaweed gives it an amazingly seafood-y flavor. The recipe takes a few hours to make, but most of it is downtime. Serve it on your fave bread.

4 cups (940 ml) low-sodium vegetable broth
1 can (20 ounces, or 570 g) young green jackfruit, packed in water or brine, drained and rinsed
¼ cup (20 g) hijiki or wakame seaweed
½ cup (80 g) finely diced red onion
½ cup (50 g) finely diced celery
½ cup (52 g) finely diced cucumber
2 tablespoons (8 g) finely chopped fresh parsley
1½ teaspoons fresh dill
½ cup (112 g) Tofu Mayo (See page 9.)

In a large pot with a tight-fitting lid, bring the broth, jackfruit, and seaweed to a boil over medium-high heat.

Reduce to simmer, cover, and simmer for 2 hours, stirring about every 30 minutes. Remove from the heat, uncover, and cool to room temperature. Drain excess liquid and place the jackfruit and seaweed in a bowl. Using your hands, break apart jackfruit until stringy and flaky. Add the onion, celery, cucumber, parsley, dill, and Tofu Mayo. Mix until well combined. Store in the fridge in an airtight container for up to 1 week or freeze for up to 4 months.

Yield: 8 servings

OUT OF TUNA SANDWICHES
This is a take on salad niçoise, which is named for the city of Nice in France. Here it's in sandwich form, which is even nicer because it says no to tuna and anchovies.

FOR CHICKPEA TUNA:
1 can (15 ounces, or 425 g) chickpeas, drained and rinsed
½ cup (120 g) Miso Dressing (See page 101.)
2 teaspoons lemon juice
½ teaspoon minced capers
1 teaspoon Dijon mustard
1 teaspoon minced shallot
½ teaspoon kelp powder
⅛ teaspoon dried dill
Salt, to taste
Black pepper, to taste

FOR THE DRESSING:
Salt, to taste
Black pepper, to taste
1 small clove garlic, pressed
2 teaspoons lemon juice
2 teaspoons white balsamic vinegar
½ teaspoon Dijon mustard
2 tablespoons (30 ml) olive oil
2 teaspoons minced shallot
1 teaspoon capers, drained and chopped
½ teaspoon vegan Worcestershire sauce

FOR THE SANDWICHES:
3 soft bread rolls, halved
18 small yellow leaves from heart of romaine
6 thin slices tomato
6 ounces (170 g) green beans, cooked until crisp-tender
12 olives, for serving

To make the chickpea tuna: In a food processor, pulse the chickpeas a few times, breaking up some of the chickpeas. Transfer the chickpeas to a large bowl. Add the remaining ingredients. Stir to combine. Cover with plastic wrap and refrigerate for about 2 hours.

To make the dressing: In a small bowl, combine all of the ingredients and whisk thoroughly. Whisk again just before using.

To assemble the sandwiches: Place ½ cup (120 g) of the chickpea tuna on the bottom of each roll. Top with 6 lettuce leaves and 2 tomato slices.

In a small bowl, combine the beans with the freshly whisked dressing. Place 2 ounces (a little under ½ cup, or 57 g) of beans on top of the tomato slices. Replace the top of the roll and with 4 olives per serving.

Yield: 3 sandwiches

THE INCREDIBLE GREEN SANDWICH
This monochromatic sandwich is a hybrid of the popular avocado toast and green smoothie recipes everyone seems to be enjoying for breakfast lately.

2 small ripe avocados, peeled, halved, and pitted
1 clove garlic, minced, optional
1½ tablespoons (15 g) minced green onion
½ teaspoon minced jalapeño, to taste
1½ tablespoons (2 g) chopped fresh cilantro
1½ tablespoons (25 ml) lime juice
Salt, to taste
Olive oil, for drizzling, optional
8 rolls, halved and toasted
3 cups (100 g) fresh baby spinach
1 ounce (28 g) sprouts

In a bowl, mash the avocado with the garlic, onion, jalapeño, cilantro, juice, and salt to taste.

Drizzle a little oil on each roll half. Spread a generous 1 tablespoon (20 g) of guacamole over each roll half. Top with a handful of spinach and then add a handful of sprouts. Top with the other roll.

Yield: 8 sandwiches

RAZZ-ELNUT SPINACH SANDWICHES

A sandwich combining mayonnaise with raspberries? Delish! You'll fall in love with the pink hue and tingling flavor of this new favorite spread.

FOR THE RASPBERRY SPREAD:
¼ cup (47 g) frozen raspberries, thawed and drained
½ cup (120 g) Miso Dressing (See page 101.)
1½ teaspoons minced shallot
Generous ¼ teaspoon fresh thyme leaves, chopped

FOR THE GOBBLERS SLICES:
½ cup (91 g) cooked navy beans
½ cup (120 ml) dry white wine
½ cup (120 ml) vegetable broth, plus more if needed
2 tablespoons (30 ml) lemon juice
2 tablespoons (30 ml) olive oil
2 teaspoons onion powder
1 teaspoon garlic powder
1 teaspoon dried parsley
¾ teaspoon dried sage
½ teaspoon mustard powder
½ teaspoon dried rosemary
½ teaspoon black pepper
½ teaspoon salt
¼ teaspoon celery seed
1¼ cups (180 g) vital wheat gluten, plus more if needed
¼ cup (30 g) nutritional yeast
2 tablespoons (15 g) chickpea flour
2 tablespoons (24 g) instant tapioca

FOR THE SANDWICHES:
4 bagels, halved and toasted
⅓ cup (38 g) coarsely chopped dry-roasted hazelnuts
2 cups (57 g) baby spinach
32 super-thin Gobbler Slices

To make the Raspberry Spread: In a small bowl, combine all the spread ingredients, making sure that no large pieces of raspberries are left.

To make the Gobbler Slices:
In a blender, combine the beans, wine, broth, juice, oil, and spices. Blend until smooth.

In a medium bowl, combine the gluten, yeast, flour, and tapioca. Pour the wet ingredients into the dry ingredients. Mix with a fork. Add an extra 1 tablespoon (15 ml) broth or (9 g) gluten if needed to make a soft, workable dough. Knead for a few minutes, squeezing to be sure all the ingredients are combined.

Transfer the mixture to a 12-inch (30.5-cm) piece of foil. Form into a roll about 6 inches (15 cm) long. Roll the foil around the mixture, twisting the ends to enclose.

Prepare a steamer. Steam the roll for 1 hour 15 minutes. Let cool. Using a sharp, serrated knife, slice thinly with a seesaw motion. Wrap tightly in plastic and store in the fridge for up to 1 week or freeze for up to 2 months.

To assemble the sandwiches: Spread 1 heaping tablespoon (16 g) Raspberry Spread on each bagel half (or enough to cover the surface of it). Top with 1 heaping tablespoon (10 g) hazelnuts. Cover with ½ cup (14 g) baby spinach, 8 Gobbler Slices, and the other bagel half.

Yield: 4 sandwiches, 20 ounces (573 g) Gobbler Slices

1 Vegan "Loose Meat" Sandwiches; 2 Summer Squash Veggie Sloppy Joes; 3 Pav Bhaji; 4 Tempeh Sloppy Joes; 5 Carnitas Sandwiches; 6 Super Stacked Veggie "Burger"; 7 Beet-n-Barley Burgers; 8 Beet Burgers

9 "Bacon 'n' Egg" Pineapple Beetroot Burger; 10 Tu-Not Salad; 11 Out of Tuna Sandwiches; 12 The Incredible Green Sandwich; 13 Razz-Elnut Spinach Sandwiches; 14 Out for the Count of Monte Cristo; 15 Bierocks; 16 Almo-Cado Sandwiches

OUT FOR THE COUNT OF MONTE CRISTO

This differs from what you might think of as a traditional Monte Cristo, but we're betting you'll be glad we did.

FOR THE FILLING AND SPREAD:
1 tablespoon (15 ml) olive oil
12 ounces (340 g) Moo-Free Seitan (See right), cut into
½-inch (1.3-cm) strips
1½ cups (210 g) sauerkraut, drained (Reserve 1 tablespoon (15 ml juice for bagels below.)
2 tablespoons (30 g) prepared horseradish, divided
1 tablespoon (15 g) Dijon mustard, divided
¼ teaspoon black pepper
Pinch of red pepper flakes
1 large avocado, peeled and pitted
2 teaspoons lemon juice

FOR FRENCH TOAST BAGELS:
¼ cup (35 g) cashews, soaked in water for 1 hour, then
rinsed and drained
½ cup plus 2 tablespoons (150 ml) nondairy milk
2 teaspoons Dijon mustard
1 tablespoon (15 ml) sauerkraut juice
1 tablespoon (15 ml) white wine vinegar
½ teaspoon salt
⅛ teaspoon black pepper
¼ cup (25 g) minced green onion
1 tablespoon (8 g) all-purpose flour
1 teaspoon baking powder
Canola oil, for cooking
4 bagels, halved

To make the filling and spread: In a large skillet, heat the oil over medium-high heat. Add the seitan. Cook until seared, 3 to 5 minutes. Add the sauerkraut, 1 tablespoon (15 g) of the horseradish, 1 teaspoon of the mustard, black pepper, and red pepper. Cook, stirring, for 4 minutes.

For the spread, in a small bowl, mash the avocado, juice, remaining 1 tablespoon (15 g) horseradish, and remaining 2 teaspoons mustard with a fork until smooth.

To make the French Toast Bagels: In a blender, process the cashews, milk, mustard, juice, vinegar, salt, and pepper until smooth. Pour the mixture into a shallow dish. Stir in the onion, flour, and baking powder.

In a skillet, heat ⅛ inch (3 mm) of oil over medium-high heat. (These are prone to sticking, so add additional oil if needed.) Dip the bagels into the mixture, let the extra batter drip back down into the dish, and transfer to the skillet. Cook for 3 to 4 minutes on one side, or until browned. Flip and cook the other side for 3 to 4 minutes. Place a bagel half on each plate and spread evenly with the avocado mixture. Divide the seitan/sauerkraut mixture evenly among the bagels. Put the bagel tops on.

Yield: 4 sandwiches

MOO-FREE SEITAN

FOR THE SEITAN:
2 cups (288 g) vital wheat gluten, plus more if needed
3 tablespoons (23 g) soy flour
1 tablespoon (8 g) nutritional yeast
2 teaspoons onion powder
1 teaspoon paprika
1 teaspoon garlic powder
½ teaspoon black pepper
1¼ cups (295 ml) vegetable broth, chilled, plus more if
needed
¼ cup (60 ml) tamari
3 tablespoons (45 g) ketchup
2 teaspoons liquid smoke

FOR THE COOKING BROTH:
4 cups (940 ml) vegetable broth, chilled
1 tablespoon (15 ml) tamari
1 tablespoon (15 g) ketchup
2 large cloves garlic, sliced
¼ small onion, sliced
Generous pinch of black pepper

To make the seitan: In a medium bowl, stir the gluten, flour, yeast, and spices with a fork.

In a small bowl, combine the broth, tamari, ketchup and liquid smoke. Mix the wet ingredients into the dry, using a fork. Add an extra 1 or 2 tablespoons (15 to 30 ml) broth or (9 to 18 g) gluten, if needed, to make a workable dough. Knead by hand for 4 minutes, or until the dough forms a cohesive ball. Form into a ball about 5 inches (13 cm) across.

To make the cooking broth: In a large bowl, combine the broth, tamari, ketchup, garlic, onion, and pepper.

Preheat the oven to 300°F (150°C, or gas mark 2). Coat a 2-quart (1.9-l) round covered casserole dish with nonstick cooking spray.

Place the seitan in the prepared dish. Cover with the broth. Place on top of a baking sheet in case of drips. Cover and bake for 3 hours. Cool in the broth. Cut into four 8-ounce (227-g) portions, or as desired. Wrap tightly in plastic and store in the fridge for up to 1 week or freeze for up to 3 months.

Yield: 2½ pounds (1.1 kg)

BIEROCKS

Reputed to be German, these buns feature flavorful cabbage, tempeh, and sauerkraut, wrapped in easy-to-make beer and caraway bread dough. Enjoy these at any temperature, topped with mustard.

FOR THE FILLING:
1½ cups (355 ml) vegetable broth
¼ cup (60 ml) red wine vinegar
2 tablespoons (33 g) tomato paste
1 tablespoon (15 ml) tamari
2 teaspoons onion powder
1 teaspoon cumin seeds
1 teaspoon paprika
½ teaspoon fennel seeds
½ teaspoon lemon pepper
2 cloves garlic, minced
1 teaspoon vegan Worcestershire sauce
8 ounces (227 g) tempeh, minced
2 tablespoons (30 ml) olive oil, divided
1 cup (160 g) minced onion
2 cups (180 g) chopped green cabbage
1 cup (142 g) sauerkraut, drained
⅓ cup (34 g) grated carrot
1 tablespoon (15 g) Dijon mustard
Salt, to taste
Black pepper, to taste

FOR THE BUNS:
3 cups (375 g) all-purpose flour
3 tablespoons (45 g) packed brown sugar
2 teaspoons instant yeast
1 teaspoon salt
1 teaspoon caraway seeds
1 cup (235 ml) dark vegan beer, flat and at room temperature
Nondairy butter, for brushing

To make the filling: In a medium saucepan, combine the broth, vinegar, paste, tamari, onion powder, cumin, paprika, fennel, lemon pepper, garlic, and Worcestershire. Bring to a boil, reduce to a simmer, and cook for 20 minutes.

Place the tempeh and the marinade in an 8-inch (20-cm) pan. Marinate for 1 hour in the fridge.

In a large skillet, heat 1 tablespoon (15 ml) of the oil over medium heat. Drain the tempeh, reserving the marinade, and add to the skillet. Cook, stirring, for 10 minutes.

Remove the tempeh from the pan. Add the remaining 1 tablespoon (15 ml) oil, onion, and cabbage to the skillet. Cook for 5 minutes. Add the sauerkraut, carrot, mustard, salt, pepper, tempeh, and reserved marinade. Cook, stirring, for 5 minutes. Let cool.

To make the buns: In a medium bowl, combine the flour, sugar, yeast, salt, caraway, and beer. Stir together. Knead for 8 minutes on a floured board. Add 1 tablespoon (8 g) flour or (15 ml) beer to make a workable dough. Form into a ball. Oil a large bowl. Place the dough in the bowl and cover

with a towel. Let rise in a warm place for 1 1/2 to 2 hours, or until doubled.

Evenly divide the dough into 8 pieces. On a floured surface, roll each into a 6-inch (15-cm) round. Scoop 1/2 cup (102 g) filling into the center and fold the sides in to seal. Pat the bun into a round and place seam-side down on a baking sheet. Repeat with the remaining dough. Let rise, covered with a towel, for 30 minutes.

Preheat the oven to 350°F (180°C, or gas mark 4).

Bake the buns for 30 minutes, or until golden. Brush with the butter. Transfer to a rack to cool.

Yield: 8 Bierocks

ALMO-CADO SANDWICHES

This recipe puts the oft-ignored beet in the spotlight. This earthy sandwich is more substantial and delicious thanks to the healthy fats in the almond butter and avocado.

6 ounces (170 g) raw beet, peeled and grated or shredded
1 tablespoon (15 ml) seasoned rice vinegar
2 teaspoons orange juice
1 small clove garlic, pressed
Salt, to taste
Black pepper, to taste
1 medium ripe avocado, halved, pitted, and peeled
1 tablespoon (15 ml) orange muscat champagne vinegar
⅓ cup (80 g) toasted, crunchy, salted almond butter
4 large slices whole-grain bread
⅓ cup (13 g) micro greens
⅓ cup (17 g) onion sprouts

Squeeze the liquid out of the grated beets if needed.

In a medium bowl, combine the beets with the rice vinegar, juice, garlic, and salt and pepper to taste.

Cut the avocado into thin slices and gently rub it with the muscat vinegar.

Spread 1 ½ tablespoons (24 g) almond butter on each slice of bread to cover. Place the greens and sprouts on two slices, reserving some. Arrange half of the beets on top of each, along with half of the avocado and the remaining greens and sprouts. Top with the other slices of bread.

Yield: 2 sandwiches

FROM RUSSIA WITH LOVE
These flavors blend together in perfect harmony.

FOR THE TEMPEH:
1½ cups (355 ml) vegetable broth
2 small pickled beets
⅓ cup (50 g) minced shallot
1 tablespoon plus 1 teaspoon (20 ml) tamari
1 tablespoon plus 1 teaspoon (20 ml) apple cider vinegar
1 tablespoon (15 ml) liquid smoke
1 teaspoon agave nectar
½ teaspoon salt
½ teaspoon black pepper
2 packages (8 ounces, or 227 g each) tempeh, each
  halved lengthwise, then across to make 8 patties

FOR THE SPREAD:
¼ cup plus 2 tablespoons (80 g) nondairy sour cream
¼ cup (60 ml) dill pickle juice
1 tablespoon plus 1 teaspoon (20 g) horseradish
2 teaspoons Dijon mustard
1 teaspoon dried dill
1 teaspoon agave nectar
½ teaspoon black pepper
¼ cup (40 g) minced onion
¼ cup (60 g) minced dill pickle

FOR THE SANDWICHES:
1 tablespoon (15 ml) canola oil
2 cups (284 g) sauerkraut, drained
1 teaspoon caraway seeds
½ teaspoon smoked paprika
½ teaspoon black pepper
¼ cup (56 g) nondairy butter
16 slices pumpernickel or rye bread, 4 inches (10 cm)
  wide

To make the tempeh: In a blender, blend the broth, beets, shallot, tamari, vinegar, liquid smoke, agave, salt, and pepper until smooth. Pour into a 9 x 13-inch (23 x 33-cm) pan. Add the tempeh and turn to coat. Marinate in the fridge for at least 1 hour.

To make the spread: In a small bowl, stir all of the ingredients together. Refrigerate in an airtight container.

To make the sandwiches: In a large skillet, heat the oil over medium-high heat. Drain the tempeh. Sauté it for 5 minutes, or until blackened. Turn and cook the other side for 4 minutes.

In a medium saucepan warm the sauerkraut, caraway, paprika, and pepper over medium heat. Preheat a panini press fitted with smooth plates on high.

Butter the bread. Smear 1 tablespoon (25 g) of the spread on the unbuttered sides of 8 slices. Place 1 tempeh patty on each slice. Top with ¼ cup (36 g) of the sauerkraut mixture. Smear the remaining spread on the remaining 8 slices. Put the tops on, buttered sides out. With the grill

open, cook for 4 to 5 minutes, or until golden. Turn and cook the other side for 3 to 4 minutes.

Yield: 8 sandwiches

DOUBLE-DECKER DELUXE
With three slices of bread, the filling stays hot while the vegetables stay cool. Marinate the seitan ahead of time, and you can have dinner on the table in minutes.

FOR THE SAUCE:
¼ cup (34 g) cashews, soaked in water for 1 hour, then
  rinsed and drained
3 tablespoons (45 ml) vegetable broth
1 tablespoon (15 ml) red wine vinegar
1 tablespoon (15 ml) lemon juice
1 tablespoon (10 g) minced shallot
1 teaspoon harissa, to taste
¼ teaspoon agave nectar
Generous pinch of black pepper
2 teaspoons minced fresh parsley

FOR THE SEITAN:
¼ cup (60 ml) vegetable broth
3 tablespoons (45 ml) brewed coffee
1 clove garlic, minced
¼ teaspoon salt
12 ounces (340 g) Moo-Free Seitan (See page 88), thinly
  sliced
2 teaspoons olive oil

FOR THE SANDWICHES:
¼ cup (56 g) nondairy butter, softened
12 slices sandwich bread
2 tablespoons (18 g) minced pepperoncinis, patted dry
1 green bell pepper, seeded and cut into strips
2 thin slices red onion, cut into half-moons, separated
2 teaspoons Dijon mustard
Lettuce leaves
1 tomato, thinly sliced
2 dill pickles, thinly sliced and patted dry

To make the sauce: In a blender, process the cashews, broth, vinegar, juice, shallot, harissa, agave, and pepper until smooth. Stir in the parsley. Refrigerate in an airtight container until ready to use.

To make the seitan: In an 8 x 12-inch (20 x 30-cm) pan, combine the broth, coffee, garlic, and salt. Add the seitan and toss to coat. Marinate in the fridge for at least 1 hour.

In a large skillet, heat the oil over medium heat. Drain the seitan, reserving the marinade. Cook until lightly browned, about 5 minutes, scraping up any stuck bits. Add the marinade and cook for 5 minutes, or until the liquid has been absorbed.

For the sandwiches: Preheat a panini press on high.

Butter one side of all the bread slices. Grill 4 slices of bread in the closed press until golden, 4 minutes. Transfer to a cooling rack. On the unbuttered side of each of 4 other slices, spread 1 tablespoon (15 ml) of the sauce. Divide the seitan evenly among them, topping with the pepperoncinis, pepper, and onion. Spread the remaining sauce evenly on the unbuttered side of the 4 remaining slices. Place the sandwiches buttered sides out on the panini press. Close and grill until golden, 4 minutes. To prepare the cold layer, spread mustard on the unbuttered sides of the first grilled bread. Layer with the lettuce, tomato, and pickles. When the grilled layer is done, carefully remove from the press and place on top of the cold layer. Turn the sandwich over, so the cold part is on the top.

Yield: 4 sandwiches

CHOW MEIN SANDWICHES
Serve this sandwich with a couple of baked (or grilled) tofu slices, for added protein on top of those carbs.

FOR THE PASTA:
8 cups (1.9 L) water
2 packages (4.4 ounces, or 125 g) vegan chow mein noodles
1 tablespoon (15 ml) peanut oil

FOR THE VEGETABLES:
1 tablespoon (15 ml) sesame oil
4 stalks center yellow part of celery heart, thinly sliced
1 green bell pepper, seeded and cut into thin strips
½ cup (80 g) thin half-moon slices red onion
4 cloves garlic, minced
1 cup (104 g) mung bean sprouts

FOR THE SAUCE:
¾ cup (180 ml) pineapple juice
¼ cup (60 ml) tamari
2 tablespoons (30 ml) apple cider vinegar
¼ cup (60 ml) vegetable broth
1 to 2 teaspoons sriracha, to taste
2 tablespoons (16 g) cornstarch
Salt, to taste

FOR THE SANDWICHES:
4 burger buns, halved and toasted

To make the pasta: In a large pot, bring the water to a boil, add the pasta, and cook, following the package instructions until just tender, about 4 minutes. Drain and cool completely.

Once the pasta is completely cooled, in a large skillet, heat the oil over medium heat. Divide the cold pasta into 4 nests. (They will be stiff and uncooperative.) Fry the nests as single units until golden brown and crispy, about 10 minutes, flipping once halfway through, reducing the heat if necessary so the pasta doesn't burn. Transfer to a wire rack.

To make the vegetables: In a skillet, heat the oil over medium-high heat. Add the celery, pepper, onion, and garlic. Cook for 2 to 3 minutes, or until the vegetables are crisp-tender. Stir in the sprouts and cook for 1 minute longer.

To make the sauce: In a medium saucepan, combine the juice, tamari, vinegar, broth, and sriracha.

In a small bowl, combine ¼ cup (60 ml) of this mixture with the cornstarch, stirring to dissolve.

Bring the pineapple juice mixture to a boil, lower the heat to medium-high, and cook for 2 minutes. Add the cornstarch slurry, stirring constantly. When the sauce is thick, remove from the heat, 1 to 2 minutes. Pour the sauce over the vegetables and stir to combine. Season with salt.

To make the sandwiches: Place a pasta nest on the bottom half of each burger bun. Top with a generous amount of the vegetables and sauce. Top with the other half of the bun.

Yield: 4 sandwiches

ZUCCWICH
Even if you're not a zucchini fan, you'll love this sandwich. You can store the spread in an airtight container in the fridge for up to 1 week.

FOR THE SPICY SPREAD:
6 ounces (170 g) drained firm silken tofu
2 tablespoons (30 ml) olive oil
1 tablespoon (15 ml) lime juice
½ teaspoon salt, to taste
Black pepper, to taste
¼ to ½ teaspoon cayenne pepper, to taste
½ teaspoon onion powder

FOR THE SANDWICHES:
1½ teaspoons olive oil
1½ teaspoons apple cider vinegar
Salt, to taste
Black pepper, to taste
5 ounces (150 g) zucchini (about 1 medium), trimmed and cut lengthwise into ⅓-inch (8-mm) slices
Four 4 x 3-inch (10 x 8-cm) panini rolls, lightly toasted and rubbed with a garlic clove
8 small hearts romaine lettuce leaves
4 roasted red bell pepper halves, drained and squeezed to remove extra moisture
4 marinated artichoke hearts, drained and squeezed to remove extra moisture

To make the spread: In a food processor, process all of the ingredients until smooth, scraping the sides with a rubber spatula as needed.

To make the sandwiches: In a medium bowl, combine the oil, vinegar, salt, and pepper. Brush the zucchini with the dressing.

Heat the grill or grill pan. Cook the zucchini for about 4 minutes per side, or until grill marks appear and the slices are tender.

Smear a heaping tablespoon (20 g) of the spread on each half of the rolls. Divide the zucchini slices equally among the sandwiches, then top each with 2 lettuce leaves, 1 pepper half, and 1 artichoke heart. Top with the other half of the rolls.

Yield: 4 sandwiches, 1 scant cup (215 g) spread

MUFFULETTA SANDWICH

This is an animal-friendly version of the New Orleans signature sandwich.

FOR THE SANDWICH:
1 Italian globe eggplant, cut into ⅓-inch (8 mm)-thick rounds
1 large zucchini, cut into ⅓-inch (8 mm)-thick rounds
1 large sweet onion, thinly sliced
2 red bell peppers, seeded and quartered
2 large tomatoes, sliced
Olive oil, for brushing

FOR THE OLIVE SALAD:
2 cups (200 g) green olives, pitted
½ cup (50 g) Kalamata olives, pitted
3 tablespoons (45 ml) brine from olives
2 tablespoons (17 g) capers
4 cloves garlic, thinly sliced
3 stalks celery, thinly sliced
1 tablespoon (4 g) finely chopped fresh parsley
1 tablespoon (3 g) dried oregano
1 teaspoon crushed red pepper flakes
⅓ cup (80 ml) olive oil
3 tablespoons (45 ml) red wine vinegar
3 green onions, finely chopped
Salt, to taste
Black pepper, to taste

1 round loaf hearty French or Italian bread

Preheat the oven to 425°F (220°C, or gas mark 7). Lightly oil a baking sheet.

To make the sandwiches, brush all sides of the eggplant, zucchini, onion, peppers, and tomatoes with oil. Arrange them on the prepared baking sheet. Roast in the oven for 5 minutes. Remove the tomatoes if done. Return the pan to the oven and roast for 15 to 30 minutes, or until browned and tender.

To make the olive salad: In a food processor, pulse the olives until finely chopped. Transfer to a large bowl. Add the olive brine, capers, garlic, celery, parsley, oregano, and red pepper. Toss to combine.

In a small bowl, whisk together the oil, vinegar, onions, and salt and pepper. Drizzle over the olive salad ingredients and stir to thoroughly combine, making sure all the vegetables are coated.

Cut the bread in half lengthwise and remove some of the soft center to provide room for the filling. Spoon the olive salad on both sides of the bread, sandwiching the layer of roasted vegetables in between.

For best results, wrap the sandwich tightly in foil and chill in the fridge for at least 1 hour and up to 3 hours before serving. Cut into 4 to 6 wedges.

Yield: 4 to 6 servings

NORI WRAPS WITH ORANGE CASHEW CREAM

Light but filling, flavorful but simple, these wraps are a favorite summertime dish. Serve as a wrap or use a sharp serrated knife to cut into 1½-inch (3.8 cm) rounds.

FOR THE ORANGE CASHEW CREAM:
1 cup (150 g) raw cashews
½ to ¾ cup (120 to 175 ml) orange juice
1 to 2 tablespoons (15 to 30 ml) tamari soy sauce

FOR THE WRAPS:
4 nori sheets (found in the Asian section of a grocery store)
2 carrots, grated or shredded
1 medium beet, grated
¼ head red or green cabbage, shredded
¼ cup (12 g) alfalfa sprouts
2 avocados, sliced or mashed
Salt, for sprinkling
Black sesame seeds, for garnish

To make the cashew cream: In a blender, process the cashews, ½ cup (120 ml) of the juice, and tamari until you have a creamy consistency. Thin with more juice, if needed. Transfer to a bowl.

To make the wraps: Place a nori sheet on a cutting board. Leaving a 1-inch (2.5 cm) border at each edge of the nori sheet, place a thin layer of carrot, beet, cabbage, and sprouts on top. Place the avocado in a horizontal line across the middle of the shredded veggies. Repeat with the orange cashew cream. Sprinkle on the salt. Working from the bottom, roll up the nori like a fat cigar, tucking in the veggies as you roll upward. Seal the "seam" with a little water. Repeat with the remaining ingredients to make 4 wraps. Sprinkle with the seeds.

Yield: 4 wraps, ¾ cup (270 g) dressing

TASTE OF TUSCANY
Garlic toasted bread gives these sandwiches a savory crunch. To make the sandwich a little heartier, add some Gobbler Slices. (See page 85.)

FOR THE ROASTED TOMATOES:
8 Roma tomatoes, quartered and seeded
1 tablespoon (15 ml) olive oil
1 teaspoon dried Italian seasoning blend
3 large cloves garlic, thickly sliced
Generous pinch of salt
Generous pinch of black pepper

FOR THE SPREAD:
¼ cup plus 2 tablespoons (84 g) vegan mayonnaise
Reserved roasted garlic from tomatoes (above)
2 tablespoons (13 g) minced Kalamata olives
2 tablespoons (13 g) minced green olives
2 teaspoons drained capers
Black pepper, to taste

FOR THE SANDWICHES:
¼ cup (56 g) nondairy butter, softened
¾ teaspoon garlic salt
8 slices Italian bread
1 cup (30 g) baby spinach
1 green bell pepper, seeded and cut into thin strips
4 thin slices red onion, separated into rings
Handful fresh basil leaves

To make the roasted tomatoes: Preheat the oven to 450°F (230°C, or gas mark 8).
   On a large rimmed baking sheet, combine all of the ingredients. Roast for 15 minutes, or until the tomatoes have a few charred spots. Remove from the oven, let cool, reserve the garlic for the spread, and slip off the tomato skins.

To make the spread: In a blender, combine the mayonnaise and the reserved garlic until smooth. Stir in the remaining ingredients.

To make the sandwiches: Preheat a panini press fitted with smooth plates on high.
   In a small bowl, combine the butter and garlic salt. Spread the outside of the bread slices with the garlic butter. Divide the mayonnaise spread evenly on the inside of the

slices. Layer on the spinach, tomatoes, pepper, onion, and basil. Top with the remaining bread slices, buttered sides out. Grill with the press open for 2 to 3 minutes, or until golden. Turn and cook the other side for 2 to 3 minutes. Cut in half on the diagonal.

Yield: 4 sandwiches

FRENCH TOFU SALAD WITH GRAPES
This is a perfect picnic sandwich. It pairs wonderfully with a dry white vegan wine.

FOR THE TOFU SALAD:
1 teaspoon canola oil, if needed
1 pound (454 g) extra-firm tofu, drained, pressed, and
   cut into ½-inch (1.3-cm) cubes
1 teaspoon tamari
¼ cup (56 g) vegan mayonnaise
¼ cup (37 g) quartered seedless green grapes
2 tablespoons (20 g) minced shallot
1 tablespoon (15 g) minced celery
1 tablespoon (15 ml) white wine vinegar
1 tablespoon (7 g) slivered almonds, toasted
1 teaspoon minced fresh chives
½ teaspoon Dijon mustard
½ teaspoon minced fresh thyme
½ teaspoon minced fresh parsley
¼ teaspoon dried tarragon, crumbled
¼ teaspoon dried herbes de Provence
Salt, to taste
Black pepper, to taste

FOR THE SANDWICHES:
1 cup (20 g) arugula
One 16-inch (40-cm) baguette, halved lengthwise

To make the tofu salad: Heat a large cast-iron skillet over medium heat. If the skillet is well seasoned, no oil is needed. If it isn't, add the canola oil. Add the tofu and cook, pressing down with a spatula and stirring, for 7 to 8 minutes, or until lightly golden and firmer. Remove from the heat and add the tamari. Transfer to a medium bowl. Add all of the remaining ingredients and season to taste. Cover and refrigerate for 1 hour.

To make the sandwiches: Place the arugula on the bottom of the baguette. Spread the tofu salad evenly over the arugula and top with the other half of the bread. Cut into 4 pieces.

Yield: 4 sandwiches

TOFU POMEGRANATE POCKETS

Savory tofu bits combine with pomegranate to make a palate-pleasing sandwich. The pomegranate adds texture and a tart sweetness, while the ume plum vinegar brings it all together.

FOR THE TOFU BITES:
1 pound (454 g) extra-firm tofu, drained, pressed, and cut into ½-inch (1.3-cm) cubes
2 tablespoons (30 ml) tamari
1½ teaspoons liquid smoke, divided
1 teaspoon maple syrup
½ teaspoon onion powder
½ teaspoon salt
¼ teaspoon black pepper

FOR THE DRESSING:
½ cup (69 g) cashews, soaked in water for 1 hour, then rinsed and drained
¼ cup plus 2 tablespoons (90) apple juice
1 tablespoon plus 1 teaspoon (20 ml) ume plum vinegar

FOR THE SANDWICHES:
4 cups (120 g) chopped baby spinach
¼ cup (40 g) minced red onion
Two 8-inch (20-cm) pita breads, halved
1 small cucumber, sliced
½ cup (91 g) pomegranate seeds

To make the tofu: Preheat the oven to 400°F (200°C, or gas mark 6). Spray an 8 x 11-inch (20 x 28-cm) pan with nonstick cooking spray.

In the prepared pan, combine the tofu, tamari, 1 teaspoon of the liquid smoke, syrup, onion powder, salt, and pepper. Stir to coat. Bake for 20 minutes, stirring once halfway though. When browned, remove from the oven and add the remaining ½ teaspoon liquid smoke. Let cool.

To make the dressing: In a blender, blend all of the ingredients until completely smooth.

To make the sandwiches: In a bowl, combine the spinach, onion, and half of the dressing. Toss to coat. Fill the pockets evenly with the salad and then layer in the cucumber. Fill evenly with the tofu and sprinkle each with 2 tablespoons (23 g) of the pomegranate seeds. Drizzle with the remaining dressing. Cut each pocket in half.

Yield: 4 half pockets

KATI ROLLS

If you're pressed for time or energy, you can buy ready-made vegan paratha, chapati, or roti at most international markets.

FOR THE CHAPATIS:
2 cups (240 g) whole wheat flour
2 cups (250 g) all-purpose flour
2 teaspoons sugar
1½ teaspoons salt
Black pepper, to taste
¼ cup (60 ml) olive oil
2 cups (470 ml) unsweetened plain nondairy milk, warmed, as needed

FOR THE FILLING:
2 tablespoons (30 ml) peanut oil
2 small potatoes, diced
½ cup (80 g) chopped green onion
3 medium tomatoes, diced
1 cup (149 g) diced red bell pepper
2 cloves garlic, pressed
1 to 2 teaspoons grated fresh ginger
1 teaspoon garam masala
½ teaspoon ground coriander
½ teaspoon ground cumin
¼ teaspoon turmeric
¼ to ½ teaspoon cayenne pepper, to taste (optional)
8 ounces (227 g) super-firm tofu, cut into ⅓-inch (8-mm) cubes
¼ cup (60 ml) water
Salt, to taste
Black pepper, to taste
Chutney, for serving (optional)

To make the chapatis: In a large bowl, combine the flours, sugar, salt, and pepper to taste. Add the oil. Add the milk a little at a time, as needed. Knead until the dough is soft and smooth. Let rest for 15 minutes. Divide the dough into 16 portions. On a lightly floured surface, roll them out thinly (like tortillas).

Lightly coat a griddle with nonstick cooking spray, preheat to medium-high, and cook each chapati until brown spots form, about 1 to 2 minutes per side. Stack each chapati on a plate, while cooking the rest.

To make the filling: In a large skillet, heat the oil over medium heat. Cook the potatoes until barely tender, about 8 minutes. Add the onion, tomatoes, and pepper, and cook until just tender, about 4 minutes. Add the garlic, ginger, and spices and cook for 1 minute longer.

Add the tofu and brown for about 6 minutes. Add the water, salt, and pepper and cook for about 4 minutes, or until the water has been absorbed.

Place one chapati on a plate, spread ¼ cup (48 g) of the filling in a line down the center, and fold the chapati over the filling. (Wrap the ends in foil for a less messy eating experience.) Serve with the chutney, if using.

Yield: 16 rolls

SEITAN SANDWICH WITH FRIED PICKLES

With fried pickles on a sandwich, how wrong can it be? Some of the best sandwiches are a little messy, so be prepared.

FOR THE SEITAN:
1 pound (454 g) Moo-Free Seitan (see page 88), thinly sliced
½ cup (120 ml) dry red wine
½ teaspoon black pepper
½ teaspoon smoked salt

FOR THE BARBECUED ONIONS:
1 teaspoon olive oil
1¼ cups (200 g) thinly sliced onion
3 tablespoons (48 g) barbecue sauce

FOR THE DRESSING:
⅓ cup (75 g) vegan mayonnaise
1 tablespoon (15 g) mustard
2 teaspoons hot sauce
2 teaspoons white wine vinegar

FOR THE FRIED PICKLES:
1¼ cups (194 g) dill pickles, cut into ½-inch (1.3-cm) rounds and patted dry
6 tablespoons (48 g) all-purpose flour, divided
Canola oil, for cooking
½ cup (120 ml) nondairy milk
½ teaspoon baking powder
¼ teaspoon smoked paprika

FOR THE SANDWICHES:
1 baguette, 20 inches (50 cm) long, halved lengthwise, some of the inside removed
2 cups (140 g) shredded lettuce
1 large tomato, sliced

To make the seitan: Preheat the oven to 400°F (200°C, or gas mark 6).

In a 9 x 13-inch (23 x 33-cm) pan, combine the seitan, wine, pepper, and salt. Bake for 10 minutes, or until the liquid has evaporated.

To make the onions: In a large skillet, heat the oil over medium heat. Cook the onion, stirring, for 10 minutes, or until softened. Stir in the sauce. Cook for 2 minutes longer. Keep warm.

To make the dressing: In a small bowl, mix all of the ingredients together until smooth.

To make the fried pickles: Line a plate with paper towels. In a medium bowl, toss the pickles with 1 tablespoon (8 g) of the flour.

In a large skillet, heat ¼ inch (6 mm) of the oil over medium-high heat.

In a pie plate, stir together the milk, remaining 5

tablespoons (40 g) flour, baking powder, and paprika. Working in batches, dip the floured pickles into the batter, and then place in the skillet. Cook for 3 minutes, or until golden. Turn and cook the other side for 2 minutes. Transfer to the prepared plate to drain.

To make the sandwiches: Spread the dressing evenly on both sides of the bread. Layer with the bottom baguette half, seitan, onions, pickles, lettuce, tomato, and top baguette half. Cut into 4 pieces.

Yield: 4 sandwiches

TEMPEH ARUGULA CAESAR WRAPS

This sandwich features the best of Caesar salad. You can store the dressing in an airtight container in the fridge for up to 1 week.

FOR THE SALAD DRESSING:
¼ cup (34 g) cashews, soaked in water for 1 hour, then rinsed and drained
2 tablespoons (30 ml) capers, with brine
2 tablespoons (30 ml) red wine vinegar
2 tablespoons (30 ml) nondairy milk
2 tablespoons (30 ml) olive oil
1 tablespoon plus 1 teaspoon (20 ml) lemon juice
2 cloves garlic, minced
2 teaspoons nutritional yeast
½ teaspoon agave nectar
½ teaspoon black pepper
1 teaspoon minced chives

FOR THE TEMPEH AND SANDWICHES:
1 pound (454 g) tempeh, steamed and cut into ½-inch (1.3-cm) slices
2 tablespoons (30 ml) tamari
Canola oil, for frying
½ teaspoon salt
¼ teaspoon black pepper
4 cups (80 g) chopped arugula
2 cups (94 g) chopped romaine
2 cups (360 g) chopped roasted red bell pepper
½ cup (80 g) minced red onion
Four 10-inch (25-cm) flour tortillas
2 tablespoons (9 g) sunflower seeds
1 tomato, sliced

To make the salad dressing: In a blender, combine the cashews, capers and brine, vinegar, milk, oil, juice, garlic, yeast, agave, and pepper until smooth. Stir in the chives.

To make the tempeh: On a large baking sheet, combine the tempeh with the tamari. Let sit for 30 minutes, or until the tamari has been absorbed.

Preheat the oven to 250°F (120°C, or gas mark ½). Line a

baking sheet with a paper towel.

In a large cast-iron skillet, heat ¼ inch (6 mm) of oil over medium heat. In batches, panfry the tempeh, turning once, for 10 minutes, or until golden. Transfer to the baking sheet and keep warm in the oven. When all of the tempeh is cooked, season with the salt and pepper.

In a large bowl, combine the arugula, romaine, pepper, and onion. Add the dressing and toss to coat.

To make the sandwiches: Divide the tempeh evenly among the 4 tortillas. Top each with one-fourth of the salad mixture, seeds, and tomato. Fold the ends in and roll.

Yield: 4 wraps

UNFISHWICH
Kelp, a seaweed that is packed with vitamins and minerals, mimics the flavor of the fish sticks.

FOR THE TARTAR SAUCE:
½ cup (120 g) miso dressing (See page 101.)
1 to 2 teaspoons lemon juice, to taste
½ teaspoon minced capers
1 teaspoon Dijon mustard
1 teaspoon minced shallot
Few drops of hot sauce

FOR THE FISH STICKS:
8 ounces (227 g) tempeh
2 tablespoons plus 2 teaspoons (40 ml) lemon juice, divided
⅓ cup plus ¼ cup (140 ml) unsweetened plain nondairy milk, divided
1 teaspoon kelp powder
1 teaspoon onion powder
2 cloves garlic, pressed
1 teaspoon paprika
½ teaspoon salt, plus a pinch
½ teaspoon dried dill
⅓ cup (42 g) arrowroot powder
1 tablespoon (2 g) Old Bay seasoning, divided
¾ cup (60 g) bread crumbs
3 tablespoons (42 g) nondairy butter, melted
¼ teaspoon cayenne pepper

FOR THE SANDWICHES:
3 sub sandwich rolls, 6 inches (15 cm) long, halved and toasted
¾ cup (78 g) thinly sliced cucumber
2 small tomatoes, thinly sliced

To make the tartar sauce: In a medium bowl, combine all of the ingredients. Store in an airtight container in the fridge until ready to use.

To make the fish sticks: Cut the tempeh widthwise into 9 sticks.

In a shallow dish, combine 2 tablespoons (30 ml) of the lemon juice, ⅓ cup of the (80 ml) milk, kelp powder, onion powder, garlic, paprika, ½ teaspoon of the salt, and dill. Add the tempeh. Marinate for 1 hour in the fridge.

Preheat the oven to 375°F (190°C, or gas mark 5). Line a baking sheet with parchment.

On a shallow plate, combine the arrowroot powder with 2 teaspoons of the Old Bay. On another plate, place the bread crumbs. Remove the tempeh from the marinade. Thin out the marinade by adding the remaining ¼ cup (60 ml) milk.

Dip the sticks into the arrowroot, shaking off any excess. Dip the sticks into the marinade, shaking off any excess. Coat with the bread crumbs. Place on the prepared baking sheet. Lightly coat all sides with nonstick cooking spray. Bake for 10 minutes.

In a small bowl, combine the butter, 2 teaspoons lemon juice, cayenne, 1 teaspoon Old Bay, and pinch of salt.

To assemble the sandwiches: Spread 2 tablespoons of the (30 ml) tartar sauce on each side of the rolls. Divide the cucumber and tomatoes among the sandwiches. Add 3 sticks to each sandwich.

Yield: 3 sandwiches

SOY-RIPAN SANDWICHES
The classic choripán sandwich features chorizo, but soyrizo is a great substitute for the traditional spicy sausage.

½ cup (30 g) fresh parsley
3 tablespoons (12 g) fresh oregano
¼ cup (60 ml) plus 1 tablespoon (15 ml) olive oil, divided
1 teaspoon salt
2 tablespoons (28 ml) lime juice
Paprika, to taste
1 to 2 tablespoons (15 to 28 ml) water to thin
½ cup (57 g) soyrizo, crumbled
2 thick slices bread
Dill relish
Vegan mayonnaise

In a food processor, whirl the parsley, oregano, ¼ cup (60 ml) of the oil, salt, juice, paprika, and water until smooth like pesto, to make a chimichurri sauce.

In a small frying pan, heat the remaining 1 tablespoon (15 ml) oil over medium-high heat, about 30 seconds. Cook the soyrizo, stirring often, just to brown, about 5 to 7 minutes.

Spread the chimichurri sauce generously on top of 1 slice of bread. Top with the soyrizo and dill relish. Cover the other slice of bread with mayonnaise and place atop the relish.

Yield: 1 sandwich

SUSHI SOY WRAPS

If sushi grew up and turned into a full-fledged sandwich, this would be it! Crispy tempura is accented by pickled vegetables, creamy avocado, and sushi rice.

FOR THE RICE:
1 cup (145 g) prepared sushi rice
¾ cup (180 ml) water
1 tablespoon (15 ml) seasoned rice vinegar
½ teaspoon tamari
¼ teaspoon toasted sesame oil
Pinch of sugar

FOR THE VEGETABLES:
1½ cups (225 g) shredded napa cabbage
½ cup (48 g) grated daikon radish
½ cup (50 g) chopped green onion
2 teaspoons ume plum vinegar
½ teaspoon grated fresh ginger

FOR THE DIPPING SAUCE:
2 tablespoons (30 ml) mirin
½ teaspoon sriracha
½ teaspoon tamari
½ teaspoon ume plum vinegar

FOR THE TEMPURA:
¾ cup (94 g) all-purpose flour
½ teaspoon salt
¼ teaspoon baking powder
⅔ cup (160 ml) sparkling water, chilled
Canola oil, for cooking
6 asparagus stalks, halved
1 large portobello mushroom cap, stemmed, gilled, and cut into ½-inch (1.3-cm) slices

FOR THE WRAPS:
4 soy wraps
½ avocado, peeled, pitted, and sliced

To make the rice: Combine the rice and water and cook according to the package directions. Scoop it into a bowl.
 In a small bowl, combine the vinegar, tamari, oil, and sugar. Pour over the rice and gently fluff. Let cool.

To make the vegetables: In a medium bowl, stir all of the ingredients together.

To make the dipping sauce: In a small bowl, combine all of the ingredients.

To make the tempura: In a deep bowl, whisk the flour, salt, and baking powder together. Whisk in the water. The mixture should be thick enough to coat the asparagus and mushroom without dripping off. If needed, add 1 tablespoon (8 g) flour or (15 ml) sparkling water.
 Line a baking sheet with paper towels.
 In a deep, heavy-bottomed saucepan, heat 1 to 2 inches

(2.5 to 5 cm) oil over medium-high heat. (Or heat 3 to 4 inches (7.5 to 10 cm) oil in a deep fryer to medium-high heat.) Working in batches, dip the vegetables in the batter to coat, slide them into the oil, and fry until golden, 4 to 5 minutes. (Do not crowd the fryer or the temperature of the oil will drop. The correct oil temperature should cause a coated vegetable to bubble.) Batter and fry all the vegetables and transfer them to the baking sheet to drain.

To make the wraps: Place the wraps on a cutting board. In the center, spread ¼ cup (46 g) of the rice and ¼ cup (20 g) of the vegetables. Top evenly with the tempura and avocado. Fold two opposite corners in and roll the wrap closed. Serve with the dipping sauce.

Yield: 4 wraps

PROTEIN-HAPPY QUINOA WRAPS

These wraps are super-packed with protein, courtesy of the quinoa and beans

FOR THE TAPENADE:
½ cup (28 g) minced sun-dried tomatoes, not oil-packed
¼ cup (25 g) minced Kalamata olives
2 tablespoons (15 g) chopped capers
2 tablespoons (30 ml) olive oil
¼ teaspoon red pepper flakes

FOR THE FILLING:
1½ cups (355 ml) vegetable broth
½ cup (84 g) dry quinoa
¼ cup (30 g) packed golden raisins, optional
1 tablespoon (15 ml) apple cider vinegar
1 tablespoon (15 ml) lemon juice
1½ tablespoons (25 ml) olive oil
¼ teaspoon red pepper flakes
1½ tablespoons (15 g) minced red onion
1 clove garlic, minced
Salt, to taste
Black pepper, to taste
2 tablespoons (15 g) roasted salted pepitas
¾ cup (197 g) cooked cannellini beans
2 tablespoons (8 g) chopped fresh parsley
1 tablespoon (2 g) minced fresh basil

FOR THE WRAPS:
Four 10-inch (25-cm) flour tortillas
1 red bell pepper, seeded and cut into strips
1 small cucumber, cut into strips

To make the tapenade: In a food processor, pulse all of the ingredients a few times, but leave it chunky. Chill in the fridge for at least 2 hours.

To make the filling: In a medium pot, bring the broth to a

17 From Russia with Love; 18 Double-Decker Deluxe; 19 Chow Mein Sandwiches; 20 Zuccwich; 21 Muffuletta Sandwich; 22 Nori Wraps with Orange Cashew Cream; 23 Taste of Tuscany; 24 French Tofu Salad with Grapes

25 Tofu Pomegranate Pockets; 26 Kati Rolls; 27 Seitan Sandwich with Fried Pickles; 28 Tempeh Arugula Caesar Wraps; 29 Unfish-wich; 30 Soy-Ripan Sandwiches; 31 Sushi Soy Wraps; 32 Protein-Happy Quinoa Wraps

boil. Cook the quinoa for 8 minutes. Add the raisins, if using, and cook for 2 to 4 minutes longer, or until the quinoa is cooked and the telltale tail appears. Drain in a fine-mesh sieve. Set aside to cool completely.

In a large bowl, combine the vinegar, juice, oil, red pepper, onion, garlic, salt, pepper, pepitas, and beans. Add the quinoa mixture, parsley, and basil to the dressing and stir until well coated.

To make the wraps: In the middle of each tortilla, spread 3 tablespoons (25 g) of the tapenade. Top with a generous ½ cup (120 g) of the filling. Divide the pepper and cucumber among the tortillas. Fold the ends in and roll closed.

Yield: 4 wraps, generous ¾ cup (100 g) tapenade

MANGO BASIL WRAPS
Store the extra coconut spread in an airtight container in the fridge.

FOR THE COCONUT SPREAD:
1 package (7 ounces, or 200 g) creamed coconut (See page 12)
1 cup (235 ml) warm water
2 tablespoons (30 ml) lemon juice
2 teaspoons onion powder
2 cloves garlic
½ teaspoon salt
½ teaspoon red pepper flakes
1 teaspoon ground ginger
½ teaspoon black pepper

FOR THE WRAPS:
Six 10-inch (25-cm) flour tortillas
2 ounces (57 g) favorite sprouts
1 large English cucumber, thinly sliced
1 large, not overly ripe mango, peeled, pitted, and cubed
3 small avocados, peeled, pitted, and sliced, optional
24 fresh basil leaves
Salt, to taste
Black pepper, to taste
6 tablespoons (6 g) chopped fresh cilantro

To make the coconut spread: In a blender, combine all of the ingredients until smooth. Chill for 1 to 2 hours, stirring occasionally. As it chills, it will thicken. If the spread is too thick, microwave it for a few seconds or leave it at room temperature until it is spreadable.

To make the wraps: Smear 2 tablespoons (50 g) of the Coconut Spread in the center of each tortilla. Place a generous handful of sprouts on top, followed by ⅓ cup (34 g) cucumber, ¼ cup (41 g) mango, the slices of ½ an avocado, and 4 basil leaves. Season with salt and pepper. Sprinkle each with 1 tablespoon (1 g) cilantro. Wrap tightly.

Yield: 6 wraps, 2 cups (800 g) spread

FAUX-LAFEL
Instead of frying this falafel, bake them for a lower-fat option. They are full of flavor. With the parts packed individually, this sandwich is ideal for on-the-go eating.

FOR THE FALAFEL:
2 cans (15 ounces, or 425 g each) chickpeas, drained and rinsed
¼ cup (40 g) minced onion
¼ cup (60 ml) lemon juice
4 cloves garlic, minced
2 tablespoons (8 g) minced fresh parsley
2 teaspoons ground cumin
2 teaspoons ground coriander
2 teaspoons toasted sesame oil
¾ to 1 teaspoon red pepper flakes, to taste
½ teaspoon salt
Pinch of black pepper
2 teaspoons baking powder
2 to 3 tablespoons (16 to 24 g) all-purpose flour
1 tablespoon (15 ml) olive oil

FOR THE TAHINI SAUCE:
¼ cup (32 g) cashews, soaked in water for 1 hour, drained and rinsed
3 to 4 tablespoons (45 to 60 ml) nondairy milk
3 tablespoons (45 ml) lemon juice
1 tablespoon (16 g) tahini
1 tablespoon (15 ml) apple cider vinegar
1 clove garlic, minced
½ teaspoon harissa
¼ teaspoon salt
Pinch of white pepper
1 teaspoon fresh minced chives

FOR THE SANDWICHES:
Four 8-inch (20 cm) whole wheat pita breads, halved across
6 cups (420 g) shredded lettuce
2 large tomatoes, cut into ¼-inch (6-mm) slices
1 medium cucumber, cut into ⅛-inch (3-mm) slices

To make the falafel: Preheat the oven to 400°F (200°C, or gas mark 6). Oil a large baking sheet.

In a medium bowl, combine the chickpeas, onion, juice, garlic, parsley, cumin, coriander, sesame oil, red pepper, salt, and pepper. Using a fork, mash to break the chickpeas into chunks. Add the baking powder and 2 tablespoons (16 g) of the flour. Mix well. Form a heaping tablespoon of the mixture into a patty 2 inches (5 cm) wide and ½ inch (1.3 cm) thick. If the patty does not hold together, add the remaining 1 tablespoon (8 g) flour. Place the patty on the prepared baking sheet. Repeat with the remaining dough to make 20 patties. Brush the patties with the olive oil. Bake for 15 minutes, or until the bottoms are golden. Turn and cook the other side for 8 minutes, or until golden.

To make the tahini sauce: In a blender, process the cashews, milk, juice, tahini, vinegar, garlic, harissa, salt, and pepper until smooth. Stir in the chives.

To make the sandwiches: Fill each pita pocket evenly with 5 of the falafel patties, lettuce, tomatoes, and cucumber. Drizzle the sauce over all.

Yield: 4 sandwiches

CROQUINOETTE WRAP PARTY
These little croquettes get beautifully crusty once you panfry them in sesame oil.

FOR THE MISO DRESSING:
4 ounces (113 g) drained firm silken tofu
3 tablespoons (24 g) white miso
3 tablespoons (45 ml) olive oil
3 tablespoons (45 ml) white balsamic vinegar
½ teaspoon black pepper
Smoked sea salt, to taste
1 clove garlic

FOR THE CROQUETTES:
1 can (15 ounces, or 425 g) chickpeas, drained and rinsed
2 tablespoons (32 g) creamy natural peanut butter
2 tablespoons (16 g) white miso
2 tablespoons (30 ml) lemon juice
2 tablespoons (15 g) nutritional yeast
2 cloves garlic, pressed
2 cups (370 g) cooked and cooled quinoa
¼ cup (20 g) bread crumbs
2 tablespoons (16 g) cornstarch
1 cup (150 g) grated zucchini
2 tablespoons (20 g) minced shallot
Salt, to taste
Black pepper, to taste
2 tablespoons (30 ml) toasted sesame oil, divided

FOR THE WRAPS:
1 English cucumber, halved lengthwise and cut into thin half-moons
Eight 8-inch (20 cm) flour tortillas
Sriracha, optional

To make the dressing: In a blender, combine all of the ingredients. Chill in an airtight container until ready to serve.

To make the croquettes: In a food processor, process the chickpeas, peanut butter, miso, juice, yeast, and garlic until smooth, stopping to scrape the sides of the bowl. Transfer to a large bowl and add the quinoa, bread crumbs, cornstarch, zucchini, shallot, salt, and pepper. Combine thoroughly without mashing too much. (The mixture will

look wet.) Cover the bowl and chill for 1 hour. Divide into 8 croquettes by scooping out a packed ⅓ cup (105 g) per croquette and shaping into a 3-inch (8-cm)-wide round.

In a large skillet, heat 1 tablespoon (15 ml) of the oil over medium-high heat. Cook the croquettes in batches for 6 minutes on each side, or until they get golden-brown, crispy crusts. Adjust the heat, if needed, and use the remaining tablespoon (15 ml) of oil if needed.

To make the wraps: Divide the cucumber evenly among the tortillas, drizzle the dressing on top, place a croquette on top, and fold the tortilla over. Add sriracha, if using.

Yield: 8 wraps, 1 cup (240 g) dressing

DAGWOOD'S SPECIAL SANDWICH
Thanks to author and blogger Nathan Kozuskanich for allowing us to use the "steam, then bake method" he features on his popular blog, Vegan Dad. You will need two long bamboo skewers, halved, to keep the sandwich stacked.

FOR THE SPREAD:
⅓ cup (75 g) vegan mayonnaise
2 tablespoons (30 g) yellow mustard
¼ teaspoon cayenne pepper, optional

FOR THE MUSHROOM TOMATO SLICES:
½ ounce (14 g) dried porcini mushrooms
1 cup (235 ml) boiling water
Broth, as needed
¼ cup (28 g) sun-dried tomatoes, not oil-packed
½ cup (91 g) cooked black-eyed peas
⅓ cup (55 g) chopped red onion
¼ cup (60 g) ketchup
¼ cup (60 ml) tamari
2 tablespoons (30 ml) olive oil
1 tablespoon (15 ml) liquid smoke
2 teaspoons smoked paprika
2 teaspoons onion powder
1 teaspoon ground coriander
1 teaspoon red pepper flakes
1 teaspoon garlic powder
1 teaspoon ground cumin
½ teaspoon white pepper
1¼ cups (180 g) vital wheat gluten, plus more if needed
¼ cup (30 g) nutritional yeast
¼ cup (32 g) soy flour
2 tablespoons (24 g) instant tapioca

FOR THE SANDWICHES:
6 slices sandwich bread, toasted
1 head romaine lettuce, torn into sandwich-size leaves
4 ounces (113 g) thin Mushroom Tomato Slices
4 ounces (113 g) thin Gobbler Slices (See page 85.)

8 ounces (227 g) tempeh bacon, cooked
1 green bell pepper, seeded and cut into rings
1 large tomato, sliced
3 thin slices red onion, cut into half-moons, separated
20 dill pickle slices
4 olives or small pickles

To make the spread: In a small bowl, mix all the ingredients together. Store in an airtight container in the fridge until ready to use.

To make the Mushroom Tomato Slices: Add the dried porcinis to the water and let soak for 30 minutes. Using a coffee filter, drain the mushrooms, reserving the liquid. Measure the liquid and add broth to make ⅔ cup (160 ml) liquid. Rinse the mushrooms well.

In a blender, combine the mushrooms, tomatoes, peas, onion, ketchup, tamari, oil, liquid smoke, paprika, onion powder, coriander, red pepper, garlic powder, cumin, and pepper. Add the reserved liquid and blend until smooth.

In a medium bowl, combine the gluten, yeast, flour, and tapioca. Pour the liquid into the dry ingredients and mix with a fork. Add an extra 1 tablespoon (15 ml) broth or (9 g) gluten if needed to make a soft, workable dough. Knead well, squeezing to combine all of the ingredients. Divide the mixture using two 12-inch (30.5-cm) pieces of foil. Form into 2 rolls about 5 inches (13 cm) long. Roll the foil around the mixture, twisting the ends to enclose the mixture.

Prepare a steamer. Steam the rolls for 1 hour 15 minutes. Preheat the oven to 350°F (180°C, or gas mark 4).

Place the steamed rolls on a baking sheet. Bake for 45 minutes. Let cool completely. Slice thinly, using a sharp, serrated knife and cutting in a seesaw motion. Wrap tightly in plastic and store in the fridge for up to 1 week or freeze for up to 2 months.

To make the sandwiches: Smear a generous 1 tablespoon (18 g) of the spread on each slice of bread. Divide the lettuce leaves evenly on 4 of the slices. Divide the Mushroom Tomato Slices, Gobbler Slices, and bacon evenly among the sandwiches. Top with the pepper, tomato, onion, and pickles. Put one topless stack on each one of the others. Top each stack with the 2 remaining slices of bread. Place 2 skewers through each sandwich and put an olive or a pickle on the skewer. Cut the sandwiches in half.

Yield: 4 sandwiches, 24 ounces (680 g) Mushroom Tomato Slices

THE PARTY MONSTER

Serve this stuffed loaf hot or at room temperature. Couple it with your favorite marinara sauce for dipping.

1 tablespoon (15 ml) olive oil
1 cup (160 g) chopped onion
2 cups (140 g) sliced mushrooms
¼ teaspoon dried oregano
¼ teaspoon dried thyme
Salt, to taste
Black pepper, to taste
1 recipe favorite bread dough
6 ounces (170 g) thin Mushroom Tomato Slices (See page 101.)
6 ounces (170 g) thin Gobbler Slices (See page 85.)
16 mild banana pepper rings

In a large skillet, heat the oil over medium-high heat. Cook the onion for 2 minutes. Add the mushrooms, oregano, and thyme. Cook for 5 minutes longer, or until the vegetables are softened. Season with salt and pepper. Let cool.

Prepare the dough and allow it to rise. Dump it onto a lightly floured work surface. Roll it into a 12 x 16-inch (30 x 40-cm) rectangle. With the short side across, on the center 6 inches (15 cm), layer half of the Mushroom Tomato and Gobbler Slices, all of the onion/mushroom mixture, the remaining Mushroom Tomato and Gobbler Slices, and the pepper rings. Leave a 1-inch (2.5 cm) strip of dough at the top and bottom without filling. Using a knife, make 6 to 8 cuts on each side of the filling, perpendicular to the filling. Make an equal number of cuts on each side. This is the part that will be braided. Starting at the top, fold an empty strip of dough over the end of the filling. Alternating sides, pull one strip from each side across the filling. Continue until you reach the last strips on each side. Fold the bottom in, and then finish the braid. Pat with your hands to help seal the strips closed.

Spray a baking sheet with nonstick cooking spray. Carefully transfer the dough to the sheet. Let rise, covered with a towel, for 30 minutes, or until nicely puffed.

Preheat the oven to 350°F (180°C, or gas mark 4).

Bake for 30 to 35 minutes, or until the bottom is browned. Transfer to a rack. Cool for a few minutes before cutting. Cut into six 2-inch (5-cm) strips.

Yield: 6 servings

PANINI WITH LEMON-BASIL PESTO

To mimic the appearance of a sandwich pressed in a panini maker, place a baking sheet, with a heavy can on top, on top of the sandwich as it cooks in the skillet. You can store the pesto tightly covered in the fridge for up to 2 days.

FOR THE PESTO:
2 cups (80 g) loosely packed fresh basil leaves
2 whole cloves garlic, peeled
¼ cup (35 g) pine nuts
Salt, to taste
2 tablespoons (30 ml) olive oil
1 to 2 teaspoons (5 to 10 ml) lemon juice

FOR THE PANINI:
2 medium roasted red bell peppers, cut lengthwise into
    slices
3 zucchini squash, sliced and roasted or grilled
1 medium red onion, sliced
1 or 2 medium tomatoes, sliced
1 ripe avocado, peeled, pitted, and sliced
8 large slices Italian bread
2 tablespoons (30 ml) balsamic vinegar
Salt, to taste
Black pepper, to taste
Olive oil

To make the pesto: In a food processor, combine the basil, garlic, nuts, and salt until smooth. Add the oil and juice and process until smooth.

To make the panini: Divide the peppers, squash, onion, tomatoes, and avocado evenly among 4 slices of bread. Drizzle each with vinegar, spread on about 2 tablespoons [30 g] of the pesto, and season with salt and pepper. Top each with the remaining bread, lightly brush outside with the oil, and press in a panini maker, until lightly browned and hot.

Yield: 4 panini

PEANUT BUTTER BANANA BACON SANDWICHES

Oh yes, we did. If you're in a pinch and prefer using pan-fried, ready-to-go tempeh bacon instead of the "fiberful" chickpea goodness here, it will work well, too.

FOR THE CHICKPEA BACON:
1 can (15 ounces, or 425 g) chickpeas, drained and rinsed
1 tablespoon (15 ml) maple syrup
1½ teaspoons apple cider vinegar
¼ teaspoon smoked paprika
½ teaspoon smoked sea salt
½ teaspoon onion powder
¼ teaspoon garlic powder
2 teaspoons to 1 tablespoon (10 to 15 ml) liquid smoke
1 tablespoon (15 ml) olive oil

FOR THE SANDWICHES:
½ cup (128 g) crunchy, unsweetened natural peanut
    butter
4 soft bread rolls, halved
2 small, just-ripe bananas, sliced

To make the Chickpea Bacon: Preheat the broiler.
    In a medium bowl, combine all of the ingredients. Spread them in a shallow, 8-inch (20-cm) baking dish, with the chickpeas in a single layer so they cook evenly. Broil for 8 minutes, stir, and broil for 6 to 8 minutes longer, checking every 2 minutes to make sure the chickpeas don't burn, or until the liquid has been absorbed and the chickpeas are crispy and dark golden brown.

To make the sandwiches: Spread 1 tablespoon (16 g) of the peanut butter on each slice of bread. Gently press down a generous ⅓ cup (90 g) of the chickpea bacon (or as much as will fit) into the peanut butter on 4 of the slices. Cover with the banana. Put the second peanut-buttered slice on top.
    Lightly coat a large skillet with nonstick cooking spray. Cook the sandwiches in batches on medium-low heat until golden brown and crispy, about 5 minutes on each side.
    (These are also great prepared in a closed panini press, for about 6 minutes in all. This will meld the ingredients together a little more than grilling the sandwich does.)

Yield: 4 sandwiches

HOT PEPPER TOASTWICHES

With a crisp crust and a creamy middle, this is a sweet and savory way to jump-start your taste buds. You can substitute whole wheat French bread and whole wheat pastry flour, if desired.

3 tablespoons (45 g) vegan cream cheese or Cashew Almond Spread (See page 46 [Fig and Nut Canapes])
16 slices (½-inch, or 1.3 cm, thick) stale French bread
3 tablespoons (60 g) hot pepper jelly
1 tart apple, cored, cut into thin slices
1½ cups (355 ml) unsweetened vegan milk, plus more if needed
2 teaspoons apple cider vinegar
1 tablespoon plus 1 teaspoon (10 g) nutritional yeast
1 tablespoon plus 1 teaspoon (16 g) Sucanat
¼ teaspoon ground cinnamon
1½ cups (188 g) all-purpose flour
2 teaspoons baking powder
High-heat neutral-flavored oil
1 to 2 tablespoons (20 to 40 g) blackberry jam
¼ cup (60 ml) maple syrup

Spread a generous 2 teaspoons of cream cheese on half of the bread slices. Spread a generous 2 teaspoons of jelly on each. Top with two or three apple slices and the remaining bread.

In a large shallow baking dish, combine the milk and vinegar. Stir in the yeast, Sucanat, cinnamon, flour, and baking powder. (The batter should be thick. Lumps are okay.) Add 1 tablespoon (8 g) extra flour if needed to thicken the batter or 1 tablespoon (15 ml) milk to thin it.

In a large skillet, heat ¼ inch (6 mm) of oil over medium-high heat. When it starts to ripple, reduce the heat to medium. In batches, dip the sandwiches in the batter, turning to coat them completely. Cook the sandwiches for 3 to 4 minutes until the bottoms are golden brown. Turn and cook the second side until golden. With tongs, turn the slices so that the filled edges of the bread also cook. Cut into halves.

In a small bowl, whisk the jam into the maple syrup. Serve on the side for dipping.

Yield: Makes 32 mini sandwiches

Hot Pepper Toastwiches

33 Mango Basil Wraps; 34 Faux-Lafel; 35 Croquinoette Wrap Party; 36 Dagwood's Special Sandwich;
37 The Party Monster; 38 Panini with Lemon-Basil Pesto; 39 Peanut Butter Banana Bacon Sandwiches

MAIN COURSES

See pages 108-109, 118-119, 130-131, 142-143, and 146-147 for main course recipe photos.

SIMPLE HOMEMADE PASTA

This is a simple pasta recipe. It's basic, and it's also gluten-free. Serve it with your favorite pasta sauce or simply dress with salt, extra-virgin olive oil, and some chopped herbs.

2 cups (277 g) superfine brown rice flour, plus more for kneading and rolling
1 teaspoon xanthan gum
1 teaspoon salt
1¼ cups (300 ml) water

Into a large bowl, sift together the flour, xanthan, and salt. Using a fork, stir in the water a little bit at a time to form a soft dough. Turn out onto a lightly (brown rice) floured surface. Knead about 2 to 3 tablespoons (14 to 21 g) flour into the dough until it is no longer sticky. Add just enough to make a slightly elastic dough.

Divide the dough in half. Pat each section with a touch more superfine brown rice flour on each side. Turn one section out onto a lightly floured safe cutting surface.

Using a lightly floured rolling pin, roll one section of dough into an 8 x 16-inch (20 x 40 cm) rectangle until the dough is about ⅛-inch (3 mm) thick. If the dough sticks to your rolling surface, add a touch more flour. (To get thinner noodles, roll out between two sheets of plastic wrap, making sure the dough is not sticky before doing so.)

Using a pizza cutter, cut the dough into long noodles, ¼-inch (6 mm) wide and 8-inches (20 cm) long. Individually remove the noodles from the surface. Delicately place them into a loose pile. Repeat with the other section of dough.

Bring at least 8 cups (1.9 L) lightly salted water to a boil in a pot. Once the water is at a rolling boil, drop in one pile of noodles, stirring gently to separate. Let the pasta cook for 3 minutes. Drain and rinse briefly under cold water. Repeat with the other pile of noodles.

Yield: 4 servings

COLD SESAME NOODLES

These noodles are best when dressed with sauce and eaten immediately because the sauce soaks into the noodles so quickly. To make it ahead, store the sauce and noodles separately.

16 ounces my tho noodles (flat, wide Asian rice noodles) or other long, wide rice noodles
2 cubes (2 teaspoons) vegetable bouillon
2 tablespoons (30 ml) Bragg's liquid aminos, plus extra to douse noodles
2 tablespoons (32 g) smooth peanut butter

3 tablespoons (45 ml) toasted sesame oil
2 tablespoons (30 ml) agave nectar
½ teaspoon turmeric
1 teaspoon cumin
1 teaspoon Chinese five-spice powder
1 teaspoon freshly grated ginger
¼ cup (25 g) chopped green onion
Toasted black sesame seeds
Chili garlic sauce

Cook the noodles according to the package directions, dissolving the bouillon cubes in the cooking water first. Once cooked, transfer the noodles to a colander and toss with cold water until they are easy to handle and any extra starch has been rinsed away. Drain and toss with liquid aminos, covering evenly until the noodles appear a golden brown all over.

In a separate bowl, combine the peanut butter and oil. Stir until smooth. Stir in the 2 tablespoons (30 ml) liquid aminos, agave, turmeric, cumin, five-spice, and ginger. Pour over the noodles. Toss until they are completely covered with a thin layer of sauce. Garnish with the onion and seeds. Stir in chili garlic sauce to taste. Refrigerate for about 30 minutes before serving, tossing occasionally to keep moist. Serve cold.

Yield: 6 servings

SPICY GOULASH

This spicy noodle dish is a fun twist on a common dinner. It's a great way to highlight the awesomeness that is soyrizo.

16 ounces (454 g) brown rice elbow noodles
1 tablespoon (15 ml) olive oil, plus more for drizzling
1 teaspoon salt, plus more for sprinkling
2 cups (300 g) chopped green bell pepper
1 Vidalia onion, diced
2 cloves garlic, minced
1 tablespoon (4 g) minced fresh oregano
1 tablespoon (2.5 g) minced fresh sage
1½ teaspoons fennel seeds
1 can (28 ounces, or 794 g) diced tomatoes, undrained
12 ounces (340 g) soyrizo
1 to 2 teaspoons crushed red pepper flakes
¼ teaspoon dried marjoram
⅔ cup (86 g) nutritional yeast

Cook the pasta according to the package directions. Drain. Drizzle with oil and salt lightly.

In a large frying pan, heat the 1 tablespoon (15 ml) oil. Sauté the pepper, onion, garlic, oregano, sage, and seeds until the vegetables are tender, about 10 minutes. Stir in the tomatoes, soyrizo, red pepper, 1 teaspoon salt, marjoram, and yeast. Simmer for about 5 minutes. Toss with the pasta.

Yield: 6 servings

STROGANOFF
This recipe holds great flavor, but it's animal-free!

¼ cup (60 ml) olive oil, divided
1 Vidalia onion, chopped
20 ounces (175 g) sliced cremini mushrooms
Salt, to taste
1 cup (235 ml) boiling water
2 beef-flavored bouillon cubes
1¾ cups (420 ml) canned full-fat coconut milk, divided
1 tablespoon (15 ml) vegan Worcestershire sauce
1 to 3 tablespoons (8 to 24 g) sorghum flour, divided
1 teaspoon black pepper, plus a dash or two
12 ounces (340 g) brown rice pasta spirals

In a large skillet, heat 1 tablespoon (15 ml) of the oil. Add the onion and mushrooms. Cook over medium to high heat until the onions begin to brown and caramelize. Salt lightly. Cook until almost all of the water has cooked out of the mushrooms and the onions are translucent, about 10 minutes. Reduce the heat to low.

In a small heat-proof bowl, combine the water and bouillon, stirring to dissolve. Add to the mushrooms and onions. Add 1 cup (235 ml) of the coconut milk. Simmer for about 20 minutes, stirring occasionally. Add the remaining ¾ cup (185 ml) coconut milk, Worcestershire, 1 tablespoon (8 g) of the flour, and 1 teaspoon of the pepper. Whisk together vigorously until very smooth. Cook over medium-high heat for about 7 minutes, stirring continuously, or until thickened. If needed to thicken, whisk in some of the remaining 2 tablespoons (16 g) flour. Season with salt.

In a large pot of salted, boiling water, cook the noodles according to the package directions. Drain and rinse briefly under cold water. Return the noodles to the pot. Toss with the remaining 3 tablespoons (45 ml) oil, a dash or two of pepper, and salt to taste. Add the mushroom sauce.

Yield: 6 servings

WALNUT RAVIOLI WITH VODKA SAUCE
This meal is very hearty and takes a bit of prep work, so it's best reserved for a special occasion or an at-home date.

FOR THE PASTA:
1 recipe Simple Homemade Pasta (See page 106.)

FOR THE FILLING:
2 cloves garlic, minced
2 cups (300 g) chopped walnuts
1 teaspoon minced fresh thyme
1 teaspoon dried sage
¾ teaspoon salt
1 teaspoon flaxseed meal
3 tablespoons (45 ml) olive oil

FOR THE SAUCE:
2 tablespoons (30 ml) olive oil
3 cloves garlic, minced
½ Vidalia onion, chopped
1 can (28 ounces, or 795 g) crushed tomatoes, plus juice
1 cup (235 ml) vodka
1 tablespoon (15 ml) balsamic vinegar
2 teaspoons sugar
2 tablespoons (5 g) fresh chopped basil
½ cup (65 g) nutritional yeast
1 cup (235 ml) canned coconut milk

To make the pasta: Make the pasta dough, but do not cook. Divide the dough in half and chill it in the fridge while you prepare the filling.

To make the filling: In a food processor, pulse the garlic, walnuts, thyme, sage, salt, and flaxseed until crumbly. Slowly drizzle in 1 tablespoon (15 ml) of the oil at a time. Pulse to blend.

To make the sauce: In a large skillet, heat the oil over medium heat. Sauté the garlic and onion until golden brown. Reduce the heat to low. Cook until the onion is translucent. Stir in the tomatoes and juice, vodka, vinegar, sugar, basil, and yeast. Simmer for about 20 minutes, or until you can no longer taste the vodka, stirring often. Remove from the heat and stir in the milk.

Between 2 pieces of plastic wrap, roll out each section of pasta, aiming to make two 12 x 16-inch (30.5 x 40.5 cm) rectangles that are about 1⅛-inch (3 mm)-thick.

Bring a large pot of salted water to a boil. Place mounds of about 2 teaspoons of filling evenly onto the dough, leaving a 1-inch (2.5 cm) radius around the filling mounds, to have around 15 mounds evenly spaced on one layer of dough. Gently cover with the second piece of rolled-out dough. (Use the plastic wrap to help flip one layer of dough evenly on top of the filling mounds.) Using a pizza cutter, cut out individual ravioli. Seal the outside of the dough with a little water. Using a fork, crimp the edges so that the ravioli are watertight.

Boil a few ravioli at a time for exactly 2 minutes. Using a slotted spoon, remove and place in a bowl. Add the ravioli to the sauce and simmer for about 5 minutes.

Yield: 5 servings, 3 ravioli and ¼ cup (60 ml) vodka sauce each

1 Simple Homemade Pasta; 2 Cold Sesame Noodles; 3 Spicy Goulash; 4 Stroganoff; 5 Walnut Ravioli with Vodka Sauce; 6 Simply Spectacular Tomato Noodles; 7 Mac 'n Cabbage Polonaise ; 8 Pasta da Fornel

9 Soy Curl Mac 'n Cheese; 10 Linguine with Purple Cabbage; 11 Tahini Noodle Bowl; 12 Triple Mushroom White Lasagna; 13 Tofu Spinach Lasagna; 14 Potato Dosa; 15 Indian Crêpes with Sorrel and Spinach; 16 Pizza Firenze

SIMPLY SPECTACULAR TOMATO NOODLES

This is a fantastic recipe: pasta with not much adornment, but a whole lotta flavor.

16 ounces (453 g) brown rice pasta shells
3 tablespoons (45 g) nondairy margarine
1 very large Vidalia onion, chopped
2 teaspoons salt, plus more to taste
Black pepper, to taste
1 can (28 ounces, or 784 g) whole tomatoes
¼ cup (34 g) jarred hot peppers, drained and minced, optional
½ cup (120 ml) olive oil

Cook the pasta according to the package directions.

In a skillet, heat the margarine over medium-high heat. Sauté the onion until soft and translucent, about 10 minutes. Add 2 teaspoons of the salt and black pepper to taste. Reduce the heat to medium-low. Cook until the onion is caramelized, stirring occasionally, about 10 minutes longer. Add the tomatoes one by one, reserving the juice in the can. Stir in the hot peppers. Using a fork, halve the tomatoes. Simmer for about 5 minutes, or until hot.

Drain the pasta well. Rinse briefly under cold water. Return the pasta to the pot and stir in the oil. Season with salt. Stir in the reserved juice. Add the onion mixture. Toss to combine. Cook over medium-low heat, stirring often, for 5 minutes longer, or until hot. Top with black pepper to taste.

Yield: 4 servings

MAC 'N CABBAGE POLONAISE

This baked mac 'n cheese is a creamy rival to traditional baked mac and cheese with a little of Polish flair thrown in. The cabbage adds a wonderful texture that's complement-ed perfectly by a crunchy crumble topping.

FOR THE MAC 'N CHEESE:
1 package (16 ounces, or 455 g) brown rice elbow macaroni
7 tablespoons (100 g) nondairy margarine
¾ cup (97 g) sorghum flour
3 cups (705 ml) plain almond milk, divided
⅔ cup (86 g) nutritional yeast
½ teaspoon salt

FOR THE CABBAGE:
1 head green cabbage, chopped into bite-size pieces
1 tablespoon (15 ml) olive oil
Black pepper, to taste
Salt, to taste

FOR THE TOPPING:
2 to 3 tablespoons (30 to 45 g) nondairy margarine
½ cup plus 2 tablespoons (81 g) sorghum flour
Dash of salt
2 cups (225 g) Cheddar-style nondairy cheese

To make the mac 'n cheese: Cook the pasta according to the package directions. Rinse under cold water. Drain.

In a saucepan, melt the margarine over medium heat. Stir in the flour until a thick roux forms. Using a whisk, stir in about 2 cups (470 ml) of the milk. Sprinkle in the yeast. Stir to smooth and thicken just slightly. Whisk in the remaining 1 cup (235 ml) milk. Cook until thick, stirring constantly, about 7 minutes. (The sauce should be quite thick and "plop" from the spoon into the pot. If you're having trouble getting the sauce to thicken, increase the heat slightly.) Add the salt and combine with the pasta.

To make the cabbage: In a large bowl, combine the cabbage with the oil. Lightly sprinkle with pepper and salt. Transfer to a well-seasoned cast-iron or nonstick skillet. Cover and cook over medium heat until the cabbage becomes soft, stirring occasionally. Uncover and cook off any moisture. (If the cabbage still has excess moisture once it's cooked thoroughly, drain in a colander.) Stir into the pasta.

To make the topping: In a bowl, cut the margarine into the flour with your hands until crumbly. (It should be like small pebbles, rather than sand.) Sprinkle in the salt.

Preheat the oven to 350°F (180°C, or gas mark 4). Lightly grease a 9 x 13-inch (23 x 33 cm) baking dish.

On the bottom of the prepared dish, spread a layer of the cabbage mixture. Top with half of the cheese and then another layer of cabbage mixture. Sprinkle with the remaining cheese. Bake, uncovered, for about 20 minutes. Two minutes before the end of the baking time, switch the oven to broil.

Yield: 8 servings

PASTA DA FORNEL

The Parmesan Cheese Mix keeps up to 1 month in the fridge. This vegan version of a dish from Northern Italy features lasagna noodles, dried fruit, poppy seeds, and Parmesan cheese.

FOR THE PARMESAN CHEESE MIX:
1½ cups (168 g) blanched almond meal
2 teaspoons salt
⅓ cup (32 g) nutritional yeast

FOR THE PASTA:
1½ cups (180 g) chopped walnuts
1 cup (150 g) dried figs, coarsely chopped

½ cup (120 ml) white wine
16 ounces (455 g) brown rice pasta
2 tablespoons (28 ml) olive oil
½ teaspoon salt
2 apples, diced
1 small red onion, chopped
1 tablespoon (9 g) poppy seeds
½ cup (50 g) vegan Parmesan Cheese Mix (See below)
7 tablespoons (98 g) vegan margarine
Salt, to taste
Black pepper, to taste

To make the Parmesan Cheese Mix:
In a large airtight container, shake together all of the ingredients about 30 times.

To make the pasta: In a bowl, soak the figs in the wine for 4 hours or up to overnight.
 Preheat the oven to 375°F (190°C, gas mark 5).
 Toast the walnuts on a baking sheet for 5 to 8 minutes. Remove to a bowl.
 Cook the pasta according to the package directions. Drain, rinse briefly in cold water, and return to the pot. Stir in the oil and salt.
 Drain the figs. In a medium frying pan, sauté the figs, apples, and onion over medium-high heat for about 10 to 15 minutes, or until the onion caramelizes. Stir the onion mixture into the pasta. Warm over low heat. Stir in the seeds, Parmesan Cheese Mix, margarine, and walnuts. Warm over medium heat until the margarine is melted and the cheese is well incorporated, stirring occasionally. Season with salt and pepper.

Yield: 6 servings

SOY CURL MAC 'N CHEESE
This dish is fantastic with just the nutritional yeast, but if you're looking for something "cheesier," perhaps to impress non-vegan friends or family, stir in your favorite vegan cheese.

2 cups (200 g) soy curls
2 cups (470 ml) warm water plus 2 cups (470 ml) cold water, or more as needed, divided
2 tablespoons (28 g) vegan butter
1 cup (160 g) diced onion
2 cloves garlic, minced
2 tablespoons (16 g) vegan chicken-flavored seasoning
¼ to ½ teaspoon black pepper
1 cup (105 g) spelt elbow pasta
2 tablespoons (14 g) nutritional yeast
½ to 1 teaspoon salt
2 ounces (56 g) shredded vegan cheese (optional)

In a large bowl, rehydrate the soy curls in the 2 cups (470 ml) warm water for 10 minutes. Drain the excess liquid.
 In an uncovered pressure cooker, heat the butter on medium-high. Sauté the onion and garlic for 3 minutes, or until the onion is translucent. Stir in the soy curls, seasoning, and pepper. Sauté for about 5 minutes. If the soy curls begin to stick, add 1 tablespoon (15 ml) water. Add the pasta and remaining 2 cups (470 ml) cold water, or as needed to cover the pasta. Stir in the yeast. Pat the soy curls and pasta down under the water. Cover and bring to pressure. Cook at low pressure for 5 minutes. Use a quick release. Remove the lid. Add the salt. Add the cheese if using and mix well. Let stand for 5 minutes to set up.

Yield: 2 servings

LINGUINE WITH PURPLE CABBAGE
Long strands of linguine combine with long strands of garlic-flavored cabbage in this delicious albeit simple dish.

¼ cup (60 ml) olive oil
2 medium red onions, thinly sliced
6 large cloves garlic, minced
1 large head red cabbage, thinly sliced (8 cups [560 g])
1 pound (455 g) linguine
Salt, to taste
Black pepper, to taste
½ cup (70 g) toasted pine nuts

In a large sauté pan, heat the oil over medium-low heat. Sauté the onion for about 10 minutes, stirring occasionally, or until tender and glistening. Add the garlic. Cook for about 3 minutes, stirring periodically. Add the cabbage, cover, and cook for about 20 minutes, stirring occasionally, or until tender.
 In a large pot of boiling water, cook the linguine according to the package directions. Drain the pasta, reserving 1 cup (235 ml) of the cooking water in a bowl. Return the pasta to the pot. Add the cabbage mixture to the pasta. Pour in the reserved water and toss well to combine. Season with salt and pepper. Transfer to serving bowls. Sprinkle with the nuts.

Yield: 4 servings

TAHINI NOODLE BOWL

You can replace the oil in the sauce with 2 extra table-spoons (30 ml) of tahini, and for the stir-fry, you can simply use vegetable broth or water in lieu of oil.

1 pound (454 g) pasta

FOR THE SAUCE:
1 cup (235 ml) tahini
¼ cup (60 ml) soy sauce
¼ cup (60 ml) balsamic vinegar
¼ cup (60 ml) water
2 tablespoons (30 ml) sesame oil, optional
1 tablespoon (15 ml) molasses
1 tablespoon (15 ml) sriracha
1 tablespoon (8 g) garlic powder
1 teaspoon Dijon mustard

FOR THE BOWL:
2 tablespoons (30 ml) vegetable oil, optional
1 block (10 to 12 ounces, or 280 to 340 g) extra- or
 super-firm tofu, drained and pressed, cut into tiny
 cubes
1 cup (108 g) shredded carrots
2 cups (270 g) chopped broccoli florets
1 cup (134 g) green peas
1 cup (170 g) shelled edamame
½ cup (145 g) cashews (raw or roasted)
½ teaspoon red chili flakes
Salt, to taste
Black pepper, to taste
4 cups (120 g) arugula
1 tablespoon (8 g) black or white sesame seeds

Prepare the pasta according to the package directions.

To make the sauce: In a small bowl, whisk all of the ingredients until smooth. Transfer to a squeeze bottle.

To make the bowl: In a frying pan, heat the oil, if using, over medium-high heat. Add the tofu, carrots, broccoli, peas, edamame, cashews, and red chili. Toss to combine. Season with salt and pepper. Sauté for 6 to 8 minutes, or until the vegetables are bright and vibrant and the tofu is slightly browned.

To assemble the bowls: Among four pasta-size bowls, divide the arugula, pasta, and stir-fry mixture. Top with the sauce. Sprinkle with the seeds.

Yield: 4 servings

TRIPLE MUSHROOM WHITE LASAGNA

Your family will rave about this unusual dish.

1 package (16 ounces, or 455 g) brown rice lasagna
 noodles

FOR THE SAUCE:
1 head cauliflower, cored and cut into florets
3 cups (420 g) raw cashews, soaked for at least 3 hours
 and drained
1¼ cups (285 ml) almond milk
2 tablespoons (12 g) nutritional yeast
1½ teaspoons salt
1 tablespoon (15 ml) lemon juice

FOR THE FILLING:
2 cups (140 g) each shiitake mushroom caps, whole
 crimini, and oyster mushrooms, sliced
1 tablespoon (1.7 g) minced fresh rosemary
2 cloves garlic, minced
1 cup (160 g) minced shallots (about 9 small)
Salt, to taste
1 tablespoon (15 ml) olive oil
2 cups (224 g) mozzarella-style shredded vegan cheese

Preheat the oven to 375°F (190°C, gas mark 5). Line 2 baking sheets with parchment.
 Cook the noodles according to the package directions, drain, rinse gently with cool water, and place on the prepared baking sheets in a single layer. Mist gently with olive oil cooking spray. Cover with another piece of parchment.

To make the sauce: Meanwhile, in a steamer basket over a large stockpot containing about 2 inches (5 cm) of water, steam the cauliflower for about 5 to 7 minutes, or until fork tender.
 In a food processor, blend the cauliflower, cashews, milk, yeast, salt, and juice until very smooth, about 7 to 9 minutes, in batches if necessary.

To make the filling: In a large frying pan, sauté the mushrooms, rosemary, garlic, shallots, salt, and oil over medium-high heat for about 12 minutes, or until most of the liquid has been cooked out of the mushrooms and they begin to caramelize around the edges.
 Lightly grease a 9 x 13-inch (23 x 33 cm) baking dish. Line the bottom with 3 noodles. Top with about 1 cup (225 g) of the sauce and then sprinkle with filling. Top with about ⅓ cup (37 g) of the cheese. Repeat with 3 more layers, ending with sauce and cheese. Cover with foil. Bake for 50 minutes, removing the foil halfway. Once cooked through and the cheese is melted, broil for 5 minutes.

Yield: 12 servings

TOFU SPINACH LASAGNA

The tofu "ricotta" has a wonderful creamy texture and boasts all the familiarity of the traditional lasagna, with which most of us grew up.

½ to 1 pound (225 to 455 g) lasagna noodles
2 packages (10 ounces, or 280 g, each) frozen, chopped spinach, thawed and drained
1 package (16 ounces, or 455 g) firm tofu (not silken)
1 tablespoon (13 g) sugar, optional
¼ cup (60 ml) nondairy milk, or as needed
½ teaspoon garlic powder
2 tablespoons (30 ml) lemon juice
2 tablespoons (5 g) minced fresh basil
1 teaspoon (6 g) salt
4 to 6 cups (980 to 1470 g) pasta sauce

Preheat the oven to 350°F (180°C, or gas mark 4).

Cook the noodles according to the package directions and drain.

Squeeze as much water from the spinach as possible.

In a blender, blend the tofu, sugar (if using), milk, garlic powder, juice, basil, and salt until smooth. (The tofu "ricotta" should be creamy but still have body.) Transfer to a large bowl. Stir in the spinach.

Cover the bottom of a 9 x 13-inch (23 x 33 cm) baking dish with a thin layer of sauce, then a layer of one-third of the noodles, then half of the tofu mixture. Repeat, using half of the remaining sauce and noodles and all of the remaining tofu mixture. End with the remaining noodles, covered by the remaining sauce. Bake for 40 to 45 minutes, or until hot and bubbling.

Yield: 8 to 10 servings

POTATO DOSA

Dosa is a filled thin crêpe eaten in southern India that's quickly gaining popularity in the United States. Even though this recipe takes three days to make, it's mostly prep time.

FOR THE DOSA BATTER:
¾ cup (140 g) urad dal (split white lentils), soaked overnight and drained
4 cups (940 ml) water, divided
1 teaspoon ground coriander powder
¼ teaspoon black pepper
¾ teaspoon salt
1 cup (158 g) white rice flour
1¼ cups (198 g) brown rice flour

FOR THE FILLING:
3 large thin-skinned potatoes, unpeeled, chopped into small pieces
2 leeks, white and light green parts only, cleaned well and thinly sliced
1 teaspoon fenugreek powder
½ teaspoon chaat masala or garam masala
2 tablespoons (30 ml) water
1 medium tomato, diced
1 cup (130 g) frozen green peas
¼ teaspoon tamarind concentrate
½ teaspoon turmeric
1 cup (16 g) chopped fresh cilantro
Salt, to taste

To make the dosa batter: In a food processor, blend the urad dal and 1 tablespoon (15 ml) of the water until a thick fluffy paste is formed, at least 5 minutes. Transfer to a large bowl. Stir in the coriander, pepper, and salt. Slowly add the remaining water and flours. Stir until well incorporated into a smooth batter. Cover with a light towel and let rest in a warm area for 8 hours. (After fermentation, the batter should thicken slightly, to be similar to heavy cream.)

To make the filling: In a large heavy saucepan, cook the potatoes, leeks, fenugreek powder, chaat masala, and water, covered, over medium heat for about 15 minutes, or until the potatoes begin to soften. Add the tomato and cook 10 minutes longer. Add the peas and cook just until heated through. Remove from the heat. Stir in the tamarind, turmeric, cilantro, and salt to taste.

Warm a large well-seasoned or nonstick skillet, griddle, or crêpe pan over medium-high heat.

Oil the pan lightly. Using a metal ladle, drop ½ cup (120 ml) of batter onto the hot griddle and immediately spread in a circular motion with the bottom of the ladle to disperse the batter into a thin pancake. Cook for 2 minutes, or until golden brown on the bottom.

Once the dosa is golden brown, spread ¼ cup (56 g) of the filling in the center of the pancake (as though you were filling up a burrito) while still on the griddle and fold over one-third of the dosa. Fold over again to close. Remove from the heat and keep warm.

Yield: 6 dosas

INDIAN CRÊPES WITH SORREL AND SPINACH

These crêpes are thicker and a little firmer than traditional French crêpes. Serve with your favorite chutney or plain coconut yogurt and fresh chopped cilantro.

¼ cup (36 g) minced mild green chile pepper (such as poblano or Anaheim)
3 shallots, minced
½ cup (8 g) chopped cilantro
1 teaspoon ajwain seeds
Pinch of turmeric
½ teaspoon baking powder
1¾ cups (210 g) + 2 tablespoons (15 g) gram flour
1 teaspoon salt
1¾ tablespoons (19 ml) olive oil, divided
1½ cups (355 ml) water
1 cup (30 g) finely chopped spinach
¼ cup (8 g) finely chopped sorrel
½ teaspoon salt
½ teaspoon olive oil

In a large bowl, combine the chile pepper, shallots, cilantro, seeds, turmeric, baking powder, flour, and salt. Stir in 1¼ tablespoons (19 ml) of the oil and water to form a medium-bodied batter.

In a small bowl, toss together the spinach, sorrel, and salt.

In a large nonstick pan, heat the remaining ½ teaspoon oil on a little higher than medium heat. Add ½ cup (139 g) of the batter and quickly move the pan in a circular motion to spread the batter into a crêpe. Cook for about 1 to 2 minutes, or until bubbles have formed on the crêpe and the top no longer has much visibly wet batter. Sprinkle on about 2 tablespoons (4 g) of the spinach and sorrel. Flip over half of the crepe to cover the chopped spinach and press down gently using a spatula. Flip and cook an additional 1 minute, or until both sides turn golden brown. Repeat with the remaining batter, adding ½ cup (139 g) at a time.

Yield: About 5 crêpes

PIZZA FIRENZE

This pizza is reminiscent of a trip to Florence, Italy!

FOR THE PIZZA CRUST:
Cornmeal, for dusting
2½ teaspoons (7 g) active dry yeast
1 cup (235 ml) warm water
1 tablespoon (13 g) sugar
1 teaspoon salt
2 tablespoons (30 ml) olive oil

1 cup (130 g) sorghum flour
1¼ cups (198 g) brown rice flour, plus extra for rolling
½ cup (55 g) potato starch
1 teaspoon xanthan gum

FOR THE SAUCE AND TOPPINGS:
3 cloves garlic, crushed
1 cup (40 g) fresh basil
¼ cup (32 g) nutritional yeast
½ cup (75 g) walnuts
¼ teaspoon salt, plus more to taste
1 tablespoon (15 ml) olive oil, plus more for drizzling
3 tablespoons (45 ml) water
2 cups (200 g) nondairy cheese
1 cup (124 g) green beans, cooked
2 roma tomatoes, thinly sliced
¼ cup (7 g) minced fresh marjoram
1 teaspoon minced fresh thyme
¼ cup (40 g) small capers, drained
10 leaves fresh spinach, chopped

To make the crust: Preheat the oven to 400°F (200°C, or gas mark 6). Lightly oil a pizza pan or baking sheet and dust with cornmeal.

In a bowl, stir the yeast into the water and sugar. Let proof until foamy, 10 minutes. Stir in the salt and oil.

In a separate bowl, sift together the flours, starch, and xanthan. Gradually add the flour mixture to the yeast mixture. Knead until a stiff dough forms. Turn out onto a parchment-paper covered surface. Lightly oil the rolling pin. Roll the dough out into a circle ½- to ¼-inch (1.3 cm to 6 mm) thick. Fold up the edges of the circle to make a lip on the crust. (If the dough begins to crack around the edges, brush on some water and rework a touch to smooth out.)

Using a flat-edged spatula, transfer the crust to the prepared pan. Let rest for about 10 minutes.

Bake on the center rack in the oven for 15 minutes.

To make the sauce: In a food processor, combine the garlic, basil, yeast, walnuts, salt, oil, and water and pulse until a smooth paste forms. Add more water if needed, to make smooth.

Spread the sauce liberally on top of the prebaked crust. Sprinkle on the cheese and remaining topping ingredients. Lightly season with salt and drizzle with oil.

Increase the oven temperature to 450°F (230°C, or gas mark 8). Return the pizza to the oven, and bake for 15 to 20 minutes, or until all the cheese has melted. Slice into 8 wedges.

Yield: 4 servings, 2 slices each

PESTO PITZAS

If you make the cheese ahead of time, you can serve this as a ready-in-no-time meal. The cheese will keep for up to 1 week in the fridge in an airtight container.

FOR THE CHEESE:
1 cup (235 ml) unsweetened coconut cream
½ cup (120 g) drained firm silken tofu
1 or 2 cloves garlic, to taste
¾ teaspoon smoked sea salt
½ to 1 teaspoon liquid smoke
½ teaspoon ground white pepper
½ teaspoon onion powder
1 tablespoon (15 ml) lemon juice
1 to 2 tablespoons (8 to 15 g) nutritional yeast, to taste
1 tablespoon (16 g) almond butter
1 tablespoon (8 g) agar powder

FOR THE PESTO:
1½ cups (36 g) fresh basil leaves
1 or 2 cloves garlic, to taste, pressed
Salt, to taste
Black pepper, to taste
1½ tablespoons (25 ml) lemon juice
¼ to ½ cup (60 to 120 ml) olive oil

FOR THE PITZAS:
Four 8-inch (20-cm) pita breads
1 cup (76 g) cheese (from recipe above)
2 tablespoons (16 g) drained capers
¼ cup (28 g) chopped oil-packed sun-dried tomatoes

To make the cheese: Lightly coat a 2½-inch (6.4-cm)-deep 16-ounce (454-g) round dish with nonstick cooking spray.

In a blender, process all of the ingredients until smooth. Transfer the mixture to a medium saucepan. Cook over medium-high heat for 5 minutes, whisking constantly to thicken. (The mixture will thicken slightly and become more cohesive; it will thicken more as it cools.) Pour the mixture into the prepared dish, cover, and chill overnight in the fridge.

To make the pesto: In a food processor, pulse the basil and garlic a few times to chop. Add salt and pepper to taste. Add the juice. Through the hole in the lid, while the machine is running, slowly drizzle in the oil until a paste forms.

To make the pitzas: Preheat the oven to 375°F (190°C, or gas mark 5).

Spread pesto on each pita to cover the surface. Sprinkle ¼ cup (19 g) of the cheese on top of each, and then add ½ tablespoon (4 g) capers and 1 tablespoon (7 g) tomatoes. Bake for 15 minutes, or until golden brown and crispy.

Yield: 4 pitzas, 1 pound (454 g) cheese

BEET AND SWEET POTATO PIZZA

This recipe is modeled after a favorite version served at a café in San Francisco.

FOR THE SUN-DRIED AND WALNUT PESTO:
1 cup (40 g) loosely packed fresh basil leaves
1 cup (60 g) packed fresh flat-leaf parsley
¾ cup (90 g) walnuts
¼ cup (30 g) oil-packed sun-dried tomatoes, drained and rinsed (5 or 6 individual sun-dried tomatoes)
3 whole cloves garlic, peeled
Juice of ½ lemon
1 to 2 tablespoons (15 to 30 ml) olive oil (or oil from sun-dried tomatoes jar)
¼ teaspoon salt

FOR THE PIZZA:
2 red beets, peeled and cubed
1 or 2 small sweet potatoes, peeled and cubed
1 package (16 ounces, or 455 g) extra-firm tofu
Olive oil, for brushing
Salt, to taste
1 disk (1 pound, or 455 g) ready-made whole wheat pizza dough
Cornmeal or flour, for dusting pizza peel and stone
1 recipe Sun-Dried Tomato and Walnut Pesto

To make the Sun-Dried Tomato and Walnut Pesto: In a food processor, blend the basil, parsley, walnuts, tomatoes, garlic, and juice until a smooth paste forms. Scrape down the sides, drizzle in 1 tablespoon (15 ml) of the oil, and blend again. Add the other 1 tablespoon (15 ml) oil, if necessary, along with salt to taste.

To make the pizza: Preheat the broiler.

Steam or roast the beets and potatoes until tender.

Cut the tofu into slices, brush with oil, and broil for 3 minutes. Flip over and broil for 3 minutes more. Sprinkle with salt.

Preheat the oven to 500°F (250°C, or gas mark 10). At least 30 minutes before baking the pizza, place a pizza stone in the oven on a rack in the lowest position. Dust a pizza peel with cornmeal.

On a floured surface, roll out the dough and shape. Fold dough over once or twice, place on the prepared peel, and unfold. Jerk the peel once or twice to make sure dough will easily slide off. If it sticks, lift dough, sprinkle more cornmeal underneath it, and replace. Spread half of the pesto on 1 pizza dough, and half on another, to make 2 pizzas. Top with the beets, potatoes, and tofu. Bake for 10 to 12 minutes, or until golden brown.

Yield: 16 slices, 1½ cups (390 g) Sun-Dried Tomato and Walnut Pesto

FARINATA PIZZA

Farinata is a crispy flatbread made from gram, or chickpea, flour. It is also known as socca in France and cecina in Italy.

FOR THE CRUST:
2 cups (240 g) gram flour
1 teaspoon salt
¼ cup (60 ml) olive oil
1 cup (235 ml) + 2 tablespoons (28 ml) water

FOR THE SAUCE:
6 ounces (170 g) tomato paste
½ tablespoon minced thyme
½ tablespoon minced oregano
2 cloves garlic, minced
1 tablespoon (13 g) sugar
2 tablespoons (28 ml) olive oil
1 tablespoon (15 ml) balsamic vinegar
Scant ½ cup (120 ml) water

FOR THE PIZZA AND TOPPINGS:
2 cups (224 g) mozzarella-style shredded vegan cheese
1 red onion, sliced very thin
6 button mushrooms, sliced very thin
½ cup (75 g) finely diced green bell pepper

To make the crust: Preheat the oven to 385°F (195°C, gas mark 6). Line a large baking sheet with parchment.

In a large bowl, whisk together all of the ingredients until smooth. Spread thinly on the prepared baking sheet so that the batter is about ¼-inch (6 mm) thick. Bake for about 13 minutes. Remove the crust from the oven.

Increase the oven temperature to 450°F (230°C, gas mark 8).

To prepare the sauce: In a bowl, combine all of the ingredients except the water. Slowly add the water and mix well to completely incorporate.

To make the pizza: Spread a thin layer of sauce onto the crust and then top with the toppings.

Bake for about 15 minutes, or until the cheese is melted and the toppings begin to brown. (Watch carefully so that it doesn't burn.) Let cool briefly and then slice.

Yield: 1 pizza, 8 to 10 slices

CHICAGO-STYLE DEEP DISH PIZZA

Classic Chicago-style deep-dish pizza is meant to be eaten with a fork, and it's good to have a napkin handy!

FOR THE CRUST:
1½ cups (240 g) superfine brown rice flour
¼ cup (51 g) sweet white rice flour
¼ cup (48 g) potato starch
1 teaspoon cream of tartar
1 tablespoon (18 g) ground psyllium husk
⅓ cup (75 ml) coconut oil
1¼ cups (285 ml) warm water, about 110°F (43°C)
1 packet active dry yeast (9 g)
1 tablespoon (13 g) sugar
1¼ teaspoons salt
1 tablespoon (12 g) ground chia seeds mixed with ¼ cup (60 ml) water

FOR THE SAUCE:
1 can (28 ounces, or 785 g) whole tomatoes, drained and crushed
1 can (6 ounces, or 170 g) tomato paste
3 tablespoons (39 g) sugar
1 tablespoon (4 g) minced oregano
1 teaspoon fennel seed
1 small onion, shredded and drained
2 tablespoons (28 ml) red wine
1 heaping tablespoon (3 g) minced basil
3 cloves garlic, grated
Dash of red pepper flakes, optional

FOR THE PIZZA:
Margarine, for greasing
Finely ground cornmeal, for dusting
2 cups (224 g) mozzarella-style shredded vegan cheese

To make the crust: In a large electric mixing bowl, combine the flours, starch, cream of tartar, and psyllium until well mixed. Using a pastry blender, cut the oil into the flour mixture until evenly incorporated.

In a small bowl, mix the water with the yeast and sugar. Proof until foamy, about 5 minutes. Add the yeast mixture, the salt, and the chia mixture to the flour mixture. Mix on medium speed until well blended, about 1 to 2 minutes.

Reserve a golf ball–size piece of dough. Place the remaining dough between 2 sheets of plastic wrap. Roll until thin, to about ¼ inch (6 mm). Place the smaller section of dough between 2 separate pieces of plastic wrap and roll as thin as possible.

To make the sauce: In a small bowl, stir together all of the ingredients until smooth.

To make pizza: Preheat the oven to 450°F (230°C, gas mark 8). Grease an 8-inch (20 cm) springform pan with margarine and dust with finely ground cornmeal. Drape the large portion of dough into the pan and shape to sit evenly in the pan, about 3-inches (7.5 cm) deep. Top with the cheese, and then the thin section of remaining rolled-out dough. Top with the sauce. Bake for 30 minutes.

Reduce the heat to 400°F (200°C, gas mark 6).

Bake for an additional 30 minutes. Broil for 5 minutes. Cool for about 15 minutes before slicing.

Yield: 1 deep-dish pizza, 8 to 10 slices

CARROT PIZZA WITH ARUGULA, CARAMELIZED ONIONS, AND TOASTED WALNUTS

This pizza is delicious and thoroughly debunks any thought that pizza is not health food. If you have a homemade dough recipe that you like, use it here.

2 tablespoons (28 g) coconut oil, divided
½ white onion, sliced
½ head cauliflower, chopped
Salt, to taste
Black pepper, to taste
1 cup (100 g) raw walnuts
1 tablespoon (15 ml) maple syrup
1 jar (2½ ounces, or 71 g) carrot baby food
1 teaspoon crushed garlic
1 disk (1 pound, or 455 g) ready-made whole wheat pizza dough
2 ounces (100 g) sliced black olives
3 baby bell peppers (preferably 1 each orange, red, and yellow), seeded and chopped
2 handfuls arugula
½ teaspoon coconut oil, melted
Balsamic vinegar, for drizzling
Crushed red pepper flakes, to taste

Preheat the oven to 425°F (220°C, or gas mark 7).

In a medium skillet over medium heat, heat 1 tablespoon (14 g) of the oil. Sauté the onion for 15 to 20 minutes, stirring occasionally, or until the onion has caramelized. Rub the cauliflower with the remaining oil. Season with salt and black pepper. Roast on a baking sheet for about 10 minutes, or until lightly brown.

Drizzle the walnuts with the syrup. Toss to coat evenly. Spread in a single layer on a baking sheet. Roast until lightly toasted, about 8 minutes, stirring often. (Check often to make sure they don't burn.)

In a small bowl, combine the baby food and garlic.

After the cauliflower and walnuts have cooked, turn the oven temperature up to 500°F (250°C, or gas mark 10).

Stretch the dough to fit a nonstick 14-inch (35.5 cm) pizza pan. Bake the dough until golden brown, about 7 minutes. Let cool slightly. Spread the carrot sauce over the dough. Top with the onions, cauliflower, walnuts, olives, and bell peppers. Bake the pizza for another 7 minutes.

Meanwhile, in a bowl, lightly dress the arugula with the melted oil and vinegar. Top the warm pizza with the microgreens and sprinkle with the red pepper.

Yield: 2 to 4 servings

ROSEMARY, LEEK, AND POTATO PIE

Serve this main dish pie with a bowl of soup for a delicious, well-rounded meal.

3 pounds (1.36 kg) thin-skinned potatoes, unpeeled and very thinly sliced (about ⅛ inch [3 mm] thick) into rounds
Salt, to taste
4 cloves garlic, minced, divided
2 tablespoons (5 g) minced fresh rosemary sprigs
1 leek, white and light green part only, cleaned well and thinly sliced
½ cup (65 g) nutritional yeast
7 tablespoons (100 g) nondairy margarine, melted, divided

Preheat the oven to 400°F (200°C, or gas mark 6). Lightly grease an 8-inch (20.3 cm) springform pan with nonstick spray.

Arrange the potatoes in an even layer to cover the bottom of the pan, overlapping, with no gaps. Sprinkle lightly with salt, about one-fourth of the minced garlic, and a little fresh rosemary. Distribute a few rings of leeks evenly on top. Dust with the yeast to well cover the potatoes. Drizzle with a little more than 1 tablespoon (14 g)] of the margarine. Cover with a second layer of potatoes, then salt, garlic, and rosemary, and a few more rings of leek, yeast and a drizzle of margarine. Repeat the layering process again and again until all the ingredients have been used. Add a final layer of potatoes around the rim. (You should end up with 4 or 5 layers of potatoes.) Bake for about 1 hour and 5 minutes, or until a knife easily slides through all layers of potatoes. If the potatoes brown too quickly, cover lightly with foil during the last 20 minutes of cooking. Let cool briefly and then carefully remove the springform rim. Slice into wedges.

Yield: 8 servings

17 Pesto Pitzas; 18 Beet and Sweet Potato Pizza; 19 Farinata Pizza; 20 Chicago-Style Deep Dish Pizza; 21 Carrot Pizza with Arugula, Caramelized Onions, and Toasted Walnuts; 22 Rosemary, Leek, and Potato Pie; 23 Shepherd's Pie; 24 English Cottage Pie

25 French Onion Pie; 26 Australian Veggie Pie; 27 Apricot Risotto; 28 Spring Vegetable Risotto; 29 Lentil, Kale, and Barley Risotto; 30 Korean Kongbap; 31 Quinoa Pilaf; 32 Easy but Memorable Quinoa Pilaf with Cacao Nibs

SHEPHERD'S PIE

This recipe calls for cooked lentils. To save time, make them up to two days in advance and store in an airtight container in the fridge.

1½ cups (355 ml) water
4 tablespoons (32 g) minced garlic, divided
4 cups (440 g) quartered fingerling potatoes
2 cups (260 g) baby carrots
1 teaspoon salt
2 tablespoons (28 g) vegan butter
1 tablespoon (15 ml) olive oil
¾ cup (120 g) diced onion
½ cup (60 g) chopped celery
3 cups (510 g) cooked lentils
1 tablespoon (15 ml) vegan Worcestershire sauce
1 teaspoon ground dried rosemary
1 teaspoon ground dried thyme
4 cups (280 g) loosely packed chopped kale
¼ cup (60 g) creamy vegan mushroom soup
Black pepper, to taste

Preheat the oven to 350°F (180°C, or gas mark 4). Grease a 13 x 7-inch (33 x 18 cm) baking dish.

In an uncovered pressure cooker, bring the water to a boil. Add 2 tablespoons (16 g) of the garlic, the potatoes, and carrots. Cover and bring to pressure. Cook at high pressure for 6 minutes. Use a quick release. Remove the lid, add the salt and butter. Using a hand masher, mash.

In a large skillet, heat the oil over medium-high heat. Sauté the remaining 2 tablespoons (16 g) garlic, onion, and celery for about 1 minute. Add the lentils, Worcestershire, rosemary, and thyme. Mix well. Add the kale and soup. Simmer on medium-low for about 5 minutes, stirring frequently.

Pour the lentil and kale filling into the prepared baking dish. Spread the carrots and potatoes on top. Season with pepper. Bake until bubbling and golden, about 30 minutes. Cool slightly on a wire rack for at least 5 minutes. (This helps the pie set).

Yield: 8 to 10 servings

ENGLISH COTTAGE PIE

Also known as shepherd's pie in other parts of the world, this classic dish was created to use leftovers. Use leftover mashed potatoes to cut down on prep time with this recipe.

FOR THE MEAT MIXTURE:
2 tablespoons (30 ml) olive oil, divided
1 large sweet onion, diced
3 cloves garlic, minced
2 carrots, diced
2 stalks celery, diced

1 teaspoon fennel seed
½ teaspoon dried sage
2 cups (192 g) TVP (textured vegetable protein)
2 cups (475 ml) boiling water
2 cubes (2 teaspoons) beef-flavored vegetable bouillon
1 tablespoon (15 ml) vegan Worcestershire sauce
1 cup (164 g) corn kernels, thawed if frozen
1 tablespoon (12 g) ground chia seeds mixed with ½ cup (120 ml) water
2 cups (260 g) peas, thawed if frozen

FOR THE MASHED POTATOES:
5 large yellow-skinned potatoes, cubed into 1-inch (2.5 cm) squares
2 tablespoons (28 g) vegan margarine
1½ teaspoons salt
3 to 4 tablespoons (45 to 60 ml) almond milk

Preheat the oven to 375°F (190°C, gas mark 5). Set a large pot of salted water on to boil.

To make the meat mixture: In a frying pan, heat 1 tablespoon (15 ml) of the oil over medium-high heat. Sauté the onion, garlic, carrots, celery, fennel, and sage until browned, about 10 to 12 minutes.

In a large bowl, combine the TVP, boiling water, bouillon cubes, and Worcestershire. Cover and cook for about 10 minutes, or until all of the water has been absorbed. Fluff with a fork. Transfer to the frying pan with the vegetables. Add the remaining 1 tablespoon (15 ml) oil and cook until lightly browned, about 7 minutes. Stir in the corn. Remove from the heat. Add the chia seed mixture until well combined.

Press into a 9 x 13-inch (23 x 33 cm) pan. Top with the peas.

To make the mashed potatoes: Once the water is boiling, add the potatoes and bring back up to a rolling boil. Boil for 13 minutes, or until fork tender. Drain.

Transfer to an electric mixing bowl. Add the margarine, salt, and 3 tablespoons (45 ml) of the milk. Mix until fluffy. (The potatoes should be creamy, so add a touch more almond milk if needed.) Spread the potatoes on top of the peas, forming a smooth layer. Using a fork, draw a few squiggles into the potatoes. Bake for about 30 minutes, or until the potatoes are browned.

Yield: 10 servings

FRENCH ONION PIE

Use a premade pie crust that you can find in the frozen section of your grocery store. Your local natural foods store will most likely carry a healthful version.

2 uncooked pie shells, thawed
5 large onions, thinly sliced

4 cloves garlic, minced
1 tablespoon (14 g) nondairy butter
1 teaspoon (4 g) sugar
½ teaspoon salt, plus a little extra
1½ cups (355 ml) nondairy milk
15 ounces (420 g) extra-firm tofu, not silken
½ teaspoon black pepper
½ teaspoon nutmeg
5 tablespoons (40 g) unbleached flour
2 tablespoons (25 g) nutritional yeast flakes, optional

Preheat the oven to 350°F (180°C, or gas mark 4).
   Bake the pie shells for 10 minutes.
   In a large sauté pan, cook the onion and garlic in the butter, stirring occasionally, until the onion becomes translucent. Add the sugar and salt. Cook for 15 to 25 minutes (or longer if you'd like the onions somewhat caramelized).
   In a blender, combine the milk, tofu, the remaining ½ teaspoon salt, pepper, nutmeg, flour, and yeast, if using, until the mixture is smooth.
   In a large bowl, stir together the tofu mixture and onions.
   Divide the mixture evenly between the two pie shells. Bake for 45 minutes, or until the crust is golden brown and the filling sets.

Yield: Two 9-inch (23 cm) pies, 10 to 12 servings each

AUSTRALIAN VEGGIE PIE

Australia's native dish is meat pie. Serve it with ketchup for an authentically Aussie-style main course. This version is family-sized, but it can easily be made into mini pies.

FOR THE FILLING:
1 tablespoon (15 ml) olive oil
1 cup (164 g) cooked corn
½ red onion, diced
2 carrots, chopped into small pieces
1 clove garlic, minced
1 red potato, diced
1 stalk celery, diced
2 teaspoons salt, divided
1 tablespoon (2.5 g) fresh minced sage
1 cup (100 g) green beans
1 cup (160 g) cooked green peas
1 tablespoon (12 g) ground chia seeds mixed with ¼ cup
   (60 ml) water
3 tablespoons (42 g) vegan margarine, softened
¼ cup (40 g) superfine brown rice flour

FOR THE CRUST:
1 recipe pastry crust from Baked Pierogi (See page 52.)

Preheat the oven to 350°F (180°C, gas mark 4). Grease a standard-size deep-dish pie pan.

To make the filling: In a large frying pan, heat the oil over medium-high heat. Sauté the corn, onion, carrots, garlic, potato, and celery until slightly tender, about 10 minutes. Add 1 teaspoon of the salt. Mix the rest of the ingredients into the sautéed veggies.

To make the crust: Prepare the crust, divide it into 2 equal pieces, and roll each out between 2 sheets of plastic wrap until ¼-inch (6 mm) thick. Gently transfer one piece of rolled dough to the bottom of the prepared pan. Using a fork, press down the edges and poke a few holes in the crust. Transfer the filling on top of the bottom crust to fill the pie pan. Top with the second piece of dough. Pinch the two pieces of dough together to seal. Cut a few small slits in the top of the crust. Bake for 30 minutes.
   Increase the oven temperature to 400°F (200°C, gas mark 6). Bake for an additional 20 to 25 minutes. Let cool about 20 minutes.

Yield: 1 standard-size pie, about 12 servings

APRICOT RISOTTO
Don't be intimidated by risotto. This one is well worth the effort.

1 onion, chopped
½ cup (65 g) chopped dried apricots
¼ cup (60 ml) olive oil
Dash of black pepper
1 cup (190 g) Arborio rice
⅓ cup (80 ml) Chardonnay, warmed slightly above room
   temperature
3 to 4 cups (705 to 940 ml) vegetable broth, warmed
⅓ cup (80 ml) nondairy milk, warmed
1 tablespoon (14 g) nondairy margarine
Salt, to taste

In a large saucepan, sauté the onion and apricots in the oil over medium heat, just until the onion turns translucent. Add the pepper. Using a slotted spoon, remove from the pan and place on a separate plate, leaving the oil in the pan. Keeping the temperature at around medium heat, add the rice to the pan. Cook for about 7 minutes, or until the rice is golden brown, stirring occasionally. Add the wine and stir. Reduce the heat slightly. Cook until all of the wine has evaporated or been absorbed. Add the onion and apricots back to the pan. Add just enough broth to cover the rice, about ½ cup (120 ml). Simmer the rice in the broth over medium heat until almost all of the liquid has been absorbed, stirring often. Add more broth. Cook until there is just a little liquid left to be absorbed. Keep repeating this process, adding liquid in increments and stirring until the rice is softened up, for around 25 minutes. If you find that you are running out of liquid too fast, reduce the heat and add less liquid at each interval. Add more broth and keep cooking if the rice is still too firm after 3 cups (705 ml) of broth have been added. Once the rice is suitably cooked, stir in the milk. Cook until most of the liquid has been absorbed. (It should look very creamy, and the rice should be tender.) Stir in the margarine.

Cover with a tight-fitting lid, turn off the heat, and let rest for about 10 minutes. Season with salt.

Yield: 4 servings

SPRING VEGETABLE RISOTTO

Use this recipe as a model for many of your favorite vegetables, so long as those on the sturdy side, such as artichoke hearts, broccoli, or beets, are precooked.

1 bunch asparagus, tough stem ends cut off, with stalks
    cut into 2-inch (5 cm) pieces
4 carrots, peeled and julienned
6 cups (1410 ml) vegetable broth, plus more if needed
½ cup (120 ml) dry white wine, optional
1 to 2 tablespoons (15 to 30 ml) olive oil
2 cloves garlic, minced
2 bunches green onions (12 to 16), white parts chopped
    and ¼ cup (25 g) of thinly sliced green parts reserved
2 cups (390 g) Arborio rice
1 cup (130 g) frozen baby green peas, thawed
Salt, to taste
Black pepper, to taste
Yellow pear tomatoes, optional

Steam the asparagus and carrots until tender but crisp, about 10 minutes. Transfer to a bowl.

In a saucepan, heat the broth and wine, if using until barely simmering. (You will typically need between 5 and 6 cups [1175 and 1410 ml] of total liquid for the risotto.)

In a large sauté pan, heat the oil over medium heat. Sauté the garlic and white parts of the onions for about 3 minutes, stirring, or until softened. Add the rice and cook, stirring constantly, for 2 minutes. Reduce the heat to medium. Add 1 cup (235 ml) of the broth. Stir until the broth is absorbed. Continue to add broth, one ladleful at a time, until almost all the liquid has been absorbed and the rice begins to soften, about 20 minutes. Stir in the peas and 1 cup (235 ml) of broth. Continue stirring constantly until the liquid has almost been absorbed and the rice begins to thicken. Stir in the steamed vegetables, adding more of the broth as needed, until the mixture is creamy, not runny, the rice is tender yet firm to the bite, and the vegetables are heated through, about 5 minutes. Remove from the heat and stir in the ¼ cup (25 g) onion greens. Season with salt and pepper. Garnished with tomatoes, if using.

Yield: 2 to 4 servings

LENTIL, KALE, AND BARLEY RISOTTO

This longer-cooking risotto features pearl barley. It calls for cooked lentils, which you can make in advance.

4 teaspoons (20 ml) olive oil
¼ cup (40 g) diced onion
2 cloves garlic, minced
1 teaspoon seeded and diced fresh jalapeño
1 cup (200 g) dried pearl barley
2 cups (470 ml) vegetable broth, or more as needed
1 cup (235 ml) water, or more as needed
¼ teaspoon salt, plus more to taste
¼ teaspoon black pepper, plus more to taste
2 cups (340 g) cooked lentils
2 cups (140 g) tightly packed chopped kale
2 to 3 tablespoons (30 to 45 ml) lemon juice
¼ cup (24 g) nutritional yeast
2 teaspoons grated vegan parmesan cheese
1 teaspoon dried sweet basil

In an uncovered pressure cooker, heat the oil on medium-high. Sauté the onion, garlic, and jalapeño for 3 minutes, or until the onion is soft. Add the barley, broth, water, salt, and pepper. Stir to combine. Cover and bring to pressure. Cook at high pressure for 18 to 20 minutes. Use a quick release. Remove the lid and stir in the lentils, kale, juice, yeast, cheese, and basil. Simmer on low for approximately 10 minutes or to the desired risotto consistency. (Add more broth or water if needed.) Season with salt and pepper.

Yield: 6 to 8 servings

KOREAN KONGBAP

Kongbap is a Korean dish comprising white or brown rice cooked with one or more beans (and sometimes also other grains). Serve it over a bed of sautéed greens with soy sauce and a garnish of freshly grated ginger.

½ cup (100 g) dried black soybeans
½ cup (100 g) dried whole peas
½ cup (95 g) brown rice
½ cup (100 g) pearl barley
7 to 7½ cups (1.6 to 1.8 L) water, divided
1 tablespoon (15 ml) sesame oil

In a large bowl, combine the soybeans, peas, rice, and barley. Add 4 cups (940 ml) of the water. Soak overnight. Rinse, drain, and add to the pressure cooker. Add the remaining 3 to 3½ cups (705 to 825 ml) water. Drizzle in the oil. Stir to combine. Cover and bring to pressure. Cook at high pressure for 22 minutes. Allow for a natural release. If after 10 minutes the pressure has still not come down fully, manually release.

Yield: 6 servings

QUINOA PILAF

You can use this basic recipe and mix and match flavors for a variety of pilaf dishes. Simply substitute the parsley and thyme for other flavor profiles, such as ginger and paprika with curry vegetable broth and chopped cashews, for a tasty Indian style pilaf.

1 cup (175 g) quinoa
1 teaspoon walnut oil
½ cup (80 g) chopped red onion
1 cup (130 g) diced carrot
1½ cups (355 ml) vegetable broth
½ teaspoon dried parsley
½ teaspoon dried thyme
½ teaspoon salt
¼ to ½ cup (30 to 60 g) chopped walnuts
Chopped fresh parsley or thyme, for garnish

Rinse and drain the quinoa.

In an uncovered pressure cooker, heat the oil on medium heat. Sauté the onion and carrot for 3 minutes. Add the broth, parsley, thyme, salt, and quinoa. Stir to combine. Cover and bring to pressure. Cook at high pressure for 1 minute. Allow for a natural release. If after 10 minutes the pressure has still not come down fully, manually release.

Fluff the quinoa. Mix in the walnuts. Garnish with parsley or thyme.

Yield: 4 servings

EASY BUT MEMORABLE QUINOA PILAF WITH CACAO NIBS

Cacao nibs are a fun taste and texture to add to pilafs. They really pop! Serve this pilaf chilled or warm.

4 cups (740 g) cooked, drained quinoa
½ cup (178 g) crushed cacao nibs
1 cup (145 g) blueberries
½ cup (85 g) sliced strawberries
½ teaspoon salt
1 to 2 tablespoons (15 to 28 ml) olive oil
2 tablespoons (28 ml) lemon juice
1 teaspoon grated lemon zest
¼ cup (16 g) chopped fresh dill
¼ cup (24 g) chopped fresh mint
4 ounces (115 g) chopped arugula
½ cup (45 g) roasted soy nuts
½ cup (80 g) finely chopped red onion
Pomegranate vinegar, optional

In a large salad bowl, toss all of the ingredients together.

Yield: 4 servings

EASY ONE-POT (JOLLOF) RICE WITH CINNAMON AND CURRY

This dish is a classic in African cuisine. Switch it up to include a variety of vegetables and spices to suit your liking.

1 tablespoon (14 g) coconut oil
2 tomatoes, blanched, peeled, and chopped
2 carrots, sliced into coins
1 red onion, diced
3 large leaves kale, cut into fine chiffonade
1 red bell pepper, seeded and chopped
1 teaspoon grated ginger
Salt, to taste
1½ cups (278 g) uncooked basmati rice
3 cups (700 ml) salted vegetable broth
2 tablespoons (32 g) tomato paste
2 bay leaves
½ teaspoon nutmeg
9 curry leaves
1 cinnamon stick
1 teaspoon cumin
½ to 1 teaspoon red chile flakes

In a deep 2-quart (2 L) saucepan with a lid, heat the oil over medium-high heat. Sauté the tomatoes, carrots, onion, kale, bell pepper, and ginger until tender, about 5 to 7 minutes. Season with salt. Once the vegetables are soft, add the rice, broth, and paste. Toss in the bay leaves, nutmeg, curry leaves, cinnamon stick, cumin, and chile flakes. Stir well to combine.

Bring to a full boil over high heat. Immediately after the mixture begins to boil, reduce the heat to a simmer and cover. Check the rice after about 15 minutes, and cook until all liquid has been absorbed, about 20 minutes. Fluff with a fork. Remove the bay and curry leaves and cinnamon stick. Season with salt.

Yield: 6 servings

POLENTA HEARTS

With cookie cutters, you can make the polenta into any shape you want, including hearts.

4 cups (940 ml) water
1½ cups (210 g) coarse cornmeal or polenta
¼ cup (60 ml) nondairy milk
1 to 2 teaspoons (6 to 12 g) salt
2 to 3 tablespoons (25 to 37 g) nutritional yeast flakes
½ cup (55 g) finely chopped sun-dried tomatoes, oil-packed or reconstituted in water if dried
2 tablespoons (5 g) minced fresh basil
2 tablespoons (8 g) minced fresh parsley
1 tablespoon (15 ml) olive oil

In a 4-quart (4.5 L) saucepan, heat the water to boiling. Add the polenta or cornmeal. Stir frequently over low-medium heat, being careful that it does not boil over. Slowly add the milk, 1 teaspoon of the salt, and the yeast. Stir until the liquid is absorbed and the polenta thickens, 5 to 10 minutes. Add the tomatoes, basil, and parsley, stir for 1 more minute, and remove from the heat. Season with salt. At this point, the polenta will be thick (and getting thicker). Once you remove it from the heat, you can serve it immediately. However, to form it into shapes, let it set up for an hour. To do this, pour it into a 9 x 12-inch (23 x 30.5 cm) glass or nonstick pan, and spread evenly with a rubber spatula. Chill in the fridge for at least 1 hour. When ready to serve, punch out shapes with a cookie cutter (or cut it into squares).

In a nonstick skillet, heat the oil over medium heat. Sear the polenta shapes until golden on both sides and heated through.

Yield: 2 to 4 servings

NAVAJO TACOS

Indian tacos are made with fried bread and topped with the typical items found on Latin-style tacos. Add nondairy sour cream and cheese on top, or keep it simple if you prefer.

FOR THE CHICKPEA CHORIZO:
1 can (15 ounces, or 425 g) chickpeas, drained and rinsed
1 tablespoon (15 ml) olive oil
¼ to ½ teaspoon cayenne pepper
1 teaspoon paprika
Smoked sea salt, to taste
1 tablespoon (15 ml) apple cider vinegar
1 tablespoon (15 ml) lime juice
1 teaspoon ground cumin
2 tablespoons (30 g) ketchup
1 teaspoon onion powder
1 clove garlic, minced

FOR THE BREAD:
1 cup (125 g) all-purpose flour, plus ½ cup (63 g) for rolling
1 teaspoon onion powder
1 teaspoon dried cilantro
½ teaspoon salt
Black pepper, to taste
1 teaspoon baking powder
½ cup (120 ml) water
Vegetable or peanut oil, for frying

FOR THE TACOS:
1 ⅓ cups (95 g) shredded lettuce
Heaping ½ cup (160 g) corn salsa
Heaping ½ cup (160 g) tomato salsa
1 avocado, peeled, pitted, and sliced, optional
Chopped fresh parsley or cilantro, for garnish
1 lime, cut into wedges

To make the Chickpea Chorizo: In a large skillet, combine all of the ingredients. Cook over medium-high heat for about 4 minutes, stirring occasionally, until all of the liquid has been absorbed.

To make the bread: In a large bowl, combine 1 cup (125 g) of the flour, the onion powder, cilantro, salt, pepper, and baking powder. Add the water, and mix thoroughly. Let stand for 15 minutes at room temperature. Divide the sticky dough into 4 equal portions.

On a floured surface, with about ½ cup (63 g) extra flour handy and your hands sufficiently floured, flatten each portion of dough (sprinkling it with flour, but not kneading the flour in) into a 6-inch (15-cm) disk.

Fill a deep 10-inch (25-cm) pot with 1 inch (2.5 cm) of oil. Preheat to 350°F (180°C) on a deep-frying thermometer. Line a plate with paper towels.

Carefully add one disk of dough at a time to the hot oil and cook for 3 minutes on each side, or until golden brown. Transfer to the paper towel–lined plate lined to absorb excess oil. Repeat with the remaining 3 disks, bringing the oil back up to temperature between batches.

To make the tacos: Top each piece of bread with ⅓ cup (24 g) lettuce, 2 heaping tablespoons (40 g) corn salsa, 2 heaping tablespoons (40 g) tomato salsa, a generous ⅓ cup (106 g) chickpea chorizo, and one-fourth of the avocado. Garnish with the parsley or cilantro and serve with the lime.

Yield: 4 tacos

ASPARAGUS AND MUSHROOM TACOS WITH CILANTRO MAYONNAISE

Try to find corn tortillas made from just corn, salt, and maybe a little lime juice, such as Trader Joe's brand.

FOR THE FILLING:
16 ounces (450 g) cremini mushrooms, thinly sliced
1 to 3 serrano chile peppers, stemmed, seeded, and minced
3 cloves garlic, minced
1 small onion, diced
2 teaspoons cumin
1 to 2 teaspoons red chile powder
¼ teaspoon chipotle chile powder
1 teaspoon minced fresh thyme leaves
1 teaspoon salt
2 tablespoons (30 ml) canola oil, divided
8 stalks asparagus, tough ends removed

FOR THE CILANTRO MAYONNAISE:
⅓ cup (5 g) finely chopped fresh cilantro
1 tablespoon (15 ml) lime juice
1 cup (225 g) vegan mayonnaise

FOR THE TACOS:
12 corn tortillas
½ cup (8 g) chopped fresh cilantro
1 cup (150 g) diced fresh tomatoes

To make the filling: In a large frying pan, toss the mushrooms, chiles, garlic, onion, cumin, red chile powder, chipotle chile powder, thyme, salt, and 1½ tablespoons (22 ml) of the oil. Cover and cook over medium heat for about 10 minutes, stirring occasionally, or until the mushrooms are tender and have released a good amount of liquid. Uncover and reduce the heat to low. Simmer for about 7 minutes, or until all of the liquid is gone.

Slice the asparagus stalks in half down the length of the spear. Place in a separate frying pan with the remaining ½ tablespoon (8 ml) oil. Sauté over medium-high heat for 2 to 3 minutes, or until bright green and tender.

To make the Cilantro Mayonnaise: In a bowl, mix all the ingredients together until well combined.

To make the tacos: In a flat skillet or cast-iron pan, warm the tortillas gently on each side until pliable and light golden brown. As each tortilla cooks, stack in a pile and cover with foil to retain heat and moisture. Among the tortillas, divide the mushroom mixture, asparagus, cilantro, tomatoes, and Cilantro Mayonnaise.

Yield: 12 tacos, or 6 servings

SWEET POTATO TACOS

Instead of the orange sweet potatoes (a.k.a. yams) in this recipe, you can use yellow potatoes instead.

2 large sweet potatoes (or yams), peeled and cubed
1 tablespoon (15 ml) olive oil
1 medium yellow onion, sliced
1 red bell pepper, seeded and finely diced
Salt, to taste
Black pepper, to taste
2 cloves garlic, minced or pressed
¼ teaspoon cayenne pepper
½ fresh jalapeño pepper, seeded and diced
8 to 10 small crispy corn or soft flour tortillas
Chopped cilantro, for garnish
Peach salsa, for topping

Place a steamer basket in a medium saucepan with enough water on the bottom of the pot to create steam. Place the potatoes in the basket, cover, and steam over medium-low heat until fork-tender, about 20 to 25 minutes, and then drain. (Keep an eye on the pot to ensure that the water doesn't evaporate, burning the saucepan.)

Meanwhile, in a medium sauté pan, heat the oil over medium heat. Add the onion and bell pepper. Cook for

about 7 minutes, or until the vegetables are translucent. Season with salt and black pepper.

When the potatoes are cooked, transfer them to a large bowl, along with the garlic, cayenne, jalapeño, and onion mixture. Season with salt. Mash the ingredients together.

Fill the tortillas with the filling, sprinkle with cilantro, and top with salsa.

Yield: 8 to 10 servings

BLACK BEAN, POTATO, AND CHEESE ENCHILADAS

The key to keeping the tortillas from splitting while rolling is to use the freshest, best-quality corn tortillas you can find. They should just include corn, salt, and maybe a touch of lime juice.

FOR THE ENCHILADA SAUCE:
1 cup (240 g) diced canned tomatoes, drained
1 can (8 ounces, or 225 g) tomato sauce
½ to 1 teaspoon salt
3 dried chile peppers (guajillos or chipotles)
2 cloves garlic, minced
1 tablespoon (7 g) cumin
1 tablespoon (15 ml) olive oil
2 cups (470 ml) vegetable broth
¼ cup (40 g) minced red onion
1 can (6 ounces, or 170 g) tomato paste

FOR THE ENCHILADAS:
2 cups (220 g) small-diced potatoes
1 tablespoon (15 ml) olive oil
Dash or two of salt
12 corn tortillas
1 can (15 ounces, or 420 g) black beans, drained
2 cups (230 g) nondairy shredded cheese

To make the sauce: In a saucepan, combine all of the ingredients and simmer over medium heat until the chile peppers are plump and rehydrated, about 20 minutes. Let cool.

Transfer the mixture to a blender. Process until very smooth.

To make the enchiladas: In a pan, sauté the potatoes in the oil with the salt over medium-high heat until lightly golden brown, stirring often. Remove from the heat and let cool briefly.

Preheat the oven to 350°F (180°C, or gas mark 4). Lightly grease a 9 x 13-inch (23 x 33 cm) baking dish.

Pour about ½ cup (120 ml) of the enchilada sauce onto a large, rimmed plate or bowl. Line up the rest of the ingredients, plus a large clean plate, to assemble the enchiladas.

Dip one corn tortilla into the sauce, ensuring both front

and back are completely covered. Transfer the single tortilla to a clean plate and fill with about 2 tablespoons (28 g) each of potatoes, beans, and cheese. Roll up to close and place in the baking dish seam side down. Repeat until all the tortillas are dipped, filled, and rolled, tucking each enchilada snugly into the baking dish, close together to keep them from unrolling. Cover the enchiladas with the remaining sauce and sprinkle with any remaining cheese, if desired. Bake, uncovered, for about 20 minutes, or until the tortillas become slightly crispy on top.

Yield: 12 enchiladas, or 6 servings

BLACK BEAN AND SUMMER SQUASH ENCHILADAS

The spiciness of the sauce will increase once the dish is baked. Try these enchiladas baked with a little Cashew "Cheesy" Sauce on top. (See page 9.)

6 ounces (170 g) tomato paste
15 ounces (434 g) tomato sauce
½ teaspoon chipotle powder
1 cup (160 g) finely diced onion
½ cup (120 ml) low-sodium vegetable broth, optional
2 cloves garlic, minced
1 medium red bell pepper, seeded and chopped
2 medium zucchini, diced
1½ cups (378 g) black beans, well rinsed and drained
1 bunch spinach, washed and chopped, or 1 small package (5 ounces, or 140 g) washed
1½ teaspoons ground cumin
¼ teaspoon black pepper
⅛ teaspoon salt
2 teaspoons lime juice
8 corn tortillas
6 green onions, sliced

Preheat the oven to 350°F (180°C, or gas mark 4).

In a large bowl, stir together the paste, sauce, and chipotle powder.

In a large pan, sauté the onion over medium heat until it starts to soften. If the onion starts to stick to the bottom of the pan, add the broth. When the onion softens, add the garlic and cook for 2 minutes. Stir in the bell pepper and zucchini. Cook, stirring occasionally, for 2 to 3 minutes, or until the squash becomes tender. If the vegetables start to stick to the bottom of the pan, add the broth. Once the squash is tender, add the beans, spinach, cumin, black pepper, and salt. Simmer for 5 minutes until the spinach wilts.

Remove from the heat and stir in the juice. Taste and add additional seasonings if desired.

In the bottom of a 9×13-inch (22 × 33 cm) ovenproof dish, spread a thin layer of the tomato mixture. Dip a tortilla in the bowl of tomato mixture to completely cover it with

sauce. Lay the coated tortilla in the bottom of the dish. Spread a large tablespoon (one-eighth) of the veggie–bean mixture across the center of the tortilla. Gently roll up the tortilla and place seam-side down in baking dish at one end. Repeat with the remaining ingredients until all of the tortillas are filled, rolled and placed next to each other in the dish. Pour the remaining tomato mixture over the enchiladas. Cover. Bake for approximately 20 minutes. (The dish doesn't need to be cooked, but just thoroughly heated through.) After 20 minutes, check to make sure dish is bubbling hot. Sprinkle with the green onions.

Yield: 8 enchiladas

WOW! CHOCOLATE DINNER ENCHILADAS

Instead of the tofu, try using 1 cup (70 g) mushrooms, (99 g) cooked eggplant, (205 g) squash, (136 g) sweet potato, (225 g) potato, or a combo!

12 to 14 corn tortillas
2 cups (475 ml) water (or enough to cover the tortillas)
¼ cup (60 ml) lime juice
3 to 4 cups (750 g to 1 kg) mole sauce or enchilada sauce, divided
1 cup (150 g) crumbled firm tofu
1 cup (30 g) chopped spinach
½ cup (80 g) diced onion
¼ cup (35 g) cornmeal
½ teaspoon chili powder
2 minced cloves garlic
½ teaspoon salt
1 tablespoon (15 ml) olive oil
1 teaspoon dried crushed oregano
2 teaspoons cider vinegar
¼ cup (24 g) raw cacao powder
¼ cup (4 g) chopped fresh cilantro
¼ teaspoon black pepper
½ cup (50 g) chopped toasted almonds

Preheat the oven to 375°F (190°C, gas mark 5). Greased a 9× 13-inch (23×33 cm) baking dish.

In a large shallow bowl, soak the tortillas in the water and juice for 2 to 3 minutes. Drain and shake the tortillas before using. (This makes them less likely to crack.) Return the tortillas to the bowl. Spread them out a little, though it's okay if they overlap.

Spoon ½ cup (125 g) of the sauce into the bottom of the prepared dish.

In a bowl, mix together the tofu, spinach, onion, cornmeal, chili powder, garlic, salt, oil, oregano, vinegar, cacao, cilantro, pepper, and nuts. Divide evenly among the tortillas, roll each one up, and place in the dish on top of the sauce. Pour the rest of the sauce over the top. Bake for 40 minutes.

Yield: 6 servings

GRILLED VEGETABLE FAJITAS

Although you can make these based only on vegetables, add some meatless chicken strips or grilled tofu for a different flavor.

Juice from 2 limes
¼ cup (60 ml) olive oil
1 teaspoon (1.8 g) dried oregano
1 teaspoon (2 g) ground cumin
¼ to ½ teaspoon chili powder
¼ cup (4 g) chopped fresh cilantro
Salt, to taste
Black pepper, to taste
1 large red onion, cut into wedges
3 bell peppers, seeded and cut into ½-inch (1 cm) strips
2 yellow squash, halved and cut into ½-inch (1 cm) strips
4 cloves garlic, halved lengthwise
12 (8-inch, or 20-cm) flour or corn tortillas
1 cup (260 g) salsa
Guacamole
Vegan sour cream

In a large bowl, stir together the juice, oil, oregano, cumin, chili powder, and cilantro. Season with salt and black pepper. Add the onion, bell peppers, squash, and garlic and toss to combine.

Prepare your grill or roasting pan. The vegetables can be made in a large grill pan, grilled outdoors, grilled on a tabletop electric grill, broiled, or roasted. Cook the vegetables until the desired doneness, 7 to 15 minutes, turning occasionally to char each side. Brush on the marinade as the vegetables cook. Transfer the vegetables to a large bowl.

Grill the tortillas, about 1 minute on each side, or microwave them on high, wrapped in a paper towel, for 20 seconds. Once warm, keep them in a low oven or wrapped in a kitchen towel to retain heat.

To serve, place the vegetables, tortillas, salsa, guacamole, and sour cream on a table. Each person can assemble his or her fajita, as desired.

Yield: 12 servings

CHICK'N STRIPS IN MOLE

Mole sauce is so popular and so varied in Mexico, it is often referred to as Mexico's curry. Serve this over rice, in a burrito, or as an addition to a taco buffet.

FOR THE CHICK'N STRIPS:
1 package (8 ounces, or 225 g) soy curls
4 cups (950 ml) very hot water
2 chick'n vegetable bouillon cubes or 2 teaspoons chick'n vegetable bouillon
1 tablespoon (15 ml) olive oil

FOR THE MOLE SAUCE:
1 tomato
4 cloves garlic
2 to 4 Mexican green chile peppers
1 serrano pepper
1 tomatillo, quartered
4 ounces (115 g) bittersweet chocolate (70 percent cocoa), melted
1 teaspoon cinnamon
½ teaspoon cloves
2 cups (230 g) corn Chex-type cereal
3 cups (700 ml) salted vegetable broth

To Make the Chick'n Strips: In a large bowl, place the soy curls, water, and bouillon. Let rest for 10 minutes. Drain well. Squeeze any excess liquid from the soy curls.

In a large, deep-sided, nonstick frying pan, sauté the soy curls in the oil over medium-high heat for about 10 minutes, or until lightly browned and crispy, stirring often. Remove from the heat.

To make the Mole Sauce: Preheat the oven to broil.

On a foil-covered, baking sheet, place the tomato, garlic, and peppers. Broil for about 45 minutes, or until blackened, turning occasionally to cook evenly. (The tomato will not be as blackened as the peppers, but it will turn very soft and wrinkly when ready. The peppers will be blackened on all sides, and the garlic should be fragrant and softened.)

Once the vegetables are roasted, rinse the peppers and tomato under cold water to gently remove the skins and stems. Let cool completely.

Transfer the vegetables to a blender. Add the tomatillos, chocolate, cinnamon, cloves, Chex cereal, and broth. Blend until smooth, about 2 minutes.

To finish: Place the sauce over the prepared soy curls in the frying pan and bring to a boil over high heat, stirring often so as not to burn the sauce. Immediately reduce the heat to medium and let simmer, covered, for about 15 minutes, stirring occasionally. (The sauce will thicken slightly upon heating.)

Yield: 6 servings

TEMPEH TACOS OR TOSTADAS

In this healthy twist on traditional Mexican fare, tempeh offers a meaty texture that is 100 percent plant-based.

FOR THE TEMPEH FILLING:
1 package (8 ounces, or 224 g) package tempeh, cut into 4 equal pieces.
2 cups (470 ml) vegetable broth, divided
2 cloves garlic, minced
½ cup (80 g) diced red onion
¼ cup (30 g) finely diced celery

2 cups (140 g) diced cremini mushrooms
1 seeded and diced fresh jalapeño
½ cup (130 g) mild salsa
1 to 2 teaspoons chili powder
Juice of ½ lime
½ teaspoon salt

FOR THE SPINACH:
1 teaspoon olive oil
2 cloves garlic, minced
8 cups (480 g) loosely packed baby spinach
Pinch of salt
Juice of ½ lime
6 taco shells or corn tortillas, baked or fried in oil until crispy
½ cup (120 g) vegan sour cream
1 lime, cut into 6 wedges

To make the tempeh: Place the tempeh in an uncovered pressure cooker with 1 cup (235 ml) of the broth. Cover and bring to pressure. As soon as pressure is achieved, use a quick release. Remove the lid and return to medium-high heat.

Using a spoon, crumble the tempeh into a "ground meat" consistency. Add the garlic, onion, celery, mushrooms, jalapeño, and salsa. Add the chili powder and remaining 1 cup (235 ml) broth. Stir well. Cover and return to pressure. Cook at high pressure for 3 minutes. Allow for a natural release. Remove the lid, add the juice and salt. Simmer on low to cook off the extra liquid.

To make the spinach: In a skillet, heat the oil over medium-high heat. Sauté the garlic and spinach for 30 seconds, tossing with tongs to prevent sticking. Add the salt and juice, toss, and remove from the heat.

Place a layer of spinach on each of the tacos shells or corn tortillas. Add the tempeh and a dollop of sour cream. Serve with the lime.

Yield: 6 servings

INDIAN-STYLE BLACK BEAN AND VEGGIE BURRITOS

The combination of Southwestern ingredients and Eastern seasonings adds a unique flavor to this burrito.

1 tablespoon (15 ml) oil
2 bell peppers, seeded and cut into strips
1 large onion, sliced
4 cloves garlic, chopped
1 teaspoon minced fresh ginger
1 sweet potato, cut into ½-inch (1.3 cm) cubes
1 teaspoon garam masala
½ cup (120 ml) vegetable broth
1 can (15 ounces, or 420 g) black beans, drained and rinsed
Salt, to taste
Black pepper, to taste
1 cup (165 g) cooked brown basmati rice
1 head romaine lettuce, shredded
Salsa
4 large burrito-size whole wheat tortillas

In a large pan, heat the oil over medium heat. Sauté the bell peppers, onion, garlic, and ginger for 7 to 10 minutes, stirring frequently, or until the peppers and onion are soft. Add the potato and garam masala and mix well. Add the broth, and cover. Reduce the heat to medium-low. Cook for 10 to 15 minutes, or until the potato is tender. At the very end of the cooking time, add the beans and stir to combine. Cook for 5 minutes longer. Season with salt and black pepper.

Spoon the vegetable and bean mixture, rice, lettuce, and salsa evenly down the center of a tortilla, and then roll it up.

Yield: 4 servings

VEGAN "BACON" AND CABBAGE

This simple, plant-based version of cabbage cooks up quickly and is sure to wow your omnivore friends and family.

4 tablespoons (55 g) vegan butter
1 package (5 ounces, or 140 g) vegan bacon, cut into ½-inch (1.3 cm) pieces
1 sweet onion, cut into half-moon slices
2 potatoes, peeled and diced into bite-size cubes
1 head cabbage, cored and thinly sliced (about 1½ pounds, or 680 g)
1 tablespoon (7 g) smoked paprika
1½ cups (355 ml) vegan chicken-flavored broth
Salt, to taste
Black pepper, to taste

In an uncovered pressure cooker, melt the butter on medium-high. Add the bacon and stir well to cover with the butter. Add the onion and sauté until soft, about 3 minutes. Add the potatoes, cabbage, and paprika. Add the broth and stir to combine. Cover and bring to pressure. Cook at high pressure for 4 minutes. Allow for a natural release. Uncover. Season with salt and pepper.

Yield: 6 servings

SEITAN SWISS STEAK

With this dish, you'll love the smell of the browning food, the thickness of the tomato gravy, and the need to eat it with mashed potatoes.

3 heaping tablespoons (24 g) flour
1 teaspoon salt
¼ teaspoon black pepper
1 package (8 ounces, or 224 g) prepared seitan strips
¼ cup (60 ml) olive oil
1 cup (160 g) half-moon slices yellow onion
½ cup (60 g) chopped celery
1 can (15 ounces, or 420 g) diced tomatoes
½ teaspoon vegan Worcestershire sauce

On a plate, mix the flour, salt, and pepper. Dredge both sides of each seitan strip in the flour.

In an uncovered pressure cooker, heat the oil on medium-high. Add the seitan and brown for 2½ minutes. Flip and brown for another 2½ minutes.

Transfer the seitan to a plate.

Add 1 tablespoon (8 g) of the leftover flour mix to the oil and seitan drippings remaining in the pressure cooker. Whisk until thickened. Add the onion, celery, tomatoes, and Worcestershire. (This should bubble from the heat right away.) Stir well. Place the seitan back into the pressure cooker. Spoon the gravy over the seitan. Cover and bring to pressure. Cook at high pressure for 2 minutes. Use a quick release.

Yield: 4 servings, 6 seitan cutlets (8 to 10 servings)

BOEUF(LESS) BOURGUIGNON

Julia Child made the classic recipe for Boeuf Bourguignon a household name in the 1960s. Serve the dish over mashed potatoes.

FOR THE MARINADE:
1 tablespoon (2.4 g) fresh thyme
⅓ cup (80 ml) vegan Worcestershire sauce
2 cups (475 ml) vegetable broth (preferably beef flavored)
7 drops of liquid smoke
1 package (8 ounces, or 225 g) soy curls
3 tablespoons (45 g) vegan margarine
¼ cup (20 g) bacon-flavored bits
Herb bouquet (bouquet garni): sprigs of parsley, sage, rosemary, and thyme tied with kitchen twine

FOR THE SAUTÉ:
5 ounces (140 g) button mushrooms, halved
4 medium carrots, sliced into rounds
1 small red onion, diced
2 cloves garlic, minced

1 tablespoon (14 g) vegan margarine
½ teaspoon salt

FOR THE SAUCE:
3 tablespoons (30 g) superfine brown rice flour
1 teaspoon or 1 cube vegetable bouillon (preferably beef-flavored)
½ cup (120 ml) full-bodied red wine (such as Zinfandel or Cabernet Sauvignon)
1½ tablespoons (24 g) tomato paste
2 cups (475 ml) vegetable broth
10 small pearl onions, peeled

Preheat the oven to 350°F (180°C, gas mark 4).

To make the marinade: In a medium saucepan, bring the thyme, Worcester, broth, and liquid smoke just to a light boil. Remove from the heat.

In a large bowl, combine the marinade and soy curls. Let rest for 15 minutes. Let the mixture come back down to room temperature and then using clean hands, squeeze out all of the liquid from the soy curls, reserving the marinade in the bowl.

In a large frying pan, heat the margarine over medium-high heat. Sauté the bacon, just until it starts to sizzle, about 5 minutes. Gently tilt the pan to evenly coat with bacon-flavored margarine. Add the soy curls and sauté until evenly browned, about 10 minutes.

Transfer to a large casserole dish and add herb bouquet.

To make the sauté: In the same saucepan, sauté the mushrooms, carrots, onion, and garlic in the margarine over medium-high heat for about 10 minutes, or until the onion is translucent and lightly brown on the edges. Add the salt while cooking.

To make the sauce: Into the bowl with the leftover marinade, whisk the flour, bouillon, wine, paste, and broth until no lumps remain. Add the onions.

In the casserole dish, combine the vegetables and soy curls. Top evenly with sauce. Cover with foil. Bake for 1 hour. Uncover and cook an additional 25 minutes, or until fragrant and bubbly on top. Remove the herb bouquet before serving.

Yield: 8 servings

33 Easy One-Pot [Jollof] Rice with Cinnamon and Curry; 34 Polenta Hearts; 35 Navajo Tacos; 36 Asparagus and Mushroom Tacos with Cilantro Mayonnaise; 37 Sweet Potato Tacos; 38 Black Bean, Potato, and Cheese Enchiladas; 39 Black Bean and Summer Squash Enchiladas; 40 Wow! Chocolate Dinner Enchiladas

41 Grilled Vegetables Fajitas; 42 Chick'n Strips in Mole; 43 Tempeh Tacos or Tostadas; 44 Indian-Style Black Bean and Veggie Burritos; 45 Vegan "Bacon" and Cabbage; 46 Seitan Swiss Steak; 47 Boeuf(less) Bourguignon; 48 Holiday Roast with Mashed Potatoes

HOLIDAY ROAST WITH MASHED POTATOES

You can buy vegan stuffed roasts in grocery stores during the holiday season. Pressure cooking is the best way to prepare these dense, precooked roasts; the outcome is a soft, succulent dish.

1 to 2 teaspoons olive oil
4 cloves garlic, minced
1 cup (160 g) diced yellow onion
2 cups (260 g) diced carrot
2 cups (220 g) diced potato
1 teaspoon salt
1 vegan stuffed roast (1 pound, or 454 g), thawed
¾ to 1 cup (180 to 235 ml) vegetable broth
1 tablespoon (15 ml) almond milk
¼ teaspoon black pepper
1 teaspoon vegan butter, optional

In an uncovered pressure cooker, heat the oil on medium-high. Sauté the garlic and onion for 1 minute. Add the carrots, potatoes, and salt. Mix well. Place the roast on top of the vegetables and pour the broth over the roast. Cover and bring to pressure. Cook at low pressure for 8 minutes. Use a quick release. Remove the lid and remove the roast to a plate.

Add the milk, pepper, and butter to the vegetables in the pressure cooker. Mash with a potato masher. Slice the roast and serve with the mashed vegetables.

Yield: 4 servings

FIESTA SOY CURL AND RICE CASSEROLE

Soy curls are a great substitute for traditional chicken dishes. Made from the whole soybean, they are packed with protein and very versatile. This loose casserole is best served in a bowl.

3 cups (300 g) soy curls
4 cups (940 ml) vegetable broth, warm, divided
1 teaspoon olive oil
2 cloves garlic, minced
½ cup (80 g) diced yellow onion
2 tablespoons (16 g) vegan chicken-flavored seasoning
1 tablespoon (8 g) taco seasoning
1 cup (190 g) long-grain white rice
1 can (15.25-ounce, or 427 g) corn, drained
1 can (28 ounces, or 784 g) diced tomatoes with green chiles
1 can (8 ounces, or 224 g) tomato sauce
½ to 1 teaspoon salt
1½ cups (180 g) shredded vegan cheese, divided
1 cup (70 g) crumbled corn tortilla chips
Black pepper, to taste

Preheat the oven to 375°F (190°C, or gas mark 5). Grease a 13 x 7-inch (33 x 18 cm) casserole dish.

In a bowl, soak the soy curls in 3 cups (705 ml) of the broth for 15 minutes. Drain the soy curls.

In an uncovered pressure cooker, heat the oil on medium-high. Sauté the garlic and onion for 3 minutes, or until the onion is soft. Add the soy curls, chicken-flavored seasoning, and taco seasoning. Sauté for 3 to 5 minutes. (Soy curls, much like tofu, need time to absorb the flavors.) Add water or vegetable broth if they begin to stick to the pan. Add the rice, corn, tomatoes and chiles, sauce, and remaining 1 cup (235 ml) vegetable broth. Mix well. Cover and bring to pressure. Cook at high pressure for 4 minutes. Use a quick release. Remove the lid. Season with salt. Stir in 1 cup (120 g) of the cheese.

Transfer the mixture to the prepared casserole dish.

In a small bowl, mix the remaining ½ cup (60 g) cheese with the chips. Sprinkle over the casserole. Bake for 10 minutes, or until the cheese has melted. Serve with pepper.

Yield: 8 to 10 servings

VEGAN "PEPPERONI" SAUSAGE

This seitan is an alternative to a favorite pizza topping. it can be made quickly and easily in the pressure cooker. You can cut thicker slices and serve as a sausage patty with breakfast.

FOR THE BROTH:
3 cups (705 ml) water
3 cups (705 ml) vegetable broth
¼ cup (60 ml) low-sodium soy sauce

FOR THE SEITAN:
1½ cups (180 g) vital wheat gluten
¼ cup (30 g) chickpea flour
2 tablespoons (14 g) nutritional yeast
½ teaspoon allspice
½ teaspoon paprika
½ teaspoon anise seed
½ teaspoon fennel seed, crumbled
½ teaspoon red pepper flakes
½ teaspoon garlic powder
½ teaspoon black pepper
1 cup (235 ml) vegetable broth, plus more as needed
1 teaspoon olive oil
½ teaspoon liquid smoke
½ teaspoon vegan Worcestershire sauce

To make the broth: In an uncovered pressure cooker, add the broth ingredients and bring to a boil.

To make the seitan: In the bowl of a stand mixer fitted with the dough hook attachment, combine the gluten, flour, yeast, and seasonings.

In a separate bowl, whisk together the broth, oil, liquid

smoke, and Worcestershire. Add the wet ingredients to the dry ingredients and stir until well combined. Knead with the dough hook for 5 minutes.

Divide the dough in half. From one half, roll 4 small sausages. Wrap them individually in cheesecloth, tying the ends with string.

Roll the other half into a larger sausage. Wrap it in cheesecloth, tying the ends with string.

Place in the boiling cooking broth, cover, and bring to pressure. Cook at pressure for 30 minutes. Allow for a natural release. Remove the sausages from the broth to cool before handling or serving.

Yield: 8 to 10 servings

FALAFELOGS WITH CUCUMBER RELISH

This dish is like a falafel hot dog! The parsley and cilantro add a bright, fresh flavor.

FOR THE FALAFELOGS:
1 can (15 ounces, or 425 g) chickpeas, drained and rinsed, or 1¾ cups (420 g) cooked chickpeas
1 cup (160 g) diced yellow onion
1 Roma tomato, roughly chopped (about ⅓ cup)
1 ounce (28 g) fresh parsley (about 1 cup [5 g] fresh leaves)
½ ounce (14 g) fresh cilantro (about ⅓ cup [5 g] fresh leaves)
2 to 4 large cloves garlic
½ cup (60 g) chickpea flour
½ cup (72 g) vital wheat gluten flour
1 tablespoon (15 ml) lemon juice
1 teaspoon salt
1 teaspoon baking powder
1 teaspoon ground cumin
¼ teaspoon cayenne pepper

FOR THE CUCUMBER RELISH:
½ cup (128 g) tahini
¼ cup (60 ml) lemon juice
3 to 4 large cloves garlic
2 teaspoons dried dill
1 medium cucumber, seeded and diced (about 1½ cups, or [205 g])
2 Roma tomatoes, seeded and diced (about ⅔ cup, or [120 g])
1 tablespoon (1 g) fresh chopped cilantro
1 tablespoon (1 g) fresh chopped parsley
Salt, to taste
Black pepper, to taste
6 to 8 pitas

To make the falafelogs: In a food processor, process all of the log ingredients until a loose dough forms. (It should be the consistency of peanut butter.)

Transfer the mixture to a bowl, cover, and chill for 20 to 30 minutes. (This step allows the gluten to develop.)

Preheat the oven to 350°F (180°C, or gas mark 4). Line a rimmed baking sheet with parchment.

Scoop about ⅓ cup (3. ounces, or 100 g) dough and form into a log shape about 6 to 7 inches long by 1½ inches wide (15 to 17 cm long × 4 cm wide). (The dough is very soft, and you may need to form the log right on the baking sheet. It will firm up when baked.)

Repeat until all of the dough is used. Bake for 20 minutes, flip, and bake for 20 minutes, or until the exterior is firm and browned. (They might look dry, but the insides will be nice and soft.)

To make the relish: In a blender, puree the tahini, juice, and garlic until smooth. (The lemon juice will curdle the tahini, similar to buttermilk, resulting in an airy, fluffy mixture.)

Transfer the mixture to a bowl. Fold in the dill, cucumber, tomatoes, cilantro, and parsley. Season with salt and pepper. Chill until ready to serve.

Assemble the pitas by placing the falafelog in the center and topping with a liberal amount of Cucumber Relish.

Yield: 6 to 8 servings

ITALIAN "SAUSAGES"

These protein-packed wieners taste great on their own or on a bun with grilled peppers, sliced or crumbled onto a pizza, or chopped and mixed into a marinara sauce to pour over pasta. Special thanks to Julie Hasson for her ingenious steaming method!

1 cup (235 ml) low-sodium vegetable broth
1 block (12 ounces, or 340 g) soft silken tofu, drained and mashed with a fork
¼ cup (66 g) tomato paste
3 tablespoons (45 ml) olive oil
½ cup (80 g) finely diced onion
½ ounce (14 g) fresh parsley, finely chopped (about ½ cup [30 g] tightly packed)
2 tablespoons (17 g) minced garlic
1 tablespoon (6 g) dried whole fennel seed
1 teaspoon dried oregano
1 teaspoon smoked paprika
½ teaspoon dried red chili flakes
½ teaspoon black pepper
½ teaspoon dried basil
½ to 1 teaspoon salt
¼ teaspoon cayenne pepper
2 cups (288 g) vital wheat gluten flour
8 sheets aluminum foil measuring about 6 × 12 inches (15 × 30 cm)

In a large bowl, mix all of the ingredients, except the flour until well incorporated.

Add the flour and mix until a stringy dough forms. Allow

the dough to rest for 20 minutes. (This allows the gluten to develop.)

Divide the dough into eight equal portions, about ½ cup (5 ounces, or 140 g each). Form each piece of dough into sausage shape and place near the long edge of one piece of foil. Roll up the foil and twist the ends tight.

These can be steamed or baked.

To steam, bring water in a steamer to a boil. Carefully place the wrapped sausages in the steamer basket and steam for 45 to 60 minutes. Remove from the steamer and allow to cool enough to handle. (They should be firm to the touch.)

To bake, preheat the oven to 350°F (180°C, or gas mark 4). Place the wrapped sausages in a single layer on a baking sheet, seam side down. Bake for 30 minutes, flip, and bake for 30 minutes longer. Remove from the oven and allow to cool enough to handle.

Once cooled, remove from the foil and refrigerate, or freeze until ready to use.

While you can eat these immediately, after they are unwrapped and cooled overnight, they get nice and firm, and the flavors stand out more. To reheat, pan-fry or grill.

Yield: 8 sausages

STRAWBERRY SPINACH TACOWICH
Stored in the fridge, the dressing will keep for up to 4 days.

FOR THE DRESSING:
¼ cup (60 ml) olive oil
¼ cup (60 g) unsweetened plain nondairy yogurt
Pinch of salt
¼ teaspoon ground white pepper
¼ cup (60 ml) orange Muscat champagne vinegar
1½ tablespoons (15 g) minced shallot
3 tablespoons (22 g) finely chopped dry-roasted hazel-
    nuts, plus more for garnish

FOR THE TACOWICHES:
Eight 6-inch (15-cm) corn or wheat tortillas
2 cups (67 g) baby spinach
16 small (1 inch, or 2.5 cm) strawberries (about 4 ounces,
    or 112 g), hulled and quartered

To make the dressing: In a blender, pulse the oil, yogurt, salt, pepper, vinegar, and shallot until combined. Transfer to an airtight container and stir in the hazelnuts before sealing.

To make the tacowiches: Spread 1 tablespoon (15 g) dressing onto each tortilla. Add ¼ cup (8 g) baby spinach, 2 quartered strawberries, and a sprinkling of chopped hazelnuts on top. Drizzle with extra dressing, if desired. Fold in half to eat.

Yield: 8 tacowiches, ¾ cup (180 g) dressing

MEAT(LESS)BALL SUBS
These are a just-right meatless ball. With gentle handling, you'll have minimal crumbling.

FOR THE MEATLESS BALLS:
⅔ cup (160 ml) boiling water
¾ cup (75 g) texturized vegetable protein (TVP)
½ cup (80 g) minced onion
3 cloves garlic, minced
1½ teaspoons Italian seasoning blend
½ teaspoon dried parsley
¼ teaspoon red pepper flakes
2 tablespoons (33 g) tomato paste
1 teaspoon vegan Worcestershire sauce
1 cup (144 g) vital wheat gluten, or more if needed
2 tablespoons (30 ml) olive oil
1 cup (235 ml) vegetable broth
¼ cup (60 ml) dry red wine, optional

FOR THE SANDWICHES:
2 tablespoons (30 ml) olive oil, divided
1 medium onion, cut into thin half-moons
1 green bell pepper, seeded and cut into strips
4 sub rolls, wedges cut out of tops, some of the bread
    removed, and toasted
1⅓ cups (333 g) marinara sauce, warmed

To make the meatless balls: In a small bowl, combine the water and TVP.

In a food processor, pulse the onion, garlic, seasoning blend, parsley, red pepper, paste, and Worcestershire until combined. Add the TVP, any unabsorbed water, and the gluten. Pulse until thoroughly combined and the mixture can be formed into balls. If it is too sticky, add 1 tablespoon (9 g) gluten and mix again. Roll about 1 rounded tablespoon (30 g) of the mixture into a tightly compressed ball. Repeat to form 16 to 20 balls.

Preheat the oven to 300°F (150°C, or gas mark 2).

In a large oven-safe skillet, heat the oil over medium-high heat. Brown the balls for about 5 minutes. Turn gently to brown all sides. Remove from the heat. Add the broth and wine, if using, to the skillet. Cover tightly with foil. Bake for 20 minutes. Remove from the oven and carefully turn the balls over. Re-cover tightly with foil and bake for 20 more minutes. Remove the foil and bake uncovered for 10 minutes, or until the liquid has been absorbed. Chill before using.

To make the sandwiches: In a large skillet, heat 1 tablespoon (15 ml) of the oil over medium heat. Add the onion and cook for 2 minutes. Add the pepper and cook for 3 minutes; the vegetables should remain crisp. Transfer to a plate.

Add the remaining oil and the balls. Cook, turning gently for 5 minutes, or until heated through. Divide the vegetables evenly among the rolls and add 4 or 5 balls each. Top each with ⅓ cup (83 g) of the sauce.

Yield: 4 subs

STUFFED ARTICHOKES
Too many people are intimidated by this gorgeous, folate-rich vegetable, which is actually a flower bud.

4 large artichokes
3 tablespoons (45 ml) oil, divided
1 yellow onion, chopped
4 cloves garlic, minced
1 cup (50 g) bread crumbs
½ cup (50 g) walnuts, toasted and finely chopped
4 medium tomatoes, seeded and diced
1 teaspoon salt
Black pepper, to taste
3 tablespoons (9 g) fresh herbs, minced
1 teaspoon lemon juice

Using a sharp knife, cut the stems off the artichokes so they sit flush. With scissors, cut the pointy tips off the outer artichoke leaves.

In a large pot with a steamer basket, steam the artichokes for 25 to 45 minutes, or until the leaves pull easily away and are tender at the base.

Meanwhile, in a large sauté pan, heat 1 tablespoon (15 ml) of the oil over medium heat. Sauté the onion and garlic for about 5 minutes, or until the onion is soft and translucent. Add more oil as necessary along with the bread crumbs and walnuts. Stir to thoroughly combine. Add the tomatoes and salt, stirring them into the mixture. Season with pepper. Stir in the herbs and juice, adjust the seasonings, and remove from the heat.

When the artichokes are steamed done and cool enough to handle, pry open the tops with your fingers and expose the cavity into which you will spoon the mixture.

Yield: 4 servings

STUFFED CABBAGE ROLLS
This is a vegan adaption of a Polish favorite.

FOR THE SAUCE:
2 tablespoons (30 ml) olive oil
2 cloves garlic, minced
1 Vidalia onion, diced
1½ teaspoons salt, divided
3 cans (6 ounces, or 170 g each) tomato paste
1¾ cups (420 ml) water
3 tablespoons (40 g) sugar

FOR THE FILLING:
1 cup (235 ml) water
1 cube (1 teaspoon) vegetable bouillon
1 cup (100 g) textured vegetable protein (TVP)
2 tablespoons (8 g) minced fresh oregano
1 tablespoon (2.5 g) minced fresh basil
2 cups (330 g) cooked brown rice

1 large head green cabbage

Preheat the oven to 325°F (170°C, or gas mark 3).

To make the sauce: In a skillet, heat the oil over medium heat. Sauté the garlic, onion, and 1 teaspoon of the salt until the onion becomes caramelized, 6 to 8 minutes. Add the paste, water, sugar, and remaining ½ teaspoon salt. Stir until smooth. Simmer on low for about 5 minutes, stirring occasionally. Remove from the heat.

To make the filling: In a small saucepan, bring the water and bouillon to a boil.

In a heat-safe bowl, toss the TVP with the oregano and basil. Pour the boiling water over the TVP. Cover and let rest for about 5 minutes, or until all of the water has been absorbed. Fluff with a fork.

In a medium bowl, combine the TVP with the rice.

To assemble, cut off the bottom of the head of cabbage and discard the two outermost leaves. Slice off a bit more of the bottom where the leaves join. Select 12 solid, unbroken cabbage leaves.

Cover the bottom of a deep 9 x 13-inch (23 x 33 cm) baking dish with sauce.

Place about ⅓ cup (57 g) of the filling in the center of a cabbage leaf and fold each side over to shape into a rectangular pouch. Place in the pan with the folded side down to hold in place. Repeat until all the rolls have been made. Generously cover with the remaining sauce. Cover with foil. Bake for 1 hour and 15 minutes, or until the cabbage is soft when pierced with a fork.

Yield: 12 cabbage rolls

FARRO AND FRESH VEGETABLE MEDLEY
You can serve this right away or the next day. Yummers!

2 cups (368 g) uncooked farro (or barley)
5 cups (1175 ml) water (or vegetable broth)
1 cup (150 g) diced bell pepper
1 cup (130 g) diced carrot (about 4 or 5 carrots)
1 cup (135 g) diced cucumber, unpeeled
1 cup (100 g) chopped green onion, white and green
    parts (about 6 green onions)
½ to ¾ cup (68 to 100 g) toasted pine nuts
½ cup (32 g) finely chopped parsley
½ cup (32 g) finely chopped mint
1 to 2 tablespoons (15 to 30 ml) balsamic vinegar
¼ to cup (60 to 80 ml) olive oil
Juice of 1 or 2 small lemons, divided
Salt, to taste
Black pepper, to taste

In a 3- or 4-quart (3.3 or 4.4 L) saucepan, combine the farro and water. Bring to a boil over high heat. Reduce the heat to low and simmer without stirring for 35 to 45 minutes until the liquid is absorbed. Remove from the heat.

Meanwhile, in a large bowl, add the bell pepper, carrot, cucumber, onions, nuts, parsley, and mint. Stir to combine. Add the vinegar, oil, and the juice of 1 lemon. Season with salt and pepper. Add the farro. Taste and add more juice and salt, if necessary.

Yield: 8 servings

RATATOUILLE WITH WHITE BEANS

This dish works best when the vegetables are in season. Serve it hot or cold and as an entrée or appetizer.

1 large globe eggplant, cut into ½-inch (1 cm) cubes
2 tablespoons (30 ml) olive oil
2 medium red onions, sliced
3 medium zucchini squash, cut into ½-inch (1 cm) cubes
2 red bell peppers, seeded and cut into ½-inch (1 cm) squares
4 cloves garlic, minced
¼ cup (60 ml) dry white wine
1 cup (235 ml) vegetable broth
4 tomatoes, seeded and roughly chopped (or 2 cans [15 ounces, or 420 g, each] fire-roasted diced tomatoes)
1 tablespoon (4 g) chopped fresh parsley
2 teaspoons (2 g) chopped fresh thyme (or ½ teaspoon dried)
2 teaspoons (2 g) chopped fresh marjoram (or ½ teaspoon dried marjoram or oregano)
2 bay leaves
2 cans (15 ounces, or 420 g, each) white beans, drained and rinsed (or 3 cups [515 g] beans made from scratch)
Salt, to taste
Black pepper, to taste
½ cup (20 g) finely chopped fresh basil
Kalamata olives, pitted and chopped, optional

Steam the eggplant for 10 minutes until soft but not mushy.

In a large sauté pan, heat the oil over medium heat. Sauté the onion and cook for about 5 minutes, stirring, or until softened. (Cook them longer to create a more caramelized effect.) Add the zucchini and bell peppers. Cook, stirring often, for about 5 minutes. Add the eggplant and cook for about 5 minutes, and then add the garlic. Add the wine and broth. Bring to a boil over high heat, and then reduce the heat to medium-high and stir in the tomatoes, parsley, thyme, marjoram, and bay leaves. Reduce the heat, cover, and simmer gently for 15 minutes, stirring occasionally.

Add the beans and stir well to combine. Cook for about 5 minutes, uncovered, or until the vegetables are tender but not mushy and the liquids have thickened, stirring occasionally. Season with salt and pepper. Remove the

skillet from the heat and stir in the basil. Garnish with the olives, if desired. Remove the bay leaves before serving.

Yield: 6 to 8 servings

PAN-GRILLED PORTOBELLO MUSHROOMS WITH HERB-INFUSED MARINADE

Serve these mushrooms as a main dish with a bunch of steamed spinach, chard, or collard greens, or with creamy mashed potatoes. Or add them to a bun with all the fixins.

8 to 12 large portobello mushrooms
1 cup (240 ml) balsamic vinegar
1 cup (240 ml) tamari soy sauce
1 cup (240 ml) water
2 or 3 sprigs fresh rosemary (or 1 teaspoon [1 g] dried rosemary)
2 or 3 sprigs fresh thyme (or 1 teaspoon [1 g] dried thyme)
2 or 3 sprigs fresh marjoram or oregano (or 1 teaspoon [1 g] dried marjoram or oregano)
Olive oil, for sautéing
Black pepper, to taste

Remove the stems from the underside of the mushrooms and lightly wipe the tops with a damp paper towel.

In a large bowl, combine the vinegar, tamari, water, rosemary, thyme, and marjoram. Stir to combine. Add the mushrooms and cover each one with the marinade, moving them if necessary so the marinade can coat the top mushrooms. Marinate the mushrooms for at least 30 minutes and up to overnight in the fridge.

When ready to cook, in a large sauté pan, heat some oil over medium heat. Remove the mushrooms from the marinade, but do not discard the marinade. Put as many mushrooms as can fit in the pan, tops down. (They will shrink as they cook.) Cook the mushrooms for 3 to 5 minutes, or until lightly browned. Turn and cook for 3 to 5 minutes longer.

Remove the herb sprigs from the marinade, and pour the marinade into the pan, reserving some for additional batches of mushrooms. Cover and cook for 5 to 7 minutes. Flip the mushrooms, and cover and cook for 5 to 7 minutes longer. When the mushrooms are fork-tender, remove them from the pan, and repeat with the remaining mushrooms. Season with the pepper.

To serve the mushrooms hot, use multiple sauté pans on the stove at once.

Yield: 4 to 6 servings

ELEGANTLY SIMPLE STUFFED BELL PEPPERS

Use any combination of peppers for this elegant but simple recipe. It's very versatile.

1 cup (235 ml) water
6 bell peppers
3 tablespoons (45 ml) oil, for brushing and oiling baking dish
Salt, to taste
Black pepper, to taste
3 tablespoons (45 ml) vegetable broth
2 medium yellow onions, roughly chopped
4 cloves garlic, minced or pressed
1 can (16 ounces, or 455 g) fire-roasted diced tomatoes
½ cup (70 g) raw almonds, finely chopped or slivered
2½ cups (415 g) cooked long-grain brown rice
3 tablespoons (18 g) chopped fresh mint
3 tablespoons (12 g) chopped fresh parsley
3 tablespoons (8 g) chopped fresh basil
3 tablespoons (27 g) raisins
2 to 3 tablespoons (12 to 18 g) ground almonds
Chopped mixed fresh herbs, for garnish, optional

Preheat the oven to 375°F (190°C, or gas mark 5). Lightly oil a shallow baking dish.

In a saucepan, boil the water.

Halve the peppers lengthwise, leaving the stems intact. Scoop out the seeds. Brush the cut sides with 1 tablespoon (15 ml) of the oil, place them cut side up in the prepared dish. Season with salt and pepper. Bake for 15 minutes, or until the peppers are soft and easily pierced with a fork but still have their shape.

In a large stockpot, heat the broth over medium heat. Sauté the onion and garlic for 5 minutes, or until the onion becomes translucent. Add the tomatoes and raw almonds. Sauté for another minute or two. Remove the pan from heat and stir in the rice, mint, parsley, basil, and raisins. Season with salt and pepper.

Spoon mixture into the peppers on the baking sheet.

Pour ⅔ to 1 cup (155 to 235 ml) of the boiling water around the peppers, just enough to touch the base of each so they don't burn. Bake, uncovered, for 15 minutes. Sprinkle the ground almonds on top. Return to the oven and bake for 15 minutes longer. Serve garnished with the herbs, if using.

Yield: 12 servings

ROASTED BRUSSELS SPROUTS WITH CARAMEL-IZED ONIONS AND TOASTED PISTACHIOS

The combination of roasted Brussels sprouts, sweet onions, and toasted pistachios puts this dish over the top.

1½ pounds (685 g) Brussels sprouts (about 40), ends trimmed and halved if large
3 tablespoons (45 ml) olive oil
½ teaspoon salt
½ teaspoon black pepper
2 tablespoons (28 g) nondairy, non-hydrogenated butter
4 small-medium yellow onions, thinly sliced
1 teaspoon (4 g) sugar
½ cup (70 g) pistachios

Preheat the oven to 425°F (220°C, or gas mark 7).

In a large bowl, toss together the sprouts, oil, salt, and pepper. Pour onto a baking sheet, and place on center rack in oven. Roast for 20 to 40 minutes, or until the sprouts are dark brown, shaking the pan every few minutes for even browning.

Meanwhile, in a large skillet, melt the butter over low-medium heat. Add the onions and sugar. Cook for about 30 minutes, stirring occasionally, or until the onions turn dark golden brown and caramelize.

Preheat a toaster oven to 200°F (100°C).

Toast the pistachios in the toaster oven for less than 4 minutes. Let cool, and coarsely chop.

In a bowl, toss together the onions, Brussels sprouts, and pistachios.

Yield: 4 to 6 servings

HARVEST-STUFFED ACORN SQUASH

The earthy colors of this dish make for a beautiful Thanksgiving dinner centerpiece. Any leftover rice mixture makes a great side dish by itself.

4 acorn squash, halved lengthwise, seeds and membranes removed
1 tablespoon (15 ml) olive oil
2 medium onions, chopped
4 stalks celery, diced
1½ cups (250 g) cooked brown rice
1 cup (165 g) cooked wild rice
1 cup (100 g) raw or toasted pecans, coarsely chopped (or walnuts, almonds, or chestnuts)
½ cup (65 g) dried diced apricots (or raisins)
2 teaspoons (4 g) ground ginger
1 teaspoon (2 g) ground cinnamon
½ teaspoon ground cardamom
¼ teaspoon ground cloves
½ teaspoon salt
Black pepper, to taste

Preheat the oven to 375°F (190°C, or gas mark 5).

Place the squash halves, cut sides down, on 1 or 2 nonstick baking sheets. Bake for 30 minutes. (The squash may not be fully fork-tender yet.)

Meanwhile, in a sauté pan, heat the oil over medium heat. Sauté the onions until they become transparent. Add the celery and sauté for several minutes.

Transfer the onion mixture to a large bowl. Stir in the rices, pecans, apricots, ginger, cinnamon, cardamom, cloves, and salt. Season with pepper.

Spoon out the cooked squash, leaving some squash in the shells, with other ingredients. Press the rice mixture into each squash shell, mounding the rice mixture as much as possible. Cover with foil and bake for 30 minutes, or until the squash flesh is thoroughly tender.

Remove the foil during the last 10 minutes of baking.

Yield: 8 servings

BUTTERNUT SQUASH TIMBALES

Timbales (drum-shaped molds) look beautiful on a plate. The vegetable combination is molded in a round ramekin and unmolded on the dinner plate. Serve these on a bread of sautéed kale.

2 cups (255 g) ½-inch (1 cm) cubes butternut squash
2½ cups (590 ml) vegetable broth
1 cup (195 g) Arborio rice, unrinsed
¼ to ½ teaspoon salt
1 tablespoon (15 ml) olive oil
1 large yellow onion, finely chopped
1 teaspoon (3 g) minced garlic
2 tablespoons (8 g) finely chopped fresh parsley
1 teaspoon (1 g) finely chopped fresh thyme
2 to 3 tablespoons (7 to 14 g) finely chopped sun-dried tomatoes
Black ground pepper, to taste
¼ cup (35 g) pine nuts, toasted, for garnish, optional

Lightly oil four 1¼-cup (280 g) ramekins, custard cups, or mini loaf pans.

Steam the squash until just tender, for 10 to 12 minutes. Transfer the squash to a bowl.

In a large saucepan, bring the broth and rice to a boil. Add the salt. Reduce the heat to low, cover, and cook until the rice is tender but some liquid remains, stirring often, for about 20 minutes. Uncover, stir, and remove from the heat.

In a large sauté pan, heat the oil over medium-high heat. Sauté the onion until translucent and turning golden brown, about 5 minutes. Add the garlic, parsley, and thyme, and stir. Cook for 2 minutes. Add the tomatoes and squash. Stir, and then remove from the heat.

To assemble, divide the veggie mixture among the ramekins. Press down with the back of a spoon to make compact. Top with rice and press down again, to make compact. Turn each timbale over on a separate plate, running a butter knife along the edge to unmold the beautiful rice/veggie mixture. Grind black pepper over the top, and sprinkle on the nuts, if using.

Yield: 4 servings

PAD THAI SUMMER ROLLS

While they look beautiful and seem difficult to make, summer rolls are actually quite simple!

FOR THE TOFU:
3 tablespoons (45 ml) tamari, divided
1 tablespoon (15 ml) toasted sesame oil
1 tablespoon (15 ml) maple syrup
½ teaspoon onion powder
½ teaspoon garlic powder
½ teaspoon ground ginger
8 ounces (227 g) extra-firm tofu, drained, pressed, and cut into ¼-inch (6 mm) slices
1 tablespoon (15 ml) neutral-flavored oil

FOR THE ROLLS:
1 cup (104 g) chopped cucumber
¼ cup plus 2 tablespoons (42 g) grated carrot
¼ cup plus 2 tablespoons (60 g) minced green onion
2 tablespoons (30 ml) seasoned rice vinegar
Eight 8-inch (20 cm) spring roll wrappers
8 fresh cilantro leaves
½ cup (52 g) mung bean sprouts
1 generous handful dry rice sticks, cooked al dente

FOR THE SAUCE:
2 tablespoons (32 g) natural creamy peanut butter
2 tablespoons (30 ml) tamari
2 tablespoons (30 ml) seasoned rice vinegar

Preheat the oven to 400°F (200°C, or gas mark 6).
To make the tofu: In an 8-inch (20 cm) square baking dish, combine 2 tablespoons (30 ml) of the tamari, the sesame oil, syrup, onion powder, garlic powder, and ginger. Add the tofu, turning to coat. Bake for 15 minutes. Turn and bake for 15 minutes longer, or until the tofu is browned. When assembling the rolls, cut the tofu slices into ¼-inch (6 mm) sticks.

In a medium skillet, heat the neutral-flavored oil over medium heat. Cook the tofu for 4 to 5 minutes, or until crisp. Add the remaining 1 tablespoon (15 ml) tamari. Stir and cook for 3 to 5 minutes, or until the tofu is coated and the tamari is absorbed.

To make the rolls: In a small bowl, combine the cucumber, carrot, onion, and vinegar. Soak one wrapper according to the package directions. Place a cilantro leaf in the center of the wrapper, add about 2 tablespoons (26 g) of the cucumber mixture, four to five pieces of tofu, 8 to 10 mung bean sprouts, and one-eighth of the rice sticks. Fold the top and bottom ends of the wrapper in and roll across the wrapper to make an eggroll shape. Continue with the remaining ingredients until all eight rolls have been prepared.

To make the sauce: In a small bowl, whisk all of the ingredients together.

Yield: 8 summer rolls

TASTY COCOA JERK TOFU

Not too spicy and full of flavor, cacao makes magic with Caribbean cuisine! Serve this dish with seasoned black beans and rice. Some fried plantains would work well, too! Garnish with grated chocolate and green onions if desired.

FOR THE SAUCE:
2 teaspoons curry powder
1 teaspoon chili powder
½ teaspoon black pepper
½ teaspoon cinnamon
½ teaspoon allspice
2 tablespoons (28 ml) hot sauce
⅓ cup (27 g) cocoa powder
¼ cup (60 ml) tamari
⅓ cup (80 ml) vegetable broth
2 to 3 crushed garlic cloves
1 tablespoon (20 g) agave nectar
2 tablespoons (28 ml) olive oil
1 tablespoon (15 ml) lemon juice
2 tablespoons (32 g) hoisin or (38 g) plum sauce, (32 g) tamarind, or a similar sauce
½ teaspoon salt
½ teaspoon ground oregano

FOR THE TOFU:
16 ounces (455 g) firm tofu
1 onion, sliced
1 red bell pepper, seeded and sliced
1 green bell pepper, seeded and sliced

To make the sauce: In a blender, combine all of the ingredients.

To make the tofu: Cut the tofu into 4 sections, and then cut each section into 4 strips.

In a casserole dish, mix the tofu with the vegetables and sauce. Allow to sit for an hour.

Preheat the oven to 400°F (200°C, gas mark 6).

Bake the tofu for 30 minutes, turning once, adding a bit more liquid if you need to or want this dish to be saucier.

Increase the heat to broil. Broil for 5 to 7 minutes to finish.

Yield: 4 servings

BULGOGI-STYLE TOFU

Bulgogi is a popular dish in Korea made from marinated thin strips of beef that literally translates to "fire meat." Try to find Twin Oaks brand tofu, which is dense and firm enough to cut into very thin strips. Serve the Bulgogi over sticky rice along with some kimchi.

1 block (16-ounces, or 455 g) extra firm, very dense tofu, very well drained

4 green onions, chopped, white and green parts
3 cloves garlic, minced
½ medium onion, sliced
1 heaping teaspoon fresh grated ginger
⅔ cup (160 ml) tamari (or soy sauce)
¼ cup (60 g) toasted sesame oil
6 tablespoons (72 g) sugar
1 teaspoon black pepper
1 teaspoon crushed red pepper flakes
¼ cup (60 ml) mirin
2 tablespoons (28 ml) rice vinegar
¼ cup (40 g) shredded pear, unpeeled
Sesame oil, for frying

Slice the tofu into very thin pieces (as thin as you can without tearing). Place the tofu in an 8-inch (20 cm) dish, about 2-inches (5 cm) deep. Stack the tofu so the marinade can easily flow through.

In a bowl, combine the rest of the ingredients. Pour over the tofu. Cover with plastic wrap. Let rest in the fridge for at least 8 hours or up to overnight.

The next day, carefully remove the tofu from the pan and reserve the marinade. (The tofu should be light brown by now.)

In a large frying pan, heat a coating of sesame oil over medium-high heat. Once the pan is hot, add 1 layer of marinated tofu and cook for 10 to 15 minutes. Once the edges of the tofu are browned on one side, flip and brown the other side. Remove the tofu to a plate and repeat with the rest of the tofu.

Once all of the tofu is browned, return all of the tofu to the pan. Simmer in the marinade until most of the liquid is gone, about 10 minutes longer.

Yield: 6 servings

SLOW-SIMMERED TOFU WITH PEANUT SAUCE

This savory tofu dish requires a little forethought because you need to freeze the tofu overnight and simmer the dish for some time, but it's well worth it.

1 block (15 ounces, or 425 g) extra-firm tofu
5 carrots, peeled and sliced
2 cans (13.5 ounces, or 378 g each) full-fat coconut milk
1 medium Spanish onion, diced
2 cloves garlic, minced
1 teaspoon freshly grated ginger
3 bay leaves
¼ cup (65 g) creamy peanut butter
⅛ teaspoon mombasa powder (or ¼ teaspoon cayenne pepper)
Salt, to taste
Cooked basmati rice

The night before you begin, drain and press the tofu, cut it into 4 equal pieces, and seal it tightly in a freezer-safe plastic bag. Freeze overnight.

The next day, in a large, heavy skillet, stir together the carrots, milk, onion, garlic, ginger, bay leaves, peanut butter, and mombasa. Place the tofu (no need to thaw) in the pan, shimmying the tofu down into the coconut mixture while gently guiding the veggies to the sides of the tofu, so that the tofu lies flat in the pan. Cook over medium heat until the sauce begins to boil, about 15 minutes. Cover, reduce the heat to medium-low, and simmer for about 2 hours, spooning sauce on top of the tofu every once in a while. Do not flip the tofu. (You want it to get caramelized on the bottom side.) Stir the sauce occasionally. Uncover the pan and cook for 1 hour longer, or until the sauce has reduced to a thick, gravy-like consistency and the edges of the carrots and onions are golden brown. The total cooking time is 3 hours. Remove the bay leaves and serve over the rice.

Yield: 4 servings

COCONUT CURRY WITH CHICKPEAS AND CAULIFLOWER

This dish is comforting and filling, yet it's full of flavor and yummy good-for-you ingredients. The coconut milk helps this dish seem creamy and decadent.

1½ cups (355 ml) water
1 cup (190 g) brown rice
2 teaspoons coconut oil
1 small yellow onion, minced
1 carrot, thinly sliced
1 small head cauliflower, chopped into florets (about 3 cups, or 300 g)
1 cup (235 ml) vegetable broth
2 tablespoons (13 g) curry powder (or paste)
1 can (15 ounces, or 428 g) chickpeas, drained and rinsed
1 can (13½ ounces, or 400 ml) coconut milk
Salt, to taste
Black pepper, to taste

In a medium pot, bring the water to a boil. Add the rice, reduce the heat to a simmer, cover, and let simmer for 30 to 40 minutes, stirring occasionally.

Meanwhile, in a large saucepan, heat the oil over medium heat. Add the onion and cook for about 5 minutes, or until the onion is translucent. Add the carrot, cauliflower, broth, and curry. Cook for about 10 minutes. Stir in the chickpeas and milk. Season with salt and pepper. Cook for another 10 minutes, or until the curry mixture thickens and the vegetables are soft. Season with salt and pepper.

Serve the curry over the rice.

Yield: Serves 4 to 6

MILD OKRA CURRY WITH FRAGRANT YELLOW RICE

You can buy curry leaves, completely unrelated to curry powder, at Indian, African, or Asian market or online. Buy a bunch. They freeze beautifully.

FOR THE CURRY:
1 onion, chopped
4 cloves garlic, minced
10 curry leaves
2 tablespoons (28 g) coconut oil
1 teaspoon cumin seed
¼ teaspoon cardamom
½ teaspoon coriander
1 teaspoon white pepper
½ teaspoon ground fennel seeds
¼ teaspoon ground cloves
1 teaspoon salt
5 ounces (150 g, about 20 heads) fresh okra
2 cups (475 ml) coconut milk
1 tablespoon (4 g) sorghum flour

FOR THE YELLOW RICE:
1½ cups (278 g) basmati rice
10 threads saffron

To make the curry: In a pan, sauté the onion, garlic, and curry leaves in the oil over medium-high heat for about 2 minutes. Add the spices and stir to coat evenly. Add the salt and cook over medium-high heat for about 7 minutes, stirring often, or until the onion is translucent. Add the okra and sauté for an additional 10 to 15 minutes, or until the okra is tender. Add the milk and cook about 10 more minutes, stirring occasionally to prevent it from sticking. Add the flour and cook about 2 more minutes, just to thicken. Remove the curry leaves. Serve over the rice.

To make the rice: Cook the rice according to the package directions, adding 10 threads of saffron to the water.

Yield: 4 servings

VEGGIE FRITTATA WITH SALSA VERDE

This frittata has countless variations. Try shredded kale instead of asparagus and zucchini in place of the carrot. Serve it warm or cold.

FOR THE FRITTATA:
1 tablespoon (15 ml) olive oil
6 stalks fresh asparagus, tough ends removed and chopped into ½-inch (1 cm) pieces
1 medium red onion, diced
2 cloves garlic, minced
1½ teaspoons salt, plus more to taste
1¾ cups (210 g) gram flour

1 cup (235 ml) water
¼ cup (24 g) nutritional yeast
⅓ cup (80 ml) olive oil
2 packages (12 ounces each, or a total of about 680 g)
    extra-firm tofu, drained and pressed for at least 4
    hours or up to overnight
½ cup (55 g) packed shredded carrot
½ cup (30 g) packed chopped fresh parsley

FOR THE SALSA VERDE:
4 tomatillos
1 serrano chile pepper, diced
4 shallots, peeled and very roughly chopped
Giant handful fresh cilantro
½ ripe avocado, peeled and pitted
½ to ¾ teaspoon salt

To make the frittata: Preheat the oven to 350°F (180°C, gas mark 4). Lightly grease a standard-size pie pan.

In a small frying pan, heat the oil over medium heat. Sauté the asparagus, onion, garlic, and dash salt for about 2 to 3 minutes, or until the asparagus turns bright green and is barely tender.

In a large bowl, whisk together the flour, water, 1½ teaspoons of the salt, yeast, and oil to make a somewhat runny, yet substantial, batter. Crumble the tofu on top of the batter. Salt lightly but evenly. Stir well to combine, gently to not purée the tofu. Fold in the asparagus mixture, carrot, and parsley. Spread into the prepared pie pan. Bake for about 60 minutes, or until golden brown on top. Remove from the oven and let cool at least 30 minutes before slicing. Top with the Salsa Verde.

To make the Salsa Verde: Peel, wash, and roughly chop the tomatillos.

While wearing kitchen-grade gloves to prevent burning of the skin, carefully seed the pepper.

In a food processor, pulse all of the ingredients until well combined to a salsa consistency. Store in an airtight container in the fridge.

Yield: 1 frittata

SPINACH MUSHROOM CURRY

This dish resembles Saag Mushroom in taste and appearance. But it's quite different from the authentic version. Serve it over basmati rice.

1 butternut squash
2½ tablespoons olive oil (37 ml), divided, plus more for
    drizzling
1 teaspoon salt, plus more to taste
8 curry leaves
1 large Vidalia onion, diced
2 cloves garlic, minced

2 coins fresh ginger, minced
10 ounces (280 g) white button mushrooms, sliced
11 ounces (310 g) baby spinach leaves

Preheat the oven to 400°F (200°C, gas mark 6).

To roast the squash, cut in half lengthwise and scoop out the seeds. Peel using a vegetable peeler. Cut the squash into 1-inch (2.5 cm) wide cubes. Place the squash on a parchment-covered baking sheet, lightly drizzle with oil, and sprinkle with salt. Bake for about 30 minutes, or until fork tender. Flip the squash halfway through the cooking time.

Transfer the squash to a bowl and mash.

In a large frying pan, heat 2 tablespoons (30ml) of the oil over medium-high heat. Sauté the curry leaves, onion, garlic, ginger, mushrooms, and 1 teaspoon of the salt, for about 15 minutes, or until the onions and mushrooms begin to caramelize and turn golden brown. Stir the squash into the mushroom mixture. Simmer over very low heat for about 10 minutes.

In a separate frying pan, heat the remaining ½ tablespoon oil over medium heat. Cook the spinach for about 5 minutes, just until wilted. Season with salt.

Drain the spinach and transfer to a food processor. Pulse briefly until well chopped but not puréed. Combine the spinach with the mushroom mixture.

Yield: 4 servings

NIGIRI AND MAKI SUSHI

Sushi can make a satisfying main course in an Asian-inspired meal. Serve these two types of sushi with wasabi, pickled ginger, and soy sauce or tamari.

FOR THE NIGIRI:
2 cups (372 g) cooked sushi rice
1 tablespoon (15 ml) sushi vinegar
½ papaya, sliced extra thin, seeds reserved
1 sheet nori, cut into strips ¼-inch (6 mm) wide
2 tablespoons (18 g) papaya seeds

FOR THE MAKI:
8 sheets nori
1 tablespoon (15 ml) sushi vinegar
2½ cups (465 g) cooked sushi rice
8 spears steamed asparagus
1 small carrot, julienned
1 small cucumber, julienned
1 to 2 avocados, pitted, peeled, and cut into thin spears

To make the Nigiri: In a bowl, mix the rice and vinegar. Using wet hands, shape into 2-inch (5 cm) logs.

Cut the papaya into 2 x 1-inch (5 x 2.5 cm) rectangles.

Place 1 nori strip on a flat surface with 1 rice log placed

49 Fiesta Soy Curl and Rice Casserole; 50 Vegan "Pepperoni" Sausage; 51 Falafelogs with Cucumber Relish; 52 Italian "Sausages"; 53 Strawberry Spinach Tacowich; 54 Meat(less)Ball Subs; 55 Stuffed Artichokes; 56 Stuffed Cabbage Rolls

57 Farro and Fresh Vegetable Medley; 58 Ratatouille with White Beans; 59 Pan-Grilled Portobello Mushrooms with Herb-Infused Marinade; 60 Elegantly Simple Stuffed Bell Peppers; 61 Roasted Brussels Sprouts with Caramelized Onions and Toasted Pistachios; 62 Harvest-Stuffed Acorn Squash; 63 Butternut Squash Timbales; 64 Pad Thai Summer Rolls

perpendicular on top of the nori. Put the cut papaya on top of the sushi logs, fold up the nori strip tightly, and use a touch of water to seal into place like a piece of tape. Top with the seeds.

To make the Maki: Place 1 sheet of nori on a flat surface. Have a small bowl of water and a sharp knife ready and easy access to a sink.

In a small bowl, mix the vinegar into the sushi rice. Smooth out about ⅓ cup (62 g) rice into a flat sheet over the lower ⅓ of the nori wrap. On top of the rice, layer 1 spear of asparagus, a few pieces of carrot and cucumber, and 2 spears avocado so that they all remain only in the center of the rice and stretch the entire surface of the nori wrap. Gently wet the very top portion of the roll (the farthest away from the rice and veggies. Using both of your hands, roll them up tightly. (A sushi mat comes in handy here, but isn't necessary.) Roll up like a cigar, as tight as possible. Using a very sharp knife, slice the roll into 1-inch (2.5 cm) coins. Repeat until all of sushi wraps have been used.

Yield: 8 Nigiri Sushi, 24 pieces Maki Sushi

BAKED POUTINE
Canadian Poutine is thick-cut French fries, slathered in a rich, salty gravy, and dotted with creamy cheese.

FOR THE BAKED FRIES:
8 large yellow or waxy potatoes
3 tablespoons (45 ml) olive oil
2 teaspoons salt
Dash of celery salt

FOR THE GRAVY:
¼ cup (56 g) vegan margarine
½ cup (80 g) superfine brown rice flour
3 cups (700 ml) water
3 cubes (teaspoons) beef-flavored vegetable bouillon powder
6 tablespoons (90 ml) soy sauce
2 tablespoons (28 ml) vegan Worcestershire sauce
Few dashes liquid smoke
1 cup (112 g) vegan mozzarella-style cheese shreds

To make the baked fries: Preheat the oven to 400°F (200°C, gas mark 6).

Cut the potatoes into thick slices to resemble steak fries. In a bowl, toss the potatoes with the oil, salt, and celery. Spread onto an ungreased, but well-seasoned, metal baking sheet. Bake for 40 to 45 minutes, turning once halfway through, or until deep golden brown on both sides and crispy.

To make the gravy: In a 2-quart (2 L) saucepan, heat the margarine over medium heat. Add the flour. Mix and cook until clumpy, about 1 minute. Whisk in the water and

bouillon and continue to cook about 5 minutes, or until it begins to thicken. Add the soy sauce, Worcestershire, and liquid smoke. Stir until pretty thick, about the consistency of a smooth cake batter.

To assemble: Place the potatoes in a bowl and top with clumps of cheese. Pour the gravy on top.

Yield: 4 servings

PHILLY CHEESESTEAK
In Philadelphia, home of the cheesesteak, plenty of vegan cheesesteak options exist. Serve with fries and seltzer.

FOR THE WHIZ:
3 medium yellow and orange bell peppers, sautéed
2 carrots, steamed
1 cup (96 g) nutritional yeast
½ cup (120 ml) almond milk
½ to 1 teaspoon salt
5 tablespoons (35 g) almond flour
½ teaspoon yellow miso
1 clove garlic

FOR THE STEAK:
1 package (8 ounces, or 225 g) soy curls
2 vegetable bouillon cubes
Very hot water (about 176°F/80°C)
½ tablespoon liquid smoke
¼ cup (60 ml) vegan Worcestershire sauce
1 tablespoon (6 g) vegetable broth seasoning
1 cup (235 ml) water
¼ cup (60 ml) soy sauce, plus more for color
2 tablespoons (30 ml) olive oil, divided

FOR THE ONIONS AND PEPPERS:
1 red onion, sliced thin
1 green pepper, sliced thin
1 tablespoon (15 ml) olive oil
1 teaspoon salt

2 Hoagie Rolls (See page 55 Pepperoni Rolls.)

To make the whiz: In a food processor, combine all of the ingredients. Whirl until creamy, about 7 minutes. Add more almond milk if needed to thin.

To make the steak: In a medium bowl, place the soy curls, bouillon, and just enough hot water to cover. Let sit about 10 minutes until the soy curls are rehydrated. Drain the soy curls and return them to the bowl. Add the liquid smoke, Worcestershire, seasoning, water, soy sauce, and 1 tablespoon (15 ml) of the oil. Let rest for at least 10 minutes and then squeeze the excess liquid from the soy curls. Toss with the remaining 1 tablespoon (15 ml) oil.

In a large frying pan, sauté the soy curls over medium-high heat for about 15 minutes, or until crispy, adding a touch more soy sauce for color.

To make the onions and peppers: In a large frying pan, sauté the onion and green pepper with the oil and salt over medium-high heat for about 10 minutes. Reduce the heat to medium and cook for about 15 minutes, or until caramelized.

To assemble: Slice a Hoagie in half lengthwise and stuff with steak, onions, and green peppers. Top with whiz.

Yield: 2 large cheesesteaks with whiz and onions

CHICKEN-FRIED TEMPEH WITH GRAVY

This finger-licking good dish is hard to resist.

FOR THE TEMPEH:
1 block tempeh (8 ounces or, 227 g), cut into 4 even "steaks"
1 cup (160 g) superfine brown rice flour
1 teaspoon salt
1 teaspoon fried chicken seasoning

FOR THE BATTER:
½ tablespoon ground chia seeds mixed with 1/4 cup (60 ml) water
½ cup (120 ml) almond milk
½ teaspoon baking powder
1 teaspoon salt
1 tablespoon (8 g) gram flour
Vegetable oil

FOR THE GRAVY:
2 tablespoons (28 g) vegan margarine, softened
1/4 cup (40 g) superfine brown rice flour
1 tablespoon (6 g) chicken-flavored vegetable broth powder
Black pepper, to taste
1 cup (235 ml) almond milk
Salt, to taste

To make the tempeh: Rinse the tempeh briefly under running water and place onto a plate.

In a bowl, whisk together the flour, salt, and seasoning.

To make the batter: In a bowl, whisk all of the ingredients together until smooth. Rest for at least 5 minutes.

Preheat the deep fryer to 365°F (182°C). Line a plate with paper towels.

Dip the moistened tempeh patties into the flour mixture, then into the batter to coat, and once again back into the flour mixture. Immediately place into the hot oil and cook for 5 minutes, or until golden brown. Place the fried tempeh steaks on the prepared plate to absorb excess oil.

To make the gravy: In a saucepan, whisk together the margarine and flour. Cook over medium heat for about 7 minutes, or until thickened. Add the rest of the ingredients

and whisk continuously to prevent any lumps from forming. Cook about 5 to 7 minutes, or until thickened. Serve the gravy over the tempeh.

Yield: 4 servings

SEARED "SCALLOPS" WITH WHITE TRUFFLE SAUCE (PHOTO PAGE 4)

With king oyster mushrooms available at natural foods stores or Asian groceries, there's no reason to eat another scallop ever again. These are wonderful served on a bed of lightly sautéed spinach leaves or zucchini.

FOR THE "SCALLOPS":
2 large king oyster mushrooms
½ cup (120 ml) sweet white wine (such as Riesling or Pinot Grigio)
½ cup (120 ml) water
3 tablespoons (42 g) vegan margarine
Salt, to taste
Black pepper, to taste

FOR THE TRUFFLE SAUCE:
3 cloves garlic, minced
1 sweet onion, minced
¾ teaspoon salt, plus dash
1 teaspoon olive oil
1 cup (235 ml) almond milk
1 cup (235 ml) vegetable broth
3 tablespoons (30 g) superfine brown rice flour
1/4 to ½ teaspoon truffle oil (white or black)

To make the "scallops": Rinse, peel, and slice the mushrooms into 1-inch (2.5 cm) thick coins.

In a bowl, soak the mushrooms in the wine and water and cover. Let rest overnight, flipping one time.

The next day, squeeze the excess liquid gently from the mushrooms.

In a medium frying pan, heat the margarine over medium-high heat, watching to make sure it does not smoke. Season each side of the mushroom with salt and pepper. Place into the margarine so that each is touching the pan evenly. Cook over medium-high heat for about 7 minutes on each side, removing the pan from the heat as necessary to prevent the margarine from scorching. Cook until golden brown on each side and very tender.

To make the Truffle Sauce: In a small saucepan, cook the garlic, onion, dash salt, and olive oil over medium heat for about 15 minutes, or until caramelized. Add the milk and broth. Allow the mixture to come up to medium-high heat, but not boil. Whisk in the flour. Cook over medium heat for about 5 minutes, or until thickened, stirring constantly.

Once thickened, stir in the truffle oil. Arrange the "scallops" on a plate. Top with the Truffle Sauce.

Yield: 10 "scallops"

65 *Tasty Cocoa Jerk Tofu; 66 Bulgogi-Style Tofu*

67 *Slow-Simmered Tofu with Peanut Sauce;* 68 *Coconut Curry with Chickpeas and Cauliflower;* 69 *Mild Okra Curry with Fragrant Yellow Rice;* 70 *Veggie Frittata with Salsa Verde;* 71 *Spinach Mushroom Curry;* 72 *Nigiri and Maki Sushi;* 73 *Baked Poutine;* 74 *Philly Cheesesteak;* 75 *Chicken-Fried Tempeh with Gravy*

SALADS, SOUPS, AND SIDES

See pages 150-151, 156-157, 164-165, 170-171, 176-177, 184-185, and 192-193
for salads, soups, and sides recipe photos.

ZESTY BLACK-EYED PEA SALAD

This salad is an incredible concoction of flavors with a zing of Cajun spice tossed in.

FOR THE SALAD:
2½ cups (375 g) cooked black-eyed peas
2 cups (330 g) cooked brown rice
2 cups (240 g) thinly sliced celery
1¾ cups (260 g) cooked sweet corn
1 cup (150 g) diced red bell pepper
½ cup (30 g) chopped cilantro
1 tablespoon (9 g) minced jalapeño (Remove the seeds if you want less heat.)
⅓ cup (33 g) chopped green onion

FOR THE DRESSING:
¼ cup (60 ml) apple cider vinegar
1 teaspoon cumin
1½ teaspoons Cajun seasoning
3 cloves garlic, minced
2 tablespoons (25 g) sugar
1 teaspoon black pepper
⅓ cup (80 ml) olive oil
1½ teaspoons salt

To make the salad: In a large bowl, combine all of the ingredients. Chill until cold, at least 1 hour.

To make the dressing: In a smaller bowl, whisk together all of the ingredients.
    Toss the salad with the dressing until well combined. Chill in the fridge for a few hours to let the flavors meld. Serve cold or at room temperature.

Yield: 12 servings

DELI-STYLE CHICKPEA SALAD

The creamy dressing has a sweet and tangy bite, which is mellowed out by the crunchy almonds and juicy grapes. This dish is equally amazing served on sliced bread or atop a bed of greens.

3½ cups (800 g) cooked chickpeas (if canned, drained and rinsed)
1 tablespoon (2.5 g) rubbed sage
1½ teaspoons chicken-flavored vegetable seasoning powder, optional
¼ teaspoon salt
3 stalks celery, thinly sliced (about 1 cup, [100 g])
2 tablespoons (30 ml) lemon juice

½ cup (120 ml) vegan mayonnaise
1 tablespoon (15 g) spicy brown mustard
1 tablespoon (15 ml) agave nectar
¼ teaspoon celery salt
½ cup (60 g) sliced, toasted almonds
1 cup (150 g) quartered seedless grapes

In a food processor, combine the chickpeas, sage, seasoning, and salt. Pulse briefly just until crumbly. For a smoother salad, pulse the chickpeas longer.
    Transfer the mixture to a bowl. Stir in the celery, juice, mayonnaise, mustard, agave, and celery salt until the salad is uniform in texture and color. Fold in the almonds and grapes.

Yield: 10 servings

WHITE BEAN AND ARTICHOKE SALAD

If you love simple bean/veggie/herb salads, you'll really love this one.

2 cans (15 ounces, or 420 g) white beans, drained and rinsed
½ or 1 can (14 ounces, or 395 g) artichoke hearts, drained and roughly chopped
1 red, orange, or yellow bell pepper, seeded and diced
⅓ cup (33 g) pitted black olives, finely chopped
1 small red onion, finely chopped
¼ cup (16 g) chopped fresh parsley
¼ cup (16 g) chopped fresh mint leaves
2 tablespoons (8 g) chopped fresh basil
¼ cup (60 ml) olive oil
¼ cup (60 ml) red wine or balsamic vinegar
Salt, to taste
Black pepper, to taste

In a large bowl, combine the beans, artichokes, bell pepper, olives, onion, parsley, mint, and basil.
    In a jar or small bowl, combine the oil and vinegar. Shake together or mix well.
    Pour the oil and vinegar over the salad and toss to coat. Season with salt and pepper.
    Cover and chill in the fridge for several hours or overnight, stirring occasionally, to let the flavors blend.

Yield: 6 servings

BLACK BELUGA LENTIL SALAD

Serve at or above room temperature. Serve as a side or starter or atop a bed of spinach or mixed greens.

1 cup (200 g) dried black beluga or French Puy lentils
2½ cups (588 ml) vegetable broth
2 carrots, finely chopped
3 green onions, chopped
1 tablespoon (4 g) chopped fresh parsley
1 tablespoon (4 g) chopped fresh oregano or (6 g) marjoram
½ cup (75 g) chopped toasted almonds
2 tablespoons (30 ml) olive oil
3 tablespoons (45 ml) balsamic vinegar
½ teaspoon salt
Black pepper, to taste

Rinse the lentils in a strainer and pick through to remove any stones or debris.

In a 3-quart (3 L) saucepan, cook the lentils and broth over medium-low heat. Cover and simmer for 30 minutes, or until the lentils are tender. Halfway through the cooking time, check to make sure the broth hasn't evaporated. If needed, add additional water to prevent the lentils from burning. Remove from the heat, drain, and transfer to a large bowl. Add the carrots, onion, parsley, oregano, almonds, oil, vinegar, and salt. Season with pepper. Stir to combine and taste.

Add any more seasonings, as needed, and either serve right away or store in the fridge for a few hours or overnight. You may need to refresh it with additional vinegar or salt before serving.

Yield: 4 servings

CREAMY POTATO SALAD

This recipe for potato salad emulates the traditional recipe.

1½ to 2½ teaspoons salt, divided
5 pounds (2.3 kg) Yukon gold potatoes, cut into 1-inch (2.5 cm) cubes
½ cup (120 ml) apple cider vinegar
5 tablespoons (70 ml) yellow mustard
2 cups (450 g) vegan mayonnaise
1 teaspoon celery salt
½ cup (75 g) minced red bell pepper
6 stalks celery, chopped to equal about 1 cup (150 g)
1 tablespoon (15 g) sweet relish
Paprika, to taste
Black pepper, to taste

Fill a large pot of water about halfway full with water, add 1 to 2 teaspoons of the salt and bring to a rolling boil. Carefully add the potatoes and return the water to a rolling boil. When the water has returned to a full boil, begin

timing. Cook the potatoes for about 7 minutes, or just until they can be pierced with a fork, but do not fall apart. (These potatoes should not be cooked to the same consistency as you would cook mashed potatoes; you want them slightly less done than that.)

Transfer the potatoes to a colander and drain well. While still in the colander, douse with vinegar, being sure to evenly cover.

Place a plate under the colander and one on top to cover. Refrigerate for about 2 hours, or until well chilled.

Transfer the potatoes to a large bowl. Stir in the mustard, mayonnaise, the remaining ½ teaspoon salt, celery salt, bell pepper, celery, and relish. Stir well. If the potatoes have held their shape too much, smash a few gently with a fork. Stir again to incorporate the dressing. Top with paprika and black pepper to taste. Serve very cold.

Yield: 10 servings

POTATO SALAD IN RADICCHIO CUPS

You can easily modify this recipe, which is perfect as a side dish, lunchtime snack, or picnic-basket staple, to include your favorite potato salad ingredients.

8 medium creamy yellow potatoes, quartered
½ cup (115 g) vegan mayonnaise, plus more if needed
4 green onions, white and green parts, finely chopped
2 small carrots, peeled and finely chopped
2 tablespoons (8 g) finely chopped fresh parsley
2 celery stalks, finely chopped
1 small red onion, finely chopped
1 tablespoon (15 ml) lemon juice
1 teaspoon (6 g) salt
Black pepper, to taste
24 small radicchio, Boston lettuce, or endive leaves

Steam or boil the potatoes until tender but not too soft. Drain, cool, and cube.

In a large bowl, combine the potatoes with the mayonnaise, onions, carrots, parsley, celery, onion, juice, and salt. Add more mayonnaise, if necessary. Season with pepper, and mix well.

To serve, place 2 tablespoons (60 g) potato salad in each leaf.

Yield: 24 servings

1 Zesty Black-Eyed Pea Salad; 2 Deli-Style Chickpea Salad; 3 White Bean and Artichoke Salad; 4 Black Beluga Lentil Salad; 5 Creamy Potato Salad; 6 Potato Salad in Radicchio Cups; 7 "No One Will Know It's Vegan" Potato Salad; 8 Russian Salad

9 Spicy Edamame Coleslaw; 10 Late Summer Salad with Creamy Dill Dressing; 11 Eggplant and Cucumber Salad; 12 Falafel Cucumber Salad with Baba Ghanoush; 13 Carrot Celeriac Remoulade; 14 Capri Salad with Pine Nuts over Arugula; 15 Roasted Fennel Salad with Caramelized Onions; 16 Chopped Endive, "Roquefort," Pecan, and Cranberry Salad

"NO ONE WILL KNOW IT'S VEGAN" POTATO SALAD

If you don't tell your family, they won't even know this potato salad is vegan.

3 (2 pounds, or 1.14 kg) red potatoes, unpeeled, cut into ¼-inch (6 mm) cubes
3 (2 pounds, or 1.14 kg) Yukon gold potatoes, unpeeled, cut into ¼-inch (6 mm) cubes
3 (2 pounds, or 1.14 kg) russet potatoes, unpeeled, cut into ¼-inch (6 mm) cubes
⅓ cup (43 g) capers
1 can (4 ounces, or 112 g) low-sodium black olives, chopped (about 1 cup)
1 cup (160 g) diced onion
1 cup (101 g) diced celery
1 red bell pepper, seeded and diced
1 tablespoon (9 g) minced garlic (about 3 cloves)
2 tablespoons (6 g) dried dill
16 ounces (284 g) frozen peas, thawed
1 tablespoon (2 g) black pepper
4 containers (24 ounces, or 681 g) unsweetened plain soy or almond yogurt
3 tablespoons (45 g) Dijon mustard, plus more to taste

Boil or steam the potatoes until firmly cooked, but not mushy. Drain the potatoes and place them in a large bowl. Add remaining the ingredients except for the yogurt and mustard. Next add half of the yogurt and mix. Continue to add yogurt and mix until it reaches your desired creaminess. (Some people like it moister than others.) Add the mustard, mix, and add more to taste. Chill for at least 2 hours before serving.

Yield: 10 to 12 servings

RUSSIAN SALAD

This potato-based salad, like its name implies, has its origins in Russia. Over the years it has gained fans in Spain, Italy, and eventually made its way to South America.

FOR THE DRESSING:
12 ounces (340 g) silken tofu, drained
1 tablespoon (15 g) spicy brown mustard
2 tablespoons (28 ml) apple cider vinegar
2 tablespoons (28 g) vegan mayonnaise
1 teaspoon salt

FOR THE SALAD:
3 medium Yukon gold potatoes, baked whole
½ cup (30 g) finely chopped, packed parsley
1 large carrot, shredded
¼ cup (60 g) dill relish
4 vegan hot dogs, diced
4 slices American-style vegan cheese, stacked and diced

5 small shallots, sliced
1 tablespoon (2.4 g) fresh thyme
Salt, to taste
Black pepper, to taste

To make the dressing: In a food processor, blend all of ingredients until smooth, scraping down the sides as necessary.

To make the salad: Cut the potatoes into bite-size pieces, salt lightly, and then toss with the other ingredients. Gently fold in the dressing to fully coat. Serve cold.

Yield: 8 servings

SPICY EDAMAME COLESLAW

This coleslaw is slightly different than the typical American-style coleslaw because it features Asian-inspired flavors and coconut cream as the dressing base rather than mayo.

FOR THE SLAW:
1 small head napa cabbage
2 cups (260 g) frozen edamame

FOR THE DRESSING:
1 ripe avocado, pitted and peeled
1 teaspoon freshly grated ginger
2 tablespoons (30 ml) mirin
3 tablespoons (45 g) white miso
2 tablespoons (30 ml) rice vinegar
1 teaspoon wasabi powder
4 heaping tablespoons (60 ml) full-fat coconut cream (the thickest part from a can of chilled, unstirred coconut milk)
¼ cup (60 ml) water
2 tablespoons (30 ml) agave nectar
1 tablespoon (15 ml) spicy chili garlic sauce (such as Sriracha)

To make the slaw: Shred the cabbage and place in a large bowl.
Boil the edamame for about 5 minutes, or just until tender. Once done, rinse under cold water until no longer hot and drain well. Toss with the cabbage and mix until the edamame is evenly distributed throughout.

To make the dressing: In a bowl, using a fork, mash the avocado. Vigorously mix in the remaining ingredients until smooth. If needed, process in a blender or food processor so there are no lumps in the dressing. Toss the cabbage and edamame with the dressing until evenly coated.

Yield: 8 servings

LATE SUMMER SALAD WITH CREAMY DILL DRESSING

This is a creamy twist on a favorite summer salad. Depending on the size of your veggies, you may be left with a little extra dressing.

4 or 5 medium tomatoes
1 or 2 medium cucumbers, peeled
3 tablespoons (45 ml) apple cider vinegar
1 block (15 ounces, or 420 g) silken tofu
1 or 2 cloves garlic
1 teaspoon salt
5 tablespoons (20 g) chopped fresh dill, divided, plus several sprigs for garnish

Chop the tomatoes and cucumbers into bite-size pieces.

In a bowl, toss the tomatoes and cucumbers with the vinegar. Marinate for at least 30 minutes in the fridge.

In a food processor, purée the tofu, garlic, salt, and 2 tablespoons (8 g) of the dill until very smooth.

Remove the cucumbers and tomatoes from the fridge, drain well, and toss with enough dressing to thoroughly coat. Stir in the remaining 3 tablespoons (12 g) dill. Chill in the fridge until cold for at least 1 hour or up to a few hours. Garnish with the dill sprigs.

Yield: 8 servings

EGGPLANT AND CUCUMBER SALAD

Korean inspiration shines through in this salad with the combination of crispy cold cucumbers and warm tender eggplant. It makes an excellent accompaniment to Cold Sesame Noodles. (See page 106.)

FOR THE EGGPLANT MIX:
3 Japanese eggplants (about 1.3 pounds, or 600 g), peeled, halved, and cut into large bite-size pieces
¼ cup (25 g) chopped green onion
1 tablespoon (10 g) minced garlic
1 tablespoon (4 g) minced fresh oregano
2 tablespoons (30 ml) olive oil
¼ cup (60 ml) water
1 teaspoon salt
1 tablespoon (15 g) horseradish (freshly grated or jarred, not powdered)

FOR THE CUCUMBER MIX:
1 large English (or thin-skinned) cucumber, diced
2 tablespoons (8 g) chopped fresh oregano
Zest and juice of 1 lemon
1 teaspoon salt
2 tablespoons (30 ml) olive oil
1 tablespoon (15 ml) agave nectar

To prepare the eggplant mix: In a medium saucepan, cook the eggplant, onion, garlic, oregano, and oil over medium-high heat for about 8 minutes, or until soft. Add the water, salt, and horseradish. Cover with a tight-fitting lid. Reduce the heat to medium-low and cook for about 10 minutes longer, stirring occasionally so that the eggplant doesn't stick to the pan. Remove from the heat and cool to room temperature.

To prepare the cucumber mix: In a large bowl, combine the cucumber, oregano, juice, zest, salt, oil, and agave. Cover and let rest in the fridge for about 20 minutes.

Drain the excess liquid from the cucumber mix and toss with the eggplant. Serve at room temperature or chill before serving.

Yield: 4 servings

FALAFEL CUCUMBER SALAD WITH BABA GHANOUSH

Serve this dish hot or at room temperature.

FOR THE CUCUMBER SALAD:
3 small tomatoes, diced
2 cucumbers, diced
1 scallion, minced
½ cup (30 g) minced parsley
½ cup (48 g) minced mint
1 tablespoon (15 ml) olive oil
1 teaspoon salt
Juice of 1 lemon

FOR THE FALAFEL:
3 cloves roasted garlic
4 cups (960 g) cooked chickpeas
1 cup (160 g) finely minced onion
2 teaspoons ground cumin
1 teaspoon salt
2 teaspoons baking powder
2 cups (240 g) chickpea flour, plus extra for shaping
½ cup (30 g) chopped fresh parsley
½ cup (8 g) chopped fresh cilantro

FOR THE BABA GHANOUSH:
3 large eggplants
Salt, to taste
1 tablespoon (15 ml) olive oil
4 cloves garlic
½ cup (120 g) tahini
1 tablespoon (15 ml) lemon juice
1 teaspoon salt

To make the Cucumber Salad: In a bowl, combine all of the ingredients.

To make the Falafel: In a food processor, pulse the garlic, chickpeas, onion, cumin, salt, and baking powder until mixed, scraping down the sides, or until thick and smooth, adding a small amount of water if needed.

Transfer the mixture into a large bowl and stir in the flour. Fold in the parsley and cilantro. Chill the mixture in the freezer for 15 minutes.

Preheat the oil in a deep fryer to 360°F (185°C). Line a plate with paper towels.

Form the Falafel mixture into fifteen 2 x 1-inch (5 x 2.5 cm) patties. Use a little extra chickpea flour to shape them if they are sticky, but try not to "coat" the patties in it.

Deep fry the falafel for about 8 minutes. Transfer to the prepared plate.

To make the Baba Ghanoush: Preheat the oven to 400°F (200°C, gas mark 6).

Slice the eggplants in half lengthwise and rub the interior flesh lightly with salt. Drizzle with the oil and then place on a baking sheet, cut side down.

Wrap the garlic loosely in foil and roast along with the eggplants. Bake for 1 hour, or until the eggplants have become very tender. Once they are roasted, remove the garlic, and then broil the eggplants for 5 minutes to add a smoky richness to the Baba Ghanoush.

Scoop out the roasted eggplant flesh, seeds and all, and place in a food processor along with the garlic, tahini, juice, and salt. Process until smooth.

Yield: 15 falafels

CARROT CELERIAC REMOULADE

This simple salad is the perfect accompaniment to the Mediterranean Croquettes. (See page 17.)

4 medium carrots, peeled
1 medium celeriac (celery root)
2 tablespoons (8 g) finely minced fresh marjoram
Juice of 1 lemon
2 tablespoons (30 g) Dijon mustard
6 tablespoons (90 g) vegan mayonnaise
3 tablespoons (45 ml) olive oil
1 tablespoons (15 g) sweet relish
3 tablespoons (40 g) sugar

Using a grater, shred the carrots to make about 2 cups (220 g).

Remove the tough outer layer from the celeriac and shred it completely to make about 3¼ cups (425 g).

In a very large bowl, toss the carrots and celeriac together.

In a medium bowl, whisk together the remaining ingredients to make a smooth dressing. Gently toss the carrot and celeriac mixture with the dressing until evenly coated.

Yield: 10 servings

CAPRI SALAD WITH PINE NUTS OVER ARUGULA

This is a traditional take on the classic Capri salad. Use vegan mozzarella wedges or sliceable vegan cheese if you can find it. Otherwise, place shredded vegan cheese on the stacks and broil.

2 large heirloom tomatoes
About 6 thick slices of vegan mozzarella-style cheese
1 tablespoon (15 ml) balsamic vinegar
1 tablespoon (15 ml) olive oil
½ teaspoon black pepper
Pine nuts
Handful of arugula
10 basil leaves

Slice the tomatoes into about three or four ½-inch (1 cm) thick slices. Stack the slices with a thin slice of mozzarella in between each tomato slice, ending with a slice of cheese on top. (You should have about 3 slices of tomato layered with 3 slices of cheese.)

Broil for about 4 minutes, or until the cheese bubbles and browns on top.

Drizzle with a little vinegar and oil. Top with the pepper and nuts. Serve over the arugula and garnish with the basil.

Yield: 2 salads

ROASTED FENNEL SALAD WITH CARAMELIZED ONIONS

Much like a wilted spinach salad, the warmth of the caramelized onions in the dressing wilts the greens softly, while the bright notes of roasted fennel liven the salad and give it depth.

1 bulb fennel, cut into bite-size chunks
1 teaspoon olive oil, divided
1¼ teaspoons salt, divided
1 large Vidalia onion, sliced very thin
4 to 5 cups (120 to 150 g) fresh spinach
2 teaspoons lemon juice
½ teaspoon black pepper
1 apple, very thinly sliced into half moons
2 teaspoons flaxseed or chia seeds
½ cup (30 g) cut-up fennel greens (the feathery greens), chopped

Preheat the oven to 400°F (200°C, gas mark 6). Line a baking sheet with parchment.

Evenly place the fennel bulb in a single layer on the prepared baking sheet. Drizzle lightly with ½ teaspoon of the olive oil and ½ teaspoon of the salt. Bake for about 30 to 35 minutes, or until tender and golden brown on the edges.

Meanwhile, in a small frying pan, sauté the onion with ½ teaspoon of the salt and the remaining ½ teaspoon oil over high heat for about 7 minutes, or until the edges turn brown and the onion begins to turn translucent. Reduce the heat slightly and continue sautéing for about 7 minutes longer, or until the onion begins to turn brown.

Reduce the heat once again and cook, on about medium heat for about 5 more minutes, stirring often, or until onion has transformed into a deep caramel brown and is very tender. Set aside to allow to cool.

In a small bowl, toss the onion, spinach, remaining salt, juice, and pepper. Gently massage into the spinach for about 15 to 30 seconds, just long enough to slightly wilt the leaves. Toss in the fennel and apple, flax or chia seeds, and fennel greens.

Yield: 4 servings

CHOPPED ENDIVE, "ROQUEFORT," PECAN, AND CRANBERRY SALAD

To quickly toast the pecans, simply place pecans on an ungreased baking sheet and roast in a preheated oven at 375°F (190°C, gas mark 5) for 5 to 7 minutes or until fragrant.

FOR THE ROQUEFORT:
1 block (about 14 ounces, or 400 g) extra-firm tofu
3 teaspoons (16 g) white or yellow miso
3 tablespoons (45 ml) white wine
2 tablespoons (28 ml) lemon juice
3 tablespoons (45 ml) water
½ tablespoon Dijon mustard

FOR THE DRESSING:
2 tablespoons (30 g) Dijon mustard
1 tablespoon (20 g) agave
1 tablespoon (15 ml) lemon juice
2 teaspoons strawberry preserves
1 tablespoon (15 ml) water

FOR THE SALAD:
1¼ pounds (630 g, or about 5 heads), endive leaves, halved
1 cup (100 g) toasted pecans, chopped
1 cup (120 g) dried cranberries

To make the Roquefort: Press the tofu until practically all the water is removed. To easily press tofu, drain all water from the package and then wrap the tofu tightly in a large, clean kitchen towel. Place the tofu on a flat baking sheet or plate and then top with another flat baking sheet or plate. Weigh down the tofu with a few heavy cans (two 30-ounce [840 g] cans of tomatoes work great) for at least 1 hour and up to 4 hours until most of the water from the tofu has been absorbed into the towel.

In a bowl, whisk together the miso, wine, juice, water, and mustard until smooth.

In a small dish, marinate the tofu in the miso mixture for at least 5 hours and up to overnight.

Preheat the oven to 225°F (110°C, gas mark ¼).

Drain the marinade from the tofu by pressing gently with your hands using a clean towel, just long enough to remove any excess liquid. Cube the tofu into about 40 small pieces.

Place the tofu on an ungreased baking dish. Bake for 45 minutes, flipping halfway through. Refrigerate before using.

To make the dressing: In a bowl, whisk all of the ingredients together until smooth, but leave chunks of strawberries from the preserves remaining.

To make the salad: In a serving bowl, toss the dressing with the endive. Top with the pecans, cranberries, and Roquefort.

Yield: 4 small side salads

ORANGE, ARTICHOKE, ARUGULA, AND FENNEL SALAD

Arugula adds a nice earthy balance to the bright notes of the fennel and orange.

2 tablespoons (30 ml) lemon juice
1 tablespoon (15 ml) olive oil
1 tablespoon (15 ml) agave nectar
2 tablespoons (30 ml) orange juice
1 teaspoon poppy seeds, plus a pinch for garnish
2 packed cups (58 g) baby arugula leaves
½ cup (100 g) thinly shaved fennel bulb, tough core removed (use a mandoline or a vegetable peeler)
8 small canned artichoke hearts, halved
2 medium seedless oranges, supremed (see Recipe Note)

In a medium bowl, whisk the lemon juice, oil, agave, orange juice, and seeds to make a thin dressing. Toss with the arugula to evenly and lightly coat. Gently stir in the fennel, artichoke, and oranges. Garnish with the seeds.

Yield: 4 servings

▶ *Recipe Note*
To supreme an orange, cut off the top and bottom of the orange, so that the fruit sits flat on your cutting board and the interior of the orange is visible. Carefully cut the remaining peel off, following the curve of the fruit until no more pith remains on the outside of the flesh. Over a bowl to catch the juice, cut along the membrane of each section with your knife from top to bottom and slice through to reveal each orange wedge. After cutting through the center of the membrane, the segments can easily be removed.

17 Orange, Artichoke, Arugula and Fennel Salad; 18 Grapefruit, Yellow Pepper, and Avacado Salad; 19 Minted Green Salad with Oranges, Lentils and Tomatoes; 20 Citrus Salad; 21 Tropical Enzyme Salad; 22 Shredded Kohlrabi and Raisin Salad; 23 Greek Salad with Tahini Dressing; 24 Drenched Pad Thai Salad

25 Red and White Quinoa Kale Salad; 26 Make a Salad a Meal; 27 Fiery Gingered Yam Salad; 28 Roasted Eggplant and Tomato Salad; 29 Warm Spinach Salad; 30 Warm Spinach and Toasty Pine Nut Salad; 31 Avocado, Tomato, and Cheddar Soup; 32 Coconut Asparagus Soup

GRAPEFRUIT, YELLOW PEPPER, AND AVOCADO SALAD

This salad is creamy from the avocado, sour from the grapefruit, sweet from the agave, cool and crunchy from the cucumber and lettuce, and hot from the red onion and jalapeño.

1 large yellow grapefruit, peeled and separated into wedges
2 yellow bell peppers, seeded and sliced
2 medium cucumbers, peeled, seeded, and cut into 1-inch (2.5 cm) matchsticks
1 medium red onion, sliced
1 tablespoon (15 ml) olive oil
1 tablespoon (20 g) agave nectar
1 jalapeño pepper, minced
¼ teaspoon salt
2 ripe avocados, peeled, halved, pitted, and sliced
8 romaine lettuce leaves, whole
Black pepper, to taste

In a bowl, combine the grapefruit, bell peppers, cucumber, and onion.

In a small bowl, combine the oil, agave, jalapeño pepper, and salt. Pour the dressing over the grapefruit mixture and toss to combine. Add the avocado and gently toss, avoiding mashing the avocado. Serve right away or marinate for 1 hour.

When ready to serve, divide the leaves among 4 plates. Top each with the marinated mixture. Season with black pepper.

Yield: 4 servings

MINTED GREEN SALAD WITH ORANGES, LENTILS, AND TOMATOES

You'll fall in love with this salad after only one bite. The earthy undertone and chewiness of the lentils pairs naturally with the robust flavors of the Middle East with the addition of fresh parsley mint.

1½ cups (297 g) cooked green lentils
1 teaspoon cumin
1 teaspoon salt
1 tomato, diced
2 seedless oranges, supremed and chopped (See Recipe Note on page 155.)
¼ cup (24 g) finely chopped mint
½ cup (30 g) finely chopped parsley

In a bowl, combine the lentils, cumin, and salt. Toss with the tomato, oranges, mint, and parsley. Chill for at least 1 hour before serving.

Yield: 4 servings

CITRUS SALAD

Enjoy this fresh, light, delicious salad any time of the year.

1 bunch curly kale, leaves stripped from rib and finely chopped
2 oranges, peeled with membranes removed and separated into wedges
1 red grapefruit, peeled with membranes removed and separated into wedges
1 small red onion, thinly sliced
1 jalapeño pepper, seeded and minced (or ⅛ teaspoon crushed red pepper flakes)
2 tablespoons (18 g) toasted pine nuts
¼ cup (60 ml) orange juice
Juice of 1 lime
1 tablespoon (15 ml) vinegar (apple cider, balsamic, or rice)
2 tablespoons (40 g) agave nectar (or other liquid sweetener)
Zest of 1 orange, for garnish

In a large bowl, combine the kale, oranges, grapefruit, onion, pepper, and nuts.

In a separate bowl, whisk together the orange juice, lime juice, vinegar, and agave nectar. Pour the dressing over the salad ingredients and toss gently to coat evenly.

Serve in individual bowls, garnished with the zest.

Yield: 4 servings

TROPICAL ENZYME SALAD

This salad is simple to prepare, refreshing, and high in vitamins. This salad is great at breakfast, lunch, or dinner, or as a snack or dessert.

1 papaya, peeled, seeded, and chopped
1 mango, peeled, pitted, and chopped
1 large avocado, peeled, pitted, and chopped
Juice of ½ lime
¼ cup (21 g) unsweetened shredded coconut

In a medium bowl, mix the papaya, mango, and avocado. Drizzle the juice over the fruit and mix gently. Sprinkle with the coconut.

Yield: 3 servings

SHREDDED KOHLRABI AND RAISIN SALAD

Kohlrabi, a member of the turnip family, has a mild flavor and crunchy texture. Serve this salad chilled or at room temperature.

2 small kohlrabi, peeled and shredded

1 carrot, peeled and shredded
1 shallot, sliced thin
1 tablespoon (2.4 g) thyme leaves
3 scallions, sliced into small rings
½ cup (30 g) loosely packed parsley leaves, minced
1 cup (145 g) raisins
Juice of 1 lemon
1 teaspoon salt
2 tablespoons (28 g) vegan mayonnaise
Dash or two nutmeg
½ tablespoon agave

In a bowl, gently mix all of the ingredients together until well mixed. Let the flavors meld for about 1 hour.

Yield: 4 servings

GREEK SALAD WITH TAHINI DRESSING

Yes, you can have a vegan Greek salad.

FOR THE DRESSING:
¾ cup (180 ml) olive oil
1 tablespoon (15 g) tahini
¼ cup (60 ml) lemon juice
½ teaspoon salt
1 tablespoon (4 g) finely minced fresh Greek oregano
2 tablespoons (5 g) finely minced fresh basil
½ teaspoon black pepper
1 tablespoon (15 ml) agave nectar
3 cloves garlic, finely minced

FOR THE SALAD:
8 cups (440 g) chopped lettuce (green leaf, romaine, or curly leaf)
1 cup (100 g) pitted Kalamata olives
1 cup (150 g) Tofu Feta (See page 14.)
⅓ cup (20 g) chopped fresh parsley
1 teaspoon lemon zest
Jarred pepperoncini (golden Greek peppers), sliced into rings, to taste
2 tomatoes, thinly sliced

To make the dressing: In a bowl, whisk together all the ingredients until combined. Store in an airtight container and let rest for at least 1 hour. Stir before using. (If refrigerating, allow to come back to room temperature before using because it will separate when cold.)

To make the salad: Shred the lettuce into bite-size pieces.
In a serving bowl, toss the lettuce with the dressing to taste. Add the olives, Tofu Feta, parsley, zest, pepperoncini, and tomatoes. Toss everything together gently.

Yield: 4 servings

DRENCHED PAD THAI SALAD

This salad is similar to pad Thai, but made with raw zucchini "noodles." It's hearty enough to serve as a meal because it contains grilled pineapple and tofu.

1 package (16 ounces, or 455 g) extra-firm tofu, well drained and pressed

FOR THE TOFU MARINADE:
¾ cup (175 ml) pineapple juice
3 scallions, thinly sliced
2 cloves garlic, minced
3 tablespoons (45 ml) wheat-free tamari (or soy sauce)
1 teaspoon Chinese five-spice powder
1 teaspoon peanut oil (or olive oil)
1 can (15 ounces, or 420 g) pineapple slices in pineapple juice

FOR THE ZUCCHINI NOODLES:
2 or 3 zucchini

FOR THE SALAD DRESSING:
¾ cup (180 ml) liquid from tofu marinade
2 tablespoons (30 ml) lime juice
4 heaping tablespoons (64 g) smooth peanut butter
Wheat-free tamari or soy sauce, to taste

FOR THE SALAD:
1 mango, cut into bite-size pieces
½ cup (110 g) roasted peanuts, crushed
Chopped fresh cilantro, optional
Hot sauce, optional

Halve the tofu, making two rectangles about ½-inch (1.3 cm) thick. Cut them into bite-size triangles.
In a medium baking dish, arrange the tofu in a single layer.

To make the marinade: In a bowl, whisk all of ingredients together. Pour the marinade over the tofu. Marinate for at least 2 hours, flipping the tofu halfway through. Remove the tofu from the dish, reserving the leftover marinade.
Grill the tofu and the pineapple rings on an electric indoor grill (or a mesh grill pan placed on an outdoor grill) for 10 to 15 minutes, or until golden brown on both sides, flipping if necessary.

To make the zucchini noodles: Remove the ends from the zucchini and peel if desired. Using a vegetable spiralizer or vegetable peeler, cut the zucchini into long noodlelike strips, chopping into shorter "noodles" if necessary, and place in a large bowl.

To make the dressing: In a bowl, whisk all of the dressing ingredients until smooth. (The dressing will be quite soupy.) Add more tamari to taste, if desired. Pour the dressing over the zucchini noodles and mix together until well coated, allowing the excess to remain at the bottom of the bowl.

To assemble the salad: Divide the zucchini noodles among six bowls, also transferring some dressing to each bowl. Top with the tofu, pineapple, mango, peanuts and cilantro and hot sauce, if using.

Yield: 6 servings

RED AND WHITE QUINOA KALE SALAD

The tahini in the dressing for this salad gives it a nice rich flavor, while the raisins add an unexpected sweetness. This salad tastes great warm or cold, which makes it the perfect dish to bring to potlucks or pack for lunches.

1 cup (168 g) white quinoa, uncooked
½ cup (84 g) red quinoa, uncooked
3 cups (705 ml) water or vegetable broth
8 ounces (227 g) chopped curly or lacinto kale
½ cup (45 g) sliced or slivered almonds (toasted or raw)
½ cup (80 g) raisins
½ cup (128 g) tahini
2 tablespoons (30 ml) soy sauce, tamari, or Bragg Liquid Aminos
2 tablespoons (30 ml) lemon juice
1 tablespoon (10 g) minced garlic

In a fine mesh strainer, rinse the quinoa. Strain out as much excess water as possible. (If you buy prewashed quinoa, you can omit this step.)

Place the quinoa in a dry pot with a lid, and heat it over medium heat for about 4 to 5 minutes, to lightly toast the quinoa, stirring constantly to prevent burning. Add the water or broth, raise the heat and bring to boil. Immediately lower the heat to low, cover, and cook for 15 minutes. Remove the pot from the heat and allow to stand, covered, for 5 minutes. Uncover and fluff with a fork.

While the quinoa is cooking, blanch the kale. Bring a pot of water to boil, drop in the kale, give it a quick stir and then quickly remove it and place into an ice water bath to stop the cooking.

Once the quinoa is cooked, place it in a bowl, along with the kale, almonds, and raisins.

In a small bowl, whisk together the tahini, soy sauce, juice, and garlic.

Toss the dressing with the salad to coat. Serve immediately or refrigerate.

Yield: 8 servings

MAKE A SALAD A MEAL

Here's an easy way to customize your favorite salad. Incorporate the suggested number of items from each of the categories. You will have a substantial salad. Select different items each time for a totally different, nutritious, and delicious salad every day. This salad is meant to be eaten as an entire family meal.

Greens: Select 2 or 3, 1 to 2 cups chopped raw per person: arugula, Belgium endive, bok choy, butter lettuce, chicory, Chinese cabbage, collard greens, escarole, kale, mache, dandelion greens, mustard greens, radicchio, spinach, Swiss chard, Romaine, red leaf, turnip greens, watercress, or other leafy greens

Vegetables: Select 4 to 5, 1 cup raw or ½ cup cooked per person: snow peas, snap peas, green beans, cucumbers, leeks, eggplant, mushrooms, green onions, bell peppers, zucchini, tomato, cauliflower, corn, sprouts, celery, radishes, jicama, beets, artichoke hearts, okra, broccoli, carrots, cabbage, or sundried tomatoes

Beans/legumes: Select 1, ¼ to ½ cup per person: black beans, garbanzo beans, black-eyed peas, pinto beans, green peas, edamame, azuki beans, cannelloni beans, lima beans, white beans, or lentils

Grains: Select 1 or 2, ½ cup cooked per person: amaranth, millet, buckwheat, rye, quinoa, sorghum, kamut, spelt, wild rice, brown rice, barley, or teff

Fruit: Select 1 or 2, ½ cup per person: apples, berries, grapes, currants, oranges, avocado, tangerines, pears, cherries, star fruit, dates, figs, or cranberries

Nuts/seeds: Select 1, ¼ cup per person: walnuts, pecans, almonds, cashews, coconut, ground flax seeds, pine nuts, chia seeds, sunflower seeds, or pumpkin seeds

In a large bowl, combine the selected ingredients.

Yield: Variable

FIERY GINGERED YAM SALAD

This salad is inspired by two of Africa's most often-used crops: ginger and yams. The ginger in this recipe dominates and adds a bit of heat to the salad. Cut it slightly if you'd prefer less spice.

3 medium-size white yams
2 cloves garlic, minced
2 tablespoons (16 g) fresh grated ginger
1 tablespoon (20 g) agave
½ teaspoon salt
Dash nutmeg

⅓ cup (5 g) finely chopped cilantro
1 tablespoon (15 ml) lemon juice
1 tablespoon (15 ml) coconut milk
8 finely chopped sun-dried tomatoes, soaked in water at least 1 hour and drained

Preheat the oven to 350°F (180°C, gas mark 4).

Place the yams on a baking sheet. Loosely cover with aluminum foil. Bake for 1 to 1½ hours, or until soft when pierced with a fork. Remove from the oven and let cool briefly until cool enough to handle. Remove the skins and cut into bite-size cubes. Place in a large bowl.

Make the dressing by mixing all the ingredients, except the tomatoes, together in a small bowl. Add the tomatoes. Drizzle the dressing onto the yams. Toss lightly to coat.

Yield: 4 servings

ROASTED EGGPLANT AND TOMATO SALAD

Serve this salad warm or cold. This tastes wonderful on top of tiny toasts made from the Pain Ordinaire recipe. (See page 12.)

Salt, to taste
1 medium thin-skinned eggplant, cut into 1-inch (2.5 cm) pieces
3 cups (450 g) assorted small tomatoes (cherry, globe, etc.)
Drizzle olive oil
½ tablespoon ground cumin
1 cup (165 g) cooked corn kernels
2 tablespoons minced (8 g) fresh dill

Preheat the oven to 400°F (200°C, gas mark 6). Line a baking sheet with parchment paper.

In a medium bowl, salt the eggplant gently. Toss with the tomatoes and drizzle with the oil. Spread the eggplant and the tomatoes onto the prepared baking sheet. Roast for about 20 minutes, or until the eggplants are golden and the tomatoes are sunken and shiny. Sprinkle the veggies with the cumin.

Transfer to a medium bowl along with the corn and dill.

Yield: 4 servings

WARM SPINACH SALAD

This salad is perfect for any season, but it's best when spinach is available locally. The warm dressing slightly wilts the spinach, and the molasses caramelizes a bit.

12 to 14 ounces (335 to 395 g) baby spinach, rinsed and dried
1 medium red onion, thinly sliced

1 cup (110 g) pecans, toasted and coarsely chopped
¼ cup (60 ml) olive oil
1 clove garlic, pressed
1 cup (235 ml) balsamic vinegar
1 tablespoon (14 g) molasses
½ teaspoon black pepper
1 teaspoon (5 ml) truffle oil, optional

In a large bowl, combine the spinach, onion, and pecans.

In a small saucepan, heat the olive oil over very low heat. Sauté the garlic for a few minutes, just to allow garlic flavor to seep into the oil. Add the vinegar, molasses, and pepper. Whisking constantly, bring almost to a boil, remove from the heat, and cool until just warm. Add the truffle oil, if using, and stir to combine.

Pour the dressing over the spinach. Toss to coat.

Yield: 4 to 6 servings

WARM SPINACH AND TOASTY PINE NUT SALAD

This salad combines spinach with heart-healthy tomatoes, free radical–killing coconut oil, and pine nuts, which contain nutrients that lower blood pressure.

2 teaspoons coconut oil, divided
2 cups (60 g) spinach leaves
2 tablespoons (18 g) pine nuts
1 cup (150 g) cherry tomatoes, sliced
1 to 2 tablespoons (15 to 28 ml) any balsamic vinaigrette dressing

In a medium skillet, melt 1 teaspoon of the oil over medium heat. Add the spinach and cook it until it wilts.

In a small skillet, heat the remaining oil over medium heat. Add the nuts and stir to make sure the oil coats the nuts evenly. Toast the nuts lightly.

Place the spinach on a serving plate. Top with the tomatoes and nuts. Drizzle the salad dressing on top.

Yield: 1 serving

AVOCADO, TOMATO, AND CHEDDAR SOUP

This slightly spicy soup is the perfect comfort food. You can make up a big batch and freeze the leftovers in individual freezer-safe plastic bags or plastic tubs.

1 green bell pepper, diced
1 large onion, diced
1 large can (30 ounces, 840 g) canned tomatoes and juice
1 tablespoon (6 g) salted vegetable broth powder (or 2 cubes bouillon)
5 cups (1.2 L) water

2 cloves garlic, minced
1 teaspoon coriander
1 teaspoon salt
1 teaspoon paprika
1 teaspoon chili powder
1 teaspoon black pepper
½ cup (56 g) Cheddar-style shredded vegan cheese
½ cup (48 g) nutritional yeast
2 avocados, peeled, pitted, and diced
¼ cup (4 g) chopped cilantro leaves

In a large pot, place all the ingredients up to the cheese. Bring to a boil. Once boiling, reduce the heat just to keep it at a constant simmer. Cook for about 35 to 45 minutes, or until the onion is very soft. Add the cheese and yeast. Cook for about 5 minutes, or until the cheese is fully melted. Stir in the avocados and cook an additional 1 to 2 minutes. Top with the cilantro right before serving.

Yield: 6 servings

COCONUT ASPARAGUS SOUP
The desiccated coconut adds a hint of texture to the puréed soup, and the asparagus incorporates a deep flavor and richness without the need for a cream base.

About 25 thin stalks asparagus, tough ends removed
1 small sweet onion, chopped (about 1 cup [160 g])
⅓ cup (30 g) desiccated coconut (unsweetened), soaked
   overnight and then drained
2 tablespoons (30 ml) olive oil, plus more for drizzling
⅔ cup (160 ml) water
Salt, to taste
2 cups (470 ml) nondairy milk or vegetable broth

Steam the asparagus for 5 to 7 minutes, or until tender.
   Meanwhile, in a shallow pan, combine the onion, coconut, the 2 tablespoons (30 ml) oil, and water. Cook over medium-high heat for about 10 minutes, or until the onion is tender and all of the water has been absorbed, stirring often to prevent sticking. Season with salt.
   Chill the asparagus and onion for about 15 minutes, or just until cold enough to place in a blender. Chop the asparagus into bite-size pieces.
   Transfer the asparagus mixture, reserving about ½ cup (50 g) of the asparagus for garnishing the soup, and the milk to a blender. Blend until smooth, about 5 minutes. Season with more salt.
   Reheat on the stove top to the desired temperature. Garnish with a drizzle of oil and the reserved asparagus.

Yield: 4 servings

SPICY KIMCHI SOUP
To help cut the heat, serve this with a bowl of steamed rice.

3 cups (450 g) kimchi, undrained
2 green onions, chopped
1 stalk celery, sliced thinly
5 cups (1.2 L) vegetable broth
2 cubes (2 teaspoons) vegetable bouillon
1½ tablespoons (23 g) yellow or white miso
2 teaspoons wheat-free soy sauce (or tamari)
2 tablespoons (30 ml) unseasoned rice vinegar
2 teaspoons crushed red pepper flakes
Cooked rice

In a deep soup pot, cook the kimchi, onions, and celery over medium-high heat for about 10 minutes, or until the kimchi is translucent and the other vegetables are tender. Add the broth and bring to a boil over high heat. Reduce the heat to low and stir in the bouillon, miso, soy sauce, vinegar, and red pepper. Simmer for about 15 minutes, or until fragrant and heated through. Serve with a bowl of hot rice.

Yield: 4 servings

SIX-SHADES-OF-RED SOUP
A rich-tasting and rich-colored soup, this recipe is a testament to how delicious low-calorie food can be.

10 cups (2350 ml) water
2 cups (400 g) red lentils, picked through and rinsed
3 red potatoes, unpeeled, chopped
2 red beets, peeled and diced
1 red onion, diced
2 carrots, finely chopped
2 cloves garlic, minced
½ teaspoon crushed red pepper flakes
1 tablespoon (2 g) finely chopped dill, plus more for
   garnish
¼ to ½ cup (65 to 130 g) red miso paste
½ cup (120 ml) vegetable juice
1 teaspoon salt
Black pepper, to taste

In a large soup pot, combine the water, lentils, potatoes, beets, onion, carrots, garlic, red pepper, and 1 tablespoon (2 g) of the dill. Cover and bring to a boil. Reduce the heat and simmer for 20 to 25 minutes, or until the potatoes are fork-tender. (Keep covered while cooking.)
   Meanwhile, in a small bowl, combine the miso and juice.
   When the soup is cooked, remove from the heat, stir in the miso mixture, and sprinkle with the dill. Season with salt and pepper.

Yield: 8 servings

FAJITA SOUP
Topping this soup with sliced avocados right before serving adds a little creaminess to this brothy vegetable soup.

½ cup (75 g) seeded and chopped red bell pepper
½ cup (75 g) seeded and chopped yellow bell pepper
½ cup (75 g) seeded and chopped orange bell pepper
2 cups (240 g) chopped zucchini
1 small red onion, thinly sliced
6 cremini or button mushrooms, sliced (about 1 cup [70 g])
2 tablespoons (30 ml) olive oil
1 can (15 ounces, or 420 g) black beans, drained and rinsed
1 can (28 ounces, or 794 g) diced tomatoes
6 cups (1410 ml) vegetable broth
2 teaspoons cumin
½ teaspoon chipotle chili powder
2 tablespoons (30 ml) lime juice, plus extra for serving
Salt, to taste
2 ripe avocados, peeled, pitted, and chopped

In a large frying pan, sauté the peppers, zucchini, onion, mushrooms, and oil over medium-high heat, for 10 to 15 minutes, or until the vegetables are tender, stirring often to prevent sticking.

Transfer the vegetables to a large soup pot. Stir in the beans, tomatoes, broth, cumin, chili powder, and 2 tablespoons (30 ml) of the lime juice. Season with salt. Simmer for about 15 minutes, or until heated through. Garnish with the avocado and more juice.

Yield: 6 servings

CHEESY BROCCOLI SOUP
The classic combination of broccoli and cheese is always a winner.

1 Vidalia onion, chopped
2 cloves garlic, minced
1 tablespoon (15 ml) olive oil
¼ cup (30 g) millet flour
¼ cup (60 g) nondairy margarine
2 cups (470 g) nondairy milk
3 to 4 cups (705 to 940 ml) vegetable broth, or to desired consistency
1 recipe Cashew Cream, unsweetened (See page 6.)
1½ cups (195 g) nutritional yeast
3 to 4 cups (210 to 280 g) broccoli florets, steamed until very tender and chopped into bite-size pieces
½ cup (45 g) nondairy shredded cheese, optional
Salt, to taste
Black pepper, to taste

In a skillet, sauté the onion and garlic in the oil over medium-high heat for about 13 minutes, or until the onion is caramelized, stirring often to prevent sticking.

In a large soup pot, cook the flour and margarine over medium heat until the margarine is melted and the mixture forms a roux. Quickly whisk in the milk and stir continuously until smooth. Add the Cashew Cream and yeast, whisking to prevent lumps from forming. Stir in the broccoli and onions and garlic. Simmer for 5 to 7 minutes over medium heat, or until thickened. If the soup becomes too thick too quickly, reduce the heat and whisk in a little more broth to thin. Stir in the cheese, if using. Simmer over low heat until melted. Season with salt and pepper.

Yield: 8 servings

CHESTNUT SOUP WITH BAKED APPLE CRISPS
You can use fresh roasted chestnuts here (which may require a bit of extra liquid to thin), but canned are fine.

FOR THE BAKED APPLE CRISPS:
Dash salt
1 medium apple, unpeeled, sliced very thinly

FOR THE CHESTNUT SOUP:
1 onion, chopped
2 leeks, cleaned and sliced, tough green tops removed
1 parsnip, sliced into thin coins
1 stalk celery, minced
1 tablespoon (15 ml) olive oil
1 teaspoon salt
1 cup (235 ml) almond milk
1 cup (145 g) whole canned chestnuts, drained
Few leaves sage, whole
2 cups (475 ml) vegetable broth or additional almond milk

To make the Baked Apple Crisps: Preheat the oven to 425°F (220°C, gas mark 7). Line a baking sheet with parchment paper.

Lightly salt the apples. Bake for 10 minutes, flipping once halfway through.

Reduce the heat to 250°F (120°C, gas mark ½).

Continue to bake the apples for about 1 to 1½ hours, or until they are dried out, checking as they bake to prevent burning. Let cool.

To make the Chestnut Soup: In a medium frying pan, sauté the onion, leeks, parsnip, and celery in the oil and salt over medium-high heat for about 8 minutes, just until browned on the edges. Add the milk. Simmer over medium heat for about 20 minutes, until the parsnips are tender and all of the liquid is gone.

In a blender, blend the vegetables, chestnuts, and sage until smooth, slowly incorporating the broth or additional milk to thin. Serve the soup topped with the Baked Apple Crisps.

Yield: 4 servings

33 Spicy Kimchi Soup; 34 Six-Shades-of-Red Soup; 35 Fajita Soup; 36 Cheesy Broccoli Soup; 37 Chestnut Soup with Baked Apple Crisps, 38 Butternut Squash Orange Ginger Soup; 39 Potato Soup; 40 Red Potato and Watercress Soup

41 Winter White Soup; 42 Vegetable Miso Soup; 43 Bump Up Your Day the Miso (Soup) Way; 44 Creamy Kale Miso Soup; 45 White Beans and Greens Soup; 46 Peanutty Parsnip and Carrot Soup; 47 Brown Lentil Soup; 48 Portobello Mushroom and Barley Soup

BUTTERNUT SQUASH ORANGE GINGER SOUP

A delightfully sweet soup, this is as healing as it is delicious.

1 tablespoon (15 ml) water
1 large onion, coarsely chopped
3 tablespoons (18 g) minced fresh ginger
4 cloves garlic, minced
¼ cup (60 ml) orange juice
1 large butternut squash, peeled, seeded, and cubed
2 medium yellow potatoes, peeled and quartered
3½ cups (823 ml) vegetable broth
Salt, to taste
Black pepper, to taste
2 tablespoons (8 g) finely chopped fresh parsley or cilantro
Zest from 2 oranges (about 2 tablespoons [6 g])
2 green onions, thinly sliced or finely chopped

In a large soup pot, heat the water over medium heat. Sauté the onion, ginger, and garlic for 5 minutes. Add the juice. Simmer for about 3 minutes. Add the squash, potatoes, and broth. Simmer slowly for about 25 minutes, or until the squash and potatoes are fork-tender.

Ladle the contents into a blender and purée. Return the soup to the soup pot and reheat over low heat. Season with salt and pepper. Garnish the individual servings with parsley, zest, and green onions.

Yield: 4 to 6 servings

POTATO SOUP

Healthier than traditional potato soup and cooked in less than half the time, this soup will warm your heart and belly just the same as the original.

2 to 3 tablespoons (28 to 42 g) vegan butter
3 cloves garlic, minced
1 package (14 ounces, or 392 g) soft tofu
1 cup (235 ml) almond milk
2 tablespoons (30 ml) lemon juice
½ teaspoon salt
1 teaspoon dried dill
4 cups (440 g) diced potatoes
2 cups (140 g) sliced mushrooms
2 cups (320 g) sliced onion, cut into half-moons
1 cup (130 g) chopped carrot
1 cup (120 g) chopped celery
4 cups (940 ml) vegetable broth
Black pepper, to taste

In an uncovered pressure cooker, heat the butter on medium-high heat. Sauté the garlic for 1 minute.

In a blender, pulse the tofu, milk, juice, salt, and dill until creamy.

Add the potatoes, mushrooms, onion, carrots, and celery to the pressure cooker, mixing well. Pour the tofu mixture into the pressure cooker. Stir in the broth. (Tip: As a way to get the remaining tofu cream out of the blender, first pour the broth into the blender and pulse quickly; then pour into the pot.) Cover and bring to pressure. Cook at high pressure for 5 minutes. Use a quick release. Season with the pepper.

Yield: 8 servings

RED POTATO AND WATERCRESS SOUP

This soup's red potato base gives it an undeniably familiar taste for anyone who loves potato soup. It's best served slightly cooled, not piping hot.

6 small red potatoes (1 pound, or 455 g), cubed
3 green onions, chopped
2 cloves garlic, minced
6 cups (1.4 L) water
1 teaspoon black pepper
2 to 3 teaspoons salt, divided
2 large handfuls (10 to 15 g) watercress, chopped
Coconut cream (the thick part from the top of a can of coconut milk)

In a large pot, bring the potatoes, onions, garlic, water, pepper, and 1 teaspoon of the salt to a boil. Once boiling, reduce to the heat to medium. Simmer for about 8 to 9 minutes, or until the potatoes smash with a bit of pressure under a fork. Add the watercress. Cook for an additional 1 to 2 minutes. Stir in 1 teaspoon of the remaining salt.

Blend the potato mixture in the pot using an immersion blender or cool it slightly and transfer to a blender. Blend until fairly smooth, making sure to leave some tiny bits of watercress floating throughout. Add up to 1 teaspoon of the remaining salt to taste. Garnish with the cream.

Yield: 6 servings

WINTER WHITE SOUP

The name alone evokes a chilly night with the fire blazing, romance swirling, and kitties purring on your lap. The red beet garnish contrasts beautifully with the white soup. Serve hot.

1 tablespoon (15 ml) olive oil
3 cloves garlic, chopped
2 shallots, chopped
1 (1-inch, or 2.5 cm) piece fresh ginger, minced
3 green onions, chopped
3 yellow potatoes, peeled and cubed
2 medium parsnips, chopped
1 apple or pear, peeled and cubed

1 can (15 ounces, or 420 g) white beans, drained and
  rinsed
1 teaspoon chopped fresh dill
1 teaspoon dried tarragon
¾ cup (180 ml) dry white wine
6 whole sprigs fresh thyme
3 cups (705 ml) vegetable broth
¼ cup (60 ml) nondairy milk (such as almond, soy, rice,
  hemp, hazelnut, or oat)
Salt, to taste
Black pepper, to taste
Grated red beet, for garnish

In a soup pot, heat the oil over medium-low heat. Add the
garlic, shallots, ginger, and onions. Cook for about 5
minutes, or until fragrant but not brown. Add the potatoes,
parsnips, apple, beans, dill, and tarragon. Cook for 5
minutes longer, stirring occasionally. Stir in the wine and
thyme and increase the heat to high. Boil for about 5
minutes, stirring constantly, or until the wine is reduced by
half. Pour in the broth. Return the mixture to a boil. Reduce
the heat to low and simmer, partly covered, for about 20
minutes, or until the vegetables are tender.

  Remove the thyme sprigs and transfer to a blender.
Purée until smooth, working in batches if necessary. Stir in
the milk, season with salt and pepper, and top with the
beet.

Yield: 4 servings

VEGETABLE MISO SOUP

*Kombu, an ingredient often called for in miso soup, is a
type of sea vegetable that can easily be found in most
Asian groceries and natural food stores, generally next to
nori and other sea vegetables.*

4 heads baby bok choy, cleaned, ends removed, and
  roughly chopped
4 carrots, peeled and sliced
One 3- to 4-inch (7.5 to 10 cm) strip kombu, optional
¼ cup (40 g) chopped green onions
1½ cups (225 g) chopped oyster mushrooms
½ cup (74 g) chopped enoki mushrooms
10 cups (2.4 L) water
2 teaspoons freshly grated ginger
1 teaspoon lemon zest
⅔ to 1 cup (165 to 250 g) miso (white, yellow, or red)
Lemon wedges

In a large pot, simmer the bok choy, carrots, kombu, onions,
mushrooms, water, ginger, and zest over medium-high heat
for about 15 minutes, or until the carrots are soft. Remove
the kombu and discard. Reduce the heat to low and stir in
the miso until all of the paste dissolves into the soup.
Simmer for a few minutes, making sure the broth never

comes to a boil. Taste and add more miso if needed for
saltiness. Serve with the lemon.

Yield: 8 servings

BUMP UP YOUR DAY THE MISO (SOUP) WAY
*Miso and cacao are a natural fit. Play around with this rich
and luxurious combination.*

5 cups (1.2 L) vegetable broth
⅓ to ½ cup (32 to 48 g) raw cacao powder
1 teaspoon minced chile pepper
1 teaspoon minced or grated ginger
1 minced clove garlic
¼ cup (64 g) miso paste (or less for a less salty taste)
8 ounces (225 g) tofu, cut into small cubes
½ cup (50 g) sliced green onions
1 or 2 tablespoons (20 or 40 g) agave nectar, optional
Lemon wedges

In a large pot, simmer the broth, cacao powder, chile,
ginger, and garlic for 10 minutes, stirring occasionally. Stir in
the miso, combining well. Add the tofu and onions. Simmer
for 3 or 4 more minutes. Add the agave, if using. Remove
from the heat. Serve with the lemon.

Yield: 4 servings

CREAMY KALE MISO SOUP
This simple soup is packed with nutrients.

1 to 2 teaspoons vegetable oil
4 cloves garlic, halved
1 small sweet onion, quartered
2 medium carrots, cut into 2- to 3-inch (5 to 7.5 cm)
  pieces
4 cups (940 ml) vegetable broth
1 package (12 ounces, or 344 g) package silken (light
  firm) tofu
1 bunch kale (about 6 ounces [168 g] off the stem), plus a
  few leaves for garnish
¼ cup (63 g) yellow miso
Black pepper, to taste

In an uncovered pressure cooker, heat the oil on
medium-high. Sauté the garlic, onion, and carrots for 5
minutes, or until the onion begins to brown. (Add liquid if it
begins to stick.) Stir frequently. Add the broth and tofu.
Using a spoon, crumble the tofu into pieces. Add the kale
and stir to combine. Cover and bring to pressure. Cook at
high pressure for 4 minutes. Allow for a natural release. If
after 10 minutes, the pressure has still not come down fully,
manually release. Remove the lid and stir in the miso.

Transfer to a blender, in batches if necessary of no more than 3 cups (705 ml) hot soup at a time, and blend for 20 to 30 seconds, or until the kale leaves are completely blended. (Note: Hot soup expands in the blender, so pay heed to using only 3 cups (705 ml) of soup at a time and place a hand towel over the top of the blender for an added measure of safety.)

Season with pepper. Garnish with the extra kale.

Yield: 6 servings

WHITE BEANS AND GREENS SOUP
Packed with leafy greens and beans, this soup is a nutrient-dense meal.

1½ cups (300 g) dried cannellini beans, soaked for 12 hours or overnight
1 tablespoon (15 ml) vegetable oil, optional
4 large cloves garlic, minced
2 cups (320 g) diced carrots
1 cup (160 g) diced onion
1 cup (120 g) diced celery
2 cups (140 g) sliced cremini mushrooms (or shiitake, maitake, or baby bella mushrooms)
1 bay leaf
2 tablespoons (3 g) dried herbes de provence
½ teaspoon black pepper, plus more for serving
1 teaspoon red pepper flakes
5 cups (1.2 L ml) vegetable broth
2 cups (470 ml) water
¼ cup (64 g) tomato paste
8 cups (400 g) loosely packed greens
Juice of 1 large lemon
1 to 1½ teaspoons salt, optional

Rinse and drain the beans.

In an uncovered pressure cooker, heat the oil on medium-high. Sauté the garlic, carrots, onion, and celery for 3 minutes. Add the mushrooms and seasonings. Sauté for another 3 to 5 minutes. Add the broth, water, and paste. Mix well. Add the beans and greens. Stir to combine.

Cover and bring to pressure. Cook at high pressure for 6 to 8 minutes. Allow for a natural release. Remove the lid, stir in the juice. Add the salt. Season with pepper. Remove the bay leaf before serving.

Yield: 6 servings

PEANUTTY PARSNIP AND CARROT SOUP
The sweetness of parsnip and carrot accent the earthy peanut flavor in this soup quite nicely.

1 bulb garlic, about 7 cloves
½ teaspoon olive oil, plus more for drizzling

5 medium carrots, peeled
5 medium parsnips, peeled
Salt, to taste
¼ cup (65 g) peanut butter
1 teaspoon curry powder
4 cups (950 ml) vegetable broth, divided

Preheat the oven to 400°F (200°C, gas mark 6).

Peel off the thick outer skin of the garlic. Using a small knife, trim about ½ inch (1 cm) off of the pointy end of the bulb to expose the individual cloves, leaving the bottom part completely intact. Place the bulb in the center of an 8 x 8-inch (20 x 20 cm) square of aluminum foil. Lightly drizzle with the oil. Create a loose pouch around the foil and seal. Place the foil pouch on a baking sheet. Bake for about 40 minutes, or until the cloves are softened and very fragrant.

Slice the carrots and parsnips into ½-inch (1 cm) wide ovals.

Place the carrots and parsnips in a medium bowl. Toss with ½ teaspoon of the oil. Spread the carrots evenly onto an ungreased baking sheet. Season with salt. Roast for 25 minutes, or until the carrots and parsnips are tender and browned on the edges. Let the vegetables cool briefly.

Transfer the vegetables to a food processor. Combine with the garlic, peanut butter, curry powder, and about 1 cup (235 ml) of the broth. Process the mixture for about 5 minutes, or until it's very smooth.

Transfer the mixture to a pot, add the remaining broth, and simmer until hot.

Yield: 6 servings

BROWN LENTIL SOUP
This semi-puréed soup is both smooth and textured.

2 tablespoons (30 ml) olive oil
1 large yellow onion, chopped
3 cloves garlic, finely chopped
2 carrots, finely chopped
2 stalks celery, finely chopped
2 cups (400 g) brown lentils, picked through and rinsed
8 cups (1880 ml) vegetable broth
1 teaspoon salt, plus more to taste
½ teaspoon freshly ground coriander
½ teaspoon freshly ground cumin
2 tomatoes, seeded and chopped
1 tablespoon (15 ml) truffle oil, optional
Black pepper, to taste
Chopped fresh parsley

In a soup pot, heat the olive oil over medium heat. Add the onion, garlic, carrots, and celery and cook for about 7 minutes, or until the onion is translucent. Add the lentils, broth, 1 teaspoon of the salt, the coriander, and cumin. Stir to combine. Increase the heat to high and bring to a boil. Reduce the heat to medium-low, cover, and cook for 35 to

40 minutes, or until the lentils are tender.

Using an immersion blender, purée the mixture to your preferred consistency. Add the tomatoes to the semi-puréed soup and stir to combine. Add the truffle oil. Season with salt and pepper.

Top with parsley.

Yield: 6 to 8 servings

PORTOBELLO MUSHROOM AND BARLEY SOUP

This homemade soup is quick to prepare and to the table.

1 teaspoon vegetable oil
2 cloves garlic, minced
½ cup (80 g) diced onion
3 stalks celery, chopped
2 carrots, diced
2 large portobello mushrooms (6 ounces [168 g]), sliced lengthwise, then sliced again
1 tomato, diced
¾ cup (200 g) pearl barley, rinsed and drained
3 cups (705 ml) vegetable broth
4 cups (940 ml) water
2 sprigs fresh thyme (or 1 teaspoon dried)
½ to 1 teaspoon salt
Black pepper, to taste

In an uncovered pressure cooker, heat the oil on medium-high. Sauté the garlic and onion for 2 to 3 minutes, or until the onion is soft. Add the celery and carrot and sauté for another 3 to 5 minutes, or until the celery is soft. Add the mushrooms, tomato, barley, broth, water, and thyme. Stir to combine.

Cover and bring to pressure. Cook at high pressure for 20 minutes. Allow for a natural release.

Remove the cover and stir in the salt. Season with pepper.

Yield: 6 to 8 servings

SURPRISINGLY GOOD GREEN SOUP

This soup will change the way people view "green."

1 cup (160 g) chopped white onion
1 large (1 cup, or 89 g) leek, diced
3 tablespoons (40 ml) vegetable broth, optional
3 carrots, peeled and diced, to make 1 cup (108 g)
4 small green zucchini, unpeeled, chopped, to make 1 cup (113 g)
8 ounces (72 g) button mushrooms, chopped
1 head broccoli rabe, chopped, to make 1 cup (40 g)
1¼ cups (295 ml) carrot juice
⅔ cup (160 ml) celery juice
2 cups (470 ml) vegetable broth

Black pepper, to taste
1 teaspoon ground cumin
1 teaspoon turmeric
½ cup (96 g) dry lentils, uncooked
½ cup (96 g) dry split peas, uncooked
1 small bunch (1 cup, or 67 g) lacinato (Dino) kale, de-stemmed and cut into strips
1 small bunch (1 cup, or 36 g) collard greens, cut into strips
1 small bunch (1 cup, or 36 g) Swiss chard, cut into strips
Cashew Cream or nutritional yeast, to taste (See page 6.)

In a large pot, cook the onion and leek over high heat for about 5 minutes, until they become translucent. If the onion and leeks begin to stick, add the broth, if using. Add the carrots, zucchini, and mushrooms. Cook over high heat for about 7 minutes, or until they begin to create liquid. Add the broccoli rabe. Cook for 5 minutes.

Decrease the heat to medium. Add the carrot juice, celery juice, broth, pepper to taste, cumin, and turmeric. When juices and broth start to boil, add the lentils and peas. Stir and cook for 20 to 45 minutes, or until the lentils and peas are soft. Add the kale, collard greens, and chard. Cook for about 7 to 10 minutes, or until the greens are cooked down.

Using a handheld mixer, purée the soup until creamy. (Or transfer small batches in a blender and blend until creamy.) Top with the Cashew Cream or yeast.

Yield: 6 servings

THREE-GREENS RIBOLLITA SOUP

Ribollita means "twice-cooked," or "reboiled," in Italian. A white bean stock is livened up with greens, carrots, and potatoes, with added slices of toasted bread.

2 cans (15 ounces, or 420 g) cannellini beans, drained and rinsed
6 cups (1.4 L) vegetable broth, divided
5 cloves garlic, minced
4 fresh sage leaves
2 bay leaves
½ teaspoon salt
2 tablespoons (30 ml) oil
2 medium yellow onions, diced
3 carrots, coarsely chopped
2 potatoes, peeled and diced
½ cup (45 g) coarsely chopped cabbage
1 bunch Swiss chard, trimmed and chopped into bite-size pieces
1 bunch kale, trimmed and chopped into bite-size pieces
Salt, to taste
Black pepper, to taste
6 or 12 (½ inch, or 1.3 cm, thick) slices hearty Italian or French bread, lightly toasted

49 Surprisingly Good Green Soup; 50 Three-Greens Ribollita Soup; 51 Lemon Rice Soup; 52 Coconut Tom Yum Soup; 53 Chik'n Lentil Noodle Soup; 54 Tofu Noodle Soup (Pho); 55 Vegan "Turkey," Bean, and Kale Soup; 56 Split Pea Soup

57 Simple-to-Make Veggie Chili; 58 Pumpkin Chickpea Chili; 59 Saffron-Infused White Chili; 60 Black-Eyed Pea and Collard Green Chili; 61 Asian Adzuki Bean Chili; 62 Tamarind-Chocolate Chili; 63 Minted Green Pea Bisque; 64 Roasted Tomato and Beet Bisque

In a saucepan, simmer the beans, 4 cups (940 ml) of the broth, garlic, sage leaves, bay leaves, and salt over low-medium heat, for about 20 minutes, or until the mixture begins to thicken and the flavor of the garlic and herbs begin to infuse the beans. (You can purée the beans first and then add to saucepan.) Discard the bay and sage leaves.

Transfer the mixture to a blender and blend until smooth. (If you purée the beans first, you can skip this step.)

In a large soup pot, heat the oil over medium-high heat. Sauté the onions for about 7 minutes, or until they are translucent. Add the carrots, potatoes, cabbage, Swiss chard, kale, the bean mixture, and the remaining 2 cups (470 ml) broth. Season with salt and pepper. Cover and cook for about 20 minutes, or until the potatoes are fork-tender, stirring at least once.

Adjust the seasonings to taste. At this point, you can either serve it right away or refrigerate it overnight and reboil it the next day.

When ready to serve, place 1 or 2 toasted bread slices in the bottom of each serving bowl. Ladle the soup over the bread.

Yield: 6 servings

LEMON RICE SOUP

This deliciously creamy soup is inspired by a traditional Greek soup called Avgolemono.

½ cup (120 ml) lemon juice
Zest of 1 lemon
2 cloves garlic, minced
1 sweet onion, diced
2 small stalks celery, thinly sliced
6 cups (1.4 L) vegetable broth
¼ cup (30 g) gram flour, mixed with ¼ cup (60 ml) water
    until very smooth
1 cup (158 g) cooked white rice
½ cup (30 g) fresh chopped parsley
6 lemon wedges

In a medium soup pot, combine the juice, zest, garlic, onion, celery, and broth. Bring to a boil.

Reduce the heat and simmer for about 20 minutes, or until the onion is soft. Slowly whisk in the flour paste. Stir well to prevent any lumps from forming. Stir in the rice and simmer for 10 to 15 minutes, or until the soup thickens. Fold in the parsley. Cool for about 10 minutes. Garnish with the lemon.

Yield: 6 servings

COCONUT TOM YUM SOUP

This sweet and sour Thai soup is a wonderful starter and also great as a light lunch or dinner. This recipe freezes especially well in individual-size freezer-safe containers.

3 tomatoes, cut into small wedges
2 cloves garlic, minced
2 carrots, cut into thin spears
4 ounces (115 g) shiitake mushroom caps, sliced
2 teaspoons vegetable broth powder or 2 cubes veg-
    etable broth
3 to 6 whole Thai bird chiles
Juice of 2 limes, plus the zest
2 coins fresh galangal
½ tablespoon finely minced lemongrass
4 kaffir lime leaves, stems removed and halved (dried
    also works well)
6 cups (1.4 L) water
2 to 3 teaspoons (10 to 15 g) salt
3 tablespoons (39 g) sugar
1 cup (235 ml) coconut milk

In a large soup pot, bring all of the ingredients except for the milk to a boil. Once boiling, reduce to a simmer. Cook for at least 25 minutes, or until the soup is fragrant and the mushrooms are very tender. Stir in the milk. Remove the lime leaves or galangal just before eating.

Yield: 10 servings

CHIK'N LENTIL NOODLE SOUP

This soup is incredibly easy to prepare and delicious!

1 teaspoon olive oil
3 cloves garlic, finely diced
1 large onion, diced
2 cups (200 g) green beans (fresh or frozen), snapped
    into bite-size pieces
1 cup (130 g) chopped carrots
1 cup (120 g) chopped celery
2 teaspoons vegan chicken-flavored seasoning
1 bay leaf
½ teaspoon dried sage
1 cup (200 g) dried brown lentils, rinsed and drained
4 ounces (112 g) soba noodles
4 cups (940 ml) vegetable broth
1 to 1½ cups (235 to 355 ml) water

In an uncovered pressure cooker, heat the oil on medium-high. Sauté the garlic, onion, beans, carrots, and celery for about 3 minutes. Add the seasoning, bay leaf, and sage. Sauté for another 2 minutes. Add the lentils, noodles, broth, and water. Stir to combine. Cover and to bring to pressure. Cook at high pressure for 8 minutes. Use a quick release.

Taste the lentils and the noodles. If they are not cooked

through, simmer on low in the uncovered pressure cooker until done, adding more water if necessary. Remove the bay leaf before serving.

Yield: 4 to 6 servings

TOFU NOODLE SOUP (PHO)

Pho is a popular Vietnamese noodle soup.

6 cups (1.4 L) vegetable broth
2 cloves garlic, minced
1 white onion, sliced very thin
2 carrots, peeled and sliced into long disks
10 broccoli florets
1 teaspoon black pepper
1 teaspoon fresh grated ginger
1 teaspoon ground cinnamon
2 star anise pods
2 to 3 heaping tablespoons (28 to 45 g) sambal oelek
2 tablespoons (30 ml) plus 2 teaspoons soy sauce, divided
1 teaspoon salt
1 block tofu (12 ounces, or 340 g), drained and pressed well for at least 3 hours
8 ounces (225 g) thin rice noodles
Juice of 1 lime
1 cup (24 g) fresh Thai basil leaves

In a large soup pot, combine the broth, garlic, onion, carrots, broccoli, pepper, ginger, cinnamon, anise, sambal oelek, 2 tablespoons (30 ml) of the soy sauce, salt, and tofu over medium-high heat. Bring to a boil. Simmer gently, for 3 to 5 minutes, or just until the broccoli is bright green and slightly tender. (Do not overcook!)

In a separate pot, cook the noodles according to the package directions. Rinse very well in cold water to remove starch. Toss with the remaining 2 teaspoons soy sauce. Divide among 2 deep bowls.

Cut the tofu into about 20 even squares. In each bowl, pour the broth and vegetables on top of the noodles. Top with the tofu, juice, and basil.

Yield: 2 servings

VEGAN "TURKEY," BEAN, AND KALE SOUP

This vegan soup uses TVP—textured vegetable (soy) protein—as a ground meat replacement. It's very popular in "multivore" homes of vegans and omnivores.

1 teaspoon olive oil
½ cup (80 g) diced onion
2 tablespoons (20 g) minced garlic
1 cup (130 g) chopped carrots
1 cup (120 g) chopped celery
1 teaspoon ground cumin
1 teaspoon chili powder
1½ teaspoons dried oregano
1 tablespoon (8 g) chicken-flavored seasoning
½ cup (50 g) Textured Vegetable Protein (TVP)
1 cup (200 g) dried Great Northern beans
4 cups (268 g) tightly packed kale, cut or torn into bite-size pieces
6 cups (1.4 L) vegetable broth
4 cups (940 ml) water
2 tablespoons (32 g) tomato paste
2 tablespoons (30 ml) lemon juice
1 teaspoon salt
½ teaspoon black pepper

In an uncovered pressure cooker, heat the oil on medium-high. Sauté the onion and garlic for 1 minute. Add the carrots and celery. Sauté for another 2 to 3 minutes. Stir in the spices and seasoning. Add the TVP, beans, kale, broth, and water. Stir to combine. Cover and bring to pressure. Cook at high pressure for 25 to 30 minutes. Allow for a natural release.

Remove the lid and stir in the paste, juice, salt, and pepper. If the beans are not quite cooked, simmer on low, with the pressure cooker uncovered, until done.

Yield: 4 servings

SPLIT PEA SOUP

This is perfect comfort food with a cooking time that offers a good excuse to relax with friends.

2 cups (450 g) green split peas, rinsed and picked over
6 to 7 cups (1410 to 1645 ml) vegetable stock
1 medium yellow onion, diced
2 creamy yellow potatoes (such as Yukon gold or fingerlings), diced
2 or 3 cloves garlic, pressed or minced
2 carrots, diced
2 celery stalks, diced
1 teaspoon dried marjoram
1 teaspoon dried basil
½ teaspoon dried parsley
¼ teaspoon ground mustard
¼ teaspoon black pepper
½ teaspoon liquid smoke, optional
Salt, to taste
Black pepper

In a soup pot, simmer all of ingredients except for salt and pepper over low-medium heat for at least 1 hour, or until the peas are tender, covered loosely. Check occasionally to make sure the water has not completely evaporated. (The resulting soup should be thick and creamy, with the peas broken down and mushy.) Season with salt and pepper.

Yield: 4 to 6 servings

SIMPLE-TO-MAKE VEGGIE CHILI

If you're serving people who are a little vegan phobic, add the soy meat substitute or some minced, reconstituted dried shiitake mushrooms.

2 cups (320 g) minced onion
2 cloves garlic, minced
3 tablespoons (40 ml) vegetable broth, optional
1 green bell pepper, seeded and chopped
1 red bell pepper, seeded and chopped
1 yellow bell pepper, seeded and chopped
15 ounces (392 g) vegetarian meat substitute, pan-cooked, optional
1 ounce (28 g) dried shiitake mushrooms, soaked in water and then minced, optional
26 ounces (750 g) aseptically packaged tomatoes or tomatoes, chopped, with juice
1 can (15 ounces, or 425 g) kidney beans, drained and rinsed
1 can (15 ounces, or 425 g) black beans, drained and rinsed
2 teaspoons chili powder
½ teaspoon ground cumin
½ teaspoon ground nutmeg
½ teaspoon turmeric
Pinch black pepper
2 cups (470 ml) vegetable broth, plus more if needed
1 to 2 cups (120 g to 240 g) nutritional yeast
Tiny pinch of salt

In a deep pot, sauté the onion and garlic over medium heat for 6 to 7 minutes, stirring occasionally, or until the onion is translucent. If the onion sticks to the pan, add the broth. Add the bell peppers and cook for 5 to 7 minutes, or until they become soft. Add the meat substitute and mush-rooms, if using. Cook for 5 minutes, or until moisture starts to come out of the meat substitute and mushrooms and collects in the bottom of the pot. Add the tomatoes, beans, chili powder, cumin, nutmeg, turmeric, black pepper, and broth. Decrease the heat to low. Cover the pot and cook on low for at least 1 hour, preferably 2 or more hours. Check occasionally and add water or vegetable broth to desired thickness. Halfway through the cooking time, add the yeast, in small amounts, tasting as you go. Stir. Add the salt.

Yield: 6 servings

PUMPKIN CHICKPEA CHILI

You can enjoy this simple recipe just about any time of year.

1 onion, diced
2 cloves garlic, minced
½ green bell pepper, diced
½ to 1 teaspoon salt
1 tablespoon (15 ml) olive oil
1 cup (130 g) frozen or fresh corn
1 can (28 ounces, or 793 g) diced tomatoes
1 can (15 ounces 420 g) pumpkin purée
1 can (15 ounces, or 420 g) chickpeas, drained and rinsed
1 can (15 ounces, or 420 g) black beans, drained and rinsed
1 to 3 teaspoons chili powder
2 teaspoons cumin
1 cup (235 ml) vegetable broth
Zest and juice of 1 lime
Black pepper, to taste
¼ to ½ cup (4 to 8 g) minced cilantro

In a large skillet, sauté the onion, garlic, bell pepper, and salt in the oil over medium heat for 10 to 15 minutes, or until tender. Stir in the remaining ingredients except for the cilantro, increase the heat to high, and bring to a boil. Immediately reduce the heat to medium-low. Simmer for 15 to 20 minutes, or until heated through. Garnish with the cilantro.

Yield: 10 servings

SAFFRON-INFUSED WHITE CHILI

The white chili powder used in this recipe can be found in Indian groceries, or you can substitute another variety of chili powder to taste.

6 cremini or mushrooms, chopped
1 Vidalia onion, diced
1 yellow zucchini, unpeeled, diced
2 jalapeño chiles, stemmed, seeded, and minced (Leave the seeds in if you like a lot of heat.)
1 yellow bell pepper, seeded and diced
1 tablespoon (3 g) total minced fresh rosemary, sage, and oregano
4 cloves garlic, minced
2½ tablespoons (38 ml) olive oil, divided
Salt, to taste
2 teaspoons cumin
1 teaspoon white chili powder
4 cubes (4 teaspoons or 8 g) chicken-flavored vegetable bouillon
6 cups (1.4 L) water
1 cup (100 g) textured vegetable protein (TVP)
2 cans (15 ounces, or 420 g each) Great Northern beans, drained and rinsed
1 can (15 ounces, or 420 g) white kidney beans, drained and rinsed
2 tablespoons (30 ml) lime juice
3 tablespoons (24 g) cornstarch mixed with 6 table-spoons (90 ml) cold water
Small pinch saffron threads, soaked in 3 tablespoons (45 ml) boiling water and allowed to rest for 2 to 3 hours

In a large stockpot, sauté the mushrooms, onion, zucchini, jalapeños, bell pepper, herbs, and garlic in 2 tablespoons (30 ml) of the olive oil over medium-high heat for about 13 minutes, or until soft, stirring often to prevent sticking. Season with salt. Stir in the cumin and white chili powder (as the vegetables are cooking).

In a pot, bring the bouillon cubes and water to a boil, whisking to dissolve the bouillon.

In a bowl, combine the TVP and 1 cup (235 ml) of the boiling broth. Cover for 5 minutes, or until fluffy.

Once the vegetables are soft, add the remaining 5 cups (1.2 L) broth. Bring to a simmer over low heat.

In a small skillet over medium-high heat, sauté the rehydrated TVP in the remaining ½ tablespoon (8 ml) oil for about 5 minutes, or just until golden brown. Stir the TVP into the vegetable mixture.

In a food processor, purée 1 can of Great Northern beans until smooth. Stir the beans into the vegetable mixture until well incorporated. Stir in the remaining 2 cans of beans, juice, and cornstarch mixture. Cook over medium-high heat for an additional 10 minutes, or until thickened, stirring occasionally. Season with salt.

Using the back of a spoon, crush the saffron threads. Add them to the chili. Cook for an additional few minutes.

Yield: 10 servings

BLACK-EYED PEA AND COLLARD GREEN CHILI

The combination of this legume and leafy greens sounds like a typical Southern dish and understandably, because in the South it is considered good luck to consume together on New Year's Day.

4 large collard green leaves
1 teaspoon olive oil
½ cup (80 g) diced red onion
3 cloves garlic, minced
2 cups (260 g) chopped carrot
2 cups (240 g) chopped celery
2 tablespoons (12 g) chili powder
1 teaspoon ground cumin
½ teaspoon ground coriander
1 teaspoon ground cinnamon
1 tablespoon (3 g) dried oregano
1 teaspoon seeded and diced fresh jalapeño
2 cups (400 g) dried black-eyed peas, rinsed and drained
2 bay leaves
1 can (28 ounces, or 784 g) diced tomatoes
1 can (8 ounces, or 224 g) tomato sauce
2 cups (470 ml) vegetable broth
1 cup (235 ml) water
¼ to ½ teaspoon salt

Using kitchen shears, halve each collard leaf lengthwise, cutting out and discarding the center ribs. Stack the leaves and cut them crosswise into ¼-inch (6 mm) wide strips.

In an uncovered pressure cooker, heat the oil on medium-high. Sauté the onion and garlic for about 2 minutes, or until the onion begins to soften. Add the carrots and celery. Sauté for another

3 to 5 minutes. Add the collard greens, chili powder, cumin, coriander, cinnamon, oregano, and jalapeño. Sauté for a minute or two. Add the peas, bay leaves, tomatoes, sauce, broth, and water.

Stir to combine. Cover and bring to pressure. Cook at high pressure for 10 minutes. Allow for a natural release. Remove the cover and taste the peas. Add the salt. If the peas are not thoroughly cooked, simmer on low, uncovered, until done. Remove the bay leaves before serving.

Yield: 4 to 6 servings

ASIAN ADZUKI BEAN CHILI

Adzuki beans are popular in Japanese cuisine. The flavors and seasoning here make a different kind of chili.

1½ cups (300 g) dried adzuki beans, soaked for 12 hours or overnight
1 tablespoon (15 ml) sesame oil
3 or 4 large cloves garlic, minced
1 cup (160 g) diced onion
1 cup (130 g) chopped carrots
4 cups (940 ml) vegetable broth
1 can (14 ounces, or 392 g) fire-roasted diced tomatoes
2 tablespoons (32 g) tomato paste
1 teaspoon Herbamare or other salt alternative
1 teaspoon dulse flakes
1 tablespoon (15 ml) yuzu pepper sauce
1 tablespoon (15 ml) soy sauce
2 cups (180 g) sliced cabbage

Rinse and drain the beans.

In an uncovered pressure cooker, heat the oil on medium heat. Sauté the garlic, onion, and carrots for 3 minutes, or until the onion is soft. Add the broth, beans, tomatoes, paste, Herbamare, dulse, pepper sauce, soy sauce, and cabbage. Stir to combine. Cover and bring to pressure. Cook at high pressure for 7 minutes. Allow for a natural release.

Yield: 6 servings

*65 Corn and Mushroom Chowder; 66 New England-Can-Kiss-My-Clam Chowder; 67 "Seafood" Stew (Encebollado);
68 Curried Mung Bean Stew; 69 Black Bean and Sweet Potato Stew; 70 Chunky Red Lentil Stew; 71 Root Veggie Tagine;
72 Brazilian Black Bean Stew*

73 Saffron-Spiked Moroccan Stew; 74 Rich Borscht with Cacao Accent; 75 Pomegranate Soup; 76 Chilled Blueberry Mango Soup; 77 Herb-Roasted Potatoes; 78 Lavender-Roasted Purple Potatoes and Purple Onions; 79 Home-Fried Potatoes; 80 Mashed Yukon Golds

TAMARIND-CHOCOLATE CHILI

This is an easy, tasty way to have a hearty chocolate stew.

2 cups (396 g) cooked lentils or other legumes
1 cup (248 g) chopped seasoned tofu or (166 g) cooked
    tempeh
½ cup (80 g) diced onion
1 cup (235 ml) vegetable broth, plus more if needed
1 cup (240 ml) crushed tomatoes
2 minced cloves garlic
2 teaspoons chili powder
1 teaspoon ground cumin
1 teaspoon minced ginger
⅓ cup (85 g) tamarind puree
1 tablespoon (15 ml) lemon juice (or balsamic vinegar)
1 tablespoon (9 g) minced chile pepper
½ cup (75 g) diced bell pepper
¼ cup (28 g) minced carrot
½ cup corn, (77 g) fresh, (82 g) frozen, or (105 g) canned
2 tablespoons (28 ml) tamari
½ teaspoon black pepper
⅓ cup (27 g) cocoa powder or 2 to 4 ounces (55 to 115 g)
    chopped dark chocolate
¼ cup (4 g) chopped fresh cilantro
Sweetener of your choice, optional
Garnish options: diced red bell pepper, cocoa powder
    or crushed cacao nibs, minced scallions, chopped
    cilantro, chopped pineapple, diced onion

In a large pot, cook all of the ingredients except for the
chocolate for 25 minutes, stirring occasionally. Add more
broth if needed to achieve the desired texture. Add the
chocolate and cilantro. Cook for 10 minutes more.

Yield: 5 servings

MINTED GREEN PEA BISQUE

*This recipe is extremely easy to make and is always a
welcome addition to almost any meal.*

1 small sweet onion, minced
1 clove garlic, minced
2 tablespoons (30 ml) water
1 teaspoon salt, divided
3 cups (450 g) frozen green peas
2 tablespoons (12 g) minced fresh mint leaves
1 cup (235 ml) nondairy milk, plus more if needed
Black pepper, to taste

In a small frying pan, sauté the onion and garlic in the
water over medium-high heat, or until translucent. Season
with ¼ teaspoon of the salt. Reduce the heat to
medium-low and simmer for about 10 minutes, or until the
onion is caramelized. Remove from the heat and let cool.

In a medium pot, bring water to a boil. Add the peas and
cook for about 5 minutes, or until tender. Drain well. Rinse

under cold water until the peas are cool to the touch.

Transfer the peas to a blender. Blend the peas, onion
and garlic, mint, milk, and the remaining ¾ teaspoon salt
for 5 minutes, or until very smooth. If the soup is too thick,
add more milk.

Transfer the mixture to a saucepan. Warm gently over
medium heat. Season with pepper.

Yield: 2 servings

ROASTED TOMATO AND BEET BISQUE

*If you love borscht and tomato soup, you'll adore this
simple yet complex-tasting bisque.*

2 medium tomatoes
1 large beet, peeled and sliced
2 cloves garlic
Salt, to taste
½ teaspoon olive oil
½ cup (120 ml) coconut cream
3 cups (700 ml) vegetable broth
Salt, to taste
Black pepper, to taste

Preheat the oven to 400°F (200°C, gas mark 6). Place a
large piece of foil on top of a baking sheet.

Place the tomatoes, beets, and garlic on the foil. Fold up
the edges to create an open pouch around the vegetables.
Season with salt. Drizzle with the oil. Loosely close the
pouch. Bake for about 1 hour, or until the beets are tender.

In a food processor, blend the beets, tomatoes, and
cream until smooth. Add broth to thin. Season with salt and
pepper.

Transfer the mixture to a saucepan and warm gently.

Yield: 4 servings

CORN AND MUSHROOM CHOWDER

*Creamy, hearty, and terribly addictive, this soup is terrific
on a chilly evening with a crusty piece of bread.*

8 ounces (227 g) cremini or button mushrooms, sliced
2 cloves garlic, minced
1 tablespoon (15 ml) olive oil
Salt, to taste
1 small red onion, chopped (about ¾ cup (120 g))
3 large yellow potatoes, unpeeled, diced (about 3½ cups
    (385 g))
3 carrots, peeled and shredded
8 cups (1.9 L) water
12 ounces (340 g) frozen or fresh corn
1 cup (235 ml) full-fat coconut milk
2 tablespoons (16 g) cornstarch mixed with ¼ cup (60
    ml) cold water
Black pepper, to taste

In a skillet, sauté the mushrooms and garlic in the oil over medium-high heat, until soft, stirring often to prevent sticking. Season lightly with salt.

In a large stockpot, bring the mushrooms and garlic, onion, potatoes, carrots, and water to a boil over high heat. Reduce the heat to medium. Cook for about 20 minutes, or until the potatoes are tender, stirring occasionally. Stir in the corn.

Reduce the heat to medium-low, and stir in the milk. Add the cornstarch slurry. Simmer for about 10 minutes, or until just slightly thickened. (If it's taking a while to thicken, increase the heat slightly.) Season with salt and pepper.

Yield: 8 servings

NEW ENGLAND-CAN-KISS-MY-CLAM CHOWDER
Get ready for weird, folks. Here is a very strange—and very tasty—clam chowder, complete with seitan clams!

8 cups (1.9 L) vegetable broth
1 ounce (28 g) dried seaweed
Cheesecloth
2 cups (470 ml) water
1 cup (235 ml) canned coconut milk
2 pounds (908 g) potatoes, peeled and cut into bite-sized cubes
1 cup (160 g) diced onion
1 cup (144 g) vital wheat gluten
1 teaspoon black pepper

Pour the broth into a soup pot with a tight-fitting lid.

Loosely tie the seaweed in a satchel made from cheesecloth. Place it in the pot with the broth. Bring to a boil, reduce to a simmer, cover, and simmer for 30 minutes. Remove ½ cup (120 ml) of the broth and set it aside to cool. Simmer the remaining broth for 30 minutes. Add the water, milk, potatoes, and onion. Cover and simmer for 1 hour.

Meanwhile, in a small bowl, combine the gluten, pepper, and the reserved ½ cup (120 ml) broth. Work it with your fingers to form a ball. Let the dough ball rest for 5 minutes. Using a non-serrated knife, cut the dough into very small pieces.

Add the dough pieces to the broth, stirring to make sure they are not all clumped together. Cover and simmer for the remainder of the hour. (At this point, there should be about 30 minutes left.) After 15 minutes, stir to prevent the "clams" from getting stuck to the bottom.

Remove the soup from the heat and remove the lid. Using a wooden spoon, break up the potatoes to thicken the soup. (Don't worry about smashing the "clams"; they are pretty unsmashable.)

Yield: 8 servings

"SEAFOOD" STEW (ENCEBOLLADO)
This stew is usually made with shellfish of various species, but here it's replaced with hearts of palm.

1 can (20 ounces, or 560 g) hearts of palm, drained and chopped into small bites
1 tablespoon (3 g) dulse flakes
1½ teaspoons salt, divided
Juice of 1 lime
1 tablespoon (15 ml) olive oil
1 green bell pepper, seeded and chopped
1 yellow onion, diced
1 teaspoon crushed red pepper
1 tomato, seeded and diced
2 cloves garlic, minced
1 can (13.5 ounces, or 400 ml) coconut milk
1 tablespoon (10 g) superfine brown rice flour mixed with 3 tablespoons (45 ml) water
½ cup (8 g) chopped cilantro
3 cups (555 g) cooked rice

In a small bowl, toss the hearts of palm and dulse flakes with ½ teaspoon of the salt and juice. Cover. Let rest for between 1 and 3 hours. Drain.

Once the hearts of palm have marinated, in a deep frying pan, sauté the oil, bell pepper, onion, red pepper, tomato, garlic, and the remaining 1 teaspoon salt over medium-high heat for about 7 minutes, or just until the peppers become tender. Add the milk and hearts of palm. Cook over medium heat for about 10 to 15 minutes, or until the bell peppers are thoroughly cooked. Drizzle in the flour slurry. Whisk quickly to combine into and thicken the sauce. Cook briefly while stirring constantly. Toss in the cilantro. Serve over the rice.

Yield: 4 servings

CURRIED MUNG BEAN STEW
The mung bean is often used in Asian cuisine. Curry bouillon cubes are great for this, or mix 2 cups (470 ml) water with 2 teaspoons curry powder.

1 teaspoon vegetable oil
2 cloves garlic, minced
1 cup (160 g) diced onion
½ cup (65 g) chopped carrot
1 cup (110 g) cubed sweet potatoes
½ cup (60 g) chopped celery
3 cups (150 g) loosely packed collard green strips
1 teaspoon ground ginger or 1 tablespoon (6 g) minced fresh
¼ teaspoon turmeric
¼ teaspoon paprika
2 cups (470 ml) curry broth
1 cup (235 ml) water

1 cup (200 g) dried mung beans
2 tablespoons (45 ml) lemon juice
½ teaspoon salt

In an uncovered pressure cooker, heat the oil on medium heat. Sauté the garlic, onion, carrot, potatoes, and celery for 5 minutes. Add the collard greens, ginger, turmeric, paprika, broth, water, and mung beans. Stir to combine. Cover and bring to pressure. Cook at high pressure for 6 to 8 minutes. Allow for a natural release. Stir in the juice. Season with salt.

Yield: 4 servings

BLACK BEAN AND SWEET POTATO STEW

Black beans and sweet potatoes are visually appealing with their vibrant color, but they are also a dynamic nutrition duo.

4 cups plus 2 tablespoons (970 ml) vegetable broth,
**   divided**
½ cup (80 g) chopped onion
4 cloves garlic, minced
2 carrots, chopped
1 large sweet potato, diced into equal, bite-size pieces
3 stalks celery, chopped
2 small tomatoes, diced
½ teaspoon ground cinnamon
1 teaspoon garam masala
1 cup (200 g) dried black beans, rinsed and drained
2 bay leaves
½ teaspoon salt, optional
¼ teaspoon black pepper

In an uncovered pressure cooker, heat 2 tablespoons (30 ml) of the broth on high. Sauté the onion and garlic for about 2 minutes, or until the onion is soft. Add the carrots and sweet potato. Sauté for another 3 minutes. Add the celery, tomatoes, cinnamon, and garam masala. Stir to coat all of the vegetables with the spices. Add the beans and bay leaves and the remaining 4 cups (940 ml) broth. Stir to combine. Cover and bring to pressure. Cook at high pressure for 22 to 24 minutes. Allow for a natural release. Remove the lid, remove the bay leaves, and stir in the salt and pepper.

Yield: 6 servings

CHUNKY RED LENTIL STEW

This very quick, thick stew is fantastic served over grains such as barley, farro, or freekeh.

2 cups plus 2 tablespoons (500 ml) vegetable broth,
**   divided**
2 cloves garlic, minced
½ cup (80 g) diced yellow onion
2 carrots, chopped
½ teaspoon garam masala
½ teaspoon curry powder
1 tomato, cut into large chunks
1 cup (200 g) dried red lentils, rinsed and drained
Juice of ½ lemon
Salt, to taste

In an uncovered pressure cooker, heat 2 tablespoons (30 ml) of the broth on high. Sauté the garlic and onion for 2 to 3 minutes, or until the onion is soft. Stir in the carrots, garam masala, and curry powder. Sauté for another 2 to 3 minutes. Add the tomato and lentils and the remaining 2 cups (470 ml) broth. Stir to combine. Cover and bring to pressure. Cook at high pressure for 6 minutes. Use a quick release. Remove the lid and stir in the juice. Taste and season with salt.

Yield: 4 servings

ROOT VEGGIE TAGINE

Tagine is a North African stew, typically made of spiced meat and vegetables in a shallow dish. Serve this dish with couscous or other grains such as barley or freekeh for a rich meal.

2 cups (220 g) diced sweet potatoes (½-inch, or 1.3 cm
**   cubes)**
2 cups (240 g) diced carrots ½-inch, or 1.3 cm)
1 cup (150 g) cubed turnips (½-inch, or 1.3 cm)
½ teaspoon ground ginger
½ teaspoon ground cumin
½ teaspoon ground cinnamon
½ teaspoon saffron strands
1 teaspoon sugar
½ cup (120 ml) orange juice
½ cup (120 ml) water
½ teaspoon salt

In a pressure cooker, combine all of the ingredients. Stir well, covering the vegetables with the juice and water. Cover and bring to pressure. Cook at high pressure for 3 to 4 minutes. Use a quick release. Remove the lid and stir.

Yield: 4 to 6 servings

BRAZILIAN BLACK BEAN STEW

The contrast in spicy and sweet flavors as well as dark and bright colors makes this a fabulous dish for guests.

1 tablespoon (15 ml) olive oil
1 medium yellow onion, chopped
2 cloves garlic, minced
½ pound (225 g) Mexican-spiced vegetarian sausage, cut into half-circles
2 medium garnet or jewel yams, peeled and diced
1 large red bell pepper, seeded and diced
2 cans (15 ounces, or 420 g) diced tomatoes
1 small jalapeño pepper, diced
1½ cups (353 ml) water
2 cans (15 ounces, or 420 g) black beans, rinsed and drained
1 mango, peeled, seeded, and cubed
¼ cup (4 g) chopped fresh cilantro, plus extra for garnish
¼ teaspoon salt

In a large soup pot, heat the oil over medium heat. Sauté the onion and garlic for about 7 minutes, or until the onion starts to turn translucent. Add the sausage, yams, bell pepper, tomatoes, jalapeño, and water. Bring to a boil, reduce the heat to low, and cover. Simmer for 15 minutes, or until the yams are tender. Add the beans. Cook, uncovered, until heated through. Stir in the mango, cilantro, and salt. Garnish with additional cilantro.

Yield: 4 to 5 servings

SAFFRON-SPIKED MOROCCAN STEW

This hearty stew is perfect over couscous or quinoa.

1½ cups (350 ml) plus 3 tablespoons (45 ml) vegetable broth, divided, plus more if needed
1 large yellow onion, finely chopped
2 large red bell peppers, seeded and chopped
2 or 3 cloves garlic, minced
2 teaspoons (10 g) light brown sugar
1 teaspoon (2 g) ground coriander
½ teaspoon ground cinnamon
½ teaspoon ground cumin
¼ teaspoon ground cayenne
1 teaspoon (2 g) grated or minced fresh ginger
½ teaspoon saffron threads
2 medium sweet potatoes or garnet or jewel yams, peeled and cut into ½-inch (1 cm) cubes
1 can (15 ounces, or 420 g) diced tomatoes, undrained
1 can (15 ounces, or 420 g) chickpeas, drained and rinsed
Salt, to taste
Black pepper, to taste

In a soup pot, heat 3 tablespoons (45 ml) of the broth over medium heat. Sauté the onion, peppers, and garlic for 5 to

7 minutes, or until the onion is translucent. If the broth begins to evaporate, add a little more. Stir in the sugar, coriander, cinnamon, cumin, cayenne, ginger, and saffron. Cook for 60 seconds, stirring constantly. Add the potatoes. Stir to coat. Stir in the tomatoes, the remaining 1½ cups (350 ml) broth, and the chickpeas. Bring to a boil, and then reduce the heat to low. Simmer for about 30 minutes, or until the potatoes are tender but not overcooked. Season with salt and pepper.

Yield: 2 to 4 servings

RICH BORSCHT WITH CACAO ACCENT

Garnish with grated chocolate on each bowl before serving.

8 cups (1.9 L) vegetable broth
1 to 1½ teaspoons salt
2 cups (220 g) diced potatoes
5 cups (1.1 kg) diced beets
½ cup (80 g) chopped red onion
½ cup (65 g) diced carrots
2 minced cloves garlic
1 teaspoon dill
½ teaspoon paprika
½ teaspoon caraway or cumin seed, crushed
⅓ cup (32 g) raw cacao powder
2 to 3 tablespoons (28 to 45 ml) lemon juice
Chopped green onions

In a large soup pot, bring all of ingredients, except for the cacao powder, juice, and onions, to a boil. Reduce the heat. Simmer for 20 minutes. Stir in the cacao powder. Cook for another 20 minutes, stirring occasionally. Add the juice and remove from the heat. Serve with the onions.

Yield: 8 servings

POMEGRANATE SOUP

This Persian soup usually contains meatballs, but it's so hearty on its own.

FOR THE SOUP:
1 onion, sliced very thin
2 cloves garlic, minced
1 tablespoon (15 ml) olive oil
4¼ teaspoons (16 g) salt, divided
¾ cup (169 g) yellow split peas
8 cups (2 L) water
1 teaspoon black pepper
1 teaspoon turmeric

1 small beet, peeled and diced
2 cups (475 ml) pomegranate juice
½ cup (30 g) chopped fresh parsley
½ cup (48 g) chopped fresh mint
½ cup (8 g) chopped fresh cilantro
1 cup (186 g) cooked rice

FOR THE MEATBALLS:
2 cups (80 g) soy curls
2 cups (475 ml) vegetable broth, warmed until just
    before boiling
1 teaspoon psyllium husk powder
1 cup (240 g) cooked chickpeas
½ cup (93 g) cooked sushi rice
1 tablespoon (12 g) ground chia seeds mixed with ¼ cup
    (60 ml) water
½ teaspoon salt
2 tablespoons (28 ml) olive oil

To make the soup: In a large soup pot, sauté the onion,
garlic, oil, and 1 teaspoon of the salt over medium-high heat
for about 10 minutes, or until translucent. Add the peas.
Sauté for an additional 1 to 2 minutes, or until golden
brown. Add the water, 1½ teaspoons of the salt, the pepper,
turmeric, and beet. Bring to a boil. Reduce the heat. Simmer
for about 45 minutes to 1 hour, or until the peas are
softened. Stir in the juice, the remaining 1¾ teaspoons salt,
the herbs, and rice. Cook for 10 to 15 minutes.

To make the meatballs: Preheat the oven to 350°F (180°C,
gas mark 4).
    In a bowl, rehydrate the soy curls in the broth for about
10 minutes, or until softened. Drain well and press out any
excess liquid.
    In a food processor, pulse the soy curls, psyllium husk,
and chickpeas just until ground.
    Transfer the mixture to a bowl, add the rice, chia
mixture, and salt. Using clean hands, knead the mixture
into a sticky dough. Roll it into around 20 small patties,
brush each with oil on all sides, and place on an ungreased
baking sheet. Bake for about 45 minutes, or until dark
golden brown and crispy.
    Serve the meatballs in the soup.

Yield: 10 servings

CHILLED BLUEBERRY MANGO SOUP
*Enjoy this totally fat-free but filling soup that makes a
striking appearance at a summer dinner with friends.*

½ cup (120 ml) orange juice
¾ cup (175 ml) pineapple juice (or white grape juice)
¼ cup (50 g) sugar
2 cups (290 g) fresh blueberries (or frozen, thawed, with
    their juice [310 g])
¼ cup mango chunks (frozen, thawed, or fresh)
1 container (6 ounces, or 175 g) plain or vanilla nondairy
    yogurt

In a saucepan, boil the orange juice, pineapple juice, and
sugar for about 1 minute, stirring constantly. Add the
blueberries and mango. Cook for 1 minute longer.
    Remove from the heat and let cool.
    In a blender, purée the blueberry mixture and yogurt
until smooth.
    Chill for at least 2 hours or up to overnight. (It will
thicken as it cools.)

Yield: 4 servings

HERB-ROASTED POTATOES
*This recipe makes great use of dried herbs that almost
everyone has on hand in the spice rack.*

2 pounds (908 g) Yukon gold potatoes
2 tablespoons (12 g) vegetable broth powder
1 teaspoon granulated garlic
1 teaspoon granulated onion
1 teaspoon dried rosemary
1 teaspoon dried thyme
1 teaspoon dried marjoram
1 teaspoon dried oregano
1 teaspoon dried dill
½ teaspoon ground paprika
2 tablespoons (30 ml) olive oil, optional
Salt, to taste
Black pepper, to taste

Preheat the oven to 425°F (220°C, or gas mark 7). Line a
baking sheet with parchment paper.
    Cut the potatoes into bite-size chunks and rinse them in
cold water. Drain them and place them in a large bowl.
    In a small bowl, combine the vegetable broth powder,
garlic, onion, rosemary, thyme, marjoram, oregano, dill, and
paprika.
    Add the oil, if using, to the potatoes and toss to coat.
Add the spice mixture to the potatoes and toss to coat.
    Arrange the potatoes in a single layer on the prepared
baking sheet. Roast for 20 minutes.
    Toss the potatoes and bake for an additional 10 minutes,

or until lightly browned and tender.
Season with salt and pepper.

Yield: 4 servings

LAVENDER-ROASTED PURPLE POTATOES AND PURPLE ONIONS

Lavender imparts a lovely flavor evocative of spring but can taste like perfume if overused. Serve these potatoes warm or at room temperature.

1½ pounds (685 g) purple potatoes, quartered if large
¼ cup (60 ml) olive oil
6 cloves garlic, minced or pressed
2 tablespoons (10 g) dried culinary lavender
2 teaspoons (3 g) fresh thyme
3 large red/purple onions, peeled, halved, quartered, and separated into strips
Salt, to taste
Black pepper, to taste
1 tablespoon (5 g) pink peppercorns, optional
Juice of 1 lemon (or lime)

Preheat the oven to 400°F (200°C, or gas mark 6).
Boil or steam the potatoes until they are just fork-tender.
Meanwhile, in a bowl, combine the oil, garlic, lavender, and thyme.
When the potatoes are cooked, transfer them to a cutting board. Using a potato masher, smash each one.
In a large bowl, combine the potatoes and onions. Pour the oil mixture over the potatoes and onions. Toss to thoroughly coat. Season with salt and pepper.
Transfer the mixture to a baking sheet. Sprinkle on the peppercorns, if using. Bake for 25 to 35 minutes, turning the pan halfway through cooking, or until the potatoes and onions are golden brown and crispy.
Remove from the oven. Immediately squeeze the juice over the potatoes and onions. (The potatoes will brighten up upon contact with the citrus juice.)

Yield: 4 servings

HOME-FRIED POTATOES

Nothing says comfort like a plate of potatoes. Enjoy these as a side dish, breakfast, or brunch with friends.

3 pounds (1365 g) creamy yellow potatoes, quartered (such as Yukon gold)
3 tablespoons (45 ml) olive oil or (42 g) nondairy, nonhydrogenated butter, divided
1 large yellow onion, sliced
2 or 3 cloves garlic, minced

1 teaspoon paprika
1 teaspoon (6 g) salt
½ teaspoon black pepper
¼ cup (15 g) fresh parsley, chopped

In a steamer basket over a 4-quart (4.5 L) pot, steam the potatoes for 12 to 15 minutes, or until tender but still firm. Let cool, and then cut into ½-inch (1 cm) cubes.
Meanwhile, in a large skillet, heat 1 tablespoon (15 ml) of the oil over medium-high heat. Sauté the onion and garlic for about 10 minutes, stirring often, or until it starts to brown. Add 1 tablespoon (15 ml) of the oil and the potatoes. Add the paprika, salt, and pepper. Cook for 15 to 30 minutes, stirring occasionally, or until the potatoes are browned. (When turning the potatoes, use a flat spatula so you don't smush them.)
Meanwhile, add the remaining 1 tablespoon (15 ml) oil and parsley to the skillet. Stir to combine.

Yield: 4 to 6 servings

MASHED YUKON GOLDS

For many, a bowl of homemade mashed potatoes is the epitome of comfort food. This is a great way to prepare mashed potatoes–slightly dry, yet still quite creamy.

1½ teaspoons salt, plus more for boiling water
5 pounds (2.3 kg) unpeeled Yukon gold potatoes
3 tablespoons (42 g) nondairy margarine, plus more if desired
½ teaspoons salt
Black pepper, to taste

In a large stockpot, bring lightly salted water to a boil.
Scrub the potatoes well. Chop them into approximately 1-inch (2.5 cm) pieces. Once the water reaches a full rolling boil, carefully add the potatoes. Allow the water to return to a rolling boil.
Once boiling, begin timing the potatoes, cooking for 11 to 13 minutes. Reduce the heat slightly if needed to avoid boiling over.
Check the potatoes at 11 minutes to see if they are easy to smash with a fork. (You should not have to put any pressure on them to make this happen. You don't want undercooked potatoes or your mashed potatoes will end up lumpy; it's better to cook them for the full 13 minutes if you are unsure.)
Once the potatoes are very fork-tender, drain in a colander and transfer to an electric mixing bowl. Mix on low speed, combining with the margarine and 1½ teaspoons of the salt until blended. Increase the speed to medium-high and mix until fluffy and smooth. Stir in more margarine if desired. Season with pepper.

Yield: 8 servings

81 Turmeric and Ginger Whipped Sweet Potatoes; 82 Mashed Peas and Potatoes; 83 Sweet Potato Fries; 84 Carrot Fries; 85 Veggies and Dumplings; 86 Quinoa Tabbouleh; 87 Spanish Rice; 88 Coconut Rice

89 Wild Rice with Dried Cherries and Cranberries; 90 Mushroom-Pepper Quinoa Risotto; 91 Crispy Crunchy Basmati Rice Fritters; 92 Beans and Rice (Gallo Pinto); 93 Italian Pearl Barley; 94 Almond Garlic Green Beans; 95 Bok Choy, Mushrooms, and Onion with Tamari Lime Dressing; 96 Mediterranean Beans with Greens

TURMERIC AND GINGER WHIPPED SWEET POTATOES

Comfort food is perfect when you feel under the weather.

2 tablespoons (28 g) coconut oil, divided
2 medium sweet potatoes, peeled and chopped
1 small onion, chopped
½ teaspoon ground turmeric
½ teaspoon grated fresh ginger
Salt, to taste
Black pepper, to taste

Preheat the oven to 425°F (220°C, or gas mark 7). Grease a baking sheet with 1 tablespoon (14 g) of the oil.
    Arrange the potatoes in a single layer on the prepared baking sheet. Roast for 20 to 25 minutes, or until soft.
    Meanwhile, in a medium skillet, heat the remaining oil over low heat. Sauté the onions until caramelized.
    In a blender, purée the potatoes, onions, turmeric, and ginger until smooth. Season with salt and pepper.

Yield: 2 servings

MASHED PEAS AND POTATOES

A colorful, quick mash, these bright green peas, a legume, pack a whopping 8 grams of protein.

Pinch salt, plus more to taste
2 pounds (908 g) butter cream potatoes (or other small, new potatoes)
8 ounces (228 g) English peas, shelled
½ cup (120 ml) almond milk
2 tablespoons (28 g) vegan butter
¼ teaspoon thyme leaves
¼ teaspoon whole rosemary

Place a trivet in the pressure cooker, place a steamer basket on top of the trivet, and add enough water to come up to, but not in, the basket. Add the pinch of salt. Bring the water to a boil.
    Scrub the potatoes. Rinse the peas. Place the potatoes in the steamer basket. Pour the peas over the potatoes. Cover and bring to pressure. Cook at high pressure for 6 minutes. Use a quick release. Uncover the pressure cooker. Using kitchen tongs, gently remove the steamer basket. Pour any remaining water out of the pressure cooker. Transfer the potatoes and peas back into the pressure cooker. (Alternatively, you can use a large bowl.) Add the milk and butter. Using a potato masher, smash the mixture until the potatoes are chunky.
    Using a mortar and pestle, crumble the thyme and rosemary. Sprinkle the spices over the potatoes and peas and stir. Season with salt.

Yield: 4 servings

SWEET POTATO FRIES

Baking is always a healthier cooking method than frying.

1 medium sweet potato
1 tablespoon (14 g) coconut oil, melted
Salt, to taste
Black pepper, to taste

Preheat the oven to 425°F (220°C, or gas mark 7).
    Slice the potato into long skinny matchsticks.
    Place the potato on a baking sheet. Coat evenly with the oil, tossing to combine and then spreading out in a single layer. Season with salt and pepper.
    Bake for 15 to 20 minutes, or until crispy.

Yield: 2 servings

CARROT FRIES

Mega amounts of beta-carotene result in these gorgeous-color fries that pack a nutritional as well as flavorful punch.

16 medium carrots, peeled and cut into matchsticks about 4 inches (10 cm) long
1 tablespoon (15 ml) oil
1 teaspoon salt
Black pepper, to taste
½ teaspoon ground cumin, optional

Preheat the oven to 425°F (220°C, or gas mark 7). Line a baking sheet with parchment paper.
    In a bowl, combine the carrots and oil. Using your hands, toss the carrots in the oil to thoroughly coat.
    Spread the carrots in a single layer on the prepared baking sheet. Sprinkle with the salt, pepper to taste, and cumin. Bake for about 45 minutes, or until they begin to crisp, checking every 15 minutes or so to toss and ensure even cooking.

Yield: 4 servings

VEGGIES AND DUMPLINGS

Serve it warm–not piping hot–or the dumplings will be soupy.

8 cups (1.9 L) vegetable broth
1 large zucchini, chopped
5 medium carrots, peeled and sliced into rounds
1 Vidalia onion, chopped
3½ ounces (120 g) shiitake mushroom caps, chopped
3 ounces (100 g) cremini mushrooms, thinly sliced
4 stalks celery, sliced
1 tablespoon (2 g) dried sage
Salt, to taste

1 cup (150 g) corn kernels (fresh or frozen)
5 cups (625 g) Bizquix (See page 12.)
1½ cups (350 ml) nondairy milk
2 tablespoons (16 g) cornstarch mixed with ¼ cup (60 ml) cold water
Black pepper, to taste

In a deep stockpot, bring the broth to a rolling boil. Add the zucchini, carrots, onion, mushrooms, and celery. Return the broth to a rolling boil. Reduce the heat to medium-low. Simmer for about 20 minutes, or until the vegetables are tender. Stir in the sage. Season with salt. Stir in the corn. Return the broth to a slow boil.

Meanwhile, in a medium bowl, place the Bizquix. Gradually add the milk until a tacky dough forms. Using your hands, gently shape the dough into about 20 golf ball-size dumplings.

Carefully drop the dumplings one at a time into the broth. Cover the pot and reduce the heat to medium. (The dumplings don't all need to be submerged to cook; a few of the dumplings will inevitably end up underneath others.) Cook the dumplings for 10 minutes, or until they are firm.

Gently move aside a couple of dumplings from the top of the mixture. Slowly add the cornstarch slurry to thicken the broth. Simmer for about 10 minutes, or until thickened. Remove from the heat. Season with pepper. .

Yield: 10 servings (2 dumplings each plus vegetables)

QUINOA TABBOULEH
Serve this dish cold.

1 cup (175 g) quinoa, rinsed and drained
2 cups (470 ml) water
¼ cup (60 ml) olive oil
1½ teaspoons salt
2 cups (120 g) finely minced fresh parsley
½ cup (30 g) finely minced fresh mint
3 medium tomatoes, seeded and diced
Zest and juice of 1 large lemon
½ teaspoon black pepper
3 green onions, finely chopped

In a 2-quart (2 L) saucepan, bring the quinoa and water to a boil over high heat. Immediately reduce the heat to low, stir gently, and cover. Simmer for about 15 minutes, or until all of the water has been absorbed. Chill the quinoa in the fridge for about 1 hour, or until cold.

Stir in the oil and salt. Gently fold in the parsley, mint, tomatoes, juice, zest, pepper, and onions until well combined. Let rest for at least 1 hour in the fridge.

Yield: 6 servings

SPANISH RICE
Spanish rice is a great side when serving a traditional Mexican meal. It's also delicious as a filling for tacos or in a taco salad.

1 tablespoon (15 ml) olive oil
2 cloves garlic, minced
½ cup (80 g) finely chopped onion
2 cups (380 g) short-grain brown rice
3 cups (705 ml) vegetable broth
1 tablespoon (16 g) tomato paste
½ cup (90 g) diced tomato
½ teaspoon cumin
½ teaspoon paprika
¼ to ½ teaspoon salt
1 teaspoon chili powder, or more to taste

In an uncovered pressure cooker, heat the oil on medium-high. Sauté the garlic and onion for 3 minutes, or until the onion is translucent. Add the rice. Sauté for about 5 minutes, or until the rice browns slightly. Add the broth, paste, tomato, and seasonings. Stir to combine. Cover and bring to pressure. Cook at high pressure for 20 to 22 minutes. Allow for a natural release.

Yield: 8 servings

COCONUT RICE
The aroma of the cooking rice will have you anxious with anticipation. Serve it with Asian-style dishes and stir-fries

1 can (15 ounces, or 420 g) light coconut milk
1¼ cups (295 ml) water
1½ cups (285 g) uncooked brown rice (or jasmine rice)
1 teaspoon coconut extract
1 teaspoon salt
3 tablespoons (13 g) unsweetened coconut flakes, optional

In a saucepan, bring the milk, water, rice, and coconut extract to a boil over medium heat. Cover and reduce the heat to low. Simmer for 40 minutes, or until the rice is tender. (Check halfway through and close to the end of the cooking time to see if the liquid has evaporated and extra needs to be added.)

Turn off the heat and let sit, covered, for 5 minutes. Remove the lid. Using a fork, fluff the rice. Stir in the salt and coconut flakes, if using.

Yield: 4 servings

WILD RICE WITH DRIED CHERRIES AND CRANBERRIES

Just right for the holidays, this is a great side with a vegan roast, or add cooked lentils to make it a festive entrée. You can replace the oil with ¼ cup (60 ml) water or vegetable broth.

1 teaspoon olive oil
¼ cup (25 g) chopped celery
¼ cup (40 g) diced onion
1 cup (160 g) wild rice
1 cup (120 g) mix of dried cranberries and dried cherries
½ teaspoon dried thyme
½ teaspoon dried sage
3 to 3½ cups (705 to 825 ml) water
Salt, to taste

In an uncovered pressure cooker, heat the oil on medium-high. Sauté the celery and onion for 3 to 4 minutes, or until the celery is soft. Add the rice, dried fruit, thyme, sage, and water. Stir to combine. Cover and bring to pressure. Cook at high pressure for 22 to 25 minutes. Allow for a natural release. Season with salt.

Yield: 4 servings

MUSHROOM-PEPPER QUINOA RISOTTO

Risotto is traditionally made with Arborio or another short-grained rice, but this version, which uses quinoa, is equally creamy. If you cannot find lemon verbena, substitute about a teaspoon of lemon zest.

3 tablespoons (45 ml) olive oil
1 sweet onion, diced
3 cups (210 g) cremini mushrooms, cut into chunks
2 bell peppers (1 yellow, 1 red), diced
1 teaspoon ground coriander
1 teaspoon salt
1¼ cups (216 g) quinoa, rinsed
½ cup (120 ml) beer, slightly flat and room temperature
3 cups (700 ml) vegetable broth, divided
1½ cups (180 ml) coconut milk
Sprinkle of paprika
3 to 4 leaves lemon verbena, whole or cut into fine chiffonade

In a large frying pan, heat the oil over high heat. Sauté the onion, mushrooms, bell peppers, coriander, and salt. Stir often and cook for about 10 to 12 minutes, or until all moisture is released from the vegetables and the mushrooms are reduced in size. Drain any excess liquid and transfer to a bowl.

Reduce the heat to medium high. Add a drizzle more oil to the pan and the quinoa. Cook the quinoa, for about 2 minutes, stirring often, or until toasted and fragrant.

Reduce the heat again to medium low. Carefully pour in the beer. Step back first because the carbonation could cause a bubbly burst. Cook until all of the liquid is absorbed. Add 1 cup (235 ml) of the broth. Cook, again stirring often, until most of the liquid has been absorbed. Add the milk, in ½ cup (120 ml) increments, until all is used. Then add up to 2 cups (475 ml) more broth until the quinoa is tender. The entire process to cook the quinoa should take about 30 minutes—taste toward the end to make sure the quinoa is tender; it should have a slightly firm but soft texture when it is done. Be sure between each addition of liquid that the quinoa is fairly dry and not much liquid remains before adding in more. If the liquid is absorbing too quickly, reduce the heat slightly.

Stir in the mushrooms and peppers, sprinkle with paprika, and top with lemon verbena. Serve warm.

Yield: 6 servings

CRISPY CRUNCHY BASMATI RICE FRITTERS

You'll absolutely adore the surprising texture and ease of this recipe; they taste a lot like hash browns but contain no potatoes. This fritter is a perfect dish to share with company.

2 tablespoons (14 g) flaxseed meal
¼ cup (60 ml) water
2 cups (370 g) cooked basmati rice
½ cup (68 g) sorghum flour
¼ cup (30 g) tapioca starch
1½ teaspoons salt
¼ cup (40 g) grated onion
Scant ½ cup (120 ml) coconut milk
Vegetable oil
Black pepper, to taste
Paprika, to taste

Preheat a deep fryer to 360°F (182°C). Line a plate with paper towels.

In a small bowl, combine the flaxseed meal with the water. Allow the mixture to rest for about 5 minutes, or until thick.

In a large bowl, combine the flaxseed meal mixture with the rice, flour, starch, salt, onion, and milk. Stir until a thick, clumpy dough is formed.

Using your hands, form the dough into rounded patties, about 1-inch (2.5 cm) thick.

Carefully place the patties into the oil. Cook for about 5 minutes, or until golden brown.

Using a slotted spoon, remove the patties from the oil and place on the prepared plate. Season with pepper and paprika.

Yield: 14 fritters

BEANS AND RICE (GALLO PINTO)

If you cannot locate Salsa Lizano, Pickapeppa or vegan Worcestershire sauce is an adequate replacement.

FOR THE BLACK BEANS:
⅔ cup (167 g) dry black beans, rinsed and picked over
Water for soaking and cooking
1 tablespoon (3 g) dried seaweed, optional

FOR THE GALLO PINTO:
1 tablespoon (15 ml) olive oil
1 red pepper, diced
3 cloves garlic, minced
Dash salt
2½ cups (415 g) cooked white rice, cold
2 cups (512 g) Black Beans with 1½ cups (355 ml) liquid
    from cooking
5 tablespoons (75 g) Salsa Lizano
½ cup (60 g) minced fresh cilantro

To make the Black Beans: Soak the beans in water (about 3 inches [7.5 cm] from top of dried beans) for at least 8 hours and up to overnight. Rinse the beans, place them in a large stockpot, and cover with water about ⅔ of the way full, or about 4 inches (10 cm) above the beans. Add the seaweed, if using. Bring beans to a boil over high heat. Once water is boiling, reduce the heat to medium. Simmer for 1½ to 2 hours, or until beans are tender. Reserve the bean liquid for use in the Gallo Pinto.

To make the Gallo Pinto: In a large frying pan, sauté the oil, red pepper, and garlic along with a dash or two of salt over medium-high heat for 10 minutes, stirring often. Add the rice. Sauté for about 2 minutes, or until slightly golden brown on the edges. Add the beans, bean liquid, Salsa Lizano, and salt. Cook for 7 to 10 minutes, or until thickened slightly.

Press the mixture to a small bowl. Invert it onto a plate to serve. Top with the cilantro.

Yield: 6 servings

ITALIAN PEARL BARLEY

Popular in hearty soups and stews, pearl barley is also used in orzotto, which is similar to risotto.

1 cup (200 g) pearl barley
3 cups (705 ml) vegetable broth
½ teaspoon dried oregano
½ teaspoon dried basil

Add all of the ingredients to the pressure cooker. Cover and bring to pressure. Cook at high pressure for 18 to 20 minutes. Use a quick release.

Yield: 4 to 6 servings

ALMOND GARLIC GREEN BEANS

When cooking vegetables in the pressure cooker, remember to use a quick release to avoid them turning to mush.

1 teaspoon sesame oil
4 or 5 cloves garlic, thinly sliced lengthwise
1 pound (454 g) green beans, cut into ½-inch (1.3 cm)
    pieces
¼ cup (60 ml) water
¼ teaspoon salt
¼ cup (27 g) almond slivers

In an uncovered pressure cooker, heat the oil on medium. Sauté the garlic for about 2 minutes, or until soft. Add the green beans and water. Cover and bring to pressure. Cook at pressure for 1 minute. Use a quick release. Remove the lid, and stir in the salt and almonds.

Yield: 4 servings

BOK CHOY, MUSHROOMS, AND ONION WITH TAMARI LIME DRESSING

Cooked up quickly with mushroom and onion, this wholesome side dish–served with an umami dressing–delivers a whole lot of flavor.

FOR THE VEGETABLES:
5 to 6 cups (450 to 540 g) chopped bok choy
2½ cups (175 g) sliced shiitake, cremini, or maitake
    mushrooms
1 cup (160 g) half-moon slices onion
¼ teaspoon salt, optional

FOR THE DRESSING:
½ cup (120 ml) tamari
1 teaspoon minced garlic
½ teaspoon red pepper flakes
2 tablespoons (30 ml) lime juice

To make the vegetables: Place a trivet in the pressure cooker, place a steamer basket on top of the trivet, and add enough water to come up to, but not in, the basket. Bring the water to a boil. Place the bok choy, mushrooms, and onion in the basket. Add the salt, if using. Cover and bring to pressure. Cook at low pressure for 5 minutes. Use a quick release. Remove the lid. Using tongs, remove the steamer basket. Using a slotted spoon, carefully spoon the vegetables into a bowl.

To make the dressing: In a bowl, whisk all of the dressing ingredients together. Pour over the vegetables in the bowl and toss lightly.

Yield: 4 servings

MEDITERRANEAN BEANS WITH GREENS

This dish epitomizes the Mediterranean diet–low in satu-rated fats, high in fiber and other nutrients.

1 cup (200 g) dried navy or cannellini beans, soaked for
    12 hours or overnight
2 cups (470 ml) vegetable broth
2 cans (14.5 ounces, or 406 g) cans diced tomatoes with
    basil, garlic, and oregano
½ cup (50 g) sliced green olives, plus extra for garnish
1 teaspoon olive oil
4 cloves garlic, finely diced
8 cups (140 g) loosely packed arugula (about 5 ounces,
    or 140 g)
½ cup (120 ml) lemon juice, divided
Pinch salt, optional
2 cups (320 g) cooked pearl barley (See page 189–Italian
    Pearl Barley)

Rinse and drain the beans.

Add the beans, broth, tomatoes, and ½ cup (50 g) of the olives to the pressure cooker. Cover and bring to pressure. Cook at high pressure for 6 to 8 minutes. Allow for a natural release.

Meanwhile, in a skillet, heat the oil over medium-high heat. Sauté the garlic for 1 to 2 minutes, or until soft but not brown. Add the arugula and ¼ cup (60 ml) of the juice. Using tongs, turn the arugula frequently for 30 seconds, or until it wilts, and remove it from the heat before it turns brown.

Remove the lid from the pressure cooker. Stir in the remaining ¼ cup (60 ml) juice. Season with the salt, if using. Serve the barley, topped with the arugula, then the beans and tomatoes, and the olives for garnish.

Yield: 4 servings

SHREDDED BRUSSELS SPROUTS WITH APPLES AND PECANS

Here is a wonderful way to enjoy Brussel sprouts.

2 tablespoons (30 ml) oil
1½ pounds (685 g) Brussels sprouts, washed and shred-ded (cut into strips)
½ teaspoon salt, plus more to taste
1 large tart apple, cubed and unpeeled
2 medium cloves garlic, minced
1 tablespoon (20 g) maple syrup
⅓ cup (50 g) pecans, toasted and chopped
Black pepper, to taste
Juice of 1 lemon, optional

In a large sauté pan, heat the oil over medium heat. Sauté the sprouts and ½ teaspoon of the salt for 7 to 10 minutes, or until the sprouts begin to brighten. Add the apple, garlic, and syrup. Cook for 3 to 5 minutes, or until the apples are

heated through but not too soft. At the end of the cooking time, add the pecans, salt and pepper to taste, and juice, if using and toss.

Yield: 2 to 4 servings

BRUSSELS SPROUTS WITH CRISPY ONIONS

A bright, creamy sauce is drizzled over crispy onions and cooked-to-perfection Brussels sprouts in this side dish.

2 tablespoons (28 g) vegan mayonnaise
½ teaspoon Dijon mustard
2 teaspoons lemon juice
Pinch salt, plus more to taste
Pinch black pepper, plus more to taste
2 thin slices onion, halved
1 teaspoon whole wheat flour
Pinch of garlic powder
1 tablespoon (15 ml) neutral-flavored oil
½ teaspoon olive oil
8 ounces (227 g) fresh Brussels sprouts, trimmed,
    rinsed, and thinly sliced

In a small bowl, stir together the mayonnaise, mustard, and juice. Season with salt and pepper. Cover and refrigerate for up to 2 days, or until using.

Preheat the oven to 300°F (150°C, or gas mark 2). Line a plate with paper towels.

In a bowl, toss the onion with the flour, garlic powder, and a pinch of salt and pepper.

In a wok or skillet, heat the neutral-flavored oil over high heat. Test it by adding a piece of onion. If it sizzles, it is ready. Add the onion and cook for 4 to 6 minutes, stirring occasionally, or until the onion is browned, but not burned. Transfer to the prepared plate and blot the excess oil. Keep the onion warm in the oven while preparing the sprouts.

Wipe the wok or skillet clean with a paper towel. Heat the olive oil over high heat. Add the sprouts and cook for 5 to 7 minutes, stirring occasionally, or until the desired tenderness. (The sprouts will get some black spots.) Season with salt and pepper.

Transfer the sprouts to a serving plate. Sprinkle the onion over the sprouts. Drizzle with the sauce.

Yield: 4 servings

PAN-FRIED ASPARAGUS WITH LIME JUICE

This side dish comes together in minutes.

1 teaspoon (5 g) nondairy, nonhydrogenated butter (such
    as Earth Balance), optional
1 tablespoon (15 ml) olive oil
2 cloves garlic, minced
1 medium shallot, minced
1 bunch fresh asparagus spears, tough ends trimmed
Juice of ¼ lime

Salt, to taste
Black pepper, to taste
Lime wedges

In a large skillet, melt the butter with the oil over medium heat. Sauté the garlic and shallot for 2 minutes. Stir in the asparagus. Cook for about 5 to 7 minutes, or until bright green and tender.

Squeeze the juice over the asparagus. Season with salt and pepper. Garnish with the lime.

Yield: 2 servings

BRAISED FIGS WITH ARUGULA

Serve this warm or at room temperature.

1 tablespoon (14 g) nondairy, non-hydrogenated butter
    (such as Earth Balance)
1 teaspoon (4 g) sugar
1 pint (300 g) whole fresh figs (10 to 12 medium-size),
    halved lengthwise and stems removed
4 to 5 tablespoons (60 to 75 ml) balsamic vinegar
1 bunch baby arugula, washed and stemmed
1 to 2 tablespoons (15 to 30 ml) olive oil
Juice of ½ lemon
Salt, to taste
Black pepper, to taste

In a large sauté pan, melt the butter and sugar. Place the figs face down in the pan, and cook for 3 to 5 minutes over medium-high heat, or until the faces of the fig become sticky and slightly golden around the edges. Remove the pan from the heat and place the figs on a plate, face up.

In the same skillet, heat the vinegar until bubbly. Reduce the heat and simmer for 4 to 5 minutes, or until the vinegar is reduced by half. Remove from the heat.

In a bowl, toss the arugula with the oil to coat. Pour the juice over top; toss again. Season with salt and pepper.

Heap the arugula on a plate and arrange the figs over the top. Drizzle with the balsamic reduction, and sprinkle on more salt.

Yield: 2 or 3 servings

SAUTÉED BROCCOLI RABE WITH OLIVES AND TOASTED PINE NUTS

Broccoli rabe, also known as broccoli raab or rapini, is a popular Italian vegetable.

2 tablespoons (18 g) pine nuts
2 bunches (about 2 pounds [910 g]) broccoli rabe, thick
    stems trimmed 1 inch (2.5 cm) from the bottom
2 tablespoons (30 ml) olive oil
2 cloves garlic, crushed, pressed, or minced

10 Kalamata olives, chopped
1 teaspoon (1 g) crushed red pepper flakes
Pinch of salt
Juice from ½ lemon (or lime or orange)

In a dry skillet, toast the nuts over medium heat (or in a toaster oven on low heat) until golden brown, tossing occasionally to ensure even toasting. Remove from the heat.

Meanwhile, add a steamer basket to a 3-quart (3.5 L) pot with just enough water to reach the bottom of the basket. Bring to a boil. Add the broccoli rabe and cover. Steam for 2 to 3 minutes, and then immediately plunge the broccoli rabe into a bowl of ice water. (This will enable it to maintain its bright green color.) After a few minutes in the water, drain the rabe in a colander.

In a large skillet, heat the oil over medium heat. Sauté the garlic for about 2 minutes, or until it turns golden brown. Add broccoli rabe, olives, red pepper, and a pinch of salt. Sauté for about 5 minutes longer, until al dente, tender but still firm at the center. Sprinkle with the nuts, squeeze on the juice, and toss.

Yield: 6 to 8 servings

MARINATED MUSHROOMS

It may not be the norm in most recipes for marinated mushrooms, but the mushrooms are uncooked here.

2 tablespoons (30 ml) red wine vinegar
1 tablespoon (15 ml) olive oil
1 tablespoon (10 g) finely minced shallot
1 tablespoon (15 ml) lemon juice
2 cloves garlic, minced
¼ teaspoon dried basil
¼ teaspoon dried oregano
¼ teaspoon agave nectar
¼ teaspoon salt
¼ teaspoon black pepper
Pinch red pepper flakes
12 ounces (340 g) button mushrooms, halved or quar-
    tered if large
¾ teaspoon minced fresh parsley

In a large skillet, add the vinegar, oil, shallot, juice, garlic, basil, oregano, agave, salt, black pepper, and red pepper. Cook for 2 minutes, stirring. Do not brown the garlic. Remove from the heat. Add the mushrooms and parsley, stirring to coat well.

Transfer the mixture to an airtight container. Refrigerate for 1 hour or up to 2 days.

Yield: 4 servings

97

97 Shredded Brussels Sprouts with Apples and Pecans; 98 Brussels Sprouts with Crispy Onions; 99 Pan-Fried Asparagus with Lime Juice; 100 Braised Figs with Arugula; 101 Satuéed Broccoli Rabe with Olives and Toasted Pine Nuts; 102 Marinated Mushrooms

DESSERTS
See pages 202-203, 212-213, 218-219, 226-227, 234-235, 242-243, and 248-249
for dessert recipe photos.

EASYGOING PIE CRUST

Having a really great pie crust recipe is an essential to every baker's repertoire. This pie crust works great in both sweet and savory recipes.

1¾ cups (277 g) superfine brown rice flour, plus more for kneading and rolling
½ cup (60 g) cornstarch
½ cup (60 g) tapioca starch
1 teaspoon xanthan gum
1 teaspoon baking powder
2½ tablespoons (45 g) sugar
1 cup plus 2 tablespoons (270 g) nondairy margarine, very cold
3 tablespoons (45 ml) apple cider vinegar
½ cup (120 ml) very cold water

In a large bowl, sift together 1¾ cups (277 g) of the flour, cornstarch, tapioca starch, xanthan, baking powder, and sugar. Using a pastry blender, cut in the margarine until the mixture is evenly crumbly. Make a well in the center. Add the vinegar and water, stirring together quickly with a fork.

Turn out the dough onto a lightly floured surface. Knead in about 1 to 2 tablespoons (7 to 14 g) additional flour, if necessary, until workable. (Do not overknead; a flip or two will do just fine.)

Using your hands, pat the dough into a disk. Chill the dough in the fridge for about 2 hours or in the freezer for 30 minutes, or until very cold.

Use as a crust in your favorite pie recipe following the recipe directions. The pie crust will be slightly sticky, especially as it returns to room temperature, so rolling between two sheets of parchment paper or waxed paper is a must.

If the crust needs to be prebaked, bake at 400°F (200°C, or gas mark 6) for about 10 to 15 minutes, or until lightly golden brown.

Yield: One deep-dish pie crust

WHITE CHOCOLATE BAKING BAR

This recipe yields a basic white chocolate bar that's great for baking. Buy cocoa butter at natural foods stores or online. It is often sold in solid chunks and is very firm (just like a chocolate bar) at room temperature.

½ cup plus 2 tablespoons (90 g) confectioners' sugar
3 tablespoons (24 g) soymilk powder

7 ounces (207 g) food-grade cocoa butter, chopped
1 teaspoon vanilla extract

In a small bowl, whisk together the sugar and soymilk powder until very well combined.

In the bowl of a double boiler, begin to melt the cocoa butter over medium-low heat, just until part of the mixture starts to become liquefied. Add 1 to 2 tablespoons of the sugar mixture to the melting cocoa butter. Using a wooden spoon, stir until it's smooth and once again liquefied.

Repeat this process until all the sugar mixture has been incorporated with the cocoa butter. The mixture should be liquid once everything is combined. Once all the solid cocoa butter has melted, remove from the heat.

Quickly stir in the vanilla and then transfer the mixture to a large chocolate bar mold or a silicone baking dish. Chill in the fridge for 2 hours, or until firm, before using.

Store in an airtight container or plastic bag in the fridge to keep from melting or becoming soft. Use in your favorite recipes where white chocolate is called for. This baking bar keeps for up to 3 months if stored in the fridge.

Yield: 10 servings, 1 ounce (28 g) each

APPLE CINNAMON BLINTZES

These tender crêpes, which are stuffed with a thick Cashew Cream and topped with warm cinnamon apples, are a sure-fire way to bring folks together over brunch.

FOR THE CRÊPES:
3 tablespoons (42 g) sugar
⅔ cup (87 g) cornstarch
⅓ cup (43 g) sorghum flour
⅓ cup (80 g) firm silken tofu
1 cup (240 ml) nondairy milk
1 teaspoon vanilla extract
½ teaspoon salt

FOR THE FILLING:
1 recipe Cashew Cream (See page 6.)

FOR THE TOPPING:
3 Granny Smith apples, peeled, cored, and thinly sliced
Dash salt
1 teaspoon cinnamon
2 tablespoons (30 ml) plus ½ cup (120 ml) water, divided
2 tablespoons (28 g) sugar

1 teaspoon cornstarch mixed with 1 tablespoon (15 ml) cold water

To make the crêpes: In a blender, process all of the crêpes ingredients until smooth.

Transfer the mixture to a bowl. Cover and refrigerate for at least 1 hour and up to overnight.

To make the topping: In a medium bowl, combine the apples, salt, cinnamon, 2 tablespoons (30 ml) of the water, and sugar.

Transfer the mixture to a well-seasoned cast-iron or nonstick pan. Cover and cook over medium heat for 7 minutes, or until the apples are soft. Add the remaining ½ cup (120 ml) water and cornstarch slurry to the pan. Cook over medium heat for about 6 to 8 minutes, or until thick, stirring occasionally. Remove from the heat.

To prepare the crêpes: Heat a crêpe pan or skillet over medium-high heat. Evenly grease with about ½ teaspoon margarine or coconut oil. Pour ⅓ cup (80 g) of the batter into the hot pan and gently swirl the pan around in a circular motion to coat with a thin layer of batter. Cook for about 2 minutes. Using a flat, sturdy spatula, flip gently. (If they are done, they should be fairly easy to flip.) Cook the other side for approximately 1 minute, or until golden on both sides. Place each crêpe on a plate as they are cooked and cover to keep warm. Repeat with the remaining batter to make about 8 crêpes.

To assemble: Fill the middle of each crêpe with about ¼ cup (50 g) of the Cashew Cream. Fold the crêpe over twice as you would fold a letter. Top with 1 to 2 tablespoons (15 to 30 g) of the apples. Serve warm.

Yield: 8 blintzes

VANILLA CREAM TARTLETS
These are best served freshly made.

FOR THE VANILLA-FLAVORED POWDERED SUGAR:
1 cup (120 g) confectioners' sugar
1 split vanilla bean

FOR THE WHIPPED COCONUT CREAM:
2 cans (14 ounces, or 414 ml each) full-fat coconut milk
½ cup plus 2 tablespoons (75 g) confectioners' sugar, sifted

FOR THE FILLING:
½ cup (60 g) Vanilla-Flavored Powdered Sugar, plus extra for garnishing
1⅓ cups (192 g) Whipped Coconut Cream
½ cup plus 2 tablespoons (163 g) Cashew Almond Spread (See page 46–Fig and Nut Canapes)
Zest of ½ lemon

FOR THE CRUSTS AND GARNISH:
1¾ cups (210 g) whole wheat pastry flour
¼ teaspoon salt
¼ cup (60 ml) neutral-flavored oil
¼ cup (60 ml) maple syrup
2 tablespoons (30 ml) cold water, as needed
1 package (6 ounces, or 170 g) fresh raspberries, rinsed and patted dry
1 package (4.4 ounces, or 125 g) fresh blueberries, rinsed, patted dry
Confectioners' sugar

To make the Vanilla-Flavored Powdered Sugar: In an airtight container, combine the sugar and vanilla bean for 2 days.

To make the Whipped Coconut Cream: Let the cans settle at room temperature. Chill the cans in the fridge for at least 24 hours, along with the bowl used to whip the cream.

Scoop the hardened cream from the top of each can, and place it in the chilled bowl along with the sugar. Using an electric mixer with a whisk attachment, whisk for about 5 minutes, or until thickened. Refrigerate in an airtight container until ready to use, up to 2 days before serving

To make the filling: In a large bowl, gently fold the Vanilla-Flavored Powdered Sugar, Whipped Coconut Cream, Cashew Almond Spread, and zest to combine but gently so as not to remove the fluff from the whipped cream. Cover with plastic wrap, and store in the fridge for 2 hours or overnight to firm up.

To make the crusts: Preheat the oven to 350°F (180°C, or gas mark 4). Lightly coat twelve 3-inch (7.5 cm) tart pans with nonstick cooking spray.

In a medium bowl, stir the flour and salt together. Drizzle in the oil and syrup, stirring with a fork to create crumbs. Add the water 1 tablespoon (15 ml) at a time if needed, stirring until a dough forms. Gather the dough on a piece of parchment paper. Divide the dough into 12 equal portions, each about 1 ounce (30 g).

Using your hands, pat each portion down into a 2½-inch (6 cm) circle. Place each circle into the prepared tart pan, and press down on the bottom and just halfway up the edges, about ½ inch (1.3 cm). Repeat with the remaining dough. Using a fork, prick the crust bottoms. Bake for 13 minutes, or until the crusts are light golden brown. Cool completely in the pans, and then remove from the pans before assembling.

Add 2 tablespoons (35 g) of filling per cooled crust. Place back into the fridge for 2 hours to set. Decorate with the berries before serving. Sift more confectioners' sugar on top.

Yield: 12 tartlets

NO-BAKE STRAWBERRY PIE WITH CHOCOLATE CHUNKS

This delicious, easy-to-prepare seasonal pie requires no baking and calls for the ripest, sweetest strawberries, which you can find at your local farmers' market.

4 cups (680 g) ripe strawberries, sliced
1 prepared pie crust
1 cup (110 g) ripe strawberries, whole
5 pitted dates, soaked 10 minutes in warm water and drained
2 teaspoons lemon juice
Nondairy dark chocolate chunks

Arrange the sliced berries on top of the crust.

In a food processor, purée the whole berries with the dates and juice until smooth. Pour the mixture over the sliced strawberries. Arrange the chocolate on top of the sauce. Refrigerate for 1 hour before serving.

Yield: 8 to 12 servings

APPLE PIE

Few things are as satisfying as making your own pie crust and filling it with crisp apples.

2 Easygoing Pie Crusts (See page 194.)
5 to 6 medium-large apples, peeled, cored, and sliced ¼-inch thick (6 cups (90 g))
½ cup (100 g) granulated sugar, plus 2 teaspoons more
2 to 3 tablespoons (16 or 24 g) all-purpose flour
1 tablespoon (15 ml) lemon juice
¾ teaspoon ground cinnamon
¼ teaspoon ground nutmeg
Pinch salt
2 tablespoons (28 g) non-hydrogenated, nondairy butter, cut into small pieces
⅛ teaspoon ground cinnamon

Roll out the bottom piece of dough into a 13-inch (33-cm) round. Fit it into a 9-inch (23-cm) pie pan. Trim the overhanging dough to ¾ inch (2 cm) all around. Roll out the dough for the top crust, fold it in half, and cover. Chill the dough in the fridge while you prepare the filling.

Preheat the oven to 425°F (220°C, or gas mark 7).

In a bowl, combine the apples, ½ cup (100 g) of the sugar, flour, juice, cinnamon, nutmeg, and salt. Let the mixture stand for 10 to 15 minutes, or until the apples soften slightly.

Pour the mixture into the bottom crust. Using the back of a spoon, gently level the filling. Dot the top with the butter. Brush the overhanging crust with cold water. Cover with the top crust, and tuck any excess pastry under the bottom crust.

Using your fingers, crimp the edges.

Using a sharp knife or skewer, make 5 slits from the center of the pie out toward the edge of the pie to allow the steam to escape. Sprinkle with the remaining 2 teaspoons sugar and cinnamon. Bake for 30 minutes.

Slip a baking sheet underneath the pie (to catch the juices), reduce the temperature to 350°F (180°C, or gas mark 4), and bake for 30 to 45 minutes, or until the fruit feels just tender when a knife is poked through a steam vent.

Remove the pie from the oven. On a wire rack, cool for 3 to 4 hours before cutting. (This allows the filling to thicken properly.)

Yield: 8 to 10 servings

PUMPKIN PIE

Make the filling and use your own favorite pie crust, a store-bought crust, or the fantastic Easygoing Pie Crust on page 194. Serve this pie chilled or at room temperature.

1 pie crust
16 pecan halves
12 ounces (340 g) silken tofu (firm)
2 cups (400 g) pumpkin purée
½ cup (170 g) maple syrup
½ cup (115 g) firmly packed light brown sugar
¼ cup (32 g) cornstarch (or arrowroot powder)
1½ teaspoons ground cinnamon
½ teaspoon salt
¼ teaspoon freshly grated nutmeg
¼ teaspoon ground ginger
⅛ teaspoon ground cloves

Preheat the oven to 350°F (180°C, or gas mark 4).

Prepare the pie crust or remove a store-bought crust from the freezer/refrigerator. (Thaw the crust if frozen.)

On a cookie sheet, toast the pecans for 7 to 10 minutes, or until the smell of nuts fills the kitchen.

In a food processor, blend the tofu, pumpkin, syrup, sugar, cornstarch, cinnamon, salt, nutmeg, ginger, and cloves until the mixture is completely smooth and creamy, scraping down the sides of the bowl a few times.

Pour the filling into the baked crust. Using a spatula, smooth the top. Bake for about 40 to 45 minutes, or until the crust is lightly browned and the outermost 1 inch (2.5 cm) of the filling is set. (Don't worry if the center is still soft; it will continue to firm up as the pie cools.)

Transfer the pie to a wire rack. Gently press the pecans into the filling in 2 concentric circles (or any design you like). Cool to room temperature. Chill for 1 to 2 hours, or until set.

Yield: 8 servings

MAPLE PUMPKIN PIE WITH CINNAMON WALNUT CRUST

This pie encapsulates both maple syrup's flavor and sweetness that complements the pumpkin beautifully.

FOR THE CRUST:
2 cups (200 g) walnuts, ground
¼ cup (60 g) packed brown sugar
1 cup (160 g) superfine brown rice flour
1 teaspoon cinnamon
¼ cup (56 g) vegan margarine
1 tablespoon (12 g) ground chia seeds
¼ cup (60 ml) cold water

FOR THE FILLING:
½ cup (120 g) brown sugar
½ cup (160 ml) maple syrup
1 teaspoon ground cinnamon
1 teaspoon fresh grated ginger
½ teaspoon ground cloves
¾ teaspoon salt
½ cup (120 g) silken tofu
¼ cup (40 g) superfine brown rice flour
1½ cups (368 g) canned pumpkin purée
½ cup (120 ml) coconut milk
⅓ cup (40 g) finely crushed walnuts

Preheat the oven to 400°F (200°C, gas mark 6).

To make the crust: In a food processor, process all the crust ingredients for about 2 minutes, or just until crumbly, scraping down the sides as necessary.

Using the bottom of a glass, press the mixture into the bottom of an ungreased pie pan. Using a fork, poke holes in the crust. Bake for 10 minutes.

Increase the oven temperature to 425°F (220°C, gas mark 7).

In a food processor, purée all of the filling ingredients except for the walnuts until very smooth. Spread the mixture evenly into the prebaked crust. Bake the pie for 13 minutes. Reduce the heat to 350°F (180°C, gas mark 4) and bake for 45 to 50 minutes more.

Let cool completely, top with the walnuts.

Chill in the fridge overnight before cutting.

Yield: 1 standard-size pie (8 servings)

FRUIT CRUMBLE COBBLER

You can use fresh, frozen, or canned fruit. If using frozen fruit, thaw it first and drain any excess liquid so you have 1 full cup (250 g) of thawed fruit.

1 cup (181 g) pineapple chunks
1 cup (180 g) mango chunks
1 cup (145 g) pitted cherries

½ cup (100 g) plus 3 tablespoons (38 g) evaporated cane juice, divided
½ cup (110 g) brown sugar, tightly packed, divided
1¼ teaspoons ground cinnamon, divided
⅛ teaspoon ground nutmeg
1 teaspoon lemon juice
2 teaspoons cornstarch
1 cup (125 g) all-purpose flour
1 teaspoon baking powder
½ teaspoon salt
6 tablespoons (90 ml) coconut oil, chilled until solid
¼ cup (60 ml) boiling water
¼ cup (30 g) shredded coconut

Preheat the oven to 425°F (220°C, or gas mark 7).

In a large bowl, combine the pineapple, mango, cherries, ¼ cup (50 g) of the cane juice, ¼ cup (55 g) of the brown sugar, ¼ teaspoon of the cinnamon, the nutmeg, juice, and cornstarch. Toss to coat evenly and pour into a 9 × 9-inch (23 × 23 cm) glass baking dish or nine individual ramekins. Bake for 10 minutes.

Meanwhile, in a large bowl, combine the flour, ¼ cup (50g) of the cane juice, the remaining ¼ cup (55 g) brown sugar, baking powder, and salt.

Using your fingers, blend in the oil until the mixture resembles coarse meal. Stir in the water until just combined.

In a separate bowl, mix together the remaining 3 tablespoons (38 g) cane juice, the remaining 1 teaspoon cinnamon, and the coconut.

Remove the fruit from the oven. Drop spoonsful of biscuit topping over it.

Sprinkle the cobbler with the cane juice mixture. Bake for about 30 minutes, or until the topping is golden.

Yield: 9 servings

BANANA BERRY COBBLER

Bananas add an unconventional spin on a timeless classic. This texture of this dessert is similar to a coffeecake on the top but with a sweet baked fruit layer on the bottom.

½ cup (112 g) plus 2 tablespoons (28 g) nondairy margarine, divided
1 cup (130 g) sorghum flour
½ cup (79 g) brown rice flour
½ cup (65 g) tapioca starch
1 teaspoon xanthan gum
1 tablespoon (15 g) baking powder
1 teaspoon salt
¼ cup plus 2 tablespoons (90 g) packed brown sugar, divided
1 cup (235 ml) nondairy milk
1 teaspoon vanilla extract
3 or 4 bananas, sliced

2 cups (290 g) berries (blueberries, raspberries, and/or
    blackberries)
3 tablespoons (38 g) granulated sugar
2 teaspoons lemon juice

Preheat the oven to 350°F (180°C, or gas mark 4).

In an 11 x 7-inch (28 x 18 cm) baking dish, place 2
tablespoons (28 g) of the margarine Bake until the
margarine melts. Remove the pan from the oven and tip it
to coat the bottom.

In a large bowl, combine the flours, starch, xanthan,
baking powder, and salt. Using 2 butter knives or a pastry
cutter, cut in the remaining ½ cup (112 g) margarine until
small crumb form. Stir in ¼ cup (60 g) of the brown sugar
until well mixed. Add the milk and vanilla, stirring until a
thick batter forms.

In a separate bowl, toss the bananas, berries,
granulated sugar, and juice. Spoon the fruit into the baking
dish over the margarine.

Drop the batter by the spoonful over the bananas and
berries to mostly cover the fruit. Sprinkle with the
remaining 2 tablespoons (30 g) brown sugar.

Bake for 45 minutes, or until the fruit is bubbly and the
top is golden brown. Let cool for about 15 minutes.

Yield: 12 servings

BLUEBERRY COBBLER

*This could easily be called Fruit Cobbler, as it invites the
inclusion of any berry or fruit, such as apples or peaches.*

FOR THE BISCUIT DOUGH:
1⅓ cups (165 g) all-purpose flour
3 tablespoons (40 g) sugar, divided
1½ teaspoons baking powder
½ teaspoon salt
5 tablespoons (70 g) non-hydrogenated, nondairy
    butter, melted
½ cup (120 ml) nondairy milk
1 to 2 tablespoons (15 to 30 ml) nondairy milk or 1 to 2
    tablespoons (14 to 28 g) non-hydrogenated, nondairy
    butter

FOR THE FILLING:
4 to 5 cups (580 to 725 g) blueberries
½ cup (100 g) sugar
2 tablespoons (15 g) all-purpose flour
1 teaspoon grated lemon zest, optional

Preheat the oven to 375°F (190°C, or gas mark 5).

To make the biscuit dough: In a bowl, combine the flour, 2
tablespoons (26 g) of the sugar, the baking powder, and
salt. Add the butter and ½ cup (120 ml) milk. Stir just until it
forms a sticky dough.

To make the filling: In a large bowl, combine the berries
with the sugar, flour, and zest, if using. Spread evenly in an
8 or 9-inch (20- or 23-cm) square baking dish.

Using a tablespoon, scoop the dough over the fruit.
Either leave the dough in shapeless blobs on the fruit or
spread it out.

Brush the top of the dough with the remaining 1 to 2
tablespoons milk or butter and the remaining 1 tablespoon
sugar.

Bake for 45 to 50 minutes, or until the top is golden
brown and the juices have thickened slightly. Let cool for 15
minutes.

Yield: 6 to 8 servings

FALL FRUIT CRISP
*You can use any autumn fruit in this delightful dessert that
fills the home with an inviting fragrance. The flavor and
sweetness of the fruit come through, while satisfying the
sweet tooth.*

FOR THE FILLING:
6 to 8 cups (900 to 1200 g) cored and sliced or chopped
    pears and/or apples
1 cup (145 g) blueberries, fresh or frozen, optional
1 cup (145 g) raisins, optional
Juice of 1 lemon
¼ cup (85 g) maple syrup
1 teaspoon cinnamon
½ teaspoon allspice

FOR THE TOPPING:
1 cup (80 g) rolled oats, not quick-cooking
1 cup (150 g) chopped walnuts or pecans, toasted for 10
    minutes
½ cup (62 g) whole wheat flour
½ cup (112 g) non-hydrogenated, nondairy butter
¼ cup (55 g) firmly packed brown sugar
1 teaspoon cinnamon
¼ teaspoon allspice
¼ teaspoon nutmeg
¼ teaspoon salt
½ teaspoon anise seeds, optional

Preheat the oven to 350°F (180°C, or gas mark 4).

To make the filling: In a medium bowl, combine the pears,
blueberries if using, raisins if using, juice, syrup, cinnamon,
and allspice. Pour into an ungreased 8- or 9-inch (20- or
23-cm) square baking pan at least 2 inches (5 cm) deep.

To make the topping: In a bowl, combine the oats, walnuts,
flour, butter, sugar, cinnamon, allspice, nutmeg, salt, and
anise seeds if using. The topping should be crumbly (and

chunky from the walnuts) and have the texture of wet sand. If it's too dry, add a little more butter or a few teaspoons of water. Evenly sprinkle the topping over the fruit mixture.

Bake for 35 to 45 minutes, or until the pears and apples are soft when pierced with a wooden pick.

Yield: 6 to 8 servings

CHOCOLATE MARZIPAN TART

This tastes like a brownie pie, but the almond flavor shines through delicately, making it undeniably all about the marzipan.

1 recipe Easygoing Pie Crust (See page 194.)
¾ cup (97 g) sorghum flour
¼ cup (32 g) tapioca starch
1 teaspoon baking powder
⅛ teaspoon salt
2 tablespoons (28 g) nondairy margarine
8 ounces (227 g) nondairy almond paste or marzipan
⅓ cup (65 g) sugar
1 tablespoon (15 ml) vanilla extract
2 tablespoons (14 g) flaxseed meal mixed with ¼ cup (60 ml) warm water
¼ cup (60 ml) almond milk
1 cup (175 g) nondairy chocolate chips

Preheat the oven to 350°F (180°C, or gas mark 4). Lightly grease an 8-inch (20 cm) tart pan.

On a floured surface, roll out the pie crust until about ¼-inch (6 mm) thick and about 14 inches (36 cm) in diameter. (You might want to do this a silicone mat because you can easily move the rolled-out dough and flip it into the tart pan.)

Transfer the dough to the prepared pan and press into the pan. Trim off the excess dough. Chill the crust in the fridge.

Meanwhile, in a food processor, blend the flour, starch, baking powder, salt, margarine, almond paste, sugar, vanilla, flaxseed mixture, and milk until smooth.

In a microwave or over a double boiler, melt the chocolate chips. Stir until smooth. Add to the food processor and process until blended. Spread the filling into the crust evenly.

Bake for 30 minutes, or until the crust is light golden brown around the edges and the filling puffs up and begins to crack. (It should look similar to what a brownie looks like when done.)

Yield: 8 servings

FLOURLESS CHOCOLATE TART

This is a chocolatey treat that, despite its richness, isn't overly sweet. It all depends on the type of chocolate you use.

1 cup (110 g) raw pecans
1 cup (120 g) raw walnuts
¾ cup (150 g) granulated sugar
4 tablespoons (56 g) nondairy, non-hydrogenated butter, melted
16 ounces (455 g) nondairy semisweet or dark chocolate chips or bar
2 cups (470 ml) nondairy milk (soy, rice, almond, hazelnut, hemp, or oat)
2 tablespoons (16 g) kudzu (or cornstarch powder)
¼ cup (60 ml) water
Sifted confectioners' sugar

Preheat the oven to 375°F (190°C, or gas mark 5).

In a food processor, pulverize the pecans, walnuts, and granulated sugar. Add the butter and process until a thick batter forms.

Press the mixture into a 9- or 10-inch (23 or 25 cm) tart pan.

Bake for 10 minutes, or until the crust is golden brown. Meanwhile, in a double boiler or microwave, melt the chocolate.

In a saucepan, heat the milk over medium heat until it is scalding hot but not boiling.

Meanwhile, in a bowl, combine the kudzu and water until the powder completely dissolves, creating your thickener.

Whisk the chocolate into the milk. Whisk in thickener, and stir well. Reduce the heat to low. Simmer for 10 minutes, stirring occasionally. (The chocolate mixture will slowly thicken.)

Pour the chocolate mixture into the tart shell.

Chill in the fridge for at least 2 hours or up to overnight.

Decorate by cutting out a stencil pattern and placing it over the tart. Dust some powdered sugar lightly over the top. Remove the stencil.

Yield: 6 to 8 servings

CHOCOLATE HAZELNUT BROWNIE CHEESECAKE

Freezing, then thawing this dessert gives it a cheesecake consistency. Use an 8-inch (20.3 cm) springform pan. You can use a bigger size, but the smaller the pan, the taller the cheesecake. Serve this cold.

FOR THE CRUST:
1 cup (110 g) raw pecans
10 Medjool dates, pitted
½ cup (50 g) almond meal
½ cup (40 g) cocoa powder

FOR THE FILLING:
3 cups (330 g) raw cashews, soaked in water to cover for at least 2 hours, then drained
1 cup (235 ml) coconut oil, melted
1 cup (235 ml) water, plus more if needed
¾ cup (180 ml) agave nectar (or maple syrup)
1 cup (240 g) nondairy Chocolate Hazelnut Spread, plus more for garnish (See page 231.)
1 teaspoon vanilla extract

To make the crust: In a food processor, pulse the pecans and dates until uniform and crumbly. Transfer the mixture to a medium bowl. Add the almond meal and cocoa powder. Stir to combine.

Press the crust into the bottom of a springform pan.

To make the filling: In a food processor, blend the cashews, oil, and water for about 5 minutes, or until very smooth. Add a touch more water if needed to get the cashews to blend well. Stir in the agave, 1 cup (240 g) of the chocolate hazelnut spread, and the vanilla.

Spread the filling evenly on top of the crust. Cover tightly with aluminum foil.

Chill in the freezer for at least 7 hours or up to overnight. Thaw in the fridge for a few hours. Garnish with a drizzle of melted chocolate hazelnut spread.

Yield: 12 servings

LEMON CHEESECAKE

Cheesecakes are dessert classics that date back to ancient Greece. They're versatile and handle any flavor you throw at them. In this case, lemons add light freshness.

4½ teaspoons (20 g) Ener-G Egg Replacer (equivalent of 3 eggs)
6 tablespoons (90 ml) water
24 ounces (690 g) nondairy cream cheese, at room temperature
1 cup (200 g) granulated sugar
½ teaspoon vanilla
2 tablespoons (30 ml) lemon juice
1 tablespoon (5 g) lemon zest
1 prepared pie crust
Sliced strawberries

Preheat the oven to 350°F (180°C, or gas mark 4). Lightly oil a 9-inch (23-cm) springform pan.

In a food processor, whip the egg replacer and water together, until it's thick and creamy. Beat in the cream cheese for about 30 seconds, or until creamy. Beat in the sugar, vanilla, juice, and zest.

Scrape the batter into the prepared crust, and smooth the top.

Bake for 50 to 55 minutes, or until the center barely

jiggles when the pan is tapped. (It's okay if it puffs up a bit and turns a golden brown on top.) Let cool in the pan on a rack for at least 1 hour, making sure it's cooled completely before unmolding. Cover

Refrigerate for at least 2 hours and preferably 24 hours. Garnish with the strawberries.

Yield: 10 to 12 servings

WHITE CHOCOLATE RASPBERRY CHEESECAKE WITH DARK CHOCOLATE CRUST

You can buy vegan white chocolate online from various retailers, many times not marked as vegan at all. Just look for a variety that doesn't contain any milk, milk fat, or butterfat.

FOR THE TOPPING:
1 cup (125 g) raspberries
½ cup (100 g) sugar
1 teaspoon vanilla
2 teaspoons cornstarch whisked with ¼ cup (60 ml) water

FOR THE CRUST:
2 cups (240 g) walnuts or pecans, ground
¼ cup (24 g) plus 1 tablespoon (6 g) dark cocoa powder
¼ cup (50 g) sugar
½ teaspoon salt
1 tablespoon (12 g) ground chia seeds mixed with 1/4 cup (60 ml) water

FOR THE FILLING:
3 tubs (8 ounces, or 225 g each) vegan cream cheese
¼ cup (50 g) sugar
1¾ cups (300 g) vegan white chocolate, chips or chunks, melted
1 block (11 ounces, or 325 g) silken tofu, drained
7 tablespoons (70 g) superfine brown rice flour
¼ cup (60 ml) lemon juice
1 teaspoon vanilla extract

To make the topping: In a small saucepan, cook the raspberries, sugar, and vanilla over medium heat for about 2 minutes, while mashing gently with a fork. Drizzle in the cornstarch slurry. Stir until thickened. Remove from the heat.

To make the crust: Preheat the oven to 400°F (200°C, gas mark 6).

In a medium bowl, combine all of the crust ingredients. Press the mixture into an 8-inch (20 cm) springform pan. Using a fork, poke holes in the crust. Bake for 15 minutes. Remove from the oven and let cool.

To make the filling: Increase the oven temperature to 425°F (220°C, gas mark 7).

In a food processor, blend all of the filling ingredients for about 7 minutes, or until very smooth and absolutely no lumps remain.

Spread the filling evenly over the crust. Bake for 10 minutes.

Leave the cake in the oven and reduce the oven temperature to 250°F (120°C, gas mark ½).

Bake for 45 minutes without disturbing.

Remove from the oven, cover with topping (or leave it separate for serving). Cool for 2 hours at room temperature and then overnight in the fridge before cutting.

Yield: 16 servings

CHOCOLATE CAKE

This chocolate cake might be the easiest cake in the world to prepare, and it's incredibly versatile, lending itself to a layer cake or a Bundt cake.

1½ cups (188 g) unbleached all-purpose flour
¾ cup (150 g) granulated sugar
½ teaspoon salt
1 teaspoon baking soda
¼ cup (30 g) unsweetened cocoa powder
1½ teaspoons vanilla extract
⅓ cup (80 ml) canola oil
1 tablespoon (15 ml) white distilled vinegar
1 cup (235 ml) cold water
Frosting
Confectioners' sugar, optional
Fresh raspberries, optional

Preheat the oven to 350°F (180°C, or gas mark 4). Lightly oil a Bundt pan, 9-inch (23-cm), springform pan, or muffin tins.

In a bowl, combine the flour, granulated sugar, salt, baking soda, and cocoa powder. Create a well in the center of the dry ingredients. Add the vanilla, oil, vinegar, and water. Mix until just combined. Pour into the prepared pan. Bake for 30 minutes, or until a wooden pick inserted into center comes out clean. If making cupcakes, check for doneness after 15 minutes.

Cool on a wire rack. To remove the cake from the pan, run a sharp knife around the inside of the pan to loosen the cake. Cool completely before frosting. Dust with sifted confectioners' sugar and top with fresh raspberries, if using.

Yield: One 9-inch (23-cm) cake or 8 cupcakes

OLIVE AND TOFU FETA TARTLETS

These salty, savory tartlets make a delicious brunch treat to share with friends and loved ones. They are best served warm from the oven.

FOR THE CRUST:
1 recipe Easygoing Pie Crust (See page 194.)

FOR THE FILLING:
1 cup (145 g) raw cashews, soaked in 1 cup (235 ml) water for at least 1 hour
2 tablespoons (30 ml) water
1 tablespoon (7 g) flaxseed meal mixed with 2 tablespoons (30 ml) warm water
1⅓ cups (300 g) Tofu Feta (See page 14.)
1½ cups (180 g) assorted coarsely chopped olives (Kalamata, green, black, or a mix), divided

To prepare the crust: Preheat the oven to 400°F (200°C, or gas mark 6).

Roll out the crust between 2 sheets of parchment paper or on top of a silicone mat until about ¼ inch (6 mm) thick. Cut the dough into 2-inch (5 cm) squares and carefully press it into sixteen 2-inch (5-cm) tart pans or standard-size muffin cups. Use a flat metal spatula to help transfer the dough, if necessary. Bake for 10 to 12 minutes, or until light golden brown. Remove from the oven and reduce the temperature to 350°F (180°C, or gas mark 4).

To make the filling: Drain the cashews and combine with the water and prepared flaxseed meal in a food processor. Blend until smooth, scraping down the sides as necessary.

Stir the mixture together with the Tofu Feta and spoon 1 cup (120 g) of the olives and 1 cup (225 g) of the feta into the tart shells, dividing evenly among the cups. Using the back of a spoon, spread the mixture evenly to fill the tart shell. Top each with a sprinkling of the remaining ½ cup (60 g) chopped olives and ⅓ cup (68 g) tofu feta.

Bake for 30 minutes, or until the crust edges are golden brown and the olives on top soften and get crispy around the edges. Let the tarts cool for about 15 minutes and then gently remove from the pans. Serve slightly warm.

Yield: 16 tartlets

1 Easygoing Pie Crust; 2 White Chocolate Baking Bar; 3 Apple Cinnamon Blintzes; 4 Olive and Tofu Feta Tartlets. 5 Vanilla Cream Tartlets; 6 No-Bake Strawberry Pie with Chocolate Chunks; 7 Apple Pie; 8 Pumpkin Pie

9 Maple Pumpkin Pie with Cinnamon Walnut Crust; 10 Fruit Crumble Cobbler; 11 Banana Berry Cobbler; 12 Blueberry Cobbler; 13 Fall Fruit Crisp; 14 Chocolate Marzipan Tart; 15 Flourless Chocolate Tart; 16 Chocolate Hazelnut Brownie Cheesecake

RAW CHOCOLATE-CARROT CAKE

This creative raw dish combines the healthy fats found in raw cacao and cashews with the fat-soluble beta-carotene found in carrots. Raisins supply much of the sweetness.

FOR THE CAKE:
½ cup (55 g) grated apple, with a little salt and lemon juice on it
1 cup (110 g) grated carrot
½ cup (43 g) dried coconut flakes
1 cup (140 g) chopped cashews
½ teaspoon salt
½ cup (75 g) golden raisins
2 to 3 tablespoons (40 to 60 g) agave nectar (or other sweetener)
½ cup (48 g) raw cacao powder
½ cup (113 g) mashed banana
1 teaspoon ground ginger
1 teaspoon ground cinnamon
¼ teaspoon ground cloves

FOR THE FROSTING:
½ cup (113 g) mashed banana
2 to 3 tablespoons (14 to 21 g) coconut powder
1 tablespoon (6 g) cacao powder
1 tablespoon (20 g) agave nectar (or other sweetener), optional
1 tablespoon (15 ml) lemon juice
¼ teaspoon salt
¼ teaspoon powdered mustard

To make the cake: In a food processor, grind all of the cake ingredients. Divide among 8 ramekins. (The serving size is a little more than ½ cup [115 g]).

To make the frosting: In a blender, process all of the frosting ingredients. Taste and adjust the seasonings. Frost the cakes and chill before serving.

Yield: 8 servings

DARK CHOCOLATE CHIPOTLE CAKE

Spicy, sweet, and spongy, this dessert makes a nice alternative to plain ol' chocolate cake. Adjust the chipotle powder to your spiciness liking.

FOR THE CAKE:
¾ cup (60 g) cocoa powder, plus more for dusting
2 cups (400 g) sugar
1½ cups (350 g) nondairy margarine, melted
1¼ cups (162 g) sorghum flour
½ cup (65 g) tapioca starch
½ cup (65 g) cornstarch

2 teaspoons xanthan gum
1 teaspoon salt
2 teaspoons baking powder
1½ teaspoons chipotle powder
1 cup (235 ml) nondairy milk
6 tablespoons (90 ml) apple cider vinegar

FOR THE CHOCOLATE GLAZE:
1 cup (120 g) confectioners' sugar
¼ cup (60 ml) nondairy milk
½ cup (40 g) cocoa powder
2 tablespoons (28 g) nondairy margarine, softened

To make the cake: Preheat the oven to 350°F (180°C, or gas mark 4). Grease a standard-size Bundt pan well and lightly dust it with cocoa powder.

In a large mixing bowl, combine the sugar, margarine, and ¾ cup (60 g) of the cocoa.

In a separate bowl, combine the flour, starch, cornstarch, xanthan, salt, baking powder, and chipotle powder.

Alternate between adding the flour mixture and the milk to the sugar mixture, scraping the sides as necessary. Once it is well mixed, stir in the vinegar 1 tablespoon (15 ml) at a time.

Spread the cake batter evenly into the prepared pan.

Bake for 60 to 70 minutes, or until a knife inserted near the middle comes out clean. Because Bundt cake pans vary, check after 55 minutes to make sure it isn't burning. Let cool completely on a wire rack.

To make the glaze: In a bowl, mix all the glaze ingredients together until super smooth.

When the cake has thoroughly cooled, gently remove it from the pan, place it on a wire rack over a piece of waxed paper, and pour on the chocolate glaze. Let the glaze harden before transferring to a clean cake plate and slicing.

Yield: 10 servings

CHOCOLATE LOLLY CAKE

This is one confection that is almost exclusively eaten in New Zealand. It typically uses malt cookies and "lollies," fruity candies resembling marshmallows that come in a variety of colors and flavors, but the stand-ins here bring a smile to kids' faces just as easily.

4 cups (400 g) crushed (pulsed in food processor) gluten-free animal cookies
2 tablespoons (10 g) dark cocoa powder
½ cup (120 ml) coconut milk
½ cup (112 g) vegan margarine, melted
½ cup (88 g) nondairy chocolate chips
2 cups (175 g) vegan marshmallows, assorted colors if possible (such as Sweet and Sara brand)

2 cups (170 g) sweetened shredded coconut

In a large bowl, combine the cookies with the cocoa until smooth. Add the milk, margarine, chocolate, and marshmallows. Form into a loaf shape. Roll the loaf into the coconut to completely cover.

Freeze for 15 minutes, or until firm.

Transfer to the fridge for storage. Cut into 1-inch (2.5 cm) thick slices.

Yield: 1 lolly cake, or 20 servings

STRAWBERRY MOCHI CAKE

Daifuku, a traditional Japanese confection made from gluti-nous sticky rice and usually stuffed with red bean paste, is a popular treat in Japan. You can buy these mochi-based treats in Asian groceries.

1 cup (204 g) mochiko (sweet white rice flour)
1 cup (235 ml) almond milk
1 teaspoon coconut oil
½ teaspoon apple cider vinegar
1 drop food coloring
Tapioca or potato starch, for dusting
½ cup (85 g) sweet red bean paste (anko)
12 small strawberries, greens removed
¼ cup (50 g) sugar

In a microwavable bowl, whisk the mochiko, milk, oil, vinegar, and food coloring until smooth. Lightly cover with plastic wrap. Microwave on high for 6 minutes. Let the mixture cool just until you are able to handle it.

Dust your hands with starch. Place the mixture in between 2 pieces of plastic wrap. Roll it out until about ½ to ¼-inch (1 cm to 6 mm) thick. Use a pizza cutter to cut into even squares, about 2-inches (5 cm) square.

Repeat with the bean paste: Dust your hands with starch, place the paste between 2 pieces of plastic wrap, and roll it out until thin, about ½ to ¼-inch (1 cm to 6 mm) thick. Cut into squares.

Using starch-covered hands, cover a strawberry with the bean paste. Then place it in the middle of a square of mochi and gently pull up each corner of the square to cover the strawberry, twisting to seal with each corner until covered. Pat to smooth it into an even patty. If at any point it gets too sticky to handle, dust again gently with starch.

Refrigerate for up to 48 hours.

Yield: 12 pieces

LAMINGTON CAKES

The spongy interior of these little beauties matches per-fectly with the soft exterior of the chocolate ganache and the chewy contrast of shredded coconut.

FOR THE CAKE:
1 cup (200 g) sugar
1 cup (160 g) superfine brown rice flour
¾ cup (90 g) gram flour
¼ cup (51 g) sweet white rice flour
¼ cup (48 g) potato starch
1 teaspoon xanthan gum
2 teaspoons baking powder
1 teaspoon salt
**2 tablespoons (24 g) ground chia seeds mixed with
    ½ cup (120 ml) water**
1 cup (235 ml) almond milk, divided
¼ cup (56 ml) coconut oil, softened

FOR THE GANACHE:
1 cup (235 ml) coconut milk
1½ cups (263 g) nondairy chocolate chips

2 cups (160 g) shredded coconut

To make the cake: Preheat the oven to 350°F (180°C, gas mark 4). Line an 8 x 8-inch (20 x 20 cm) pan with parchment paper.

In a large bowl, whisk together the sugar, flours, starch, xanthan, baking powder, and salt until well blended.

In a separate bowl, combine half of the flour mixture with the chia seed mixture, ½ cup (60 ml) of the milk, and the oil. Mix well. Add the remaining flour mixture and the milk. Spread the batter in the prepared cake pan.

Bake for 35 minutes, or until the cake is spongy to the touch and light golden brown. Let cool completely and then cut into small squares.

To make the ganache: In a saucepan, warm the milk over medium heat for about 5 minutes, just until it plops, but is not boiling.

In a heat safe bowl, melt the chocolate in the warm milk. Stir to melt. Let rest for 15 minutes.

To assemble: Dip the cut cakes into the ganache. Let harden in the freezer for about 10 minutes, just until firmed up a bit. Roll in the coconut to coat. Return to the fridge to completely harden.

Yield: about 30 cakes

PINEAPPLE UPSIDE-DOWN CAKE

A real crowd-pleaser, this cake—somewhat retro—is perfect for a 1950s or 1970s theme party.

9 tablespoons (126 g) nondairy, non-hydrogenated butter, melted, divided
¾ cup (170 g) firmly packed light or dark brown sugar
¾ cup (175 ml) unsweetened pineapple juice, divided
1 small pineapple, peeled, cored, and cut into rings (or 1 can sliced pineapple [20 ounces, or 560 g])
¼ cup (60 g) maraschino cherries, optional
1½ cups (190 g) all-purpose flour
2 teaspoons (9 g) baking powder
½ teaspoon salt
½ cup (100 g) granulated sugar
¼ cup (60 ml) nondairy milk (soy, rice, almond, hazelnut, hemp, or oat)
1 container (6 ounces, or 170 g) nondairy yogurt (vanilla or plain)
½ teaspoon vanilla extract

Preheat the oven to 400°F (200°C, or gas mark 6). Lightly oil a 9 x 13-inch (23 x 33 cm) cake pan.

In a bowl, mix 5 tablespoons (70 g) of the butter with the brown sugar and ¼ cup (60 ml) of the juice. Place the mixture in the bottom of the prepared pan. Arrange the pineapple on top, in a decorative pattern. Fill the middle of each pineapple ring with a cherry, if using.

In a bowl, stir together the flour, baking powder, salt, and sugar. Create a well in the center of the dry ingredients. Add the remaining ½ cup (60 ml) pineapple juice, milk, yogurt, the remaining 4 tablespoons (56 g) butter, and the vanilla. Stir to combine, but do not overmix.

Pour the cake batter on top of the brown sugar and pineapple rings. (It may seem very wet, but it will all come together.)

Bake for 30 minutes, or until a wooden pick inserted into the center comes out clean. Let the cake cool in the pan for 10 minutes. Cover tightly with a serving dish and invert it so the pineapple rings are facing up.

Yield: 10 to 12 servings

PINEAPPLE CARROT CAKE

Carrot cake is a terrific special occasion cake. The pineapple provides an extra dose of moisture while not competing with the flavor and texture of the carrots.

FOR THE DRY INGREDIENTS:
1¼ cups (162 g) sorghum flour, plus more for dusting
¾ cup (90 g) buckwheat flour
½ cup (65 g) potato starch
1 teaspoon xanthan gum
2 teaspoons baking soda
1 teaspoon baking powder
1 teaspoon salt
Dash of cardamom
1 teaspoon ground cinnamon

FOR THE WET INGREDIENTS:
1¾ cups (350 g) sugar
½ cup (112 g) nondairy margarine, melted
3 tablespoons (21 g) flaxseed meal mixed with 6 tablespoons (90 ml) warm water
1 teaspoon vanilla extract
2½ cups (375 g) peeled and shredded carrots
1 cup (165 g) crushed pineapple, drained
½ cup (75 g) applesauce

FOR THE FROSTING:
½ cup (95 g) firm coconut oil
½ cup (115 g) nondairy cream cheese
4 to 5 cups (540 to 600 g) confectioners' sugar
2 tablespoons (30 ml) almond milk

Preheat the oven to 350°F (180°C, or gas mark 4). Lightly grease and dust with sorghum flour two 9-inch (23 cm) cake pans or a 9 x 13-inch (23 x 33 cm) sheet cake pan.

To prepare the dry ingredients: In a large bowl, combine all of the dry ingredients and mix well.

To prepare the wet ingredients: In a separate bowl, mix together all of the wet ingredients until smooth. Add the wet ingredients to the dry. Mix thoroughly until you have a fairly thick batter.

Divide the batter evenly between the two cake pans. Bake on the middle rack of the oven for 30 minutes, or until a knife inserted into the middle comes out clean. If using a sheet cake pan, bake for about 5 minutes longer, or until a knife inserted into the middle comes out clean. Keep a watchful eye on the cake toward the last 5 minutes or so to check for doneness.

Let the cakes cool in the pans for about 20 minutes. Invert the cakes onto cooling racks. Let cool completely before frosting.

To make the frosting: In a bowl, combine all of the frosting ingredients and beat with an electric mixer.

Yield: 16 servings

GERMAN APPLE CAKE

The original version of this cake, which includes raw apples and no topping, is called "Apfelkuchen, sehr fein," which translates loosely to "Apple cake, very delectable."

FOR THE CAKE:
3 apples, peeled and cut into slices

½ cup (112 g) nondairy, non-hydrogenated butter
½ cup (100 g) granulated sugar
½ cup (125 g) unsweetened applesauce
2 tablespoons (30 ml) nondairy milk
1½ cups (188 g) all-purpose flour
2½ teaspoons baking powder

FOR THE TOPPING:
¼ cup (60 g) firmly packed brown sugar
½ teaspoon cinnamon
½ teaspoon ground ginger

Preheat the oven to 350°F (180°C, or gas mark 4). Lightly grease a 9-inch (23-cm) springform pan.

To make the cake: In a saucepan, cook the apples in a little bit of water, just until they're a little soft but not mushy.

In a bowl, using an electric hand mixer, cream together the butter and sugar. Add the applesauce and milk. Add the flour and baking powder. Stir until just combined.

Add the batter to the prepared pan. Arrange the apples in a circle on top of the cake.

To make the topping: In a bowl, mix together the sugar, cinnamon, and ginger. Sprinkle over the apples, covering the top of the cake.

Bake for 30 to 40 minutes, or until a wooden pick inserted into the center comes out clean. Let cool for 15 minutes before unmolding from the cake pan.

Yield: 8 to 10 slices

BLUEBERRY ORANGE BUNDT CAKE

This is a lovely cake that cries out to be served at a tea party. You can also make Blueberry-Orange Muffins.

1 cup (145 g) blueberries, fresh or frozen
¼ cup (115 g) silken tofu (soft or firm)
½ cup (120 ml) water
¾ cup (175 ml) orange juice
½ cup (120 ml) canola oil
1 teaspoon lemon extract (or orange extract)
2½ cups (315 g) all-purpose flour (or whole wheat pastry flour)
1 cup (200 g) granulated sugar
1½ teaspoons baking soda
½ teaspoon salt
Zest from 2 oranges, optional

Preheat the oven to 350°F (180°C, or gas mark 4). Lightly oil a Bundt pan or muffin tins.

If using frozen blueberries, allow them to thaw slightly, about 15 minutes at room temperature.

In a blender, combine the tofu, water, juice, oil, and extract until smooth.

In a separate bowl, combine the flour, sugar, baking

soda, salt, and zest, if using. Make a well in the center of the flour, pour the wet mixture into the center, and mix just until combined. Do not overstir. Fold in the blueberries (draining them a little if the frozen ones start to defrost).

Pour into the prepared pan. Bake for 45 to 50 minutes for a cake, 20 to 25 minutes for muffins, or until a wooden pick inserted into the center comes out clean. Let cool in the pan for 10 minutes. Invert and cool on a wire rack.

Yield: 1 Bundt cake or 12 muffins

BEET BUNDT CAKE

We use vegetables in other desserts (think carrot cake, zucchini bread, and pumpkin pie), so why not beets? No one would ever guess that the incredible moisture and beautiful color of this cake comes from an earthy root vegetable!

½ cup (120 ml) canola oil
1½ cups (340 g) packed dark brown sugar
2 cups (450 g) puréed cooked (boiled or steamed) red beets (about 3 medium beets)
½ cup (90 g) nondairy semisweet chocolate chips, melted
1 teaspoon (5 ml) vanilla extract
2 cups (250 g) all-purpose flour
2 teaspoons (9 g) baking powder
¼ teaspoon salt
Fresh blueberries, optional
Confectioners' sugar

Preheat the oven to 375°F (190°C, or gas mark 5). Lightly oil a Bundt pan.

In a bowl, cream together the oil and brown sugar. Add the beets, chocolate, and vanilla. Mix well.

In a separate bowl, combine the flour, baking powder, and salt. Add the flour mixture to the beet mixture. Stir until just combined.

Pour into the prepared Bundt pan. Bake for 45 minutes, or until a wooden pick inserted near the center comes out clean.

Cool in the pan for 10 minutes before removing to a wire rack. Cool completely. Top with the blueberries, if using. Dust with confectioners' sugar.

Yield: 16 servings

RED VELVET CAKE WITH BUTTERCREAM FROSTING

Also known as devil's food cake, this dessert is characteristically known for its deep reddish brown color.

FOR THE CAKE BATTER:
3½ cups (440 g) all-purpose flour (or whole-wheat pastry flour)

1½ cups (300 g) granulated sugar
2 teaspoons (9 g) baking soda
1 teaspoon (6 g) salt
2 teaspoons (9 g) cocoa powder
2 cups (470 ml) nondairy milk (soy, rice, almond, hazel-
    nut, hemp, or oat)
⅔ cup (155 ml) canola oil
3 tablespoons (45 ml) red food coloring
2 tablespoons (30 ml) white vinegar
2 teaspoons (10 ml) vanilla extract
Ground pecans, optional

FOR THE BUTTERCREAM FROSTING:
½ cup (112 g) nondairy, non-hydrogenated butter, at
    room temperature
3 cups (300 g) confectioners' sugar
1½ teaspoons (8 ml) vanilla extract
2 tablespoons (30 ml) nondairy milk (soy, rice, almond,
    hazelnut, hemp, or oat, or water)
Assorted food colors, optional

Preheat the oven to 350°F (180°C, or gas mark 4). Lightly oil
two 8-inch (20 cm) round cake pans.

To make the batter: In a large bowl, combine the flour,
sugar, baking soda, salt, and cocoa. Create a well in the
center. Add the milk, oil, food coloring, vinegar, and vanilla.
Mix until thoroughly combined.
    Divide the cake batter evenly between the prepared
cake pans. Place the pans in the oven spaced evenly apart.
Bake for about 35 minutes, rotating 45 degrees halfway
through, or until the cakes pull away from the side of the
pans and a wooden pick inserted into the center of each
comes out clean.
    Let the cakes cool for 10 minutes in the pans. Run a
knife around the edges to loosen them from the sides. One
at a time, invert the cakes onto a plate and then reinvert
onto a cooling rack, rounded-sides up. Let the cakes cool
completely.

To make the frosting: In a bowl, using an electric hand
mixer, cream the butter until it is smooth and begins to
fluff. With the mixer on low speed, add the sugar. Fluff for
another few minutes. Add vanilla, milk, and food coloring, if
using.
    Once all of the ingredients are well combined, beat the
frosting on high speed for 3 to 4 minutes, or until it's light
and fluffy. To achieve the desired consistency, add l or 2
tablespoons (15 to 20 ml) additional milk. Cover the icing
with plastic wrap to prevent it from drying out until ready to
use. Rewhip before using.

To frost the cake: Place one layer, rounded-side down, on
a plate or cake stand. Using a palette knife or offset
spatula, spread some frosting over top of cake. Carefully set
other layer on top, rounded-side down, and repeat. Cover
cake with remaining frosting. Sprinkle with pecans, if using.

Yield: 8 to 10 servings

RUM PLANTAIN CAKE

*This cake is a lot like a baked sticky pudding (think date or
fig pudding) with an irresistible outer crust and notes of
rum and sweetly ripened plantain.*

1 cup (225 g) packed brown sugar
3 very ripe (blackened) plantains
⅓ cup (80 ml) melted coconut oil (or olive oil)
1½ teaspoons vanilla extract
½ cup (120 ml) dark rum
1 cup (127 g) sorghum flour
½ cup (80 g) superfine brown rice flour
⅓ cup (68 g) sweet white rice flour
1½ teaspoons xanthan gum
3 teaspoons (14 g) baking powder
1 teaspoon salt
1 cup (235 ml) + 2 tablespoons (28 ml) almond milk
3 tablespoons (45 ml) lime juice

Preheat the oven to 350°F (180°C, gas mark 4). Lightly
grease and flour a standard-size tube pan.
    In a large bowl, mash together the sugar, plantains, and
oil. Stir in the vanilla and rum.
    In a small separate bowl, whisk together the flours,
xanthan, baking powder, and salt. Slowly add the flour mix
into the plantains, alternating with the milk, adding a little
at a time until all is well mixed. Once all the milk and flour
have been added, stir in the juice.
    Pour the batter into the prepared pan. Bake for about 1
hour and 25 minutes, or until the outside crust is thick and
chewy but the middle is still soft. Let cool completely. Store
in the refrigerator.

Yield: 12 servings

CHILEAN-STYLE SWEET GINGER CAKE

*This spongy and irresistible cake is studded with crystal-
lized ginger and raisins, which make for a very sweet and
sophisticated treat.*

⅔ cup (150 g) vegan margarine
¾ cup (150 g) sugar
1 teaspoon vanilla extract
2 to 3 teaspoons (3 to 8 g) fresh grated ginger
⅓ cup (30 g) tapioca flour
½ teaspoon salt
1 teaspoon xanthan gum
3 teaspoons (14 g) baking powder
2 cups (240 g) gram flour
¼ cup (80 ml) agave
1½ cups (355 ml) almond milk
½ cup (48 g) crystallized ginger
½ cup (75 g) raisins

Preheat the oven to 350°F (180°C, gas mark 4). Lightly grease and (gram) flour a medium metal tube or Bundt pan or six large muffin tins.

In a large bowl, cream together the margarine, sugar, and vanilla until smooth. Add the fresh ginger, tapioca flour, salt, xanthan, and baking powder. Add the gram flour, agave, and milk. Mix vigorously for about 2 minutes, or until smooth. Fold in the crystallized ginger and raisins until well mixed.

Spoon the batter into the prepared pan. Bake for 50 minutes, or until golden brown on the top and a wooden pick inserted into the middle of the cake comes out clean. Let cool completely before attempting to remove from the pan. Using a butter knife, loosen the cake gently and then invert to remove from the pan.

Yield: 1 standard Bundt cake or 6 large muffins

PIÑA COLADA CUPCAKES

These cupcakes bring a taste of the Caribbean right to your kitchen with a pineapple cupcake base and an intensely flavorful coconut rum icing. Don't forget the cocktail umbrellas!

FOR THE CUPCAKES:
¾ cup (180 g) nondairy margarine, melted
1 cup (200 g) sugar
½ cup (80 g) crushed pineapple, well drained (Reserve the juice for the frosting.)
1 teaspoon baking powder
½ teaspoon salt
1 cup (130 g) sorghum flour
½ cup (65 g) cornstarch
1 teaspoon xanthan gum
¼ cup (60 ml) light rum
¼ cup (60 ml) nondairy milk
3 tablespoons (45 ml) apple cider vinegar

FOR THE FROSTING:
½ cup (95 g) coconut oil, at room temperature (firm)
2 tablespoons (30 g) nondairy margarine
2¼ cups (270 g) confectioners' sugar, divided
2 tablespoons (30 ml) pineapple juice (Reserved from the canned pineapple in the cupcakes.)
1 teaspoon rum extract
2 teaspoons coconut extract

To make the cupcakes: Preheat the oven to 350°F (180°C, or gas mark 4). Grease or line 9 cups of a standard-size cupcake pan.

In a large bowl, combine the margarine, sugar, and pineapple.

In a separate bowl, combine the baking powder, salt, flour, cornstarch, and xanthan.

In a small bowl, combine the rum and milk.

Gradually add the flour mixture to the margarine mixture about ¼ cup (30 g) at a time. After each addition of flour, add a little of the milk mixture. Repeat until all of the flour and liquid have been added. Mix vigorously until smooth. Add the vinegar 1 tablespoon (15 ml) at a time.

Divide the mixture among the cupcake liners. Bake for 25 minutes, or until a wooden pick inserted into the middle comes out clean. Let cool completely on a wire rack before frosting.

To make the frosting: In a bowl, using an electric mixer, beat the oil, margarine, and 1 cup (120 g) of the sugar until smooth. Add 1 cup (120 g) more of the sugar. Gradually add the juice, rum, and coconut. Whip on the highest speed until fluffy. Add the remaining ¼ cup (30 g) sugar. Beat until stiff.

Using a pastry bag or a small plastic bag with a corner cut off, or with an offset spatula, pipe the frosting onto the cupcakes. Store the cupcakes in an airtight container in the fridge.

Yield: 9 cupcakes

AMARETTO CUPCAKES

There are hundreds upon hundreds of kid-friendly cupcake recipes out there. This is not one of them. This sophisti-cated cupcake is made for grown-ups! The cupcake itself has no added fat, so if you are watching your fat, you can make these without frosting, or try the Chocolate Ganache. (See page 205.) For a nice decorative touch, sprinkle the tops with sliced or slivered almonds

FOR THE CUPCAKES:
1 cup (235 ml) almond milk
2 tablespoons (30 ml) white vinegar
½ cup (120 ml) amaretto liqueur (such as DiSaronno)
1 teaspoon vanilla extract
½ cup (100 g) evaporated cane juice (or granulated sugar)
2 cups (250 g) all-purpose flour
½ cup (40 g) unsweetened cocoa powder
1 teaspoon baking soda
½ teaspoon baking powder
½ teaspoon salt
¼ teaspoon ground cardamom

FOR THE FLUFFY ALMOND VANILLA FROSTING:
½ cup (112 g) nondairy butter
1 teaspoon vanilla extract
2 to 5 cups (240 to 600 g) powdered sugar, as desired
½ cup (120 ml) amaretto liqueur (such as DiSaronno)

To make the cupcakes: Preheat the oven to 350°F (180°C, or gas mark 4). Line a standard muffin tin with cupcake papers.

In a small bowl, mix the milk and vinegar. (It will curdle and become like buttermilk.) Stir in the amaretto, vanilla, and cane juice.

In a large bowl, sift together the flour, cocoa, baking soda, baking powder, salt, and cardamom.

Add the wet ingredients to the dry ingredients. Stir to combine. Don't overmix.

Fill the cupcake papers three-quarters full with the batter. Bake on the center rack for 18 to 20 minutes, or until a wooden pick inserted in the center comes out clean. Remove from the oven, allow to cool enough to transfer to a cooling rack, and cool completely before frosting. (This step is important to prevent the bottoms of your cupcakes from getting soggy.)

To make the frosting: In a bowl, beat the butter and vanilla with an electric mixer until smooth. Add the sugar, 1 cup (120 g) at a time, until the desired consistency is reached. (For a thinner icing use 2 to 3 cups [240 to 360 g]; for a fluffy, pipeable frosting use 4 to 5 cups [480 to 600 g].) Add the liqueur 1 tablespoon (15 ml) at a time as needed to taste and for the desired consistency

Yield: 12 cupcakes

GREEN TEA AND PISTACHIO CUPCAKES
The green color from the matcha tea is breathtaking, and these cupcakes are absolutely moist and magnificent.

FOR THE CUPCAKES:
2 cups (240 g) all-purpose flour (or whole wheat pastry flour)
½ to ¾ cup (100 to 150 g) granulated sugar
2 tablespoons (18 g) plus 1 teaspoon powdered green tea (such as matcha)
½ teaspoon ground cinnamon
1½ teaspoons baking powder
½ teaspoon salt
1 cup (235 ml) nondairy milk (such as almond, soy, rice, hazelnut, hemp, or oat)
⅓ cup (80 ml) canola oil
1 teaspoon pure vanilla extract

FOR THE GREEN TEA FROSTING:
½ cup (112 g) nondairy, non-hydrogenated butter
1½ cups (150 g) confectioners' sugar, sifted
1 teaspoon powdered green tea (such as matcha)
3 to 4 tablespoons (45 to 60 ml) nondairy milk (such as almond, soy, rice, hazelnut, hemp, or oat), divided
¼ cup pure vanilla extract
⅛ teaspoon almond extract
½ cup (63 g) coarsely ground pistachio nuts

To make the cupcakes: Preheat the oven to 350°F (180°C, or gas mark 4). Lightly oil a muffin tin or fill with cupcake

liners.

In a large bowl, combine the flour, sugar, green tea, cinnamon, baking powder, and salt.

Create a well in the center of the dry ingredients. Pour in the milk, oil, and vanilla. Stir to combine, breaking up any large lumps and being careful not to overstir.

Distribute the batter among the 12 prepared muffin cups. Bake for 20 minutes, or until a wooden pick inserted into the center comes out clean. Let cool on a rack.

To make the frosting: Meanwhile, in a bowl, using an electric hand mixer, cream the butter until smooth. Add the sugar, green tea, 2 tablespoons (30 ml) of the milk, vanilla, and almond. Beat for a few minutes until the frosting is light and fluffy, adding 1 or 2 tablespoons (15 or 30 ml) additional milk, if needed.

Cover the icing with plastic wrap. Store it in the fridge for about 1 hour. If the icing gets too warm in the kitchen, it will be thin rather than fluffy. Store it in a covered container in the fridge for up to 2 weeks. Rewhip before using.

When ready to use, frost each cupcake and top with the pistachios.

Yield: 12 cupcakes

FULL-O-NUTS MINI CUPCAKES
Do you remember the pretty famous (and not vegan) milk chocolate candies that have finely chopped hazelnuts in them? We're told these tender, finger-friendly little cakes are reminiscent of the candies in question. If you're not a fan of hazelnuts, you can make them with almonds instead. The longer these sit, the more their flavor develops.

FOR THE CREAM FILLING:
½ cup plus ⅓ cup (146 g) vegan semisweet chocolate chips, divided
½ cup (130 g) Cashew Almond Spread (See page 46–Fig and Nut Canapes)
¼ cup plus 2 tablespoons (75 g) coconut cream, scooped from the top of a chilled can of full-fat coconut milk
¼ cup (30 g) vanilla-flavored powdered (See page 195– Vanilla cream tartlets) or regular powdered sugar
½ teaspoon pure almond extract

FOR THE CUPCAKES:
½ cup plus 2 tablespoons (150 g) vegan yogurt (plain or vanilla)
¾ cup (144 g) evaporated cane juice
¼ cup (60 ml) plain or vanilla nondairy milk
¼ cup (60 ml) neutral-flavored oil
½ teaspoon salt
1 teaspoon vanilla extract
1 cup (120 g) whole wheat pastry flour
1 cup (120 g) shelled hazelnuts (or whole nonskinned almonds)

2 tablespoons (16 g) cornstarch
1½ teaspoons baking powder
½ teaspoon baking soda
½ cup (88 g) chopped vegan chocolate
1 recipe cream filling

To make the cream filling: In a double boiler, melt ½ cup (88 g) of the chocolate chips over medium heat, stirring until smooth. (If you don't have a double boiler, simply place a metal mixing bowl over a pot of simmering water.) Be careful not to get any of the water in the chocolate, or it will seize.

In a food processor, process the spread, coconut cream, sugar, almond, and chocolate until perfectly smooth and combined, scraping down the sides with a rubber spatula. Transfer to a medium bowl. Cover with a lid or plastic wrap. Refrigerate for 4 hours to thoroughly firm up.

To make the cupcakes: Preheat the oven to 350°F (180°C, or gas mark 4). Line 42 cups of two mini muffin pans with paper liners.

In a medium bowl, combine the yogurt, cane juice, milk, oil, salt, and vanilla.

In a food processor, process the flour and hazelnuts until the hazelnuts are very finely ground. Transfer to a large bowl, and combine with the cornstarch, baking powder, and baking soda. Pour the wet ingredients into the dry ingredients. Stir just until combined. Gently fold the chocolate into the batter.

Divide the batter among the lined cups, about 2½ teaspoons per liner, filling the liners about two-thirds full. Do not overfill the liners. Bake for 18 to 22 minutes, or until the tops are lightly browned and spring back when touched.

Remove the cupcakes from the muffin pans. Let cool completely on a wire rack. Store in an airtight container at room temperature.

Spread or pipe a small amount of cream filling onto each cupcake

Yield: 42 mini cupcakes

MINI RUM RAISIN CUPCAKES
Hopefully, you're not tired of the vegan cupcake revolution yet (imagine us looking at you in disbelief if you actually are), because we just couldn't not include a few mini cupcake recipes to make the dessert chapter of this cookbook complete.

FOR THE CUPCAKES:
½ cup (80 g) raisins
½ cup (120 ml) dark rum
½ cup (120 ml) vegan milk
¼ cup (60 ml) neutral-flavored oil
½ cup plus 2 tablespoons (120 g) Sucanat
1½ teaspoons vanilla extract

2 cups (240 g) whole wheat pastry flour
1 teaspoon baking powder
1 teaspoon baking soda
1 teaspoon ground nutmeg
½ teaspoon fine sea salt

FOR THE FROSTING:
6 tablespoons (84 g) vegan butter, softened
6 tablespoons (78 g) vegan shortening
2¼ cups (270 g) powdered sugar
Generous ¼ teaspoon maple extract (or ½ teaspoon pure vanilla extract and ¼ teaspoon ground cinnamon)
⅛ teaspoon salt

To make the cupcakes: In a small saucepan, bring the raisins and rum to a boil. Remove from the heat immediately. (Or in a microwave safe bowl, heat for 30 seconds and remove from the oven.) Let stand for about 10 minutes so the raisins plump up and the mixture cools.

Preheat the oven to 325°F (170°C, or gas mark 3). Line 40 cups of two mini muffin pans with paper liners.

In a large bowl, combine the rum mixture, milk, oil, Sucanat, and vanilla.

Into a medium bowl, sift the flour, baking powder, baking soda, nutmeg, and salt. Add to the wet ingredients. Stir until just combined.

Fill each paper liner about two-thirds full. Bake for 12 to 14 minutes, or until a wooden pick inserted into the center comes out clean.

Place the cupcakes on a wire rack to cool completely before frosting.

To make the frosting: In a bowl, using an electric mixer, cream the butter and shortening. Slowly add the sugar, and beat until combined. Add the maple extract and salt. Beat for about 2 minutes, until fluffy.

Spread or pipe a small amount of frosting onto each cupcake.

Store the leftovers in an airtight container at room temperature for up to 2 days. Store the frosting leftovers in an airtight container in the refrigerator for up to 2 days. Allow to soften at room temperature to decorate the cupcakes just before serving.

Yield: 40 mini cupcakes

17 Lemon Cheesecake; 18 White Chocolate Raspberry Cheesecake with Dark Chocolate Crust; 19 Chocolate Cake; 20 Raw Chocolate-Carrot Cake; 21 Dark Chocolate Chipotle Chake; 22 Chocolate Lolly Cake; 23 Strawberry Mochi Cake (Ichigo Daifuku); 24 Lamington Cakes

25 Pineapple Upside-Down Cake; 26 Pineapple Carrot Cake; 27 German Apple Cake; 28 Blueberry Orange Bundt Cake; 29 Beet Bundt Cake; 30 Red Velvet Cake with Buttercream Frosting; 31 Rum Plantain Cake; 32 Chilean-Style Sweet Ginger Cake

COCONUT-GINGERED BLACK BEAN BROWNIES

These pressure cooker brownies are not very sweet, so consider serving them with your favorite vegan ice cream.

1½ to 2 cups (300 to 400 g) dried black beans, soaked for 12 hours or overnight
6 tablespoons (90 ml) maple, date, or brown rice syrup, divided
1 (13.5-ounce, or 378 g) can light coconut milk
¾ cup (184 g) no-sugar-added applesauce
2 teaspoons vanilla extract
1 tablespoon (8 g) freshly grated ginger (or 1 teaspoon ground ginger)
½ cup (60 g) cacao powder
½ cup (60 g) millet flour (or oat, quinoa, or sorghum flour)
2 tablespoons (20 g) chunks dark chocolate, chopped from a bar, divided
¼ cup (30 g) chopped walnuts, divided

Preheat the oven to 350°F (180°C, or gas mark 4). Line a 9 x 9-inch (23 x 23 cm) baking dish with parchment paper.

Rinse and drain the beans. Add the beans, 2 table-spoons (30 ml) of the syrup, and the milk to the pressure cooker. Stir to combine. Cover and bring to pressure. Cook at high pressure for 12 minutes. Allow for a natural release. Remove the lid. If beans are not done, simmer uncovered for 5 to 10 minutes, or until cooked through.

Transfer the beans to a food processor fitted with an S blade. Process the applesauce, vanilla, ginger, and the remaining 4 tablespoons (60 ml) syrup until smooth. Add the cacao powder and flour. Blend until smooth, resembling cake batter. Add half of the dark chocolate and half of the walnuts. Quickly pulse (don't blend) so the pieces are mixed in but still chunky.

Pour the batter into the prepared baking dish. Sprinkle the remaining half of the chocolate and walnut pieces on top. Bake for 40 to 50 minutes, or until a wooden pick inserted into the center comes out almost clean. (These brownies are fudgy, so the pick will have some moist crumbs clinging to it.) If necessary, bake for 5 to 10 minutes longer.

Remove the brownies and the parchment paper from the baking dish. Let cool on a rack for 20 minutes.

Slice into squares.

Yield: 12 brownies

S'MORE BROWNIES

Most graham crackers have honey in them. Unless you bake your own graham crackers, or have a good source for vegan ones, just use animal crackers instead.

¼ cup (26 g) flaxseed meal
½ cup (120 ml) warm water
2 cups (250 g) all-purpose flour
1 cup (80 g) cocoa powder
½ teaspoon baking soda
½ teaspoon baking powder
¼ teaspoon salt
1 cup (200 g) sugar
½ cup (120 ml) canola oil
1 banana, mashed
1 cup (235 ml) nondairy milk
1 teaspoon vanilla extract
2 cups (352 g) vegan chocolate chips
1 (10-ounce, or 283 g) package vegan marshmallows
1 cup (120 g) crushed vegan graham crackers, divided

Preheat the oven to 350°F (180°C, or gas mark 4). Coat a 9 x 13-inch (23 x 33 cm) baking dish with nonstick cooking spray.

In a small bowl, whisk together the flaxseed meal and warm water.

In a large bowl, sift together the flour, cocoa, baking soda, baking powder, and salt.

In a separate bowl, whisk together the sugar, oil, banana, milk, and vanilla until smooth. Add to the flour mixture and mix until well combined. Fold in the chocolate and half (5 ounces [142 g]) of the marshmallows.

Spread the mixture evenly into the prepared baking dish. Using the back of a spoon, smooth the top. Press the remaining marshmallows into the batter evenly across the top. Sprinkle the crackers evenly over the top.

Bake for 30 to 40 minutes, or until firm and the marshmallows are golden and browned.

(It's hard to check for doneness with the wooden pick method, and all of the gooey goodness on top kind of makes it difficult to do the "dent" test, so you kinda have to jiggle the dish gently. It should be firm, not jiggly.)

Allow to cool completely before cutting into squares.

Yield: 15 brownies

"POT" BROWNIES

Sure, it's a silly play on words, but it is a really cute way to make brownies!

Vegetable oil or melted shortening
½ cup (110 g) firmly packed brown sugar
1½ cups (188 g) all-purpose flour
½ teaspoon baking soda
½ teaspoon baking powder
½ teaspoon salt
½ cup (40 g) unsweetened cocoa
1 cup (200 g) evaporated cane juice (or granulated sugar)
¾ cup (180 ml) nondairy milk
1 cup (176 g) vegan semisweet chocolate chips
⅓ cup (80 ml) vegetable oil

⅓ cup (113 g) applesauce
2 teaspoons vanilla extract

Preheat the oven to 350°F (180°C, or gas mark 4). Prepare 8 unglazed 3-inch (7.5 cm) terra-cotta pots for baking. Remove any labels, rinse the pots in clean water, and allow them to dry. Do not wash with soap, because terra cotta is very porous and will absorb the detergent. Cut parchment paper or foil circles to fit into the bottom of the pot to cover the drainage hole. Brush the entire inside surface of the pots liberally with vegetable oil or melted shortening.

In a bowl, stir together the sugar, flour, baking soda, baking powder, salt, cocoa, and cane juice until well combined.

In a small saucepan, bring the milk to a boil. As soon as it begins to boil, add the chocolate and stir until completely melted. Remove from the heat and stir in the oil, applesauce, and vanilla.

Add the chocolate mixture to the dry ingredients. Stir until well combined.

Pour the batter into the prepared pots just under three-fourths full. Do not overfill or the brownies will spill over.

Place the pots on a baking sheet and bake for 55 to 60 minutes, or until a wooden pick inserted into the center comes out clean.

Allow to cool completely before packaging for gifts.

Yield: 8 pot brownies

COCONUT BANANA FOUR-INGREDIENT BARS
Try out this recipe, and then experiment with your own healthy ingredients to put a personal twist on your bars! Just remember to keep things balanced, like this bar, with carbs (banana and dates), protein (walnuts), and a healthy fat (coconut butter). Dates help hold the bar together.

1 cup (80 g) dried banana chips
1 cup (178 g) chopped pitted dates
2 tablespoons (28 g) raw coconut butter
1 cup (100 g) raw walnuts

In a food processor, blend the banana chips, dates, and coconut for 1 to 2 minutes, or until blended.

Transfer the "batter" to a bowl.

In the food processor, pulse the walnuts until chopped.

Transfer the walnuts to the bowl with the dates and bananas. Fold all of the ingredients together evenly.

Place a piece of plastic wrap on a cutting board. Place the batter on top and cover it with another piece of plastic wrap. Using a rolling pin, flatten the batter into a ⅓-inch (1 cm) thick square.

Chill the batter in the fridge for at least 1 hour.

Unwrap the chilled bars and cut into 8 large bars or 16 small squares.

Store the bars wrapped in plastic wrap in an airtight container in the fridge or freezer.

Yield: 8 large bars or 16 small squares

MANGO FRITTERS WITH COCONUT DIPPING SAUCE
You'll need a deep fryer for these or a skilled hand at deep-frying in a pot. If that's not too big of a concern, make these as soon as you can. You will not regret it.

FOR THE FRITTERS:
2 ripe mangoes
Vegetable oil
½ cup (88 g) yellow cornmeal
⅓ cup (42 g) plus ½ cup (65 g) potato starch, divided
½ cup (120 ml) almond milk
½ teaspoon salt
1 teaspoon ground cinnamon
Confectioners' sugar

FOR THE DIPPING SAUCE:
½ cup (120 ml) crème de coco
1 tablespoon (15 ml) lime juice
Zest of 1 small lime

To make the fritters: Peel and remove the pits from the mangoes. Slice the fruit into strips about 1 inch (2.5 cm) wide.

Pour the oil into a deep fryer to a depth of 5 inches (13 cm) and bring to 360°F (182°C).

Meanwhile, in a small bowl, whisk together the cornmeal, ⅓ cup (42 g) of the starch, the milk, salt, and cinnamon to make a slightly thick batter.

Spread the remaining ½ cup (65 g) starch on a plate. Line a plate with paper towels.

Dredge each piece of mango in the starch, and then immediately dip it into the batter to cover completely. Hold over the bowl to allow extra batter to drip from the mango pieces. Drop the mango immediately one by one into the hot oil. Fry for 4 minutes, or until golden brown. Using a skimmer, remove the mango from the hot oil and place on the prepared plate to drain. Repeat with the remaining fritters. Dust with the confectioners' sugar. Let cool.

To make the dipping sauce: In a bowl, using an electric mixer, mix together the crème de coco, juice, and zest until fluffy.

Serve the fritters with the sauce.

Yield: 6 servings, 2 fritters each

PUMPKIN FRITTERS

Much like Chilean-style sopapillas, these fritters are inspired by the classic fritters of Latin American cuisine, which use pumpkin in their base. They are perfect with coffee or tea.

FOR THE PUMPKIN FRITTERS:
Vegetable oil
2 cups (490 g) puréed pumpkin
1¼ cups (150 g) gram flour
½ cup (64 g) cornstarch
¾ cup (102 g) sorghum flour
1 teaspoon baking powder
½ teaspoon baking soda
1 teaspoon salt

FOR THE BROWN SUGAR SYRUP:
½ cup (115 g) packed brown sugar (or ½ cup [160 g] agave)
1 tablespoon (15 ml) orange juice
1 peeled orange slice

To make the Pumpkin Fritters: Preheat oil in a deep fryer to 360°F (182°C). Line a plate with paper towels.

In a large bowl, combine the pumpkin, gram flour, cornstarch, sorghum flour, baking powder, baking soda, and salt until a sticky batter forms.

Using an ice cream scoop, drop by 2-tablespoon (28 g) size balls into the heated oil. Let cook for 6 minutes, gently stirring to prevent them from sticking together.

Using a slotted spoon, remove the fritters from the oil. Drain them on the prepared plate.

To make the Brown Sugar Syrup: In a saucepan, warm the sugar, juice, and orange slice over low heat until the sugar is completely dissolved. Cook for 1 minute and then remove the orange slice.

Serve the Pumpkin Fritters with the Brown Sugar Syrup.

Yield: about 20 fritters

CHERRY-APRICOT POCKET PIES

These flaky little pocket pies are the perfect treat to whip up when you're craving a fruit-filled pastry, but pulling together an entire pie seems overwhelming.

FOR THE GLAZE:
½ cup (60 g) confectioners' sugar
2 tablespoons (30 ml) nondairy milk
1 teaspoon corn syrup or agave nectar, plus more if needed
Vanilla extract (or other extract)

FOR THE FILLING:
2 cups (470 ml) water
⅓ cup (50 g) dried cherries
1 cup (150 g) chopped dried apricots
¼ cup (50 g) plus 2 tablespoons (25 g) sugar, divided
1½ tablespoons (12 g) cornstarch
2 teaspoons flaxseed meal
Dash of salt
¼ teaspoon ground cinnamon
1 recipe Easygoing Pie Crust (See page 194), chilled for at least 2 hours

Preheat the oven to 375°F (190°C, or gas mark 5).

To make the glaze: In a bowl, whisk the sugar and milk until smooth. Stir in the syrup until shiny. Add the vanilla.

To make the filling: In a medium saucepan, bring the water to a boil over high heat. Add the dried fruits and reduce the heat to medium. Cook for 5 to 7 minutes, or until the apricots are very soft but not mushy. Drain the fruit.

In a bowl, combine the fruit, ¼ cup (50 g) of the sugar, the cornstarch, flaxseed, salt, and cinnamon.

Place the dough between 2 large pieces of parchment paper. Roll out to ¼ inch (6 mm) thick. Using a large biscuit cutter or a small bowl (about 5 inches [13 cm] wide) turned upside down, cut out 6 circles of dough, gathering up the dough and rerolling as necessary.

Place about 2 tablespoons (30 g) of the filling onto half of each circle crust, leaving about a ½-inch (1.3 cm) edge around the filling. Fold the dough over the fruit filling, pressing together the edges to seal.

Using a fork, crimp the edges. Cut a few slits in the top of the crust. The dough will be slightly fragile, so handle with care. Sprinkle with the remaining 2 tablespoons (28 g) sugar. Place on an ungreased baking sheet.

Bake for about 28 minutes, or until lightly golden brown on the edges. Let cool. Drizzle with the glaze.

Yield: 6 pocket pies

MANGO SAFFRON MOUSSE

This delicious mousse takes 5 minutes to put together, especially if you're using frozen mangoes. Saffron and mango blend beautifully together, not only in terms of flavor but also in terms of color.

1 bag (10 ounces, or 280 g) frozen mangoes (or 1 small mango, cubed), thawed
1 box (12 ounces, or 340 g) organic silken tofu, firm or extra-firm
¼ cup (50 g) sugar
3 drops saffron extract

In a blender, process the mangoes, tofu, sugar, and saffron until smooth.

Transfer to a container and refrigerate for at least 1 hour. This helps it set up but also provides the characteristic chill of a good mousse.

Yield: 3 cups (670 g)

CHOCOLATE MOUSSE

You won't miss the dairy in this quick, delicious, rich, and creamy mousse that's also perfect as a pie filling.

1 cup (175 g) nondairy semisweet chocolate chips
12 ounces (340 g) silken tofu (soft or firm)
½ cup (120 ml) nondairy milk
½ teaspoon vanilla extract
Fresh berries for serving, optional

In a microwave-safe bowl, heat the chocolate in the microwave for 1 minute. Stir the chips and heat for 1 minute more. Stir again. (They should be melted. You can also melt the chocolate by creating your own double boiler. Place the chocolate in a small saucepan. Set this pan in a larger pot that's filled with ¼ to ½ cup (60 to 120 ml) water. Heat over medium heat on the stove and stir the chocolate in the small pot until it's melted.)

In a blender, process the tofu, chocolate, milk, and vanilla until completely smooth, scraping down the sides and under the blade, if necessary.

Pour the mixture into serving bowls. Chill in the fridge for at least 1 hour. Add the berries just before serving, if using.

Yield: 6 servings

RICE PUDDING

This is simplicity at its best. You can make it with any non-dairy milk. If you'd like to be like the medieval Europeans, use almond milk, which was their top choice.

2½ cups (590 ml) nondairy milk
⅓ cup (65 g) long- or short-grain white or brown rice
⅛ teaspoon salt
¼ cup (50 g) sugar
1 teaspoon vanilla extract
1 teaspoon cinnamon, plus more for sprinkling
¼ cup (35 g) raisins, optional

In a 3-quart (3.4-L) saucepan, combine the milk, rice, and salt. Place the saucepan over high heat and bring the mixture to a boil, watching so it doesn't boil over. Reduce the heat to medium-low. Simmer for about 25 minutes, or until the rice is tender. Using a heatproof rubber spatula or wooden spoon, stir the rice frequently to prevent it from sticking to the bottom of the pan.

When the rice is tender, remove the saucepan from the heat. Add the sugar, vanilla, and the 1 teaspoon cinnamon. Return the saucepan to the heat. Cook for 5 to 10 minutes, or until the rice pudding thickens.

Remove from the heat. Add the raisins, if using. Spoon the pudding into serving bowls, sprinkle with cinnamon, and cover with plastic wrap. If you want a skin to form on the puddings, allow them to cool before covering with plastic wrap. Chill in the fridge for 1 to 2 hours.

Yield: 2 to 3 servings

DARK CHOCOLATE ORANGE CUSTARD

This is ridiculously easy, ridiculously rich, and oh so good. This custard is dense and delicious. It's best reserved for an occasion when your taste buds deserve a little something special. This is best served cold.

1 tablespoon (6 g) orange zest
1 teaspoon vanilla extract
1 bag (12 ounces, or 340 g) nondairy chocolate chips
1 can (13.5 ounces, or 378 ml) coconut milk

In a large heat-safe bowl, combine the zest, extract, and chocolate.

In a small pan, bring the milk to a boil over medium heat. Pour the milk over the chocolate. Whisk together vigorously but carefully until smooth and uniform.

Transfer the mixture to 6 single-serving dishes and cover. Chill in the fridge for at least 3 hours, or until firm.

Yield: 6 servings

33 Piña Colada Cupcakes; 34 Amaretto Cupcakes; 35 Green Tea and Pistachio Cupcakes; 36 Full-O-Nuts Mini Cupcakes; 37 Mini Rum Raisin Cupcakes; 38 Coconut-Gingered Black Bean Brownies; 39 S'more Brownies; 40 "Pot" Brownies

41 Coconut Banana Four-Ingredient Bars; 42 Mango Fritters with Coconut Dipping Sauce; 43 Pumpkin Fritters; 44 Cherry-Apricot Pocket Pies; 45 Mango Saffron Mousse; 46 Chocolate Mousse; 47 Rice Pudding; 48 Dark Chocolate Orange Custard

COCONUT PUDDING

This creamy and slightly addictive coconut pudding is a classic dessert often eaten in Puerto Rico. You can place the easy and beautiful pudding in decorative molds, chill them overnight, and then invert them to capture intricate designs, although you can stick with the simple and very efficient large muffin pan, which generally fits 6 servings.

2 cans (13.5 ounces, or 400 ml each) coconut milk
2 cups (475 ml) water
2 cups (400 g) sugar
1 cup (128 g) cornstarch mixed with ½ cup (120 ml) water
1 teaspoon salt
1 teaspoon vanilla extract
1 tablespoon (15 g) equal amounts ground cloves, nutmeg, and cinnamon, mixed

Lightly grease 4 to 6 molds (large muffin tins work well) with coconut oil or nondairy margarine.

In a 2-quart (2 L) saucepan, combine the milk, water, and sugar. Cook over a little higher than medium heat for about 5 minutes, or until the mixture is hot. Add the cornstarch mixture, salt, and vanilla. Cook over medium heat for about 7 minutes, or until it thickens, stirring constantly with a whisk.

Pour the mixture into the prepared molds. Chill in the fridge overnight.

Invert onto a serving tray and dust with the cloves, nutmeg, and cinnamon mixture.

Yield: 4 large or 6 small servings

COCONUT RICE WITH PEACHES AND RUM RAISINS

This recipe is a more exotic take on the average rice pudding with its extra-creamy texture and sweet and tart flavors of fruit laced throughout. For a non-boozy option, soak the raisins in ½ cup (120 ml) pineapple juice mixed with 2 teaspoons rum extract. Serve this hot or cold.

½ cup (120 ml) light rum
1 cup (145 g) raisins
2 cups (390 g) uncooked jasmine rice
4 cups (940 ml) water
1 can (13.5 ounces, or 378 ml) coconut milk
1 cup (200 g) sugar
Salt, to taste
2 or 3 ripe peaches, chopped
Ground cinnamon

The night before, in a small bowl, combine the rum and raisins. Cover. Chill in the fridge overnight.

In a 1½-quart (1.4 L) saucepan, heat the rice, water, and milk over medium-high heat, stirring to combine. Bring the rice just to the beginning of a boil (not rolling). Reduce the heat to low and cover. Simmer for 20 to 25 minutes, or until all of the liquid has been absorbed and the rice is fluffy. Do not stir the rice while it is cooking and avoid lifting the lid more than absolutely necessary.

Once the rice is fully cooked, stir in the sugar. Season with salt.

In a small saucepan, cook the peaches and rum raisins with liquid over medium heat for about 2 minutes, or until the peaches are soft, stirring occasionally. Drain.

Gently stir the fruit into the rice. Sprinkle with a touch of cinnamon.

Yield: 8 servings

FRUIT AND NUT RICE PUDDING

The ultimate comfort food, rice pudding is reimagined in the pressure cooker! Serve this pudding warm or chilled.

4 tablespoons (56 g) vegan butter
1 cup (190 g) Arborio rice
3½ cups (822 ml) unsweetened vanilla almond milk
2 to 3 tablespoons (30 to 45 ml) maple, date, or brown rice syrup
1 teaspoon vanilla extract
½ teaspoon almond extract
¼ teaspoon ground cinnamon, plus more for garnish
¼ cup (35 g) golden raisins
¼ cup (35 g) chopped dried apricots
½ cup (55 g) slivered almonds

In an uncovered pressure cooker heat the butter on medium. Add the rice and stir to cover. Stir in the milk. Cover and bring to pressure. Cook at high pressure for 7 minutes. Use a quick release.

Remove the cover and stir in the syrup, extracts, cinnamon, raisins, apricots, and almonds.

Sprinkle with more cinnamon.

Yield: 6 servings

BAMBARA PEANUT BUTTER RICE PUDDING

This easy and oh-so-peanutty dessert is a great way to use up any extra basmati rice you may have in your fridge. This porridge is a favorite for Central Africans, where they prepare it similarly using rice, peanut butter, and sugar.

2 cups (316 g) cooked jasmine rice, cold
¼ cup (60 ml) coconut milk
¼ cup (80 ml) agave or brown rice syrup, plus more for drizzling
1 teaspoon salt
½ cup (130 g) creamy natural peanut butter
1 cup (145 g) crushed peanuts
Cinnamon

In small saucepan, heat the rice, milk, agave, salt, and peanut butter over medium-low heat until warm and creamy. Garnish with more syrup. Top with peanuts and cinnamon.

Yield: 4 servings

PINEAPPLE, MANGO, COCONUT, AND CHIA SEED PUDDING

This cool tropical treat is full of naturally sweet fruit goodness. It's also packed full of omega-3 fatty acids from the chia. You'll love the texture of the seeds.

2 to 3 cups (470 to 705 ml) canned coconut milk, divided
1½ cups (280 g) frozen pineapple chunks, plus more for garnish, optional
1½ cups (280 g) frozen mango chunks, plus more for garnish, optional
2 tablespoons (30 ml) lemon juice
½ cup (60 g) shredded coconut
½ cup (120 g) chia seeds
Zest of 1 lemon
Sweetener, to taste, optional

In a blender, purée 2 cups (470 ml) of the milk, the pineapple, mango, and juice until smooth. (It should be the consistency of a thin milkshake, not too thick.)

Pour the mixture into a bowl. Stir in the coconut, chia seeds, and zest. Cover and chill to thicken. Stir before serving. If needed, stir in extra milk to achieve desired consistency. Top with additional pineapple and mango chunks, if using. Sweeten, if desired.

Yield: 8 servings

CHOCOLATE, COCONUT, AND CHIA PUDDING

This dessert is sweet and full of texture and healthy nutrients. From our beloved superfood coconut to the chia seeds, maple syrup, and raw cacao powder, it's a powerhouse of a pudding! You can substitute unsweetened natural cocoa powder, if necessary. Serve chilled.

2 tablespoons (28 ml) maple syrup
1 to 2 teaspoons water
1 cup (235 ml) canned coconut milk
1 cup (235 ml) unsweetened vanilla-flavored almond milk
¼ teaspoon ground cinnamon
1 tablespoon (15 g) unsweetened raw cacao powder
¼ cup (50 g) chia seeds

In a medium bowl, combine the syrup and 1 teaspoon of the water. Whisk together to form a thin syrup. Add up to 1 additional teaspoon water, if necessary. Whisk in the

coconut milk, almond milk, and cinnamon. Whisk in the cacao. Add the chia seeds and whisk them into the pudding mixture. Chill in the fridge for at least 4 hours and up to overnight to allow the pudding consistency to develop.

Yield: 2 servings

CHOCOLATE CHIP COOKIES

When you make these cookies, don't be surprised to hear "I'd never know this was vegan!" That's the highest compliment for a vegan chef.

4½ teaspoons Ener-G Egg Replacer (equivalent of 3 eggs)
6 tablespoons (90 ml) water 1 cup (225 g) nondairy, non-hydrogenated butter, softened
¾ cup (150 g) granulated sugar
¾ cup (170 g) firmly packed brown sugar
2 teaspoons vanilla extract
2¼ cups (280 g) all-purpose flour
1 teaspoon baking soda
1 teaspoon salt
1 to 2 cups (175 to 350 g) nondairy semisweet chocolate chips
1 cup (150 g) chopped nuts, optional

Preheat the oven to 375°F (190°C, or gas mark 5). Line a baking sheet with parchment paper.

In a food processor, whip the egg replacer and water together, until thick and creamy. (Blending it in a food processor or blender results in a better consistency than what you could get if you did it by hand.)

In a large bowl, cream the butter, granulated sugar, brown sugar, and vanilla. Add the egg replacer mixture to this wet mixture, and thoroughly combine.

In a separate bowl, combine the flour, baking soda, and salt. Gradually beat the flour mixture into the wet mixture until it begins to form a dough. When it is almost thoroughly combined, stir in the chips and nuts, if using.

Place spoonsful of the mixture onto the prepared baking sheet. Bake for 8 to 10 minutes, or until golden brown. Let cool on the baking sheet for 2 minutes. Remove to wire racks to cool completely.

Yield: 1 dozen cookies

MEXICAN WEDDING COOKIES

These melt-in-your mouth cookies are called many names: Russian Tea Cakes, Mexican Wedding Cakes, Pecan Balls, Snowdrops, and Snowballs. They're often baked during the winter holidays, but they're also popular at weddings and other festive occasions.

1 cup (225 g) nondairy, non-hydrogenated butter
¼ cup (50 g) granulated sugar
2 teaspoons vanilla extract
2 cups (250 g) all-purpose flour, sifted
2 cups (250 g) raw pecans, finely chopped
2 cups (200 g) confectioners' sugar, sifted

Preheat the oven to 300°F (150°C, or gas mark 2). Line 3 cookie sheets with parchment paper.

In a bowl, using an electric hand mixer or by hand, cream the butter, granulated sugar, and vanilla for 1 to 2 minutes, or until light and fluffy. Add the flour, and mix until thoroughly combined. Add the nuts and mix for about 30 seconds, or until well blended.

Measure out generously rounded teaspoonfuls of dough and roll them into balls.

Place the balls about 1 inch (2.5 cm) apart on the prepared cookie sheets. Bake for about 30 minutes, or until they just begin to turn golden. To test for doneness, remove one cookie from the sheet and cut it in half. There should be no doughy strip in the center.

Place the confectioners' sugar in a bowl.

Remove the cookies from the oven. Roll the cookies in the sugar while they are still warm, and then cool them on the cookie sheets.

Yield: 3 dozen cookies

SHORTBREAD FINGERS

Because the main flavor in these not-very-sweet cookies comes from nondairy butter, choose wisely. Some nondairy butters are not as yummy as others. Try Earth Balance Coconut Spread in these, but regular Earth Balance and Nucoa both work well, too.

½ cup (110 g) firmly packed brown sugar
1 cup (224 g) nondairy butter
¼ teaspoon salt
2¼ cups (281 g) all-purpose flour, divided

Preheat the oven to 325°F (170°C, or gas mark 3). Line a baking sheet with parchment paper.

In a bowl, using an electric mixer, cream together the sugar and butter. Add the salt and mix to combine. Add 2 cups (250 g) of the flour and mix well. The mixture will be crumbly.

Turn the mixture out onto a floured work surface and knead for about 5 minutes, adding the remaining ¼ cup (31 g) flour as needed to make a soft dough.

Roll out into a rectangle 5 x 12 inches (12.5 x 30 cm). Cut into twelve 1 x 5-inch (2.5 x 12.5 cm) fingers. Using a fork, prick the tops.

Arrange the fingers on the prepared baking sheet, spacing them 1 inch (2.5 cm) apart.

Bake for 20 to 25 minutes, or until golden. Allow to cool completely before removing from the baking sheet.

Yield: 12 fingers

OATMEAL RAISIN COOKIES

The addition of the nutmeg makes these classics extra-special. Baked just right, they are moist and crispy at the same time and will fill your kitchen with a homey aroma. Rolled oats work best in these cookies, but you can use quick-cooking oats if that's what you have on hand. The cookies will just be a little less chewy.

2 tablespoons (30 g) ground flaxseed (equivalent
    of 2 eggs)
6 tablespoons (90 ml) water
1 cup (225 g) nondairy, non-hydrogenated butter,
    softened
1½ cups (340 g) firmly packed brown sugar
¼ cup (50 g) granulated sugar
2 teaspoons vanilla extract
1¾ cups (220 g) all-purpose flour
½ cup (50 g) oat bran
¾ teaspoon baking soda
¾ teaspoon baking powder
½ teaspoon salt
½ teaspoon ground cinnamon
½ teaspoon ground nutmeg
3 cups (240 g) rolled oats
1 cup (145 g) raisins

Preheat the oven to 350°F (180°C, or gas mark 4). Lightly oil 3 cookie sheets or line them with parchment paper.

In a blender, whip the flaxseed and water until thick and creamy. The consistency will be somewhat gelatinous.

In a bowl, by hand or using an electric hand mixer, cream together the butter, sugars, vanilla, and flaxseed mixture until well blended.

In a separate bowl, thoroughly combine the flour, oat bran, baking soda, baking powder, salt, cinnamon, and nutmeg. Add to the butter mixture and mix until well blended and smooth. Stir in the oats and raisins until thoroughly combined.

Using a tablespoon, scoop up some dough and, with lightly greased hands, lightly press the cookies to form ½-inch-thick (1.3-cm) rounds. Bake for 12 to 15 minutes, or until the cookies are golden brown.

Remove from the oven and allow the cookies to firm up for a few minutes on the baking sheet. Transfer the cookies to a wire rack to cool.

Yield: 3½ dozen cookies

GAZELLE HORNS

The intoxicating flavor of almond dominates these filled cookies. Use plastic wrap to help roll the dough as thin as possible without tearing and cut off any excess dough from the tips once they have been rolled up or else you'll have an uneven dough-to-filling ratio. You're not going to want to miss out on this cookie's almondy ambrosia, so don't let the dough become too thick.

1 cup (160 g) superfine brown rice flour, plus 1 to 2 additional tablespoons (10 to 20 g) for kneading
¼ cup (39 g) sweet white rice flour
½ cup (65 g) sorghum flour
½ cup (85 g) potato starch
2 teaspoons xanthan gum
¼ cup (50 g) sugar
7 tablespoons (98 g) vegan margarine
½ cup (120 ml) ice-cold water
4 ounces (115 g) almond paste (Make sure it's gluten free, such as Solo brand.)
⅓ cup (48 g) white sesame seeds

Preheat the oven to 400°F (200°C, gas mark 6).

In a large bowl, whisk together the flours, starch, xanthan, and sugar until well combined. Using a pastry blender, cut in the margarine until it's evenly mixed into the dry ingredients. Form a well in the center of the flours.

Using a fork, stir in the water until a tacky dough is formed. Sprinkle the dough lightly with an additional 1 to 2 tablespoons (10 to 20 g) superfine brown rice flour. Knead until soft and pliable.

Chill the dough briefly in the fridge.

Between 2 sheets of plastic wrap, roll out the dough quite thin. Cut out a 4-inch (10 cm) square and place a small rounded cylinder of almond paste in the middle. Roll the dough up around the almond paste like a cigar and gently coax the dough into a half-moon shape around the filling. (This takes a bit of practice to get perfect, so don't worry if yours look a little ragged around the edges the first time. They will still taste good!)

Using your fingertips, seal the dough.

In a small bowl, place the seeds. Press the tops of the rolled cookies into the seeds.

Place the cookies on an ungreased cookie sheet, about 1 inch (2.5 cm) apart. Bake for 25 minutes, or until the cookies are golden around the edges. Let cool completely.

Yield: 12 cookies

ALMOND CRESCENTS

A simple almond-flavored, crescent-shaped shortbread cookie dusted with powdered sugar makes for an especially pleasing treat during the finger food–friendly holiday season. But these cookies taste so great, and the recipe is so straightforward, that you will probably make them all year long!

½ cup (60 g) almond meal
1¼ cups (150 g) whole wheat pastry flour
3 tablespoons (36 g) evaporated cane juice
¼ teaspoon salt
¼ cup (60 ml) light agave nectar or maple syrup
¼ cup (56 g) solid coconut oil, melted
1 teaspoon almond extract
½ teaspoon vanilla extract
3 tablespoons (23 g) confectioners' sugar

Preheat the oven to 325°F (170°C, or gas mark 3). Line a baking sheet with parchment paper.

In a food processor, pulse the almond meal, flour, cane juice, and salt. Add the agave nectar, oil, and extracts, pulsing to combine until a dough forms.

Place the dough on the prepared baking sheet. Knead it a couple of times. Using 1 packed tablespoon (20 g) of dough per cookie, form a log, then a small crescent shape, flattening it slightly so that the cookie bakes evenly. You can slightly wet your fingers with water to help make the shaping easier. Leave about 1 inch (2.5 cm) of space between the cookies.

Bake for 18 minutes, or until the cookies are golden brown around the edges and on the bottom. (Your nose will tell you when they're just about ready to come out of the oven, so pay close attention.)

Carefully transfer the cookies to a wire rack to cool completely. Sift confectioners' sugar over the cooled cookies.

Store leftovers in an airtight container at room temperature for up to 2 days.

Yield: 17 cookies

SOULHAUS COOKIES

These chewy chocolate chippers are a delicious excuse to heat up your oven, and they will inevitably have a warming effect on your soul. Inspired by the classic Nestlé Tollhouse Cookie, these cookies alone make gluten-free vegan baking so very worth the extra flours required.

1 cup (225 g) nondairy margarine
¾ cup (170 g) packed brown sugar
¾ cup (150 g) granulated sugar
1 teaspoon salt
1 teaspoon baking soda
2 teaspoons vanilla extract

2 tablespoons (21 g) flaxseed meal mixed with ¼ cup
  (60 ml) warm water
1½ cups (195 g) sorghum flour
1 cup (158 g) brown rice flour
½ cup (65 g) tapioca starch
1 teaspoon xanthan gum
1 cup (175 g) nondairy chocolate chips

Preheat the oven to 375°F (190°C, or gas mark 5).
    In a bowl, using an electric mixer, cream together the margarine, sugars, salt, baking soda, and vanilla. Stir in the prepared flaxseed meal.
    In a separate, smaller bowl, combine the sorghum flour, brown rice flour, starch, and xanthan.
    On low speed, gradually add the flour mixture to the sugar mixture until well combined. At first, your dough will be crumbly. Keep mixing (you may need to increase your speed a touch) until a soft cookie dough forms. Fold in the chocolate.
    Chill the dough briefly in the freezer until cold.
    Scoop about 1 tablespoon (15 g) of dough onto an ungreased baking sheet, leaving about 2 inches (2.5 cm) between each cookie. Chill extra dough in the fridge while waiting to bake.
    Bake for 11 minutes and immediately remove them from the oven. The cookies will not look done at this point, but they are.
    Cool completely on the baking sheet for up to 1 hour, or until the chocolate chips have returned to a firm state. (If you try to move them too soon, they will most definitely fall apart, so let them cool!)

Yield: 24 cookies

PEANUT BUTTER COOKIES
Naturally flourless, these cookies pack in a whole lotta peanutty flavor, and they have a soft texture to boot! Be sure to let them cool completely before trying to pick them up, or they'll most definitely crumble.

2 cups (500 g) smooth natural peanut butter
1¾ cups (350 g) sugar, plus extra for sprinkling
1 teaspoon salt
2 teaspoons baking soda
2 teaspoons vanilla extract
2 tablespoons (15 g) flaxseed meal mixed with ¼ cup
  (60 ml) warm water

Preheat the oven to 350°F (180°C, or gas mark 4).
    In a bowl, mix together the peanut butter, 1¾ cups (350 g) of the sugar, the salt, baking soda, and vanilla. Mix in the prepared flaxseed meal. Roll into 1-inch (2.5 cm) balls, place 2 inches (5 cm) apart on 2 ungreased baking sheets. Sprinkle the tops with the extra sugar.
    Using a fork, flatten the cookies slightly to form a crisscross pattern.
    Bake for 9 minutes, or until slightly golden brown on the edges. Let cool completely before removing from the baking sheets.

Yield: 20 cookies

PEANUT BUTTER AND JELLY COOKIES
These cookies are perfect for a children's party, a treat to send with your kids to school, or for those of us who still love this classic combination.

⅓ cup (75 g) nondairy, non-hydrogenated butter
½ cup (115 g) packed light brown sugar
½ cup (130 g) natural peanut butter (creamy or chunky)
2 tablespoons (30 ml) nondairy milk plus extra, if necessary (soy, rice, almond, hazelnut, hemp, or oat)
1 teaspoon (5 ml) vanilla extract
1¼ cups (160 g) all-purpose flour (or whole-wheat pastry
  flour)
¾ teaspoon baking powder
2 to 3 tablespoons (40 to 60 g) strawberry (or any flavor
  you prefer) preserves or jam

Preheat the oven to 375°F (190°C, or gas mark 5). Line a baking sheet with parchment paper.
    In a large bowl, beat the butter, sugar, peanut butter, milk, and vanilla until creamy.
    In a small bowl, combine the flour and baking powder. Add the dry ingredients to the wet ingredients, and mix until combined.
    Test the batter to make sure you can roll it into balls. If you need extra moisture, add a small amount (1 teaspoon [5 ml]) of nondairy milk.
    Roll the batter into 1-inch (2.5 cm) balls. While holding a ball in one hand, use your other thumb to make a well in the center, flattening the ball but keeping it intact. Patch the ball as needed. (The sides may crack as you press into the center.) Place the flattened balls 2 inches (5 cm) apart on the prepared baking sheet.
    Using a ¼-teaspoon measuring spoon, fill the well in each cookie with the preserves.
    Bake for 10 to 11 minutes. Remove the cookies from the oven, and let cool on the baking sheet for 2 minutes. Cool completely on a wire rack.

Yield: 2 to 2½ dozen cookies

SWEETHEART COOKIES

Because we love these cookies so much, we call them "sweetheart cookies." We think you will agree.

1 cup (225 g) nondairy margarine
1 cup (200 g) sugar
2 tablespoons (14 g) flaxseed meal mixed with ¼ cup (60 ml) warm water
1½ teaspoons vanilla extract
1¼ cups (162 g) sorghum flour
¾ cup (118 g) brown rice flour (Superfine is best, but not required.)
⅔ cup (86 g) potato starch
1 teaspoon xanthan gum
1 teaspoon baking powder
½ teaspoon sea salt

Preheat the oven to 400°F (200°C, or gas mark 6).

In a large bowl using an electric mixer, cream together the margarine and sugar until smooth. Add the prepared flaxseed meal and vanilla. Mix together gently.

In a separate bowl, sift together the sorghum flour, brown rice flour, starch, xanthan, baking powder, and salt. Gradually add the flour mixture to the margarine mixture and stir until all of the flour has been added. Mix vigorously (or on medium speed of an electric mixer) until the dough clumps together.

Drop the dough by rounded tablespoonsful (15 g) onto 2 ungreased cookie sheets about 2 inches (5 cm) apart. You should have 30 cookies.

Bake for 8 to 10 minutes, or until medium golden brown on the bottoms.

Transfer the cookies to a wire rack to cool completely.

Yield: 30 cookies

NO-BAKE THUMBPRINT COOKIES

These cookies are easy to make, great for holidays, and absolutely delicious. Try a variety of different preserves each time you make them.

¾ cup (110 g) pitted dates
Hot water
3 cups (245 g) rolled oats
1½ cups (375 g) creamy almond butter (or peanut butter)
½ cup (40 g) shredded coconut
Zest of 1 orange
Juice of 1 orange
½ teaspoon ground cinnamon
⅛ teaspoon salt
¾ cup (240 g) cherry or apricot fruit preserves

Line a rimmed baking sheet with parchment paper.

In a medium bowl, place the dates. Add hot water to the bowl until it just covers the dates. Set the bowl aside for 10 to 15 minutes to let dates become soft.

Meanwhile, in a food processor, pulse the oats until they are coarsely ground.

Transfer the oats to a large bowl.

In a blender, purée the dates and half of the soaking liquid until smooth. (If the dates aren't blending easily, add more soaking water until it blends easily.)

To the bowl with the oats, add the dates, almond butter, coconut, zest, juice, cinnamon, and salt. Knead the mixture together to make a dough.

Take a small amount of dough and roll it into a ball. Place the ball onto the prepared baking sheet. Continued until you have rolled all of the dough.

Using your thumb, make an indentation in the middle of each dough ball to slightly flatten the dough and leave a well in the middle. Spoon a bit of the fruit preserves into each indentation. Chill the dough in the fridge for at least 1 hour.

Yield: about 2 dozen cookies

BANANA OAT DATE COOKIES

Children and adults alike love this incredibly healthful, delicious, sugar-free cookie that can be put together in no time and nibbled throughout the day.

3 large ripe bananas
1 teaspoon vanilla extract
¼ cup (60 ml) coconut butter or nondairy butter (such as Earth Balance), warmed until smooth
2 cups (160 g) rolled or quick-cooking oats
⅓ cup (23 g) unsweetened shredded coconut
½ teaspoon ground cinnamon
½ teaspoon salt
1 teaspoon baking powder
6 or 7 large dates, chopped (about ¼ cup, or 38 g)

Preheat the oven to 350°F (180°C, or gas mark 4). Line 2 baking sheets with parchment paper.

In a large bowl, mash the bananas until smooth. (Alternatively, you may purée them in a blender.) Add the vanilla, coconut butter, oats, coconut, cinnamon, salt, and baking powder. Using your hands, mix until fully combined. Fold in the dates.

Drop dollops of the dough, each about 2 teaspoons in size, 1 inch (2.5 cm) apart, onto the prepared baking sheets. Press down a bit to flatten them to the desired size. (They won't spread very much, so consider at this point what shape/size you want your finished cookies to be.) Bake for 15 minutes, or until the cookies are golden brown on the bottom.

Yield: 2 dozen cookies

49 Coconut Pudding; 50 Coconut Rice with Peaches and Rum Raisins; 51 Fruit and Nut Rice Pudding; 52 Bambara Peanut Butter Rice Pudding; 53 Pineapple, Mango, Coconut, and Chia Seed Pudding; 54 Chocolate, Coconut, and Chia Pudding; 55 Chocolate Chip Cookies; 56 Mexican Wedding Cookies

57 Shortbread Fingers; 58 Oatmeal Raisin Cookies; 59 Gazelle Horns; 60 Almond Crescents; 61 Soulhaus Cookies; 62 Peanut Butter Cookies; 63 Peanut Butter and Jelly Cookies; 64 Sweetheart Cookies

SWEET COCONUT ORANGE COOKIES

These cookies resemble macaroons, but they also have the lovely addition of almond flavor, which adds a touch of sweetness and a lovely bite to the classic cookie.

2 cups (160 g) sweetened shredded coconut
1 cup (112 g) almond flour
½ cup (115 g) packed dark brown sugar
¼ cup (60 ml) nondairy milk, plus more if needed
1 tablespoon (6 g) orange zest

Preheat the oven to 350°F (180°C, gas mark 4). Line a baking sheet with parchment paper.

In a large bowl, stir together the coconut, flour, sugar, milk, and zest until it comes together into a thick dough. At first it will seem crumbly, but the more you stir, the quicker it comes together. If needed, add a tablespoon (15 ml) or more milk to form the dough, but don't add too much.

Divide the dough into 12 cookies and place them on the prepared baking sheet. Bake for 20 to 25 minutes, or until lightly golden brown on the edges. Let the cookies cool completely.

Yield: 12 cookies

CHOCOLATE CHERRY COOKIES

These cookies look as great as they taste.

1 tablespoon (7 g) ground flaxseed (equivalent of 1 egg)
3 tablespoons (30 ml) water
½ cup (112 g) nondairy butter, softened
1 cup (200 g) sugar
1½ teaspoons vanilla extract
1½ cups (180 g) all-purpose flour
½ cup (60 g) unsweetened cocoa powder
¼ teaspoon baking soda
¼ teaspoon baking powder
¼ teaspoon salt
12 maraschino cherries, with juice
½ cup (88 g) nondairy chocolate chips (semisweet or dark)
¼ cup (60 ml) nondairy milk (such as almond, soy, rice, hazelnut, hemp, or oat)

Preheat the oven to 350°F (180°C, or gas mark 4).

In a food processor, whip the flaxseed and water together for 1 to 2 minutes, or until thick and creamy. (You can do this by hand, but a food processor or blender does a quicker, better job.)

Transfer the "flax egg" to a medium bowl. Add the butter and sugar. Using an electric hand mixer, beat until the mixture is creamy and fluffy. Add the vanilla and mix well.

In a separate bowl, combine the flour, cocoa, baking soda, baking powder, and salt. Add the dry ingredients to the butter and sugar mixture. Using your hands, mix until just combined. (The batter might be too thick for the hand mixer.)

Roll the dough into twenty-four 1-inch (2.5 cm) balls. Place them 2 inches (5 cm) apart on 2 ungreased baking sheets.

Using your thumb, make an indentation in the center of each cookie.

Drain the cherries, reserving the juice. Remove the stems and cut the cherries in half. Place one cherry half into the indentation in each cookie.

In a small saucepan, heat the chocolate and milk over low heat, stirring, until the chocolate is melted. Stir in 4 teaspoons (20 ml) of the cherry juice. Spoon ½ to 1 teaspoon of the chocolate mixture over the top of each cherry, covering it completely.

Bake for 10 minutes, or until the cookies are firm to the touch and golden brown on the bottom. Transfer to a wire rack to cool.

Yield: 2 dozen cookies

COOL LEMON COOKIES

These are reminiscent of the lemon coolers of years past. Sweet and tart and cool, these delicious little cookies are so yummy, you won't mind the sugary mess on your fingers!

FOR THE COOKIES:
½ cup (60 g) confectioners' sugar
½ cup (100 g) granulated sugar
⅓ cup (64 g) vegetable shortening
6 ounces (170 g) nondairy yogurt
1 teaspoon vanilla extract
1 teaspoon lemon extract
¼ teaspoon salt
2½ cups (313 g) all-purpose flour
1½ teaspoons baking powder
1 teaspoon baking soda

FOR THE COATING:
1 cup (120 g) confectioners' sugar
1 envelope (¼ ounce, or 7 g) unsweetened lemonade drink mix powder, such as Kool-Aid

Preheat the oven to 325°F (170°C, or gas mark 3). Line 2 baking sheets with parchment paper.

To make the cookies: In a large bowl, combine the confectioners' sugar, granulated sugar, shortening, yogurt, vanilla, lemon, and salt. Using an electric mixer, beat until creamy.

In a separate bowl, sift together the flour, baking powder, and baking soda. Slowly add to the sugar mixture and beat until smooth.

Drop spoonsful of about 1 ounce (28 g) of the dough

onto the prepared baking sheets. Place 15 cookies evenly spaced on each baking sheet. Bake for 18 to 20 minutes, or until lightly browned.

To make the coating: Meanwhile, in a resealable plastic bag, place the sugar and drink mix. Shake to combine.

Remove the cookies from the oven. Let them cool on the baking sheets for about 5 minutes.

Place the cookies, about 4 or 5 at a time, in the bag. Shake to coat.

Yield: 30 cookies

LEMON BARS

Think lemon meringue pie without the meringue! Who needs whipped egg whites anyway, when you can experience the sweet/tart lemon filling in a buttery shortbread crust?

FOR THE CRUST:
½ cup (112 g) non-hydrogenated, nondairy butter, at room temperature
¼ cup (25 g) confectioners' sugar
1 cup (125 g) all-purpose flour

FOR THE FILLING:
½ cup (112 g) silken tofu (soft or firm)
1 cup (200 g) granulated sugar
Zest of 2 lemons
⅓ cup (90 ml) lemon juice
2 tablespoons (8 g) all-purpose flour
1 tablespoon (8 g) cornstarch
Confectioners' sugar, sifted

Preheat the oven to 350°F (180°C, or gas mark 4). Grease an 8 × 8-inch (20 × 20-cm) baking pan with nonstick cooking spray and sprinkle with a light dusting of all-purpose flour.

To make the crust: In a bowl, using an electric mixer, cream the butter and sugar until light and fluffy. Add the flour. Beat until the dough just comes together.

Press the dough into the bottom of the prepared pan. Bake for about 20 minutes, or until lightly browned. Remove from the oven and cool on a wire rack.

To make the filling: Meanwhile, in a food processor, blend the tofu for about 1 minute, or until creamy. Add the granulated sugar and blend until smooth. Add the zest, juice, flour, and cornstarch.

Pour the filling over the baked shortbread crust. Bake for about 20 minutes, or until the filling is set. Remove from the oven and cool on a wire rack.

Cut the bars into squares. Just before serving, dust with the sifted confectioners' sugar. (Wait until you're just about

to serve the bars before you sprinkle them with the confectioners' sugar. Otherwise, it will soak into the bars and you'll miss out on that pretty presentation.)

The bars can be covered and stored in the refrigerator for up to 2 days.

Yield: 16 squares

LEMON-FENNEL SCONE BITES

These flaky, savory bites are so perfect when enjoyed straight from the oven that we feel they don't need anything to accompany them. But if you really must, they will pair beautifully with any of our small plate vegetable recipes or with trays of vegan cheeses.

1½ cups (180 g) whole wheat pastry flour
2 teaspoons baking powder
Generous ½ teaspoon salt
2 tablespoons (24 g) Sucanat
½ cup (128 g) tahini or other nut or seed butter
¼ cup (60 ml) lemon juice
Zest of 1 lemon
2 small cloves garlic, minced
2 teaspoons fennel seeds
¼ cup (60 ml) plain unsweetened vegan milk, plus more if needed

Preheat the oven to 400°F (200°C, or gas mark 6). Line a baking sheet with parchment paper.

In a food processor, combine the flour, baking powder, salt, and Sucanat. Add the tahini. Pulse a few times to combine. Add the juice, zest, garlic, and fennel seeds. Pulse a few times. Add the milk through the hole in the lid, 1 tablespoon (15 ml) at a time, while pulsing until a dough ball forms. The dough should be moist, but not too wet to handle. If it crumbles, pulse in a little more milk 1 teaspoon at a time.

Place the dough on another piece of parchment paper. Using your hands, pat it down to a little over ½-inch (1.3 cm) thickness. Avoid using a rolling pin, which would make for tough scones.

Using a 2-inch (5 cm) biscuit cutter, cut the dough into scones. Place them on the prepared baking sheet. Gather the scraps of dough and repeat the process to make approximately 16 scones and use all of the dough.

Bake for 12 to 14 minutes, or until golden brown around the edges on the bottom and light golden on top. Remove from the oven and let cool on a wire rack.

Store leftovers in an airtight container for up to 2 days. Toast leftovers slightly.

Yield: 16 small scones

MINI SAVORY SCONES

Although these scones may be on the smaller side, they sure pack a serious flavor punch! You might enjoy munching on them with a bowl of extra Cashew Almond Spread (see page 46—fig and nut canapés) on the side, sprinkled with a little extra salt.

2 cups (240 g) whole wheat pastry flour
1 tablespoon (12 g) baking powder
¾ teaspoon salt
2 teaspoons mild to medium chili powder
2 teaspoons onion powder
3 large cloves garlic, minced
2 tablespoons (8 g) soft sun-dried tomato halves (not oil-packed)
½ cup (130 g) Cashew Almond Spread (see page 46—fig and nut canapes)
2 tablespoons (30 ml) neutral-flavored oil
3 tablespoons (45 ml) unsweetened plain vegan milk, plus more if needed

Preheat the oven to 375°F (190°C, or gas mark 5). Line 2 baking sheets with parchment paper.

In a food processor, pulse the flour, baking powder, salt, chili powder, onion powder, garlic, and sun-dried tomatoes to mince the tomatoes and combine. Add the Cashew Almond Spread and oil and pulse to combine. Using a rubber spatula, scrape down the sides if needed. Add the milk and pulse to combine. The dough crumbs should hold together well when pinched. If the mixture is crumbly, add extra milk 1 teaspoon at a time, pulsing to combine.

Pack 1 tablespoon (20 g) with dough crumbs to make one scone. Place on the prepared sheets, and flatten just slightly. Repeat with the remaining dough to make about 27 scones.

Bake for 14 minutes, or until golden brown on the bottom. Transfer to a wire rack to cool.

Store leftovers in an airtight container for up to 2 days.

Yield: 27 mini scones

LEMON BISCOTTI

This biscotti has a light lemony flavor, making it the perfect accompaniment to a hot mug of tea. These biscotti are somewhat softer than those found at your local coffeehouse. If you'd like an extra-crunchy cookie, bake them for 1 or 2 minutes longer than recommended on each side. These are best served a few hours after cooling.

1 cup (200 g) sugar
½ cup (120 ml) olive oil
3 tablespoons (45 ml) lemon juice
1 teaspoon vanilla extract
1 teaspoon lemon zest
3 tablespoons (45 ml) nondairy milk

3 tablespoons (21 g) flaxseed meal mixed with 6 tablespoons (90 ml) warm water
1½ cups (195 g) sorghum flour
¾ cup (96 g) brown rice flour
¾ cup (96 g) potato starch
¼ cup (32 g) tapioca starch
1 teaspoon xanthan gum
1 teaspoon salt
1 tablespoon (15 g) baking powder

Preheat the oven to 375°F (190°C, or gas mark 5). Line 2 baking sheets with parchment paper.

In a large bowl, stir together the sugar, oil, juice, vanilla, zest, milk, and flaxseed mixture.

In a separate bowl, sift together the sorghum flour, brown rice flour, potato starch, tapioca starch, xanthan, salt, and baking powder. Gradually add the flour mixture to the sugar mixture and combine until a stiff dough forms. If mixing by hand, you'll have to knead it a bit to get it smooth. The dough will be slightly tacky when handling.

Divide the dough in half. On the prepared baking sheets, using slightly wet hands, shape the dough into 2 long ovals, each about 3½ inches (9 cm)-wide, 9 inches (23 cm)-long, and ¾ inch (2 cm) tall. Bake for 25 minutes. Remove from the oven and let cool for at least 20 minutes.

Once cooled, slice across the dough diagonally, cutting each log into approximately twelve ¾-inch-wide x 4½-inch-long (2 x 11.5 cm) cookies, varying slightly in length. Place each cookie on its side on the baking sheets. Bake for an additional 9 minutes. Flip and bake the other side for 9 to 11 minutes, or until golden brown on the edges. Let cool completely before serving.

Yield: 24 biscotti

BUTTERSCOTCH AMARETTI

The delicate flavors of almond and brown sugar come together to make a slightly chewy and crispy cookie that's very hard to resist. Use almond meal made from blanched almonds, such as Bob's Red Mill brand, with no skins in the ground mix, so you achieve a more uniform color.

3 tablespoons (21 g) flaxseed meal
6 tablespoons (90 ml) water
3 cups (300 g) almond meal
½ teaspoon salt
1 cup (200 g) granulated sugar
½ cup (115 g) packed light brown sugar

Preheat the oven to 300°F (150°C, or gas mark 2). Line 2 or 3 baking sheets with parchment paper.

In a medium bowl, mix together the flaxseed meal and water. Let rest for about 5 minutes, or until goopy.

In a large bowl, stir together the almond meal, salt, granulated sugar, and brown sugar until well combined.

Slowly add the flaxseed mixture to the almond meal mixture. Using an electric mixer, beat vigorously until a slightly sticky dough forms. (You can do this by hand, but it takes a bit of elbow grease to bring the dough together.) The dough will be crumbly at first, but eventually it will come together into a clumpy dough.

Drop the dough by slightly rounded tablespoonfuls (15 g) onto the prepared baking sheets to make 36 cookies. Bake for 30 minutes, or until lightly golden brown around the edges.

Let cool on the baking sheets for a few minutes. Transfer to wire racks to cool completely.

Yield: 36 cookies

RED WINE HOT FUDGE SAUCE
Hot fudge sauce for grown-ups! Hooray!

FOR THE SAUCE:
4 cups (700 g) vegan semisweet chocolate chips
2 cups (470 ml) Cabernet Sauvignon (or your favorite wed wine)
2 cups (400 g) sugar
¼ cup (56 g) nondairy butter
½ cup (64 g) cornstarch mixed with ¼ cup (60 ml) soy milk
2 tablespoons (30 ml) vanilla extract
4 teaspoons (20 ml) almond extract

FOR CANNING:
6 (8-ounce, or 235 ml) jars
6 rings and lids
Other "Canning Materials Needed" (See page 8.)

In a saucepan, bring the chocolate, wine, sugar, and butter to a boil over medium heat. Boil for 3 minutes, stirring constantly. Add the cornstarch mixture. Stir until thickened.

Remove from the heat and continue to stir. Add the vanilla and almond. Stir until shiny and smooth.

Follow the canning instructions as outlined in "Canning Basics" on page 8. The processing time is 15 minutes. Any jars that didn't seal need to be stored in the refrigerator and used within 1 week. Refrigerate after opening.

Yield: 6 (8-ounce, or 235 ml) jars

CHOCOLATE HAZELNUT SPREAD
Inspired by Nutella, this vegan version leaves out the cow's milk and focuses on the delicious combination of roasted hazelnuts and rich chocolate with a hint of sweetness.

2 cups (300 g) whole roasted hazelnuts, skinned
¼ cup (50 g) superfine granulated sugar

¼ cup (20 g) cocoa powder
¼ teaspoon salt
¼ cup (60 ml) nondairy milk, plus more if needed

In a food processor, blend the hazelnuts, sugar, cocoa powder, and salt until crumbly.

Slowly add the milk, about 1 tablespoon (15 ml) at a time, and blend until smooth. (Depending on how dry the hazelnuts are, you might need to add more or less milk.) Blend for about 5 minutes, or until very smooth.

Transfer the mixture to a sealed jar. Store in the fridge for up to 2 weeks.

Yield: 20 servings, about 1 tablespoon (15 g) each

CHOCOLATE SALTED CARAMELS
A candy thermometer is extra helpful when making these fun, yet sophisticated, candies.

2 cups (470 ml) canned coconut milk
½ cup (90 g) semisweet chocolate
2 cups (400 g) sugar
1 cup (235 ml) light corn syrup
½ cup (112 g) nondairy margarine
1 tablespoon (15 ml) vanilla extract
Flaky sea salt, for topping

Line a 9 x 9-inch (23 x 23 cm) baking pan with parchment paper.

In a 2-quart (1.8 L) saucepan, bring the milk to a boil over medium heat. Stir in the chocolate until melted. Add the sugar and corn syrup and cook, stirring constantly, until the sugar is completely dissolved. Add the margarine and stir until the mixture comes to a boil.

Once the mixture boils, stop stirring! Let it boil over medium heat for about 35 minutes, without stirring, until it reaches 240°F (116°C) on a candy thermometer. If you don't have a candy thermometer, dip the tip of a wooden spoon into the top of the bubbly mixture. When the syrup sticks to the spoon, it's almost done.

When the candy comes to temperature, take a teaspoon of the syrup and quickly drop it into a cold glass of water; if it's ready, you'll be left with what looks like a caramel. This is referred to as the "firmball" stage. It's ready when the ball is firm enough to allow you to remove it from the glass with your fingers and will flatten if you give it a little squeeze.

When the mixture is at the right temperature, stir in the vanilla.

Pour the mixture into the prepared pan. Let cool at room temperature for a few minutes.

Transfer to the fridge for about 1 hour.

Once firm, cut the caramels into 40 pieces. Sprinkle with the sea salt. Wrap in waxed paper and store in the fridge.

Yield: 40 caramels

ALMOND BUTTER CUPS

This recipe is slightly time-consuming, but that mostly lies in painting the cups with the melted chocolate. After that, it's smooth sailing. If you're a die-hard chocolate and almond fan, these little treats are well worth the effort. Serve these chilled.

1 bag (12 ounces, or 340 g) nondairy chocolate chips, divided
1 cup (250 g) smooth or crunchy unsalted almond butter
1 teaspoon vanilla extract
2 tablespoons (15 g) confectioners' sugar
Dash or two of salt
2 tablespoons (30 ml) almond milk

Line 16 mini muffin cups with mini muffin liners.

In a double boiler, melt half of the chocolate over medium-low heat until smooth.

Drop about 1 teaspoon of chocolate into each mini muffin cup. Using the back of a spoon, smoosh the chocolate to coat the liners. Aim for making the chocolate about ⅛-inch (3 mm) thick.

Chill the chocolate-coated liners in the freezer for about 10 minutes, or until solid.

Meanwhile, in a small bowl, mix together the almond butter, vanilla, sugar, salt, and milk until smooth.

Once the chocolate shells are chilled, divide the almond butter mixture evenly among all 16 cups. Chill again in the freezer.

Meanwhile, in a double boiler, melt the remaining half of the chocolate over medium-low heat until smooth. Top the filled cups with a smooth layer of chocolate. Use the back of a spoon to spread the chocolate out to the edges of the paper liners.

Chill again in the freezer for 5 to 10 minutes, or until firm. Store the cups in the fridge or freezer in an airtight container.

Yield: 16 candies

MOCK TURTLES

This is a healthier version of "turtle" chocolates, with a very easy caramel made from Medjool dates.

20 Medjool dates, pitted
3 tablespoons (45 g) nondairy margarine
1 vanilla bean pod, split lengthwise and seeds scraped
40 whole pecan pieces
4 cups (700 g) nondairy chocolate chips
1 teaspoon coconut oil

Line a baking sheet with waxed paper.

In a food processor, pulse the dates, margarine, and scraped vanilla seeds until uniformly sticky. Scoop out 1 to 2 teaspoons of the mixture, shape into a patty, and place 2 or

3 pecans on top. Flip over so that the pecans are on the bottom. Place on the prepared baking sheet. Repeat with the remaining date mixture and pecans to form 20 candies.

In a double boiler, melt the chocolate over medium-low heat. Stir in the oil. Dip bottoms of the candies into the chocolate to coat evenly and return to the baking sheet. Drizzle the tops with the remaining melted chocolate.

Chill in the fridge for at least 2 hours, or until firm. Store in the fridge to prevent melting.

Yield: 20 candies

ORANGE CHOCOLATE LINZERS

Specialty linzer cookie cutters are widely available at baking supply shops and online. If you don't have one (or don't want one) you can simply use graduated round cookie cutters, 2 inches (5 cm) for the outer circle and 1 inch (2.5 cm) for the inner circle.

FOR THE COOKIES:
1⅔ cups (280 g) all-purpose flour
¼ teaspoon baking powder
¼ teaspoon salt
¾ cup (150 g) evaporated cane juice (or granulated sugar)
½ cup (112 g) nondairy butter
¼ cup (60 ml) orange juice
1 teaspoon vanilla extract
1 teaspoon orange extract
Confectioners' sugar, for sprinkling

FOR THE GANACHE FILLING:
½ cup (120 ml) nondairy cream (full-fat coconut milk, MimicCreme, or soy or coconut creamer)
1 cup (176 g) vegan chocolate chips
1 tablespoon (15 ml) orange extract

To make the cookies: In a small bowl, sift together the flour, baking powder, and salt.

In a large bowl, beat together the evaporated cane juice, butter, orange juice, vanilla, and orange extract until well combined. The butter will separate; that is normal. Slowly add in the flour mixture and beat until well combined.

Turn out the dough onto a floured surface. Knead into a soft, smooth dough. Shape into a ball, wrap in plastic, and chill in the fridge for at least 2 hours, or until ready to bake.

Preheat the oven to 375°F (190°C, or gas mark 5). Line several baking sheets with parchment paper.

Remove the dough from the refrigerator. Divide the dough in half, so it is easier to work with. On a well-floured surface, roll out the dough until it is about ⅛ inch (3 mm) thick. Use a linzer cookie cutter or two circular cutters to cut 36 tops and 36 bottoms. Gather up the scraps and reroll the dough as needed.

Place the cookies on the prepared baking sheets. Bake for 8 to 10 minutes, or until golden on the bottom and browned on the edges.

Remove the cookies from the oven and transfer to a cooling rack to cool completely. Sprinkle the confectioners' sugar all over the tops.

To make the filling: Meanwhile, in a small saucepot, heat the cream until it just begins to boil. Remove from the heat and stir in the chocolate and orange until completely melted, combined, and smooth.

When the cookies are cool, spread about 1 teaspoon of ganache onto a cookie bottom and place a cookie top on top. Return to the rack and allow the ganache to cool and stiffen completely.

Yield: 36 sandwich cookies

PEANUT BUTTER BALLS

Who doesn't love peanut butter and chocolate? These balls take a little more time to make, but the result is a delicious one.

1 cup (256 g) creamy peanut butter
1 cup (120 g) confectioners' sugar
12 ounces (340 g) vegan chocolate chips
16 toothpicks

Line a baking sheet with waxed paper.

In a bowl, knead together the peanut butter and sugar until a smooth dough is formed with the consistency of playdough. Depending on the moisture content of the peanut butter, you might need a little more or a little less sugar.

Using about 1 tablespoon (21 g) of dough at a time, form it into 16 balls. Place the balls on the prepared baking sheet.

Stick a toothpick into each ball. Chill the balls in the freezer to harden. (This step makes it easier to dip them into the chocolate.)

Meanwhile, in a double boiler, melt the chocolate. Dip each ball into the chocolate to coat, and return it to the baking sheet.

Carefully remove the toothpicks. Using the flat side of a butter knife, carefully smooth over the hole where the toothpick was removed, adding a swirl design if desired. Let cool and harden.

Yield: 16 balls

SALTINE BUTTER TOFFEE

There's just no way that anyone would ever suspect the vegan-ocity here. They are too buttery and delicious. Feel free to experiment and play with different toppings, such as sprinkles, crushed candy canes, or even coarse sea salt.

35 to 40 saltine crackers
1 cup (224 g) nondairy butter
1 cup (200 g) evaporated cane juice (or granulated sugar)
2 cups (352 g) vegan chocolate chips
1 cup (120 g) chopped nuts (Any nut will do!)

Preheat the oven to 350°F (180°C, or gas mark 4). Line a rimmed baking sheet with foil and spray lightly with nonstick cooking spray.

Place the crackers on the prepared baking sheet in a single layer.

In a saucepan, melt the butter and evaporated cane juice over medium heat, until completely dissolved. Pour the mixture evenly over the crackers.

Bake for 10 to 12 minutes, or until golden.

Carefully remove from the oven. Place on a flat surface, and immediately sprinkle the chocolate evenly all over the crackers. Using a spreader or butter knife, spread the chocolate evenly over the crackers as it melts. Sprinkle with the nuts.

Allow to cool and harden completely before breaking into pieces.

Yield: 35 to 40 pieces

65 No-Bake Thumbprint Cookies; 66 Banana Oat Date Cookies; 67 Sweet Coconut Orange Cookies; 68 Chocolate Cherry Cookies; 69 Cool Lemon Cookies; 70 Lemon Bars; 71 Lemon-Fennel Scone Bites; 72 Mini Savory Scones

73 Lemon Biscotti; 74 Butterscotch Amaretti; 75 Red Wine Hot Fudge Sauce; 76 Chocolate Hazelnut Spread; 77 Chocolate Salted Caramels; 78 Almond Butter Cups; 79 Mock Turtles; 80 Orange Chocolate Linzers

CHOCOLATE BARK

Let's face it, almost anything tastes fabulous when it's mixed with chocolate. Bark lets you get creative with your mix-ins. Who knows, maybe you will come up with the next crazy food combo!

12 ounces (340 g) vegan chocolate chips
2 ounces (58 g) food-grade paraffin wax, such as Paro-wax, optional
1 tablespoon (15 ml) flavored extract from the list below
2 cups (250 g) crushed mix-ins, divided, such as
- **Crushed pretzels and vanilla extract**
- **Crushed candy canes and peppermint extract**
- **Smoked almonds and liquid smoke**
- **Mixed nuts and almond extract**
- **Chopped-up marshmallows (Don't mix with the chocolate, just arrange on the baking sheet and pour the chocolate over them, then sprinkle extra on top) and vanilla extract**
- **Crushed chocolate cookies (such as Oreos) and vanilla extract**
- **Homemade vegan bacon bits and liquid smoke**
- **Pumpkin seeds and 1 teaspoon chipotle powder**

Line a rimmed baking sheet with parchment paper.

In a double boiler, melt the chocolate and wax, if using, over medium heat, stirring until smooth. (If you don't have a double boiler, place a metal mixing bowl over a pot of water.) Take care not to get water in your melting chocolate.

If you aren't using the wax, stir the extract into the chocolate before melting it. (If you add the extract to melted chocolate, it will cause it to seize.)

If you are using the wax, just before you are ready to pour the chocolate, stir in the extract.

Add half of the mix-ins and stir to combine.

Pour the chocolate evenly onto the prepared baking sheet. Sprinkle the remaining mix-ins evenly all over the top.

Allow to cool and harden completely. Break into pieces.

Yield: 24 ounces (672 g)

VANILLA BEAN ICE CREAM

Creamy, rich, and wholeheartedly decadent, you'd never know this ice cream was made without dairy.

2 cans (13.5 ounces, or 378 ml each) full-fat coconut milk
1½ cups (300 g) sugar
2 vanilla bean pods, split lengthwise and seeds scraped
¾ teaspoon salt

In a saucepan, warm the milk, sugar, scraped vanilla seeds, and vanilla bean pods briefly over medium heat for about 2 minutes, or until the sugar has dissolved, stirring occasionally. Remove the pods from the mixture and add the salt.

Pour the mixture into a bowl.

Chill in the fridge for at least 30 minutes, or until cold.

Process in an ice cream maker according to the manufacturer's instructions. Once it's finished, place in a flexible airtight container and freeze for a few hours, or until firm enough to scoop.

Yield: 8 servings, ½ cup (100 g) each

MANGO RUM ICE CREAM

This delicious tropical ice cream tastes a lot like a piña colada, without the pineapple. Instead, it featuring the tangy sweetness of mango. Because it uses alcohol, this is an adult-only indulgence.

2 large mangoes, peeled and pitted
¼ cup (60 ml) rum, dark or light
½ cup (100 g) sugar
2 cans (13.5 ounces, or 400 ml each) full-fat coconut milk
Dash of salt

In a food processor, blend all of the ingredients together until smooth.

Transfer the mixture to an ice cream maker. Process the mixture according to the manufacturer's instructions. Freeze it in a flexible, airtight container overnight.

Yield: 1 quart (1 L) ice cream

AVOCADO GELATO

The texture of this gelato is great straight from the ice cream maker, but if you prefer a firmer consistency, place it in an airtight flexible plastic container and chill in the freezer for at least 6 hours.

1 can (13.5 ounces, or 378 ml) full-fat coconut milk
1¼ cups (250 g) sugar
3 ripe avocados, peeled, halved, and pitted
1 teaspoon vanilla extract
1½ tablespoons (23 ml) lemon juice
½ teaspoon salt

In a small pan, heat the milk and sugar over medium heat just until the sugar has fully dissolved.

Remove from the heat.

Pour the mixture into a bowl. Chill in the fridge for about 25 minutes, or until cold

In a food processor, blend the avocados, milk mixture, vanilla, lemon juice, and salt until smooth.

Pour the mixture into an ice cream maker. Process according to the manufacturer's instructions.

Yield: 14 servings, ½ cup (120 g) each

WATERMELON GRANITA

Next to eating fresh watermelon, this might become favorite way of enjoying this juicy summer fruit. It's pretty, it's easy, and it contains lots of beta-carotene and lycopene.

⅓ cup (132 g) sugar
⅓ cup (80 ml) water
4 cups (560 g) seedless watermelon chunks, reserving
     the wedges for garnish
Juice of 1 lime
Mint leaves, for garnish

In a saucepan over high heat, make a simple syrup by heating the sugar and water over high heat, stirring until all of the sugar has dissolved. Let cool.

In a blender, purée the cooled sugar syrup, watermelon chunks, and juice until smooth.

Pour into a shallow, wide pan. Freeze for 1 hour.

Using a fork, rake the mixture. Freeze for another hour.

Using a fork, rake the mixture again. Freeze for 1 more hour. (The whole process takes about 3 hours.)

Rake before serving. Store in an airtight container in the freezer for up to 2 days.

Garnish with the watermelon wedges and mint leaves.

Yield: 4 servings

FUDGY GOOD FROZEN TREATS

The only problem you'll have with these treats is keeping them from being eaten too quickly! Because they don't last very long, you may want to double or triple this recipe.

12 pitted dates
Hot water
2 tablespoons (32 g) peanut butter
2 tablespoons (10 g) unsweetened cocoa powder
1 package (340 g) firm, silken tofu
2 teaspoons vanilla extract, optional
¼ cup (60 ml) unsweetened almond milk, optional

In blender, soak the dates in enough hot water to cover for 10 to 15 minutes, or until softened.

When the dates have softened, add the peanut butter, cocoa, tofu, and vanilla. Blend until smooth and creamy. If there isn't enough liquid to blend, add the milk 1 tablespoon (15 ml) at a time, adding just enough to get the mixture to blend. (If you use too much milk alternative, the treats will be icy and not creamy when frozen.)

Pour the mixture into Popsicle molds and freeze.

Yield: 3 to 4 large or 6 small Popsicles

GINGER-MANGO ICE LOLLIES

These treats are like frozen sunshine.

½ cup (120 ml) water
¼ cup (48 g) evaporated cane juice
¼ cup (48 g) Sucanat
3 to 4 tablespoons (18 to 24 g) peeled, sliced fresh ginger, or 1 to 1½ teaspoons ground ginger, to taste
1 pound (454 g) fresh or frozen mango chunks (thawed if frozen)
½ cup (120 ml) orange juice
12 wooden ice lolly sticks

In a medium, heavy-bottomed saucepan, bring the water, evaporated cane juice, and Sucanat to a boil over medium-high heat. Lower the heat. Cook for about 2 minutes, or until the sugar crystals are dissolved, stirring occasionally. Add the ginger.

Remove from the heat. Steep the mixture for at least 30 minutes.

Pour the syrup through a fine-mesh sieve, directly into a blender. Discard the ginger slices. (If using ground ginger instead of fresh, add it alongside the sugars and water to boil; there's no steeping time needed.) Let cool.

Add the mango and juice to the blender. Blend until perfectly smooth.

Pour a scant ¼ cup (60 ml) of the mixture into twelve 2 ¼-ounce (67 ml) shot glasses, leaving a little under ¼-inch (6 mm) space from the top to allow for expansion as the mixture freezes. Freeze for approximately 2 hours, or until the preparation is solid enough to hold the lolly stick upright.

Insert the sticks in the center of all lollies. Freeze overnight.

To release the lollies from their molds easily, run tepid water on the outside of the molds for a few seconds.

Store leftovers in an airtight container in the freezer for up to 2 weeks.

Yield: 3 cups (705 ml) mixture, 12 small lollies

SESAME BERRY ICE CREAM SANDWICHES

In this sandwich, a pair of surprisingly caramel-like cookies surrounds a delicately flavored, pink-hued frozen concoction that will put all the other ice cream sandwiches you've ever had to shame.

FOR THE ICE CREAM:
1 cup (235 ml) full-fat coconut milk
8 ounces (227 g) drained firm silken tofu
¾ cup (252 g) agave nectar
1 heaping cup (250 g) frozen raspberries, thawed
1 tablespoon (15 ml) rose water
1 teaspoon vanilla extract

FOR THE COOKIES:
¾ cup (192 g) tahini
⅓ cup (105 g) agave nectar
½ cup (110 g) packed light brown sugar
2 teaspoons vanilla extract
1 cup (125 g) all-purpose flour
3 tablespoons (24 g) sesame seeds
¼ teaspoon baking powder
½ teaspoon salt
Unsweetened plain nondairy milk, as needed

To make the ice cream: Freeze the tub of an ice cream maker for at least 24 hours.

In a blender, blend all of the ice cream ingredients until perfectly smooth.

Transfer the mixture to the frozen tub. Following the manufacturer's instructions, prepare the ice cream until it is firm. Place in the freezer until ready to use to firm up even more.

To make the cookies: Preheat the oven to 325°F (170°C, or gas mark 3). Line two baking sheets with parchment paper.

In a large bowl, combine the tahini, agave, sugar, and vanilla.

In a separate bowl, combine the flour, sesame seeds, baking powder, and salt. Add on top of the wet ingredients, and stir until combined. The texture of the dough will vary depending on the thickness of the tahini. If it's too dry, add just enough milk for the dough to be manageable and not crumbly.

Scoop out 2 tablespoons (50 g) dough per cookie, place it on the prepared baking sheets, six per sheet, and flatten slightly. (The cookies won't spread too much, but there won't be enough room for all of them on a single sheet.) Repeat to make 12 cookies. Bake for 12 to 14 minutes, or until golden brown. Let cool on the baking sheets for a couple of minutes.

Transfer the cookies to a wire rack to cool completely.

Place the cookies in the freezer for 1 hour before sandwiching with the ice cream.

To assemble the sandwiches: Let the ice cream sit at room temperature for about 15 minutes to soften. Place about 2 tablespoons (30 ml) ice cream between 2 cookies. Squeeze lightly to spread the ice cream to the edges. Wrap tightly in plastic and place the sandwiches on a plate.

Chill in the freezer for 30 minutes, or until the ice cream firms up.

Yield: 6 ice cream sandwiches, 1 quart (935 ml) ice cream

MANGO BUTTER AND GINGER WHOOPIE PIES

These whoopie pies are perfect for autum.

FOR THE MANGO BUTTER:
2 cups (280 g) frozen mango chunks
2 tablespoons (30 ml) water
1 tablespoon (15 ml) lemon juice
¼ cup (55 g) packed light brown sugar

FOR THE COOKIES:
⅓ cup (75 g) nondairy butter, at room temperature
¾ cup (165 g) packed light brown sugar
¾ cup (216 g) Mango Butter
2 tablespoons (16 g) cornstarch
1½ teaspoons ground ginger
½ teaspoon salt
2¼ cups (281 g) all-purpose flour
1 teaspoon baking powder
½ teaspoon baking soda

FOR THE FROSTING:
2 tablespoons (24 g) vegan shortening
2 tablespoons (28 g) nondairy butter
¼ teaspoon ground ginger
1½ cups (180 g) confectioners' sugar, sifted
1 tablespoon (15 ml) nondairy milk
½ teaspoon pure vanilla extract

To make the Mango Butter: In a medium saucepan, combine all of the Mango Butter ingredients. Bring the mixture to a boil. Lower the heat to medium. Cook for 8 minutes, or until the mango is tender enough to mash.

Transfer the mixture to a blender. Blend until perfectly smooth. Let cool completely.

To make the cookies: In a medium bowl, using an electric mixer, beat the butter and sugar until fluffy. Add the Mango Butter, cornstarch, ginger, and salt and beat until combined.

In another bowl, sift and combine the flour, baking powder, and baking soda. Add on top of the wet ingredients, and beat until just combined. The dough should be fluffy, but thick enough to be held in your hand.

Preheat the oven to 350°F (180°C, or gas mark 4). Line two baking sheets with parchment paper.

Scoop out 2 tablespoons (45 g) dough per cookie. Roll it between your hands and flatten slightly. Place 2 inches (5 cm) apart on the cookie sheets. Repeat to make 16 cookies.

Bake for 12 minutes, or until set.

Transfer the cookies to a wire rack to cool.

To make the frosting: In a bowl, using an electric mixer, cream the shortening and butter until smooth. Add the ginger and sugar. Mix on low speed, then beat until combined. Add the milk and vanilla. Mix on low speed until combined, then beat on medium speed for 2 minutes, or until fluffy, occasionally stopping to scrape the sides of the bowl with a rubber spatula.

To assemble the whoopie pies: Spread 1 generous tablespoon (30 g) frosting on the bottom of one cookie and top with another cookie, pressing down gently to spread the frosting.

Yield: 8 whoopie pies

BANANA FOSTER CAKE SANDWICHES
Over-the-top can be a good thing, as this particular treat proudly demonstrates.

FOR THE ICE CREAM:
1 recipe Vanilla Dipping Sauce (See page 28-Plum-tillas)

FOR THE CAKES:
1 heaping cup (240 g) mashed ripe bananas
Scant ⅔ cup (120 g) sugar
⅓ cup (80 ml) light olive oil
1 tablespoon (8 g) arrowroot powder
1 teaspoon vanilla extract
1½ cups (188 g) all-purpose flour
2 teaspoons baking powder
½ teaspoon salt

FOR THE CARAMEL:
2 tablespoons (28 g) nondairy butter
½ cup (110 g) packed brown sugar
Pinch of salt
1 tablespoon (15 ml) dark rum
¼ cup plus 1 tablespoon (75 ml) unsweetened plain nondairy creamer, divided
2 teaspoons cornstarch

To make the ice cream: Freeze the tub of an ice cream maker for at least 24 hours. Place the Vanilla Dipping Sauce in the frozen tub. Following the manufacturer's instructions, prepare the ice cream until it is firm. Place the ice cream in the freezer.

To make the cakes: Preheat the oven to 350°F (180°C, or gas mark 4). Lightly coat two 5¾ x 3-inch (14 x 8-cm) loaf pans with nonstick cooking spray.

In a large bowl, combine the bananas, sugar, oil, arrowroot, and vanilla.

In a separate bowl, sift and combine the flour, baking powder, and salt. Add on top of the wet ingredients, and stir until just combined.

Divide the mixture between the prepared pans. Bake for 35 minutes, or until a wooden pick inserted into the center comes out clean.

Carefully remove the loaves from the pans. Let cool completely on a wire rack.

To make the caramel: In a medium saucepan, cook the butter, sugar, salt, rum, and ¼ cup (60 ml) of the creamer over medium-high heat for about 3 minutes, or until the sugar dissolves.

In a small bowl, combine the remaining 1 tablespoon (15 ml) creamer with the cornstarch, stirring to form a paste. Add the paste to the syrup and cook for about 1 minute, or until slightly thickened. Remove from the heat and keep warm.

To assemble the sandwiches: Let the ice cream sit at room temperature for about 15 minutes to soften. Cut both mini loaves into 8 slices. Place about 3 tablespoons (45 ml]] ice cream on top. Drizzle warm caramel sauce over all. Top with another slice of cake.

Yield: 8 sandwiches, 12 ounces (355 ml) ice cream, ¾ cup (180 ml) caramel

NECTARINE AGAVE PANINI
Panini—hot pressed sandwiches—are not just for savory meals!

1 container (6 ounces, or 170 g) nondairy yogurt (plain, vanilla, or fruit-based)
2 tablespoons (40 g) agave nectar, plus more for drizzling
¼ teaspoon vanilla extract
8 thin slices bread, crusts removed
2 ripe nectarines, peaches, or plums, unpeeled and thinly sliced
Ground cinnamon, for sprinkling
3 tablespoons (42 g) nondairy butter, divided, optional
Blueberries or raspberries, for garnish

Preheat a panini maker or use a sauté pan on the stove top.

In a small bowl, stir together the yogurt, agave, and vanilla until thoroughly combined.

Carefully spread about 1 tablespoon (15 ml) of the yogurt mixture on one side of each slice of bread. Arrange a layer of fruit over the yogurt, sprinkle on some cinnamon, and top with the remaining 4 slices of bread.

If using a panini maker, lightly coat the panini maker with nonstick cooking spray to ensure the sandwiches don't stick. Place 1 or 2 sandwiches (depending on the size of your machine) in the panini maker, press down, and cook for 4 minutes. Repeat with the remaining sandwiches.

If using a sauté pan, melt 1 tablespoon (14 g) of the butter in the sauté pan over medium heat. Place 1 sandwich in the pan, place a flat heavy object on top, such as a cutting board, and cook for about 3 minutes on each side. Remove from the pan, transfer to a plate, and repeat with the remaining 2 tablespoons (28 g) butter and remaining 3 sandwiches.

Slice each sandwich in half on the diagonal, place on 4 dessert plates, drizzle with additional agave, and garnish with the berries.

Yield: 4 servings

OREO WAFFLEWICHES

Have you ever bitten into an Oreo cookie feeling that it's too small for your demanding needs? Here's the perfect excuse to have an Oreo cookie, made bigger and "wafflier."

FOR THE WAFFLES:
1 cup (235 ml) plain, vanilla, or chocolate soymilk
⅓ cup (67 g) sugar
¼ cup (56 g) nondairy butter, melted
¼ teaspoon salt
1 teaspoon vanilla extract
1 cup (125 g) all-purpose flour
¼ cup (20 g) Dutch-processed cocoa powder
1 teaspoon baking powder
1½ tablespoons (12 g) cornstarch

FOR THE FROSTING:
2 tablespoons (24 g) vegan shortening
2 tablespoons (28 g) nondairy butter
1½ cups (180 g) confectioners' sugar, sifted
1 tablespoon (15 ml) nondairy milk
½ teaspoon vanilla extract

FOR THE TOPPING:
Vegan chocolate syrup, optional

To make the waffles: In a large bowl, combine the milk, sugar, butter, salt, and vanilla.

In a separate bowl, combine the flour, cocoa, baking powder, and cornstarch. Add on top of the wet ingredients. Whisk to combine and eliminate lumps, being careful not to overmix.

Coat the waffle iron with nonstick cooking spray. Cook the waffles according to the manufacturer's instructions for about 6 minutes, or until the waffles look dry on the surface.

Repeat with the remaining batter to make 1½ Belgian-size waffles or 2 or 3 standard-size waffles.

To get the crispness that Oreo cookies are known for, toast the waffles in a toaster oven. Let the waffles cool on a wire rack for about 20 minutes before frosting.

To make the frosting: In a bowl, using an electric mixer, cream the shortening and butter until smooth. Slowly add the sugar. Mix on low speed, and then beat until combined. Add the milk and vanilla. Beat on low speed until combined, and then beat on medium speed for 2 minutes, or until fluffy, occasionally stopping to scrape the sides of the bowl with a rubber spatula.

To assemble the wafflewiches: Break the waffles into quarters. Divide the frosting equally between half of the quarters, or to taste. Top with the remaining waffle quarters. Drizzle the chocolate syrup on top, if using.

Yield: 3 or 6 wafflewiches

STRAWBERRIES WITH LAVENDER SYRUP

This dish is a summer delight, especially if you get your strawberries and lavender from your backyard or from your local farmers' market.

⅓ cup plus ½ cup (165 g) sugar, divided, or less, to taste
1 teaspoon grated lemon zest
½ cup (120 ml) water
2 tablespoons (40 g) agave nectar
2 teaspoons dried culinary lavender
3 pints (870 g) strawberries, sliced
5 mint leaves, finely minced

In a small bowl, combine ⅓ cup (65 g) of the sugar and the zest. Blend well and either use right away or store in the refrigerator in a covered container.

In a saucepan, bring the remaining ½ cup (100 g) sugar, the water, agave, and lavender to a boil over medium-high heat, stirring until the sugar dissolves. Reduce the heat to medium. Simmer for about 5 minutes, or until the lavender flavor is detectable.

Strain the syrup into a small bowl or store in a container, cover, and let stand at room temperature.

Reheat the syrup before using.

When ready to serve, place the strawberries in large serving bowl. Pour the warmed syrup over the berries and stir to coat. Divide the syrup-covered strawberries among 8 plates or bowls and sprinkle with the lemon sugar and mint.

Yield: 8 servings

CARAMELIZED BANANAS WITH CHOCOLATE CHIPOTLE SAUCE

In a matter of minutes, you can serve this elegant sweet snack. If you're not a fan of bananas, use pineapple chunks instead. We like using the pretzel sticks here because of the added bonus of dipping them directly into the chocolate, but you can use toothpicks.

2 tablespoons (28 g) vegan butter
¼ cup (56 g) packed brown sugar
2 teaspoons maple syrup
Pinch ground nutmeg
Pinch salt
2 bananas, cut into 1-inch (2.5 cm) pieces (12 to 14 slices total)
1 tablespoon (11 g) vegan semisweet chocolate chips
1 tablespoon (15 ml) vegan milk
1 teaspoon vanilla extract
Pinch chipotle chile powder
12 to 14 thin pretzel sticks or toothpicks
6 or 7 strawberries, stems removed, sliced in half length-wise if large

In a small skillet, melt the butter over medium heat. Add the sugar, syrup, nutmeg, and salt. Cook for 2 to 3 minutes, stirring, or until the mixture is bubbly and the sugar has dissolved.

Add the bananas. Cook for about 2 minutes, stirring gently to avoid breaking the bananas. The bananas should remain somewhat firm. Using a slotted spoon, remove the bananas to a plate.

Remove the skillet from the heat, and add the chocolate, milk, vanilla, and chile powder. Stir continuously until the chocolate is melted.

Pour the mixture into a shallow serving bowl. Using pretzel sticks or toothpicks, skewer a strawberry half, and then a banana slice. Continue until all the fruit is used. Serve the fruit with the Chocolate Chipotle Sauce

Yield: 12 to 14 skewers

CHOCOLATE ALMOND BRITTLE

"Brittle" is a fitting name for this easy-to-make treat, because it resembles peanut brittle in its rough-hewn appearance and buttery flavor. It takes much less time to make, however, and it's simply delicious.

½ cup (112 g) non-hydrogenated, nondairy butter, room temperature
½ cup (88 g) nondairy semisweet chocolate chips
4 ounces (115 g) graham crackers (about 6 rectangles)
1¼ cups (180 g) raw almonds, toasted and chopped

Lightly butter a 9-inch (23-cm) square or round cake pan.

In a medium saucepan, melt the butter and chocolate over low heat.

Meanwhile, break the crackers into small pieces, but not crumbs.

Once the butter and chocolate are melted, remove from the heat. Stir in the crackers, their crumbs, and the almonds. Spread the mixture into the prepared baking pan. Cover.

Chill in the fridge for at least 2 hours, or until set. Store in an airtight container.

Yield: 10 servings

PEPITA BRITTLE

This is the traditional method of making pepita brittle, which is unlike many nut brittles in that you allow the sugar to completely recrystallize while making the candy. Use a good-quality candy thermometer for easy candy making. This recipe has a very glassy sheen and distinctive crunch.

1½ cups (300 g) granulated sugar
¾ cup (175 ml) water
½ teaspoon salt
½ vanilla bean, scraped

1 cup (140 g) pepitas (pumpkin seeds)

Line a baking sheet with parchment paper.

In a 2.5-quart (2.4 L) saucepan, heat the sugar, water, salt, and vanilla bean over medium heat. Bring the mixture to 238°F (114°C), firm ball stage, checking with a candy thermometer, stirring often with a wooden spoon and washing down the sides of the pan with a silicone brush.

Once the candy mixture reaches the proper temperature, remove from the heat and stir in the pumpkin seeds. Return to the heat. Cook for about 7 minutes, or until the mixture crystallizes and gets very clumpy and then literally turn into green-tinged sugar. Cook, stirring constantly until the sugar completely remelts. Time it for about 5 minutes after the sugar crystallizes.

Pour onto the prepared baking sheet and quickly spread thin. (It hardens quickly.)

Let the candy cool for about 1 hour. Break it into small pieces once the candy is completely cool.

Yield: about 30 pieces candy

CINNAMON-GLAZED NUTS

Perfectly spiced and not overly sweet, these walnuts are quick and easy and get rave reviews.

3 tablespoons (45 ml) maple syrup
2 tablespoons (28 g) packed brown sugar
1 tablespoon (15 ml) neutral-flavored oil
¾ teaspoon ground cinnamon
½ teaspoon vanilla extract
Generous pinch ground allspice
Pinch salt
2 cups (227 g) walnut or pecan halves, or a mix of the two

Preheat the oven to 325°F (170°C, or gas mark 3). Line a large rimmed baking sheet with parchment paper. Lightly coat the paper with nonstick cooking spray.

In a medium bowl, stir together the syrup, sugar, oil, cinnamon, vanilla, allspice, and salt. Add the nuts, and stir to coat.

Spread the nuts on the prepared baking sheet in a single layer.

Bake for 15 to 17 minutes, or until the glaze is bubbly on the nuts.

Let cool on the baking sheet, stirring occasionally to coat the nuts with any glaze remaining on the parchment paper. Once the nuts have cooled completely, break them apart. Store in an airtight container at room temperature.

Yield: 2 cups (255 g) glazed nuts

81 Peanut Butter Balls; 82 Saltine Butter Toffee; 83 Chocolate Bark; 84 Vanilla Bean Ice Cream; 85 Mango Rum Ice Cream; 86 Avocado Gelato; 87 Watermelon Granita; 88 Fudgy Good Frozen Treats

89 Ginger-Mango Ice Lollies; 90 Sesame Berry Ice Cream Sandwiches; 91 Mango Butter and Ginger Whoopie Pies; 92 Banana Foster Cake Sandwiches; 93 Nectarine Agave Panini; 94 Oreo Wafflewiches; 95 Strawberries with Lavender Syrup; 96 Caramelized Bananas with Chocolate Chipotle Sauce

SUGARED SPANISH ALMONDS

A popular treat in the streets of Spain, it's hard to argue with the intoxicating flavor of these candies. These keep well if kept in an airtight container or loosely wrapped paper bag, but honestly, they won't last very long.

1½ cups (300 g) sugar
½ cup (120 ml) + 2 tablespoons (28 ml) water
Pinch salt
Half vanilla bean, scraped
2½ cups (363 g) whole raw almonds

Line a baking sheet with waxed paper.

In 2-quart (2 L) saucepan, bring the sugar, water, salt, and vanilla bean to a boil over medium heat, stirring often with a wooden spoon. Once the mixture comes to a boil, add the almonds.

Set a timer for 16 minutes. Keep the mixture at a boil. Stirring continuously, let the syrup in the mix completely recrystallize into sugar granules. This should happen at around the 10-minute mark. Continue stirring, and by the time the 16 minutes is up, the sugar should have mostly turned back into a syrup to coat the almonds.

Remove from the heat just as the sugar turns back into a glaze and spread onto the prepared baking sheet. Separate into individual almonds. Let cool completely.

Yield: 3 cups (550 g) candied nuts

BETTER BUCKEYES

Buckeyes are a tradition in Ohio, but we opted to update them. We reduced the amount of sugar, so ours aren't cloyingly sweet, and added puffed rice cereal for a surprising crunch! While we were at it, we added a bit of cinnamon, too, because peanut butter loves cinnamon.

2 tablespoons (28 g) nondairy butter
½ cup (128 g) creamy peanut butter
1 teaspoon vanilla extract
½ cup (60 g) confectioners' sugar, sifted
½ teaspoon ground cinnamon
1 tablespoon (15 ml) nondairy milk, if needed
¾ cup (23 g) natural puffed rice cereal
¾ cup (132 g) vegan semisweet chocolate chips
Kosher salt, to garnish
12 toothpicks

Line a rimmed baking sheet with wax paper.

In a bowl, using a hand mixer, cream the butter, peanut butter, and vanilla. Mix in the sugar and cinnamon. The mixture may be slightly crumbly. Add up to 1 tablespoon (15 ml) of the milk, if needed, to make an easy-to-form dough that's the consistency of very thick frosting.

Using your hands, mix in the cereal.

Chill the mixture in the freezer for 15 to 45 minutes, or until the mixture is firm enough to shape easily.

Roll the dough into 12 balls, using 1 tablespoon (20 g) of dough per ball. Place the balls on the prepared baking sheet. Chill in the fridge.

Meanwhile, in a double boiler, melt the chocolate over simmering water, stirring constantly.

Remove the balls from the refrigerator. Stick a toothpick into a ball, and then dip the ball into the chocolate mixture to nearly cover, but still leaving a bit of the dough exposed to look like a buckeye. Return the ball to the baking sheet, and repeat with the remaining balls. Sprinkle each with salt.

Chill in the fridge for 30 minutes, or until the chocolate is set.

Store in the fridge in an airtight container for up to 1 week.

Yield: 12 buckeyes

BROWNIE NUT BUTTER CUPS

We've taken a look at the best thing ever (also known as peanut butter cups) and gone one step further, replacing the chocolate candy bottom with a mini brownie. You'll realize what a brilliant idea it was when you get your fingers on (and sink your teeth into) the resulting chewy, goodness!

FOR THE BROWNIES:
4 ounces (113 g) vegan chocolate, chopped
3 tablespoons (42 g) solid coconut oil
½ cup (120 g) blended soft silken tofu or plain vegan yogurt
1 cup (200 g) light brown sugar, not packed
½ teaspoon salt
2 teaspoons vanilla extract
1¼ cups (150 g) whole wheat pastry flour

FOR THE FILLING:
¾ cup (192 g) creamy natural almond or peanut butter, at room temperature
3 tablespoons (23 g) confectioners' sugar
Pinch salt
2 ounces (57 g) vegan chocolate, chopped

To make the brownies: Preheat the oven to 350°F (180°C, or gas mark 4). Lightly coat thirty-four cups of two mini muffin pans with nonstick cooking spray.

In a microwave-safe bowl, heat the chocolate and oil in 1-minute increments, until the chocolate is melted and can be easily stirred. (Alternatively, place the chocolate and oil in a small saucepan and slowly warm over low heat until melted.)

In a medium bowl, combine the chocolate with the tofu, sugar, salt, and vanilla. Sift the flour on top. Stir until well combined. Place about 2½ teaspoons batter in each cup, filling each cup two-thirds full.

Bake for 12 minutes, or until the brownies still look a

little wet and will slightly collapse while cooling; this will create the indentation for the filling. If your brownies don't collapse within a few minutes, use the curved back of a ½ teaspoon to indent. Let cool in the pans on a wire rack.

Chill in the fridge for 45 minutes, to easily remove from the pans.

To make the filling: Meanwhile, in a small bowl, combine the nut butter, sugar, and salt. If the nut butter is on the thin side, add a little extra sugar to thicken.

Remove the chilled cups from the pans, and place 1 teaspoon filling per indentation. Sprinkle a tiny handful of chocolate on top, pressing down slightly. Serve chilled.

Store leftovers in an airtight container in the refrigerator for up to 1 week.

Yield: 34 mini brownie cups

BLACK FOREST JARS
This dessert is in a jar and needs to be eaten with a spoon.

½ cup (120 ml) nondairy milk
½ cup (96 g) evaporated cane juice
2 tablespoons (30 ml) neutral-flavored oil
½ teaspoon vanilla extract
½ teaspoon almond extract, divided
¼ teaspoon salt
¾ cup (90 g) whole wheat pastry flour
¼ cup (20 g) unsweetened cocoa powder
1 teaspoon baking powder
½ teaspoon cornstarch
2 teaspoons Kirschwasser, optional
1¼ cups (295 ml) black cherry tea, steeped from 2 teabags, cooled
¼ cup plus 2 tablespoons (120 g) cherry jam or chopped vegan maraschino cherries
1½ cups plus 3 tablespoons (270 g) Whipped Coconut Cream (See page 195.)
2 tablespoons (17 g) grated vegan chocolate

Preheat the oven to 350°F (180°C, or gas mark 4). Lightly coat eighteen cups of two standard muffin pans with nonstick cooking spray. Line a baking sheet with parchment paper.

In a large bowl, combine the milk, cane juice, oil, vanilla, ¼ teaspoon of the almond extract, and the salt. Sift the flour, cocoa, baking powder, and cornstarch on top. Using an electric mixer, mix until perfectly smooth.

Place 1 generous tablespoon (18 g) of batter into each prepared muffin cup.

Bake for 6 to 8 minutes, until the top springs back when touched. Leave the oven on. Carefully remove the cakes from the pan. Let cool for 5 minutes.

Place the cakes on the prepared baking sheet. Bake for another 10 minutes; this will prepare the cakes for the tea-soaking. Place on a cooling rack.

Have ready six half-pint (8 ounces, or 235 ml) mason jars with a diameter of more than 2½ inches (6 cm) (or same diameter as your muffin pan holes) so that the cakes fit easily.

Stir the Kirschwasser and remaining ¼ teaspoon almond extract into the tea. Fully soak each cooled cake in the tea for about 10 seconds, one at a time as you assemble the jars, letting the excess liquid drip back into the bowl.

Place a cake at the bottom of a jar. Top with 1½ teaspoons jam. Top with 1½ tablespoons (15 g) whipped cream. Top with another cake. Top with the same quantity of jam and the same quantity of whipped cream. Top with another cake. Top with whipped cream, spreading it evenly. Top with 1 teaspoon grated chocolate. Repeat with the remaining jars. Cover the jars with lids, and refrigerate overnight to let the flavors meld.

Serve chilled, and enjoy within 2 days of preparation. You can also freeze the jars for up to 3 months, thawing them in the refrigerator overnight before serving.

Yield: 6 jars

APPLE STRUDEL (APFELSTRUDEL)
Working with phyllo dough is not as hard as some might think. The trick is to have all of your ingredients prepared in advance and to work quickly so the pastry sheets don't dry out. Germans never eat their strudel cold but rather enjoy it lukewarm with vanilla sauce, which you can make by warming nondairy milk, cornstarch, and vanilla extract.

FOR THE FILLING AND PASTRY:
5 apples, peeled and sliced
½ cup (100 g) sugar
2 teaspoons ground cinnamon
¼ cup (35 g) golden raisins
¼ cup (27 g) slivered almonds, toasted, optional
1 tablespoon (8 g) all-purpose flour
Juice of 1 small lemon
6 to 8 sheets phyllo pastry
¼ cup (55 g) nondairy, non-hydrogenated butter, melted

FOR THE TOPPING:
2 tablespoons (25 g) sugar
1 tablespoon (8 g) cinnamon
½ cup (65 g) ground almonds, toasted, optional

Preheat the oven to 400°F (200°C, or gas mark 6). Line a baking sheet with parchment paper.

To make the filling: In a bowl, mix together the apples, sugar, cinnamon, raisins, almonds if using, flour, and juice, stirring thoroughly to combine.

Place 1 sheet of phyllo on a clean work surface. (It should be placed so you are looking at it vertically.) Keep the remaining phyllo sheets covered with a damp cloth.

Brush the entire phyllo sheet with butter. Lay down another phyllo sheet directly on top of the buttered sheet and brush again with some melted butter. Repeat until you use all 6 or 8 sheets.

Spoon the apple filling across the lower third of the phyllo stack, leaving a 2-inch (5-cm) border along the bottom and sides. Roll the phyllo over once to begin creating a log, and then fold in the sides. Continue to roll gently until you have a compact log, ending seam side down.

Place the strudel seam side down on the prepared baking sheet, and brush the top with butter.

To make the topping: In a small bowl, combine the sugar, cinnamon, and almonds, if using. Sprinkle the mixture on the top of the strudel.

Bake for 20 minutes, or until golden brown. Allow to cool before slicing with a serrated knife.

Yield: 8 servings

RUGELACH

These rich, sweet little pastries, a favorite in Jewish cuisine, have as many spellings (Rugulach, Rugalach, Rogelach, Rugalah) as they do filling options.

1 cup (225 g) non-hydrogenated, nondairy butter, cold
1 (8-ounce or 225-g) package nondairy cream cheese
2 cups (250 g) unbleached all-purpose flour
¼ teaspoon salt
⅓ cup (77 g) nondairy sour cream
½ cup (100 g) granulated sugar
1 tablespoon (8 g) ground cinnamon
1 cup (150 g) finely chopped walnuts
½ cup (75 g) finely chopped raisins
1 cup (320 g) fruit jam or preserves (apricot, strawberry, raspberry)

Cut the butter and cream cheese into small pieces.

In the food processor, pulse together the flour, salt, butter, cream cheese, and sour cream until crumbly.

Shape the mixture into 4 equal disks. Wrap each disk and chill for at least 2 hours or up to 2 days.

When you're ready to prepare the pastry, preheat the oven to 350°F (180°C, or gas mark 4). Line 2 cookie sheets with parchment paper. (You may use ungreased cookie sheets, but the jam mixture tends to ooze onto the sheet, making it difficult to clean.) In a bowl, combine the sugar, cinnamon, walnuts, and raisins. Set aside.

Lightly flour a work surface area, and roll each disk into a 9-inch (23-cm) round, keeping the other disks chilled until you're ready to roll them. Spread each circle of dough with a light layer of the jam. Divide the sugar/nut filling among the disks, and press lightly into the jam. With a sharp knife or pizza cutter, cut each round into 12 wedges or triangles.

Roll the wedges from the wide end to the narrow end, so you end up with a point on the outside of the cookie. Place on the prepared baking sheets with the point side down.

Bake in the center rack of the oven for 22 minutes, or until lightly golden. Cool on wire racks. Store in airtight containers. They also freeze very well for up to 2 months.

Yield: 3 dozen cookies

CARAMEL POPCORN

Package this treat as a winter holiday gift for friends, neighbors, and coworkers. This is a tasty, easy-to-make, and easy-to-double recipe. You'll never resort to store-bought again.

14 cups (1400 g) popped popcorn (air- or oil-popped)
1 cup (145 g) dry roasted peanuts, optional
1 cup (225 g) firmly packed light brown sugar
¼ cup (75 g) light corn syrup
½ cup (55 g) non-hydrogenated, nondairy butter
½ teaspoon salt
¼ teaspoon baking soda
½ teaspoon vanilla extract

Lightly grease a shallow pan, such as a roasting pan, jellyroll pan, or high-sided cookie sheet.

Place the popped popcorn in the pan. Add the peanuts, if using, to the popped corn. Set aside.

Preheat the oven to 250°F (120°C, or gas mark ½).

Combine the brown sugar, corn syrup, butter, and salt in a saucepan. Bring to a boil over medium heat, stirring enough to blend. Once the mixture begins to boil, boil for 5 minutes, stirring constantly.

Remove from the heat, and stir in the baking soda and vanilla. The mixture will be light and foamy. Immediately pour over the popcorn in the pan, and stir to coat. Don't worry too much at this point about getting all of the popcorn coated.

Bake for 1 hour, removing the pan every 15 minutes and giving the popcorn and nuts a good stir. Line the countertop with waxed paper. Dump the popcorn out onto the waxed paper and separate the pieces. Allow to cool completely, then store in airtight containers or resealable bags. Package as gifts!

Yield: 14 servings

DECADENT CHOCOLATE TRUFFLES

For a lighter treat after a heavy meal, these truffles will do the trick.

1 cup (145 g) raw almonds or walnuts
20 large (Medjool) dates, pitted
1 tablespoon (15 g) unsweetened cocoa powder

Zest from 1 medium orange
2 tablespoons (40 g) agave nectar
½ teaspoon ground cinnamon
¼ teaspoon ground nutmeg
⅛ teaspoon salt
Cocoa powder, for rolling

Grind the almonds in a food processor until fine. Add the dates, cocoa powder, orange zest, agave nectar, cinnamon, nutmeg, and salt, and process until the mixture forms a ball.

If the mixture doesn't stick together, add more agave nectar.

Form 30 small balls out of the mixture. Roll in the cocoa powder, and serve on a pretty candy dish. They also store well in the refrigerator and freezer.

Yield: 30 servings

COCONUT CACAO TRUFFLES

This dessert is raw, which helps keep the nutritional value of each nutrient high and mighty (in a good way!). Cacao is rich in heart healthy flavonols, which help to improve blood circulation. (If necessary, you may substitute unsweetened natural cocoa powder for the raw cacao powder.) Creamy coconut butter and raw nuts contain the antioxidant vitamin E. Antioxidants are important for helping to reduce aging and damage from free radicals, which can affect heart health. These truffles are one of our absolute favorite desserts, because they are quick to make, delicious, and satisfy any chocolate lover's chocolate craving!

¾ cup (180 g) raw unsweetened raw cacao powder
2 cups (290 g) raw almonds
¼ cup (36 g) raw cashews
½ cup (120 ml) maple syrup
¼ cup (60 ml) water
1 heaping tablespoon (14 g) coconut oil
Pinch of kosher salt

In a food processor or high-speed blender, combine all of the ingredients and blend until you have a thick batter.

Roll into small balls about 1 inch (2.5 cm) in diameter and place on a plate. Cover and keep in the freezer until ready to eat. The truffles will keep for up to 2 weeks in the freezer and are best served chilled.

Yield: 8 to 10 truffles

CRUNCHY COCONUT PEANUT CANDY

This candy is similar to a brittle peanut butter fudge. It's a quick and delicious treat to whip up because the sugar in the recipe only needs to cook a few minutes, much less than the long cooking times of other homemade candies.

2⅓ cups (467 g) sugar
¼ cup (60 ml) coconut milk
1 cup (85 g) shredded unsweetened coconut
1½ cups (218 g) crushed peanuts

Prepare an 8x8-inch (20 x 20 cm) baking pan by lining it with parchment paper. Set it aside but keep it close to your cooking area so it will be handy as soon as the candy is fully cooked.

In a 2-quart (2 L) saucepan, over medium heat, warm up the sugar and coconut milk and continue to cook, stirring constantly, until the sugar has turned into a liquid, about 2 minutes. The sugar will still be grainy, but it should be able to flow.

Remove from heat and stir in the coconut and peanuts until well mixed and quickly transfer to the prepared pan. Press down firmly with a fork, or clean hands, to pack the sugar mixture into the mold. The mixture will be loose and crumbly at this time, but if well packed, it will come together nicely when cooled.

Let rest at least 1 hour until completely cooled. Invert the pan to remove the candy and then carefully cut into bite-size pieces.

Store in an airtight container for up to 1 week.

Yield: 20 pieces of candy

FIG PASTRIES

This pastry is especially delicious when served with a fresh "sweetened cream," which can be made by mixing together equal parts vegan cream cheese and vegan sour cream, a touch of sugar, and a little lemon zest.

FOR THE PASTRY:
1½ cups (240 g) superfine brown rice flour
¼ cup (51 g) sweet white rice flour
2 teaspoons xanthan gum
¼ cup (50 g) granulated sugar
½ cup (112 g) cold vegan margarine, chopped into 1-inch (2.5 cm) square pieces
½ cup (120 ml) ice-cold water

FOR THE FILLING:
1⅓ cup (200 g) dried mission figs
½ cup (115 g) packed dark brown sugar
2 teaspoons vegan margarine
Dash salt
2 dashes angostura bitters, optional

To make the pastry: In a large bowl, mix together the flours, xanthan gum, and sugar until well blended. Using a pastry blender, cut the margarine into the flour mixture until it forms coarse crumbs. Make a well in the center. Use a fork to slowly stir the ice-cold water into the flour mixture just until it comes together into a dough. Quickly knead the dough a couple of times to form a disk. Wrap in waxed paper and chill in the refrigerator until cold, about 1 hour. In the meantime, prepare the filling.

To make the filling: Dice the dried figs finely and combine with remaining filling ingredients. Smash using a large fork or potato masher, just so that the ingredients blend well.

Large chunks of fruit remaining in some spots are desirable.

To assemble: Preheat the oven to 375°F (190° C, gas mark 5). Once the dough is cold, divide in half and roll out between 2 sheets of plastic wrap on a flat surface, creating a rectangle that is about ¼-inch (6 mm) thick from each half. Cut out 14 disks of dough, each about 2 inches (5 cm) in diameter (a small bowl works well as a cookie cutter here) for a total of 28 pieces of dough. Place about 1 heaping tablespoon (15 g) filling in the center of one circle and then cover with another circle of dough and crimp down the edges of the dough to seal.

Slice a slit into the tops of each pocket and bake on a parchment-covered cookie sheet for about 25 minutes or until lightly golden brown on edges. Serve warm or cold.

Yield: 14 pastries

97 Chocolate Almond Brittle; 98 Pepita Brittle; 99 Cinnamon-Glazed Nuts; 100 Sugared Spanish Almonds; 101 Better Buckeyes; 102 Brownie Nut Butter Cups

103 Black Forest Jars; 104 Apple Strudel (Apfelstrudel); 105 Rugelach; 106 Caramel Popcorn; 107 Decadent Chocolate Truffles; 108 Coconut Cacao Truffles; 109 Crunchy Coconut Peanut Candy; 110 Fig Pastries

BEVERAGES

See pages 254-255 and 258 for beverage recipe photos.

ALMOND MILK

Almond milk is a great nondairy milk to use in baking, cooking, and just simply drinking. It's available in many supermarkets and natural foods stores, but making your own at home is a cinch and allows you to control exactly what does (and doesn't) go in it. This milk is just as delicious with the sweetener and vanilla left out, if you prefer.

2 cups (300 g) raw whole almonds, soaked overnight in water to cover, drained
6½ cups (1.5 L) filtered water, divided
⅓ cup (80 ml) agave nectar
2 teaspoons (2 ml) vanilla extract

In a blender, blend the almonds, 4½ cups (1,060 ml) of the water, the agave, and vanilla for about 4 minutes, or until very smooth.

Strain the mixture through a cheesecloth, and then stir in the remaining 2 cups (470 ml) water.

Store in an airtight container in the refrigerator

Yield: About 7 servings, ¾ cup (180 ml) each

ORANGE JULIA

Modeled after the classic shopping mall treat, this creamy and dreamy smoothy is a healthier (and more feminine) version of the Orange Julius.

1¼ cups (300 ml) frozen orange juice (You can freeze it in ice cube trays.)
1 cup (235 ml) almond or rice milk
1 banana, peeled, sliced, and frozen
½ teaspoon vanilla bean paste or extract
Extra orange juice or nondairy milk to thin, if desired

In a blender, blend all of the ingredients until smooth.

Yield: 4 servings

RASPBERRY LEMONADE

This lemonade, with its sweet and tangy flavor and fun pink color, is sure to please everyone, both young and old.

2 cups (300 g) fresh raspberries
1½ cups (355 ml) lemon juice, divided
2 cups (400 g) sugar
¼ cup (60 ml) plus 8 cups (1.9 L) cold water, divided

In a saucepan, heat the raspberries, ½ cup (120 ml) of the juice, the sugar, and ¼ cup (60 ml) of the water over medium heat, stirring constantly and breaking apart the raspberries, until the sugar is dissolved and a chunky syrup is formed. Let cool to room temperature. Mix in the remaining 1 cup (235 ml) juice and the remaining 8 cups (1.9 L) water.

Pour the mixture into a large pitcher with a strainer attached to the lid or pour through a strainer before transferring to the pitcher. Serve chilled over ice.

Yield: 10 servings, 1 cup (235 ml) each

FLU FIGHTER JUICE

Juicing is an excellent way to consume high doses of raw nutrients. Drink this beverage, and colds and the flu will have no chance!

6 carrots, chopped
3 stalks celery
1 large apple, sliced
1 handful fresh Italian parsley
Juice of ½ lime
2 teaspoons coconut oil, melted
Ice cubes, as desired

In a masticating juicer, juice the carrots, celery, apple, parsley, juice, and oil. Serve over ice.

Yield: Makes 2 servings

CHOCOLATE PEANUT BUTTER (GREEN) SMOOTHIE

Chocolate and peanut butter make a cunning disguise for the spinach that hides inside this smoothie, making it the perfect starter "green" smoothie for both kids and adults.

1 banana, peeled, sliced, and frozen
1 cup (30 g) packed fresh spinach
2 tablespoons (32 g) creamy peanut butter
1 teaspoon vanilla extract
1 tablespoon (15 ml) agave nectar
2 to 3 tablespoons (16 to 24 g) cocoa powder
1 cup (235 ml) very cold water

In a blender, blend all of the ingredients until smooth. Divide among 4 glasses.

Yield: 4 servings

CHERRY BERRIES 'N CREAM SMOOTHIE

Cherries and berries combine in this delicious drink.

1 cup (155 g) chopped fresh cherries
1 cup (145 g) sliced strawberries
1 cup (235 ml) almond milk
½ cup (120 ml) light canned coconut milk
½ teaspoon almond extract

In a blender, blend all of the ingredients until smooth. Divided among 4 glasses.

Yield: 4 servings

SPARKLING CREAMY COCONUT ELIXIR WITH LIME

Feeling under the weather? Staying hydrated when you are sick, and to keep the body from becoming sick, is so important! This sparkling elixir provides the body with hydration, as well as immunity-boosting ingredients such as lime.

1 cup (235 ml) sparkling water or club soda
¼ cup (60 ml) coconut cream or canned coconut milk
Juice of ½ lime
1 tablespoon (20 g) favorite sweetener
3 or 4 ice cubes

In a blender, blend all of the ingredients until smooth.

Yield: 1 servings

IMMUNITY SMOOTHIE

This smoothie is just what the doctor ordered to help you stay well.

1 cup fresh or frozen raspberries (125 g fresh or 250 g frozen)
1 medium banana
½ lime, peeled
1 cup (235 ml) coconut water
3 or 4 ice cubes

In a blender, blend all of the ingredients until smooth.

Yield: 1 serving

MOCHACCINO MILKSHAKE

The sultry combo of chocolate and coffee come together perfectly in this thick milkshake. For extra flair, top with whipped coconut cream and nondairy chocolate shavings.

3 cups (720 g) nondairy vanilla bean ice cream
¾ to 1 cup (180 to 235 ml) nondairy milk
1 tablespoon (8 g) espresso powder or instant coffee
2 tablespoons (10 g) cocoa powder

In a blender, blend all of the ingredients until smooth.

Yield: 2 servings

PEANUT BUTTER CHOCOLATE PROTEIN SHAKE

Have a hankering for a Reese's Peanut Butter Cup? This shakes satisfies your craving for that peanutty chocolate fix, and it's also a great way to get some good-quality protein in the most yummy way.

12 pitted dates
Hot water, as needed
½ cup (120 ml) unsweetened almond milk
2 tablespoons (32 g) creamy, no-sugar-added peanut butter
2 tablespoons (10 g) unsweetened cocoa powder
12 ounces (340 g) soft silken tofu
Handful ice cubes

In a blender, cover the dates with water. Soak the dates for 10 to 15 minutes.

When the dates have softened, add the milk, peanut butter, cocoa, and tofu to the blender. Blend until smooth. Add ice cubes at the end to make it cold.

Yield: 1 large or 2 small shakes

CHOCOLATE BANANA SHAKE

Enjoy this easy-to-make shake that doesn't require any ice cream. It tastes much richer than you would expect from just a few simple ingredients, and you can reduce some of the cocoa powder if you like. Just make sure to use frozen bananas.

2 cups (470 ml) nondairy milk
2 ripe bananas, cut into chunks and frozen
4 tablespoons (32 g) unsweetened cocoa powder
1 to 2 teaspoons sugar, optional
Banana slices, for garnish
Grated chocolate, for garnish

In a blender, combine the milk, bananas, and cocoa until everything is mixed together and there are no lumps of cocoa. Add the sugar, if using. Garnish with the banana slices and chocolate.

Yield: 2 servings

INSTANT SWEET LEMON ICED TEA MIX

This instant iced tea mix is a perfect host or hostess gift when attending a summertime barbecue or get-together. The ingredients are simple, and it is a snap to throw together in a hurry.

2 cups (67 g) unsweetened instant 100% tea crystals
    (The only ingredient on the label should be tea.)
3 cups (600 g) evaporated cane juice
2 (⅓-ounce, or 9 g each) packets unsweetened lemonade
    drink mix or 2 tablespoons (18 g) citric acid
Zest of 2 lemons

In a bowl, combine all of the ingredients together.

Yield: 4 cups (896 g) mix

To use the tea:
- *To make 1 cup (235 ml): Combine 2 tablespoons (28 g) mix with 1 cup (235 ml) warm water.*
- *To make 1 quart (1 L): Combine ½ cup (112 g) mix with 4 cups (1 L) warm water.*
- *To make ½ gallon (2 L): Combine 1 cup (224 g) mix with 8 cups (1.8 L) warm water.*
- *To make 1 gallon (4 L): Combine 2 cups (448 g) mix with 16 cups (3.8 L) warm water.*
- *Chill before serving.*

STRAWBERRY SIMPLE SYRUP

Simple syrups can be used to make cocktails, sweeten teas, and even brush on cakes before frosting to add moisture.

4 cups (940 g) water
16 ounces (448 g) frozen strawberries
4 cups (800 g) evaporated cane juice or sugar

In a saucepan, boil the water and strawberries over high heat for 5 minutes, crushing the fruit to release all of its goodness. Reduce the heat to low and add the sugar. Stir until the sugar is completely dissolved.

Remove from the heat and allow to cool completely. Strain out the solids, and pour into jars or bottles. Keep refrigerated.

Yield: 6 cups (1.4 L)

ORANGE SIMPLE SYRUP

You can make a plain simple syrup using equal parts sugar and water. Here's a little fancier one.

4 cups (940 g) water
2 oranges, sliced with skin on
4 cups (800 g) evaporated cane juice or sugar

In a saucepan, boil the water and oranges over high heat for 5 minutes, crushing the fruit to release all of its goodness. Reduce the heat to low and add the sugar. Stir until the sugar is completely dissolved.

Remove from the heat and allow to cool completely. Strain out the solids, and pour into jars or bottles. Keep refrigerated.

Yield: 6 cups (1.4 L)

VANILLA SIMPLE SYRUP

You'll love this café inspired syrup.

4 cups (940 g) water
1 (4-inch, or 10 cm) vanilla bean, split lengthwise
4 cups (800 g) evaporated cane juice or sugar

In a saucepan, boil the water and vanilla over high heat for 5 minutes, crushing the fruit to release all of its goodness. Reduce the heat to low and add the sugar. Stir until the sugar is completely dissolved.

Remove from the heat and allow to cool completely. Strain out the solids, and pour into jars or bottles. Keep refrigerated.

Yield: 6 cups (1.4 L)

BLOODY MARY MIX

This is a great host or hostess gift, but it does require refrigeration.

3 cups (705 ml) tomato juice
¼ cup (60 ml) lemon juice
¼ cup (60 ml) lime juice
2 tablespoons (30 ml) vegan Worcestershire sauce
1 tablespoon (7 g) celery salt
1 teaspoon black pepper
¼ teaspoon cayenne pepper
¼ teaspoon red pepper flakes

In a bowl, combine all of the ingredients together. Pour into a bottle or jar.

Keep refrigerated.

Yield: 4 cups (1 L)

To serve: *Fill a pint glass with ice. Add 2 ounces (60 ml) vodka, and top off with Bloody Mary Mix. Pour into a shaker and shake.*

Salt the rim of a glass with celery salt. Pour the shaken Bloody Mary into the glass.

Garnish with a celery stalk, a green olive, a clove of garlic, and a sprinkle of freshly cracked pepper.

HOLIDAY SPICED RUM

This is some serious stuff. It's sometimes hard to find homemade gifts that appeal to men. Liquor fits that bill quite nicely.

2 whole cinnamon sticks
10 whole cloves
10 whole allspice berries
1 (4-inch, or 10 cm) vanilla bean, split lengthwise
1 teaspoon dried orange peel
½ teaspoon whole fennel seed
¼ teaspoon ground nutmeg
¼ teaspoon ground ginger
2 cups (470 ml) clear rum

Add all the spices to a container with a tight-fitting lid. Pour the rum over the spices and seal the container. Shake to mix. Let sit for 5 days, shaking once each day, before straining out all of the solids through a sieve lined with cheesecloth to get as many of the fine particles as possible. Pour into a bottle and seal.

Yield: 2 cups (470 ml)

TO SERVE: SPIKED HOLIDAY CIDER

2 ounces (60 ml) Holiday Spiced Rum
2 ounces (60 ml) cinnamon schnapps
4 ounces (120 ml) hot apple cider
Cinnamon stick, for garnish

Add the rum and schnapps to a coffee mug. Stir in the hot apple cider. Garnish with a cinnamon stick.

Yield: 1 serving

VANILLA MINT VODKA

This is a snap to make. Depending on how long you let it steep, you can make it a mellow vanilla mint or a deep vanilla that will make even an anti-vodka person fall in love. This recipe is for 2 cups (470 ml). You can make bigger batches and make lots of gifts at a time. Double, triple, or quadruple the recipe as needed.

2 cups (470 ml) vodka
1 vanilla bean, split lengthwise
10 mint leaves

Add all the ingredients to a jar or bottle with a tight-fitting lid and shake. Allow to steep for 24 hours up to 5 full days, or until the desired flavor is achieved, shaking a couple of times a day.

Strain out the solids, and then pour into a bottle and seal.

Yield: 2 cups (470 ml)

TO SERVE: CANDY CANE MARTINI

2 ounces (30 ml) Vanilla Mint Vodka
1 ounce (15 ml) peppermint schnapps
1 ounce (15 ml) nondairy vanilla creamer
1 ounce (15 ml) grenadine
Ice
Sugar, for rimming the martini glass
Mint leaves and a candy cane or peppermint stick, for garnish

To a cocktail shaker, add the vodka, schnapps, creamer, grenadine, and ice.

Shake to mix. Rim a martini glass with sugar. Pour the cocktail into the glass, and add the mint leaves and candy cane as a garnish.

Yield: 1 serving

1 Almond Milk; 2 Orange Julia; 3 Raspberry Lemonade; 4 Flu Fighter Juice; 5 Chocolate Peanut Butter (Green) Smoothie; 6 Cherry Berries 'n Cream Smoothie; 7 Sparkling Creamy Coconut Elixir with Lime; 8 Immunity Smoothie

9 Mochaccino Milkshake; 10 Peanut Butter Chocolate Protein Shake; 11 Chocolate Banana Shake; 12 Instant Sweet Lemon Iced Tea Mix; 13 Strawberry Simple Syrup; 14 Orange Simple Syrup; 15 Vanilla Simple Syrup; 16 Bloody Mary Mix

GIN-GER SNAP

This stuff is no joke. It's made with gin and definitely has a snap!

2½ ounces [70 g] fresh ginger, sliced (unpeeled is fine)
2 cinnamon sticks
1 teaspoon dried orange peel
4 cups [940 ml] gin

Add the ginger, cinnamon sticks, and orange peel to a container with a tight-fitting lid. Pour in the gin, seal, give it a good shake, and let it sit for 1 full week, shaking once daily.

Strain out the solids, pour into bottles and seal.

Yield: 4 cups [940 ml]

TO SERVE: HOT CRANBERRY GINGER TEA
4 ounces [120 ml] hot brewed black tea [Earl Grey is
    fabulous here!]
2 ounces [60 ml] cranberry juice
2 ounces [60 ml] Gin-ger Snap
Drizzle of agave nectar

Stir all the ingredients together and serve hot.

Yield: 1 serving

BERRY SMOOTHIE

It's difficult to create a "recipe" for smoothies, because there are so many options and variations depending on your likes and dislikes. Berries are the most healthful option, because they're packed with antioxidants and nutritional goodness; bananas add much-needed potassium as well as thickness, and flaxseed adds the ever-important omega-3 fatty acids. You can make it thinner or thicker depending on your preference by varying the juice and milk for the consistency you prefer.

1 or 2 ripe bananas, frozen or fresh
½ cup [75 g] or more frozen blueberries
¼ cup [75 g] frozen strawberries
2 teaspoons ground flaxseed
¼ cup [60 ml] orange juice
½ cup [120 ml] nondairy milk
1 to 2 tablespoons [16 to 32 g] almond butter, optional

In a blender, blend all of the ingredients until smooth.

Yield: 2 servings

COCOA-MANGO LASSI

Who doesn't love a lassi? It's a refreshing and nutritious yogurt drink, and chocolate is an obvious match. Mango adds vitamin C and beta-carotene, the precursor of vitamin A. How about strawberries, honeydew melon, or peach? The sky [or your imagination] is the limit! If coconut is not your milk of choice, others will work here as well! Add more liquid if needed for a drinkable texture.

½ cup [40 g] cocoa powder
2 or 3 tablespoons [40 or 60 g] sugar syrup or agave
    nectar, or to taste
1½ cups [355 ml] coconut milk with cream [or [345 g]
    coconut yogurt, even better!]
¼ cup [60 ml] lemon juice
Couple pinches salt
½ teaspoon cardamom
1 cup [175 g] chopped mango [Frozen works great.]
½ cup [120 ml] mango juice
Ice

In a blender, blend all of the ingredients until smooth. Pour over ice in tall glasses.

Yield: 2 large or 4 small lassis

AZTEC-STYLE CHOCOLATE DRINK [COOKED]

This drink is based on the original Aztec cacao beverage, where they ground the beans into a mealy powder and cooked it with water and spices. Some drank it obsessively back in the day, and if anything can get you excited about unsweetened chocolate, this can.

½ cup [48 g] raw cacao powder or [112 g] nibs
3 cups [700 ml] water
1 teaspoon fresh or dried minced chile pepper
1 cinnamon stick, crushed
Pinch of salt
1 vanilla bean

With a mortar and pestle or in a food processor, grind the nibs into a powder, or if your powder has pieces in it, grind that to a finer texture.

In a medium saucepan, bring the water, chile, and cinnamon stick to a boil. Reduce the heat. Simmer for 10 minutes.

Drain, saving the chile water.

In the saucepan, mix the chile water with the cacao, cinnamon stick, and salt. Bring to a boil, stirring. Reduce the heat. Simmer for 15 to 20 minutes. Scrape the vanilla bean and add both the scrapings and the bean to the concoction for the last few minutes of simmering. Serve hot or warm.

Yield: 4 servings

AZTEC-STYLE CHOCOLATE DRINK (UNCOOKED)

Think of this drink like coffee, chicory, or maté. This is the cold beverage version, for your experimental pleasure.

½ cup (48 g) raw cacao powder or (112 g) nibs
¼ cup (35 g) cornmeal
¼ cup (35 g) squash seeds
Pinch of salt
1 dried chile pepper, crushed and seeded
2 cups (475 ml) water

In a sturdy medium bowl, grind all of the ingredients except the water with a pestle. Continue grinding while adding the water slowly until a thick but drinkable consistency is reached, about 4 to 5 minutes. (You may not have to use all of the water to get this to your satisfaction.)

Whisk the mixture until a bit frothy, which will only take a few minutes.

Note: You can also serve this beverage heated. This will make for a slightly smaller amount than the hot chocolate recipe at left, but you can still put it in 4 mugs.

Yield: 4 servings

WHITE CHOCOLATE AMARETTO HOT COCOA

White chocolate hot cocoa with the subtle flavor of almond makes an intoxicating combo and a perfect beverage for when the temperature dips.

2 cups (470 ml) almond milk
½ cup (75 g) chopped white chocolate chunks (See page 194-White chocolate baking bar)
¼ cup (50 g) sugar
1 teaspoon almond extract
Dash of salt

In a saucepan, bring the milk to a boil over medium heat.

In a heat-safe bowl, place the chocolate. Pour the milk over the chocolate. Add the sugar, almond, and salt. Stir until the chocolate is melted and the sugar is dissolved. Divide among 4 mugs.

Yield: 4 servings

17 Holiday Spiced Rum; 18 Vanilla Mint Vodka; 19 Gin-ger Snap; 20 Berry Smoothie; 21 Cocoa-Mango Lassi; 22 Aztec-Style Chocolate Drink (Cooked); 23 Aztec-Style Chocolate Drink (Uncooked); 24 White Chocolate Amaretto Hot Cocoa

CREDITS

With thanks to recipe authors:

Gerrie Lynn Adams

J.L. Fields

Allyson Kramer

Joni Marie Newman

Tamasin Noyes

Colleen Patrick-Goudreau

Joshua Ploeg

Megan Roosevelt, RD, LD

Matt Ruscigno, MPH, RD

Celine Steen

INDEX

S
N
L